S0-DQZ-175

LANDLORDS & CAPITALISTS

Landlords & Capitalists

THE DOMINANT CLASS OF CHILE

by

MAURICE ZEITLIN AND

RICHARD EARL RATCLIFF

PRINCETON, NEW JERSEY

PRINCETON UNIVERSITY PRESS

1988

PUBLISHED BY PRINCETON UNIVERSITY PRESS, 41 WILLIAM STREET
PRINCETON, NEW JERSEY 08540
IN THE UNITED KINGDOM: PRINCETON UNIVERSITY PRESS, GUILDFORD, SURREY

LIBRARY OF CONGRESS CATALOGING IN PUBLICATION
DATA WILL BE FOUND ON THE LAST PRINTED PAGE OF THIS BOOK

ISBN 0-691-07757-6 (cloth)

ISBN 0-691-02276-3 (pbk.)

PUBLICATION OF THIS BOOK HAS BEEN AIDED BY THE
WHITNEY DARROW FUND OF PRINCETON UNIVERSITY PRESS

THIS BOOK HAS BEEN COMPOSED IN LINOTRON BASKERVILLE

CLOTHBOUND EDITIONS OF
PRINCETON UNIVERSITY PRESS BOOKS
ARE PRINTED ON ACID-FREE PAPER, AND
BINDING MATERIALS ARE CHOSEN FOR
STRENGTH AND DURABILITY. PAPERBACKS, ALTHOUGH SATISFACTORY FOR
PERSONAL COLLECTIONS, ARE NOT
USUALLY SUITABLE FOR
LIBRARY REBINDING

PRINTED IN THE UNITED STATES OF
AMERICA BY PRINCETON UNIVERSITY PRESS
PRINCETON, NEW JERSEY

Al pueblo unido
para que nunca más será
vencido

CONTENTS

LIST OF TABLES

LIST OF FIGURES

PREFACE

Some twenty years ago, unbeknownst to him, the senior author began what was to become a sort of "neo-Balzacian" study of Chilean society, focusing on its basic class relations. Alas, he (and later Ratcliff) made the mistake of taking seriously a passage in Paul A. Baran's review of W. W. Rostow's *The Stages of Economic Growth.* Rejecting Rostow's view that "generalizing the sweep of modern history" is a sensible way to grasp the causes of social change and historical development, Baran wrote that

> historical configurations . . . have to be studied *concretely*. . . . The foregoing is not intended to advocate renunciation of theory in favor of plodding empiricism. Rather, it suggests the necessity of an interpenetration of theory and concrete observation, of empirical research illuminated by rational theory, of theoretical work which draws its lifeblood from historical study. . . . Pigeonholing [a country] in one of Rostow's 'stages' does not bring us any closer to an understanding of the country's economic and social condition or give us a clue to the country's developmental possibilities and prospects. What is required for that is as accurate as possible an assessment of the social and political forces in the country pressing for change and development: [1] the economic condition and the stratification of the peasantry, its political traditions and its ideological make-up; [2] the economic and social status, internal differentiation and political aspirations of the bourgeoisie, the extent of its tie-up with foreign interests and the degree of monopoly prevailing in its national business, the closeness of its connection with the landowning interests and the measure of its participation in existing government; [3] the living and working conditions and the level of class consciousness of labor and its political and organizational strength. Nor is this by any means the entire job [Baran 1961, pp. 61–62; italics in original].

It may not be, but it was enough to engage the efforts of Zeitlin and several co-workers, including Ratcliff, for rather too long, in research and analysis designed to get at Baran's agenda. Previous publications have dealt with the first and third items on that agenda, and the present work addresses the second.

In this book, we aim to reveal the constituent inner relations of Chile's dominant class. Necessarily, our analysis treats those relations as if they had been frozen in that moment in time, in the mid-1960s, to which our data apply; it thus cannot address the process of class formation. So, the reader is advised that *Landlords & Capitalists* is the "sequel" to another book, which sought to overcome this limitation. Its leading questions pressed themselves upon us while we were engaged in producing the present work, and emerged out of it: once having revealed the inner structure of Chile's "coalesced bourgeoisie," we then had to ask how it was formed and how it consolidated its dominion. That question led to others, compelled by the logic of historical inquiry, and resulted in Zeitlin's *The Civil Wars in Chile (or the bourgeois revolutions that never were).* (It, Zeitlin again wishes to stress, incorporated ideas that arose in the course of our common labors on the present work.)

Here, we put forward both an original theory—constructed in a dialectic with the empirical inquiry itself—and a systematic analysis of a contemporary dominant class. Thus, this work rests on the implicit theoretical presupposition (contrary to that prevailing in academic social science in the United States) that such a class actually exists, in contemporary capitalist democracies, as a definite and coherent, if internally differentiated, social form.

In turn, our methodological premise is that this social form can be revealed empirically only through an inquiry that is guided by an appropriate paradigm (and, alas, that paradigm, however "simple," has, in practice, for far too long imposed its own demands on the authors). Thus, our inquiry *began* with data on particular individuals located at the heights of three institutionally differentiated (but, in class theory, closely related) spheres of social domination: namely, "bureaucratic economic organization," "private property relations," and the "state." Then, however, our inquiry moved, in successive approximations, from data on *individuals* to data on the *family* and other effective *kinship units* of which they are an integral part, so that the internal ensemble of social relations constituting the class could be revealed. Next, we located these individuals and the kinship units to which they belong not only within each institutional realm (interorganizational, kinship, economic, and political), but also in the constellation of relations making these separate realms cohere and interpenetrate.

In order to "locate" these individuals and their kinship connections theoretically, we found it necessary to coin a number of concepts (for instance, "kinecon group," "inner group," "finance capitalists," and "class segments") which delineate the axes of intraclass differentiation. In order to locate them empirically, we had to devise specific methods that would allow us to grasp their intraclass situations in measurable form (for instance, to transform qualitative relationships of kinship into quantitative equivalents or to establish the boundaries of distinct kinship groups). Only by adhering to this paradigm and attempting to fulfill, to the extent possible, its cruel intellectual and practical demands, was it possible to demonstrate the actual existence of, and reveal the internal structure of, that composite social/economic form observed as a dominant *class*.

At the same time, by laying out a historically specific set of interrelated substantive propositions about the inner relations structuring *any* dominant class in a highly concentrated capitalist economy—and, in that light, conducting a sustained empirical analysis of an actually existing dominant class—we have (we think) done more than reveal the internal structure of *that* class. We have also provided a theory, method, and exemplary body of findings that can closely guide future studies of other dominant classes, especially in the "advanced societies" of the West. Those studies, in turn, will make it possible to gauge the fruitfulness, and test the validity, of our theory of the internal structure of the dominant class under contemporary capitalism.

This work, though it is based on mid-1960s data, is written in the present tense (except when referring to more specifically historical events or descriptions) in order to simplify the exposition. Whether and to what extent our analysis here also reveals Chile's dominant class, in its basic inner contours, as it still is—whatever changes of personnel have since occurred, during Salvador Allende's short-lived government and the restoration that followed under Augusto Pinochet's right-wing military dictatorship—is, of course, a question that can be answered only by research conducted in a future, democratic Chile.

ACKNOWLEDGMENTS

UNFORTUNATELY, those colleagues who contributed to the early research on this project in Chile cannot be thanked here. The mere mention of their names in a book on the nation's dominant class (even a scientific work written in the language of academic discourse) would, under the bloody military dictatorship of Augusto Pinochet, put them in jeopardy.

Lynda Ann Ewen collaborated with us on the early research and analysis on which Chapter 1 is based, as did W. Lawrence Neuman on Chapter 5. We gratefully acknowledge their important contributions.

Willard F. Mueller read and provided helpful comments on our analysis in Chapter 1 of the concentration of domestic and foreign capital. Alfredo del Río and Gøsta Esping-Andersen gave important advice concerning the analysis presented in Chapter 5. John Stephens and Michael Schwartz commented very helpfully on the entire manuscript, and Schwartz suggested specific revisions in the presentation of our quantitative findings that have considerably enhanced its clarity. Our research was supported in part by the Ford Foundation, the Louis M. Rabinowitz Foundation, the University of Wisconsin Ibero-American Studies Program, the Wisconsin Alumni Research Foundation, and the Academic Senate of the University of California at Los Angeles, none of which is responsible in any way for this work's content. The final draft of the book was word-processed by Dixie Lee King, with much-appreciated care and skill, from Zeitlin's sometimes quite unintelligible, cut-and-pasted typescript. Copy editor Charles B. Purrenhage edited the final manuscript with exacting attention and fine intelligence; he caught several errors and rid the manuscript of some rather obscure passages, besides enhancing its overall clarity. Finally, the comments and suggestions on the original manuscript by Sanford G. Thatcher, Editor-in-Chief of Princeton University Press, surely made this a better book.

As cited in the References, portions of this work, extensively revised since then, have appeared in articles in the *American Sociological Review*, the *American Journal of Sociology*, *Industrial Organization Review*, *Latin*

American Research Review, *Papers: Revista de Sociología* (edited by the late Francisco Marsal in Barcelona), and *Chile: Politics and Society*, edited by Arturo Valenzuela and J. Samuel Valenzuela (Transaction Books, 1976). Various aspects of our analysis have benefited from the penetrating comments provided by their editors and anonymous referees.

LANDLORDS & CAPITALISTS

"We, the owners of land and capital, own Chile. The rest, the masses, do not matter."

— EDUARDO MATTE PÉREZ, *banker*
(*El Pueblo*, March 19, 1892)

INTRODUCTION

Inside the Dominant Class

"CLASS" always refers to the interpenetration of economy and society: whether of the "market" and "communal action" or of "production relations" and "class struggle." Thus, the central question raised by the concept of class is, What are the connections between "economic relations" and "social relations"? How do classes, rooted in a concrete set of economic relations, take on historically specific social forms? This, on the most abstract level, is the originating theoretical question of the present study. No doubt, as Anthony Giddens remarks, "the most important blank spots in the theory of class concern the processes whereby 'economic classes' become 'social classes' and whereby in turn the latter are related to other social forms."[1]

But these *theoretical* "blank spots" cannot be filled in by theoretical work alone; rather, only empirical research, addressing *empirical questions* that are both derived from and intended to contribute to a theory of classes, can fill them in with fruitful theoretical content. This, at least, is the methodological presupposition of the present empirical analysis. For rather too much that passes for sophisticated theory about classes tends to argue by postulation and logical inference from conceptual categories, thereby "knowing" class realities, as it were, a priori and thus eliminating the need to bother with the vulgarities of empirical inquiry. This penchant for theorization, and even "investigation," by postulation has tended especially to afflict sociological conceptions of the dominant, or "upper," class in contemporary Western societies. On the one hand, in functionalist theory, the capitalist class simply has been assumed away because it has no conceptual place within a preconceived harmonious system of "social stratification" revolving about mere occupational differentiation. On the other hand, in structuralist Marxism, the nature and internal structure of the "bourgeoisie" can simply be "read off" from the "global functions of capital" in an abstract capitalist mode of production.[2] For both of these theories, what has to be known

[1] Giddens 1973, pp. 72, 105.

[2] Thus, for example, the architectonic functionalist theorist Talcott Parsons

is rather conveniently already known, because it is pre-given, and plain ignorance about social reality can thus masquerade in its place. So, the present work, at a minimum, is an attempt to discover and delineate the *concrete ensemble of social relations within an actually existing dominant class in a Western capitalist country*.

That "concrete ensemble of social relations," however, which we seek to reveal through close, sustained, and systematic empirical analysis, scarcely presented itself to us as the result of mere patient observation, demarcation, and inductive logic. Our empirical inquiry was not thought through in some theory-free language of observation, but, on the contrary, was impregnated with the theory that classes and their contradictory interrelations are both the constitutive units of the social whole and the decisive elements in historical development. Thus, in our conception, class theory is a *social* theory whose originating questions are essentially *historical* questions, and whose core propositions and analytical categories are simultaneously sociological and historical. Nary a question addressed in the present work, therefore, does not—whether implicitly or explicitly—have this double edge to it: What is the history-making relevance of the actual structure of class relations revealed by our empirical analysis? What are the historical possibilities inherent in such structured social relations?

Intraclass Relations

Our focus in this work, however, is not on relations between classes but rather on intraclass relations, in particular, on the social relations within the dominant class itself. This analysis is both empirically novel and responds to and raises certain theoretical questions that neither the classic works of Karl Marx or Max Weber nor those of their most influential successors address systematically, although their conceptions surely inform our own understanding of the place of classes in society and history. So this study, by its attempt at sustained analysis of the social relations within *a* dominant class, charts new ground. Its objective

simply postulates the central managerialist notions: "The primary structural emphasis no longer falls on the orientation of capitalistic enterprise to profit and the theory of exploitation but rather on the structure of occupational roles within the system of industrial society" (1954, p. 324). Because, in Parsons' postulated world, one "can clearly no longer speak of a 'capitalistic' propertied class which has replaced the earlier 'feudal' landed class," he is led also to the logical necessity of "divorcing the concept of social class from its historical relation to both kinship and property as such" (1970, p. 24). On structuralist Marxism's similar analytical postulation as a substitute for empirical inquiry or genuine explanation, see Connell 1979.

is to grasp not only the constellation of concrete relations within that class—the dominant class of Chile—but also to delineate the relations that an adequate analysis of *any* dominant class in contemporary capitalist democracies must examine.

Every real social class, it must be emphasized, is also a historical class, not a mere social category or analytical abstraction, and its internal relations have been shaped by the specific historical experience of the society of which it is a decisive constituent. "Any theory of class structure, in dealing with a given historical period, must include prior class structures among its data. . . . Any theory of classes and class formation," as Joseph Schumpeter puts it metaphorically, "must explain the fact that classes coexisting at any given time bear the marks of different centuries on their brow."[3] In Chile, as in other Western capitalist countries and Japan, the protracted presence of agrarian (if not precapitalist or feudal) elements has been critical in the process of class formation. So, too, foreign capital has long played a crucial role in Chile's historical development. Therefore, our focus is, first, on the interrelations between the higher functionaries and principal owners of capital, and then, successively, on their interrelations with the great landowners and the major foreign firms.

The chapters of this book are thus self-contained but cumulative empirical attempts to "answer" three closely related sociological questions: (1) How has the ascendance of the large corporation affected the internal social relations of the dominant class? At issue are the social relevance of the "separation of ownership and control," the interconnections between the large corporation's owners and managers, and the intraclass role of bankers and, in particular, "finance capitalists," i.e. the men who interlock the leading banks and top nonfinancial corporations. (2) Given that an agrarian prehistory and regnant landed class have profoundly shaped Chile's capitalist development, how is the "coexistence" of the owners of land and capital structured socially? At issue is whether landlords and capitalists constitute separate (and contending) classes or the decisive "segments" of the same, if internally diverse, dominant class. How, in turn, do their contradictory interests and social relations affect their relative exercise of political hegemony? (3) How and to what extent has there been a coalescence of domestic and foreign capital, and what social forms does it take within the dominant class itself? At issue is whether the structural integration of domestic and foreign interests takes place on the margin or at the core

[3] Schumpeter 1955, p. 111.

of that class and what this implies for the existence and political role of a so-called national bourgeoisie. Answering these questions, we believe, is essential to the elaboration of a fruitful comparative theory of dominant classes under contemporary capitalism.

The leading empirical questions of the present work, then, are intrinsically theoretical; they derive from the proposition that the economy, particularly the specific historical form of ownership and control of the decisive means of production, tends to be *socially reconstituted in the structure of intraclass relations of dominant "bourgeois" classes*.

To lay bare how Chile's disparate but decisive units of production, the great landed estate and the large corporation, are integrally related to the internal structure of its dominant class has involved a logic of inquiry and methods of analysis that are indispensable, we suggest, to the adequate analysis of other dominant classes. A primary methodological assumption of this work, then, is that its basic concepts and propositions, as well as its concrete procedures of investigation, will also apply, allowing for the necessity of historical specification, to the discovery and analysis of the innermost structural secrets of the dominant classes of "advanced" capitalist societies. In reality, while we were working on the present book, we were also separately involved in studies of the internal structure of the dominant class in our own country. The scope of our sensibilities, the precision of our references, and the depth of our reasoning about the internal relations of both dominant classes have been enhanced, we think, by the parallel analyses we have carried out on each.[4]

To delve deeply into the real structure of the internal relations of Chile's dominant class, it was necessary to identify and then trace the complex proprietary, corporate, banking, and kinship connections among—and the political offices held by—the nation's higher corporate executives, major bankers, principal owners of capital, and great landowners. Concretely, this involved a systematic investigation of the connections, as of the mid-1960s, among individuals in four universes: (1) the officers and directors of Chile's top 37 nonfinancial corporations (229 men); (2) their counterparts in the Big Six commercial banks (68 men); (3) the "top landowners," or owners of the largest landed estates (132 men and women); and (4) the "top investors" (measured by the aggregate market value of their shareholdings) in the 16 leading commercial banks, the top 37 nonfinancial corporations, and 11 of the top

[4] See Ratcliff et al. 1979, 1979/80, 1980a, 1980b; Zeitlin 1974a, 1976, 1977; Zeitlin and Norich 1979; Soref and Zeitlin 1988.

foreign-owned corporations (502 men and women). For the individuals in the first three universes, we identified and analyzed the connections among their landholdings, capital ownership, managerial positions, kinship relations, and political offices held (party, legislative, and executive); for the fourth universe, we "merely" traced their kinship relations to the members of the first three universes. All told, to trace the kinship web encompassing the individuals in these four universes entailed identifying and analyzing the kinship relations of some 6,000 of their close relatives.

This extensive tracing of kinship relations was undertaken on the supposition that they provide the basis for a class's internal integration and historical continuity: freely intermarrying families, not individuals, are the constitutive units of classes, especially of the dominant class, where ownership and control of capital and of landed property tend to be held by the family or other effective kinship units. Our analysis will reveal that, appearances to the contrary notwithstanding, Chile's large corporations are ordinarily controlled not by their managements, but rather by a specific family or set of closely interrelated kindred and their associates, based on their combined ownership interests and strategic representation in management, reinforced through an intricate system of intercorporate holdings and interlocking relationships. The large corporations (and, too, the major banks) are controlled, in short, by what we have termed a "kinecon group," a complex social unit in which common economic interests and close kinship relationships are indissoluble. The concepts of the kinecon group and of social class are therefore integrally related; both refer to the fusion of the kinship and property systems—and this fusion, in turn, tends to reproduce (literally and figuratively) the existing dominant class over time.

If large corporations were not controlled by such a specific capitalist family or kinecon group, however, it would scarcely mean that power had passed from capital to the "new princes" of the managerial realm. For although, much like their counterparts in England or the United States, the higher executives of the large corporations in Chile typically appear to be mere "bureaucrats" rather than "capitalists," our analysis will reveal that multiple strands of intertwining consanguineal and affinal bonds extending far beyond the immediate family unit, at kinship distances nonetheless measurable and specifiable, bind the families of these managers and the families of the principal owners of capital together into the same relatively cohesive class.

Among these managers, it is precisely those in the inner group—sitting at the center of the elaborate network of interlocking directorates that anchors the corporate community of interest, and acting as the leading organizers of the corporate system of classwide property—who are most fully integrated into the principal capitalist families by close kinship relations. Thus, the relevant analytical unit in an adequate explanation of the interlocking directorate—its pattern of interlocking and the selection of the interlocking directors themselves—is not the corporation or the bank as an organization or even as a firm, but the internal structure of the class that owns and controls them both. Large corporations and major banks (as well as other financial institutions) tend to be units in, and instrumentalities of, the complex intercorporate system of propertied interests controlled by principal capitalist families and their entire class. Not a radical separation of the systems of property and the family, but rather an interpenetration of bureaucratic authority and class power, characterizes the higher managerial realm in Chile's top corporations.

The interlocking, in particular, of the top corporations and major banks is an organizational expression of the coalescence of interest-bearing capital and industrial capital, and the consequent inner transformation of the capitalist class itself. In Marx's time, "money capitalists" and "industrial capitalists" constituted, in his view, "rival fractions . . . of the appropriating class."[5] They were, in our conceptual terms, separate and opposed "class segments," occupying—despite their common ownership of the means of production—relatively distinct locations in the productive process (and in the accumulation and appropriation process in particular) and, consequently, possessing inherently contradictory interests.[6]

[5] Marx 1967, III, pp. 372–379; 1952, p. 86.

[6] Wolf (1955) has used the term "peasant segments" in a sense roughly similar to our own concept of "class segments." By our concept, however, we wish to denote explicitly the theoretical content usually implicit in Marx's term "Fraktion." Although he never offered a formal definition of "Fraktion," the primary conceptual content is relatively clear from his many specific discussions, and from references to the "economic foundations" (1948, p. 110; 1973a, p. 59) of the various parts of the bourgeoisie, "held together by great common interests and marked off by specific conditions of production" (1963, p. 27; 1965, p. 21) or "different kinds of property" (1963, p. 47; 1965, p. 42), among whom it was necessary to protect and advance "the common class interest without giving up their mutual rivalry" (1948, p. 110; 1973a, p. 59). But we prefer a new term, "class segment," with relatively clear conceptual meaning. First of all, Marx used a variety of terms interchangeably and not always consistently, such as "Teil" (part), "Abteilung" (section or division), "Gegenspartie" (opposing faction or party), "Faktion" (faction) and "Fraktion" (which itself is translated "faction"). Second, and most important, Marx often referred by the same term

The confluence of loan capital and industrial capital under the domain of the big bank and large corporation, however, produces a new, self-contradictory form of capital, "finance capital." The finance capitalists who personify this process, i.e. who sit simultaneously on the boards of the major banks (or other financial institutions) and large corporations, thereby also form a new coalesced class segment. In Chile, the finance capitalists have played a special role in coordinating and integrating the classwide interests embodied in these banks and corporations. The finance capitalists both exercise the decisive power in the higher corporate world and are, indeed, also the veritable embodiment not only of the coalescence of bank and corporate capital, but also of the fusion of property, family, and class—as well as the close allies of foreign capital.

Standing alongside the major banks and large corporations in Chile are the large estates, the decisive units of production in agriculture and the base of social domination in the countryside. Rather, however, than forming the disparate economic foundations of contending classes, they tend, in reality, to be owned by the very same families, simultaneously "capitalist" and "landlord," who are integrated into particular clusters of multiply intermarried propertied families, or "maximum kinship groups," constituting the central core of Chile's dominant class. Indeed, the central core itself is an incomparably large effective kinship unit consisting of closely intermarrying landlord and capitalist families,

("Fraktion") not only to parts of the same class, but also those of the same party, and even to each of the parties themselves. While he occasionally referred to politically organized parts of the bourgeoisie ("Bonapartists" or "Tricolor Republicans") that did *not* rest on common economic foundations as a mere "collection" (*Sammlung*) (1948, p. 112; 1973a, p. 60) or "coterie" (*Koterie*) (1948, pp. 109–110; 1973a, pp. 58–59), he usually also termed such a group a "Fraktion." The fact that translators have usually rendered the German term "Fraktion" as "faction" in English, and occasionally as "division," "section," or "part," but only rarely as "fraction," has also been confusing. It also accounts, in part, for this concept's virtual absence from English-language writings on Marx or by Marxists until recent years. The term "fraction" is often employed by French Marxists (e.g. Poulantzas, 1973a and 1973b). Cf. Weber 1946, pp. 181–186, 301, on his concept of "class situation." Although he usually focuses on the "mode of distribution" (in contrast to Marx's focus on the production and appropriation of the social product in a "mode of production" constituted by contradictory class relations), the content of Weber's concept of "class situation" in his actual sociological analyses is in fact quite similar to Marx's sense of "class location" (or "class position"). In what follows, we adapt Weber's term "class situation" and Marx's term "class location" to accord with the conceptual content of our term "class segments," and we refer interchangeably to their distinctive and contradictory "intraclass situations" or "intraclass locations."

thus reinforcing their common class monopoly of the decisive units of production.

In theory, even segments of the same class, given their differential location in the productive process and consequent contradictory interests, have the inherent potential of developing their own specific variants of intraclass consciousness and common action vis-à-vis each other as well as against contending classes. So pervasive, however, are the intimate social relations among Chile's "landlords" and "capitalists," that even conceptualizing them as distinctive class segments tends to distort how thoroughly they have coalesced into a single, indissoluble, dominant class.

But if Chile's historical development had thus effected the abolition of the distinction between capitalist and landowner, the particular families and kinecon groups who own both capital and landed property retain nonetheless a distinctive social and political identity within their class, rooted in their specific, self-contradictory intraclass situation. For the interests of land and capital, depending on the specific historical circumstances and phase of capitalist development, have often been at odds and have formed the potential bases of intraclass conflict. The coalesced segment of landed capitalist families is thus the bearer of the general interest of its class in a quite specific historical/sociological sense; the families within it have been impelled by their self-contradictory economic location to try through political activity, and by means of state policy, to transcend the contradictions between land and capital. They stand out, in reality, as the preeminent source of the political cadre of their class, sending their members to serve disproportionately in the leadership of its political parties and as members of the congress, the judiciary, and the cabinet ministries. To belong to a landed capitalist family is thus also to belong to one of the nation's reigning political families.

These selfsame families also engross the helms of the only other (and possibly rival) bases of economic power, the large foreign corporations: the landed capitalists who belong to a political family are thoroughly tied to foreign capital. Holding political hegemony in their class and power in the state, the great families of landlords and capitalists thus form not a threat or even a counterbalance to "imperialism," but its very bulwark—as, too, and reciprocally, is foreign capital a rampart of their own class dominion.

The empirical analysis in this work focuses on the nexus between social relations and property relations within the dominant class; but its premise is that these intraclass relations are themselves based on the relations among classes. For the large corporation administers production and commands labor to enforce the extraction of profit, which, in turn, is privately appropriated by the principal owners of capital; it is thus (as this work seeks to demonstrate) the decisive unit in a class-controlled apparatus of private appropriation. Similarly, the agrarian estate exists as such only within (and is simultaneously the social form taken by) the historically specific relations of production and appropriation between the estate owner and the agricultural producer, whether tenant, laborer, or dependent small holder.

If these are our theoretical premises, however, no systematic attempt is made in the empirical analysis itself to link intraclass and interclass relations (though we occasionally comment upon them). For, as the reader will no doubt quickly realize, the "mere" effort to reconstruct analytically and reveal empirically the inner social relations of Chile's dominant class has involved an extraordinarily demanding research process. Thus, at this writing, this work is still unparalleled in the extent to which it shows in concrete detail the ensemble of interconnections among economic and social relations—i.e. ownership and control of land and capital as well as social integration and differentiation—within a dominant class. A systematic empirical analysis of how such intraclass relations themselves are rooted in class relations is a task that others can now carry out.

That the present analysis focuses on the real internal relations of a single (if dominant) class does not imply that they are necessarily, as Frank Parkin avers, "on the same theoretical plane as inter-class divisions." Whether or not the structural relations between classes and within classes are, in Parkin's words, "related but essentially different phenomena requiring separate levels of analysis" is surely a crucial theoretical question.[7] This work does not, nor can it, address that question directly. A crucial premise of our analysis, however (especially in Chapters 4–6), is that if any struggle *between* classes tends to minimize or even erase the relevance of social relations *within* classes, the latter (i.e. intraclass relations) are also undoubtedly involved (the question is how and to what extent) in shaping that very struggle. For the internal relations of a class set limits on, if indeed they do not actually determine, the way it recognizes, articulates, organizes, and acts on its own immediate and historical interests as a class—and engages other, dominant or subordinate, classes in struggle. Intraclass relations affect the unity of a class

[7] Parkin 1979, p. 30.

and the possibility of its political alliances with other classes, and, consequently, how that class confronts its main class antagonist.

An originating question of this work, then, was the bearing of the internal structure of the dominant class—in particular, in the analysis of relations between landlords and capitalists, and among them and foreign capital—on what was historically possible in Chile. Much of our analysis thus bears on the question of what Erik Olin Wright calls "structural class capacities," i.e. the consequences of the social relations within a class for class conflict. The "structure of social relations within a class," as Wright observes, "generates a capacity for the struggle over class objectives." A class's internal structure is, in short, "the potential basis for the realization of [its] class interests within the class struggle."[8] But how "class capacities" are causally relevant, in practice, cannot be answered abstractly or "in general." Rather, the bearing of intraclass relations on any concrete political struggle can be discovered only through a historically specific analysis of the struggle itself.[9] No such analysis can be undertaken here. At appropriate points in the present analysis, however, we suggest how the political strategy of the dominant class has been affected by its internal structure.

Chile's Social Contours

Chile's class structure during the period encompassing the present empirical analysis was akin to that of its more "advanced" counterparts. In the mid-1960s, the nation had a "rather well diversified industrial structure" and a working class whose social weight in its society was similar to that of the French, Italian, and Japanese working classes a decade earlier. Chile's agricultural labor force was smaller than Japan's and Italy's in the 1950s, and it was on a par with France's.[10] Wage workers in the towns and cities constituted about half the population. Roughly 30 percent of the labor force were employed in manufacturing, construc-

[8] Wright 1978, p. 99.

[9] See Zeitlin 1984.

[10] Ehrman 1966, p. xix; also see Bohan and Pomeranz 1960, p. 3; CORFO 1966, p. 523. Chilean censuses provided no occupational breakdowns. Other official estimates, cited in Petras 1969, p. 131, put "urban workers" at 47.7 percent of the population in the 1960s. According to CORFO, Chile's development agency, the proportions of the economically active population in each sector were as follows: manufacturing, 18.1 percent; construction, 7.4 percent; mining, 4.4 percent. Comparative percentages, in the early 1950s, are as follows: France, 25.8, 7.1, and 2.1; Italy, 21.9, 7.1, and 0.9; Japan, 17.8, 4.6, and 1.4. Japan had 41.1 percent, France 27.2 percent, and Italy 40 percent employed in agriculture in the early 1950s compared with Chile's 28.6 percent in 1960. See Bain 1966, p. 16; CORFO 1966, p. 523.

tion, or mining. There were abundant near-artisan shops. But large plants owned by the top corporations employed most industrial workers, over a quarter of whom worked in plants employing 500 or more workers; well over half (55 percent) worked in plants employing at least 100 workers.[11] A central labor federation (CUT) unified the country's major unions under the predominant leadership of Socialists and Communists; by the late 1960s, some 18 percent of the entire labor force belonged to CUT's affiliated unions. But in concerns employing at least 25 workers, which was the legal minimum for organizing an industrial union, roughly 70 percent of the workers belonged to CUT unions.[12]

A heterogeneous *pequeña burguesía*, consisting of shopkeepers, small-business owners, and artisans merged imperceptibly, on one side, with elements of the *clase popular*, the poor urban "self-employed" providing services to the affluent. On the other, it merged with the *empleados*: the clerks, sales people, technicians, professionals, managers, and kindred employees, usually lumped together under the rubric of the "middle class." All told, these highly variegated intermediate social strata may have accounted for 20 to 30 percent of Chile's entire population, and for more in the major cities.[13]

Chilean capitalists, in the apt words of the International Committee of the United States Chambers of Commerce, are "members of that select company of men who are part of the mainstream of twentieth-century capitalism."[14] Despite the virtual monopoly of large-scale copper mining by American capital, and foreign penetration of much of the nation's industry and commerce, Chilean capitalists in the 1960s possessed a highly concentrated economic base of their own.[15] The largest 100 Chilean-owned nonfinancial corporations (not counting

[11] Ehrman 1966, p. 32.

[12] Angell 1972, p. 46; *New York Times*, October 6, 1970. There were 4,000 unions affiliated with CUT, most led by Communists and Socialists, but about a fourth by Christian Democrats.

[13] An unofficial estimate put "urban non-manual employees," mainly white-collar workers, at 18.6 percent in 1964 (Frank 1967, pp. 106–107). In 1970, *New York Times* correspondent Juan de Onís guessed that some 30 percent of Chile's population of roughly 10 million were "middle class" (*New York Times*, October 26, 1970).

[14] Nehemkis 1964, p. 220. A presidential campaign task force of Salvador Allende estimated "urban owners of capital" at 4.7 percent of the population in 1964 (Frank 1967, pp. 106–107). How this estimate was arrived at is not explained; it doubtlessly includes a host of owners of owner-operated small enterprises employing family members, and very much inflates the real size of the class of "owners of capital" employing wage labor on a significant scale.

[15] See Chapter 6 for an analysis of the structural interpenetration of domestic and foreign capital.

state enterprises) controlled 59 percent of the aggregate net capital assets of all Chilean corporations, and the top 10 alone controlled 25 percent.[16] Reinforced by state investment, Chile's large corporations controlled most industry (outside of mining), commerce, and finance in the country in the 1960s.

In the provinces of the Central Valley, containing most of the rural population and some three-fourths of the nation's irrigated land, the large estate was the decisive unit of agricultural production and the dominant institution of rural life. Fewer than a thousand estates, owned by great landed families and worked by labor-service tenants (*inquilinos*) and wage laborers, held almost half of the most valuable arable land in the Central Valley.[17] Only in the near-south zone around Concepción was there a class of independent commercial farmers working their own land. Foreign investment was negligible in agriculture, although it was of some significance in the huge sheep- and cattle-ranching companies of the far Patagonian south.

Politically, Chile was—until the horrific military coup of September 11, 1973—one of the world's most stable constitutional democracies; for over a century it had been ruled by a mixed system of presidential and parliamentary government. Chile's "record of representative government" had been "unsurpassed in Latin America"; in fact, as of the 1960s, that record was matched by few countries anywhere.[18] In sum, though not one of the West's major powers, Chile was a proudly sovereign capitalist democracy.[19] An empirical analysis of the ensemble of social relations among that country's reigning capitalists and landowners is, therefore, as we shall show in concrete detail, surely germane to an understanding of the internal structure of other dominant classes in the contemporary capitalist world.

[16] See Chapter 1 for detailed figures on the concentration of capital.

[17] See Chapter 4 for detailed figures on the concentration of landownership.

[18] Johnson 1958, pp. 72, 92. Zeitlin (1984) addresses the historical question as to how a society that never quite became bourgeois itself became governed by "bourgeois democracy."

[19] From the middle through the end of the past century, Chile strode the Pacific Coast of South America as a rapidly developing hegemonic power. Chile seemed, as its statesmen proclaimed, to possess its own "manifest destiny" and "civilizing mission" as an independent capitalist power in the Americas. But by the early decades of the present century it was already becoming a country remarkable for the sharp contrast between the vibrancy of its political democracy and the stagnation, if not "underdevelopment," of its economy. See Zeitlin (1984) for an analysis of the social causes of Chile's stunted capitalist development.

CHAPTER ONE

Corporate Ownership and Control: The Large Corporation and the Capitalist Class

THE LARGE corporation is the decisive unit of production in "highly concentrated capitalist economies."[1] Its ascendance surely has significantly affected the class relations and internal dynamics of contemporary capitalist societies. But has the result actually been "the breakup of family capitalism" and the transformation of "the capitalist class . . . into the managerial class"[2]—and thereby also the abolition of the internal contradictions, exploitative relations, and social domination characteristic of private ownership and control of capital? That is the originating question of the empirical analyses in this and the following chapter.

The theory of managerial capitalism, implied by our question, has hoary antecedents. Indeed, managerial theory has Marxian antecedents long antedating its widespread acceptance by liberals as a valid reflection of social reality in the West. Not only did Marx himself make some rather confusing Hegelian comments about the implications of the rise of the "joint stock company," but the theory of the emergence of a society whose capitalist class has gradually been replaced by an administrative stratum no longer bound by the interests of property, was already being enunciated in Germany at the turn of the century. Eduard Bernstein and Konrad Schmidt, Social Democratic theoreticians of what later became known as "revisionism," argued that (a) the property form of the corporation, and the consequent dispersion of its ownership among "armies of shareholders," in Bernstein's phrase, and (b) the simultaneous and inseparable "concentration of businesses" were gradually abolishing capitalism's exploitative relations of production. The capitalist class, in Schmidt's view, was going through

[1] Bain 1966, p. 102, referring to the economies of the United States, Canada, England, France, Italy, Japan, and Sweden, whose levels of concentration he analyzes and compares.

[2] Sorokin 1953, p. 90.

a process of "expropriation by stages." The "decomposition of capital" was extending the rights of "sovereignty" over property to society as a whole, and the capitalist was being transformed "from a proprietor into a simple administrator."[3]

This was more or less the thesis of a work that appeared in the United States three decades later, in 1932, and that has been the most enduring fount of the theory of managerial capitalism and its functionalist sociological variant: *The Modern Corporation and Private Property*, by Adolf Berle, Jr., and Gardiner C. Means. "The dissolution of the atom of property," they wrote, "destroys the very foundation on which the economic order of the past three centuries has rested."[4] An economy had emerged in which the decisive business units concentrated the bulk of productive property among them but were themselves so dispersed in their ownership that they were slipping under the control of their nonowning managers. This thesis became, in subsequent years, a virtually unchallenged assumption in the prevailing conception of the reality of contemporary capitalism, now variously called "capitalism without capitalists," "managerial capitalism," or "post-capitalist society."[5] So "every *literate* person," political theorist Robert Dahl has assured us, "now *rightly takes for granted* what Berle and Means established . . . decades ago in their famous study."[6]

What Dahl assures us should be "rightly taken for granted" as "incontrovertible," however, has been under suspicion in some quarters of being a "pseudofact," a notion about reality that is as plausible and persuasive as it is deceptive. In an extensive critical review of managerial theory and of the methods of analysis and empirical evidence used to support it, Zeitlin concludes that, at best, the theory rests on a shaky and shallow empirical foundation and, at worst, is a major pseudofact that has for years profoundly misguided the analysis of contemporary capitalism and its determinate class relations.[7] As Robert K.

[3] Bernstein 1961, p. 54. For a contemporary analysis and polemical critique of these views, written in 1899, see Luxemburg 1970, pp. 16–20. On Marx's confusing Hegelian comments, see Zeitlin 1974a, pp. 1113–1115.

[4] Berle and Means 1967, p. 8.

[5] See Zeitlin 1974a.

[6] Dahl 1970, p. 125; italics added. In fact, as is shown in detail by Zeitlin (1974a, pp. 1081–1082), Berle and Means by no means "established" the so-called separation of ownership and control in their study; on the contrary, "they had information which permitted them to classify as definitely under management control [i.e. firms ostensibly shorn of control by principal owners of capital] only 22% of the 200 largest corporations [in the United States], and of the 106 industrials, only 3.8%!"

[7] See Zeitlin 1974a.

Merton reminds us, "it might at first seem needless to say that before social facts can be 'explained,' it is advisable to ensure that they actually are facts. Yet, in science, as in everyday life, explanations are sometimes provided for things that never were. . . . In sociology, as in other disciplines, pseudofacts have a way of inducing pseudoproblems, which cannot be solved because matters are not as they purport to be."[8]

The "astonishing consensus" that took for granted the assumptions and assertions of managerialism as "incontrovertible," "undoubted," and "critical facts," resulted in the virtually complete deflection—for more than a generation in the United States—of serious attention from the empirical analysis of actually existing, rather than abstractly misconceived, capitalist societies.[9] For if it is right to take for granted that the political and economic effects of the concentration of capital in huge corporations are benign because they are run by managers and technocrats, no longer driven by the imperatives of capital and the calculus of profit maximization, and beholden not to capitalists but to the "public" who owns them, why, then, bother with their empirical analysis? If we already know, as Talcott Parsons and Neil Smelser tell us, that the families who once "controlled through ownership most of the big businesses . . . by and large failed to consolidate their positions as the dominant class in the society,"[10] then occupational differentiation, the flow of rewards, and status attainment in a pluralist polity, rather than class relations, exploitation, and social domination in a capitalist democracy are the appropriate (and "logical") foci of analysis. If "changes in the structure of the economy," such as the concentration of capital, bureaucratization of enterprise, and dispersion of ownership have resulted in the "shift of control of enterprise from the property interests of founding families to managerial and technical personnel who as such have not had a comparable vested interest in ownership," and thereby, as Parsons pithily puts it, have "lopped off" the capitalist class, then how can it be necessary (or possible) to examine that class and its interrelations empirically?[11]

[8] Merton 1959, pp. xiii–xv.

[9] The ostensible separation of ownership and control and its implications are described this way by such authorities as Dahrendorf (1959, p. 42), Parsons (1953, p. 123), Dahl (1970, p. 125), and Bell (1958, p. 248; 1961, p. 45), among many others. In Dahrendorf's words: there is an "astonishing degree of consensus among sociologists on the implications of joint-stock companies . . . for the wider structure of society."

[10] Parsons and Smelser 1957, p. 254.

[11] Parsons 1953, p. 123.

But, as Zeitlin has put it elsewhere, "news of the demise of capitalist classes, particularly in the United States, is, [we] suspect, somewhat premature." Instead of assorted pseudofactual generalizations,

> extrapolated from an insufficiently examined American experience or deduced from abstract ahistorical theoretical premises, detailed empirical studies are necessary. . . . [They] must focus at the outset on the complex relationships in which the corporation is itself involved: the particular pattern of holdings and their evolution within the corporation; and the relationships between it and other corporations; the forms of personal union or interlocking between corporate directorates and between the officers and directors and principal shareholding families; the connections with banks, both as "financial institutions" and . . . agents of specified propertied interests, including those who control the banks themselves; the network of intercorporate and principal common shareholdings. In a word, it will be necessary to explore in detail the institutional and class structure in which the individual large corporations are situated. . . . Studies of contemporary dominant classes . . . not only [in] "advanced" but [also] less developed and misdeveloped countries, are also essential. Such studies, aside from their intrinsic importance, may help reveal theoretical gaps and errors, as well as inadequate methodologies, in the present body of research and writing, and allow us to . . . provide the basis for a comparative theory of capitalist classes that is more comprehensive and valid than the extant one embodied in the astonishing consensus among social scientists. In place of abstract models based on ostensible "universal" elements in social structures, we need analyses of the structures of specific capitalist classes, related to the actual historical processes within which they have been formed.[12]

[12] Zeitlin 1974a, pp. 1107 and 1112. For a comprehensive discussion of recent analyses of "ownership and control of corporations," see Glasberg and Schwartz 1983. They rightly remark (p. 327) that "the debate about ownership and control has pushed beyond the narrow confines of evaluating managerial theory and has become a broad controversy over the nature of intercorporate interaction and the structure of business unity. The mass of evidence and creative analyses of the 1970s have exposed the inadequacies of managerial theory . . . and laid the foundation for a new round of theoretically grounded and socially useful empirical work." But, despite its weakened hold on the sociological imagination, it is doubtful that such "creative analyses," as Glasberg and Schwartz aver, have "definitively ended the 30-year domination of the managerial perspective." For instance, a widely used introductory sociology textbook still teaches beginning students this silliest of all managerialist pseudofacts: "Those who control the corporation—the managers and to a lesser extent the direc-

The Concentration of Capital

This is the agenda, then, for much of the present work, which is, first of all, an empirical analysis of the internal structure of an actually existing dominant class in a highly concentrated capitalist economy in which the large corporation has long been decisive.[13] The bulk of the assets, sales, and profits in the major industries and in the overall economy of Chile are held by a few large corporations that effectively

---

tors—are for most purposes *responsible to nobody but themselves*" (Robertson 1983, p. 473; italics added). In a more serious vein, some neo-managerialists of the left (see note 16, Chapter 2, below) also consider it, in Herman's words, an "established truth" that "top managers generally control large corporations." In this "theory of constrained managerial control of the large corporation," however, ownership of capital "persists as a powerful influence and constraint on managerial ends and behavior," supplemented by "internal structural changes and rules of behavior that preserve and reinforce a profitability goal." Herman, alone among managerialists of the left, rests this thesis on the results of his own original research; he tries both to identify the locus of control in the top 200 nonfinancial corporations in the United States in the mid-1970s and to measure the effects of ostensible "management control" vs. "ownership control" on the "performance" of 72 large companies from 1967 through 1976. On the basis of the latter analysis, he concludes that "managers [are] a far cry from neutral technocrats. . . . [I]n fact, . . . the profit motive has suffered no discernible eclipse as a result of the rise of management control" (1981, pp. 14–15).

The problem with any empirical analysis of the relative performance of ostensibly management-controlled vs. owner-controlled corporations, though, is that "since independent investigations concerning the control of the large corporations . . . have come to very different conclusions [as does Herman with respect to Burch 1972], we cannot know if the 'independent variable' has even been adequately measured. In reality, the allegedly management-controlled corporations may—appearances aside—continue to be subject to control by minority ownership interests and/or 'outside' centers of control" (Zeitlin 1974a, p. 1097). (This stricture also applies, of course, to the study of Zeitlin and Norich of types of control [using the control classifications of Burch 1972 and Palmer 1973] and profit performance in the top 300 U.S. industrial corporations of 1964; they, like Herman, also find that "so-called management control has no measurable effect on the rate of return of the large corporation" [1979, p. 45].) As to Herman's research on the locus of corporate control, we believe that what he says of Burch's research (Burch [1972] found management control and family control at an approximate standoff in numbers among large U.S. corporations) surely applies to Herman's work on that question also: Herman's "own definitions and methods are not beyond criticism." Herman's analysis of the locus of corporate control is susceptible to most of the same criticisms that have been made here (and in Zeitlin 1974a) of other such research. Most important, Herman scarcely inquires (and then in only a cursory and unsystematic way) into the fusion of property and family in the large corporation, and thus he cannot help but confirm the "established truth" with which he began his research and which he took as its "premise—not as something to be proved" (Herman 1981, p. 14). In the present work, to the contrary, no "established truth" on this issue is presupposed.

[13] On the growth of the corporation in Chile, see Escobar Cerda 1959.

control their markets. Of course, foreign-owned firms are prominent among them and, during the period under analysis, held a shared monopoly of large-scale copper mining (until its nationalization by the unanimous vote of congress under the presidency of Salvador Allende). But outside of mining, not foreign but Chilean-owned firms were preponderant in the nation's economy. Of the combined net capital assets held by the 182 largest nonfinancial corporations in Chile, the top 139 Chilean-owned firms accounted for slightly over half (52 percent). But of the combined assets of the top 169 *non*mining firms, the top 134 Chilean-owned companies held nearly three-quarters (72 percent). In fact, together with several state enterprises, they held most of the corporate assets in agriculture, manufacturing, utilities, transportation, and commerce, as well as in coal mining and petroleum extraction and refining.[14] Table 1.1 shows the distribution of assets among the top 193 domestic (private and state) and foreign firms in Chile during the mid-1960s.

State investment has heavily reinforced private Chilean capital and

[14] Corporations made up 17 percent of all registered business enterprises in 1967 (including partnerships, proprietorships, limited companies, and corporations); but they owned 90.4 percent of the total assets held by all of these enterprises (Garretón and Cisternas 1970, p. 6). Corporations were, as we mentioned earlier, of negligible significance in agriculture, where the large estate constituted the overwhelmingly preponderant organizational form of economic activity.

Our analysis of corporate concentration is based on data obtained from the Superintendencia de Cías. de Seguro, Sociedades Anónimas y Bolsas de Comercio (the Commission on Insurance Companies, Corporations, and Stock Exchanges). The commission completed the first official compilation of data on the 200 largest firms in the country several years after our own research on corporate ownership and control had commenced. In late 1969 it made available its compilation of data on the 200 largest firms for 1966, ranked by net capital assets and classified by three-digit standard industrial classification (SIC) categories. Included in the compilation were listings of each of the 200 firms' assets, three-digit SIC category, directors (but not officers), top-10 shareholdings (but not the number or percentage of outstanding shares held by each), and the latter's distribution among domestic and foreign shareholders. In addition, the commission's compilation provides data on the aggregate net capital assets of the country's 1,729 corporations, including domestic (state and private) and foreign firms, in the various three-digit SIC categories; it also lists the firms in each category that were among the 200 largest in the country. The top 200 firms were, in fact, distributed as follows: 11 state enterprises; 6 financial companies (5 Chilean and 1 foreign); 139 nonfinancial corporations, majority-owned by Chilean private investors; and 43 foreign-owned nonfinancial firms. One firm remained unidentified. We estimated the aggregate assets held by the Chilean state and private companies and by the foreign firms in various industries from figures in the commission's compilation, after correcting some minor discrepancies and errors. See Chapter 6 for an analysis of these data, showing the extent of the interpenetration of ownership among domestic and foreign firms.

TABLE 1.1. Distribution of the Top 193 Firms in Chile and Their Assets in Major Industrial Categories, 1966

	Chilean Firms				Foreign Firms[a]	
	State[b]		Private[c]			
	N	% Assets	*N*	% Assets	*N*	% Assets
Agriculture						
forestry and fishing	*0*	*0*	*11*	*90.6*	*3*	*9.4*
Mining	2	*24.6*	*5*	*6.2*	*8*	*69.2*
coal	0	0	1	100.0	0	0
iron	0	0	1	16.1	1	83.9
copper	1	0.9	3	4.3	6	94.2
petroleum	1	100.0	0	0	0	0
nitrates	0	0	0	0	1	100.0
Manufacturing	*4*	*5.4*	*87*	*78.3*	*20*	*16.3*
Construction	2	*93.1*	*3*	*6.9*	*0*	*0*
Utilities	2	*58.2*	*7*	*11.8*	*3*	*30.0*
electricity	1	78.8	4	10.7	1	10.4
gas	0	0	3	100.0	0	0
telephone	1	4.6	0	0	2	95.4
Transportation						
railroads[d]	*0*	—	*0*	*0*	*1*	—
shipping	*0*	*0*	*5*	*100.0*	*0*	*0*
Commerce	*0*	*0*	*21*	*60.9*	*8*	*39.1*
wholesale	0	0	8	53.1	5	46.9
retail	0	0	6	66.5	1	33.5
real estate	0	0	2	100.0	0	0
other	0	0	5	65.4	2	34.6
Services						
hotels	*1*	*100.0*	*0*	*0*	*0*	*0*
All firms	11	25.1	139	38.9	43	35.9

[a] Majority-owned by foreign investors.
[b] Majority-owned by state.
[c] Majority-owned by Chilean private investors.
[d] The Chilean State Railway owns and operates the public-service railroads; no data on these railways were included in the commission on corporations' compilation of the top 200 firms.

has acted as a substantial counterweight to foreign capital for decades, especially in those activities where foreign capital might otherwise be heavily involved. Since 1931, the ownership of petroleum deposits has been vested in the state, which has also retained exclusive control over refining, making it possible in the following years for Chile's National Petroleum Enterprise (ENAP, founded in 1950) to meet the country's petroleum needs from domestic sources and to reinvest a portion of its profits in other development projects. As the integrated state-owned petroleum industry, controlling exploration, extraction, and refining, ENAP has not only indirectly subsidized private industry by providing low-cost fuels, but has also ensured it lucrative profits from the sale of gasoline, kerosene, bottled gas, and other petroleum products. The law guaranteed the privately owned Petroleum Company of Chile (COPEC) at least 50 percent of domestic sales, with ESSO and Shell splitting the rest of the distribution market between them.[15]

The National Electricity Enterprise (ENDESA), established in 1945, tripled the country's public-service generating capacity within the next 15 years.[16] Until ENDESA's establishment, American and Foreign Power's subsidiary Chilectra had held a virtual monopoly in that industry. In the mid-1960s, ENDESA controlled 79 percent of the assets in electric light and power, and the rest was split about evenly between Chilectra and four private Chilean companies. Over the years there have also been major state enterprises, as well as "mixed" enterprises (involving both state and private investment), operating in manufacturing (pharmaceuticals, chemicals, cement), sugar refining, telecommunications, transport, mining, and the construction of public works. Once operating profitably, however, mixed enterprises have usually been turned over gradually to private ownership.[17]

Thus, if state investment undoubtedly has contributed substantially to Chile's development, it has also been guided by the profit considerations of private industry and the interests of the private sector as a whole.[18] Much as in such major capitalist countries as France, Austria, Italy, and England, where limited and selective state enterprise operates cooperatively with "private-sector interests," Chile also has been characterized by "an established intimacy between the representatives of public authority and the practitioners of private enterprise."[19]

The top 139 Chilean nonfinancial corporations, buttressed by selective state investment, constituted, in the mid-1960s, the highly concen-

[15] Puga Vega 1964, chaps. 5–7; Bohan and Pomeranz 1960, pp. 183–187. Chile's oil deposits narrowly escaped becoming the property of international oil companies more than half a century ago. In 1927, legislation (subsequently rescinded) had authorized granting concessions amounting to 1.25 million acres, for which Standard Oil, Royal Dutch Shell, and Panamerican Petroleum filed applications in Magallanes and Tierra del Fuego (Puga Vega 1964, p. 74). On the causes of the ascendance of foreign capital in the copper industry in Chile, see Zeitlin 1984, esp. pp. 190–210.

[16] Bohan and Pomeranz 1960, p. 181. On the role of state investment in Chile, see ECLA 1971.

[17] Ehrman 1966, pp. 117–132.

[18] Bohan and Pomeranz 1960, p. 219.

[19] Shonfield 1965, pp. 109, 179, 184–186, 193.

trated base of Chilean capitalism. In the aggregate, these top 139 Chilean corporations (excluding state enterprises) held roughly two-thirds of the combined net capital assets of all 1,611 Chilean nonfinancial corporations. But even among these top corporations, concentration was high: the top 10 alone held a quarter, the top 50 nearly half (48 percent), and the top 100, 59 percent of all Chilean corporate assets.[20]

Nearly two out of three of Chile's top 139 corporations were in manufacturing: 87 Chilean companies held 78 percent of the combined assets of the top 111 domestic and foreign manufacturing firms, and 58 percent of *all* corporate manufacturing assets in the country; 4 state enterprises held another 4 percent of all manufacturing assets, compared with the 12 percent held by the top 20 foreign firms.[21]

These top 111 domestic and foreign manufacturing firms were represented in 39 different industries, all of which were also highly concentrated, and Chilean-owned corporations were dominant in the vast majority of them.[22] The single-largest private Chilean industrial corporation alone owned half or more of the assets in 12 of the 39 specific manufacturing sectors and a quarter or more, but less than half, of the assets in another dozen of them.[23] Among the actual or

[20] These aggregate concentration figures understate the actual level of "centralization of capital," or the centralized control over production, for three basic reasons: (1) The subsidiaries and affiliates of top-200 firms that are themselves subsidiaries of others (whether or not they are also in the top 200 or rank below them) are treated here as separate and independent firms. Similarly, top-200 firms that are themselves subsidiaries of others (whether or not they are also in the top 200 or rank below them) are also not consolidated in these figures. (2) No account is taken here of the role of substantial (but not majority) mutual ownership of stock by various firms. (3) Nor do these aggregate concentration figures in any way take account of the role of substantial overlapping shareholdings in several different corporations by the same principal stockowners. But both intercorporate and overlapping shareholdings are significant potential levers of centralized control over ostensibly (and legally) independent corporations. The relevance of these forms of ownership for exerting corporate control is shown below in our detailed analysis of the ownership and control of the top 37 nonfinancial corporations.

[21] The commission on corporations' compilation does not provide data on the amount of manufacturing assets controlled separately by those foreign and domestic firms not included in the top 200. Only aggregate data were provided for each manufacturing industry.

[22] The industries here are three-digit SIC "manufacturing sectors," rather than four-digit industrial categories, and, as such, are broader groupings than the latter, which would be more appropriate for measuring concentration in specific industries. But, for lack of an alternative, we used the three-digit categories, as have specialists on concentration in the United States who also lacked four-digit data. See, for instance, U.S. Congress 1964, pp. 116–120, 212–213.

[23] By asking what share of the assets in the major manufacturing industries was

virtual single-firm monopolies were the Copper Products Company (MADECO), holding 100 percent of nonferrous metal manufacturing assets; United Breweries Company, with 96 percent of the assets in brewing and malt manufacturing; Paper and Cardboard Manufacturing Company, with 75 percent of its industry's assets; "El Melón" Industrial Enterprises, with 62 percent of the cement industry's assets; and Pacific Steel Company (CAP, a "mixed" company having a substantial minority holding by the state), with 82 percent of the assets in basic iron and steel manufacturing. The three largest private Chilean industrial corporations held at least one-quarter, but less than half, of the total assets in 15 of the 39 manufacturing industries, and one-half or more of the assets in another 16 industries.[24] In contrast, the three largest foreign companies (or fewer) held at least a quarter of the assets in 7 of the 39 industries in which the top 111 manufacturers were represented. In 7 industries, the combined assets of the top foreign firms exceeded those of the private Chilean firms represented (see Table 1.2). This was surely a significant level of foreign penetration, but domestic companies were, nonetheless, overwhelmingly preponderant in manufacturing.

The Dispersion of Ownership

The overwhelming bulk of the productive property of Chile is held by the largest corporations. But the ownership of these corporations is dispersed among numerous shareholdings, which are actively traded on the nation's stock exchanges.

Analysis of the distribution of shareholdings in the very largest non-

---

held by firms in the top 111, we arrive at a measure of "overall concentration" in manufacturing. Typically, "concentration ratios" show the percentage of assets held by the single-largest firm, or the three, four, or eight largest firms, *in a given industry*, whether or not they rank among the largest in manufacturing or in the economy as a whole. Our measures, however, refer specificallly, and only, to the assets share in a given manufacturing industry held by firms that ranked among the top 200 in the entire economy (and thus also in manufacturing as a whole). This is the only effort, to our knowledge, to show the assets held by the largest manufacturing companies in Chile's individual industries. A similar effort, to estimate overall concentration in manufacturing in the United States, was first made in 1964 by John H. Blair, then chief economist of the U.S. Senate Antitrust and Monopoly Subcommittee, who considered it "something of a new contribution" (U.S. Congress 1964, pp. 211–212).

[24] There were fewer than three top-111 firms represented in some industries, in which case only their aggregate assets are counted when we refer to the top 3 in an industry. See Table 1.2 for the distribution of firms and assets in specific manufacturing industries.

TABLE 1.2. Distribution of the Top 111 Manufacturing Firms in Chile and Their Assets in Various Sectors, 1966 (*cont.*)

U.N. SIC Code	Sector	Chilean Firms						Foreign Firms			All Firms	
		Private			State		All					
		% Assets Held by Top Firm	% Assets Held by All Top Firms	*N*[a]	% Assets Held by Top Firm	*N*[a]	% Assets Held by All Top Firms	% Assets Held by Top Firm	% Assets Held by All Top Firms	*N*[a]	% Assets Held by up to Top Three Firms[b]	*N*[a]
202	Dairy products	8.9	8.9	1		0	8.9	63.0	71.2	2	80.1	3
203	Canning and preserving of fruits and vegetables	27.6	27.6	1		0	27.6			0	27.6	1
204	Canning and preserving of fish and other seafoods	17.4	29.5	2	19.8	1	49.3			0	49.3	3
206	Bakery products	48.1	48.1	1		0	48.1			0	48.1	1
207	Sugar factories and refineries	25.0	25.0	1	61.3	1	86.3	12.1	12.1	1	98.4	3
208	Cocoa, chocolate, and sugar confectionaries	40.0	40.0	1		0	40.0	43.5	43.5	1	83.5	2
209	Miscellaneous food preparations	35.1	73.4	6		0	73.4			0	56.5	3
211	Distilling, rectifying, and blending of spirits	43.0	43.0	1		0	43.0			0	43.0	1
212	Wine industries	22.4	44.1	2	20.7	1	64.8			0	64.8	3
213	Breweries and malt manufacturing	95.7	95.7	1		0	95.7			0	95.7	1
214	Soft drinks and carbonated water industries	53.3	82.3	2		0	82.3			0	82.3	2
220	Tobacco			0		0		100.0	100.0	1	100.0	1

TABLE 1.2. Distribution of the Top 111 Manufacturing Firms in Chile and Their Assets in Various Sectors, 1966 (*cont.*)

U.N. SIC Code	Sector	Chilean Firms: Private: % Assets Held by Top Firm	Chilean Firms: Private: % Assets Held by All Top Firms	Chilean Firms: Private: N[a]	Chilean Firms: State: % Assets Held by Top Firm	Chilean Firms: State: N[a]	Chilean Firms: All: % Assets Held by All Top Firms	Foreign Firms: % Assets Held by Top Firm	Foreign Firms: % Assets Held by All Top Firms	Foreign Firms: N[a]	All Firms: % Assets Held by up to Top Three Firms[b]	All Firms: N[a]
231	Spinning, weaving, and finishing of textiles	20.4	73.8	15		0	73.8	3.2	7.3	3	40.0	3
232	Knitting mills	18.2	36.5	2		0	36.5			0	36.5	2
233	Cordage, rope, and twine	61.8	61.8	1		0	61.8			0	61.8	1
241	Footwear, except rubber footwear	8.1	15.7	2		0	15.7	38.1	38.1	1	53.8	3
243	Wearing apparel, except footwear	17.3	51.8	4		0	51.8			0	44.3	3
251	Sawmills, planing, and other woodmills	21.4	41.4	2		0	41.4			0	41.4	2
271	Pulp, paper, and paperboard mills	74.6	95.1	2		0	95.1			0	95.1	2
280	Printing, publishing, and allied industries	32.4	74.0	5		0	74.0			0	63.6	3
291	Tanneries and leather-finishing plants	32.4	32.4	1		0	32.4			0	32.4	1
293	Leather products, except wearing apparel	71.4	71.4	1		0	71.4			0	71.4	1
300	Rubber products	10.9	10.9	1		0	10.9	77.2	77.2	1	88.1	2
311	Basic industrial chemicals, including fertilizers	12.4	12.4	1		0	12.4	23.0	36.1	2	48.5	3

313	Paints, varnishes, and lacquers			0		0		22.6	22.6	1	22.6	1
319	Miscellaneous chemical products	34.6	42.9	2	8.5	1	51.4	10.0	10.0	1	52.9	3
331	Structural clay products	62.7	62.7	1		0	62.7			0	62.7	1
332	Glass and glass products	43.3	71.7	2		0	71.7			0	71.7	2
333	Pottery, china, and earthenware	89.6	89.6	1		0	89.6			0	89.6	1
334	Cement (hydraulic)	62.0	67.8	2		0	67.8	32.2	32.2	1	100.0	3
339	Nonmetallic minerals not elsewhere classified	65.6	65.6	1		0	65.6			0	65.6	1
341	Iron and steel basic industries	81.6	84.6	2		0	84.6	4.5	7.6	2	89.1	3
342	Nonferrous metal basic industries	100.0	100.0	1		0	100.0			0	100.0	1
350	Metal products, except machinery and transport equipment	15.8	51.4	7		0	51.4			0	34.4	3
360	Machinery, except electric machinery	66.5	84.9	3		0	84.9			0	84.9	3
370	Electric machinery, apparatus, appliances, and supplies	24.2	34.1	3		0	34.1	11.0	24.3	3	49.0	3
381	Shipbuilding and repairing	48.9	93.0	2		0	93.0			0	93.0	2
383	Motor vehicles	22.7	55.7	3		0	55.7			0	55.7	3
399	Industries not elsewhere classified	30.9	30.9	1		0	30.9			0	30.9	1

[a] The number of top-111 industrials, Chilean (private or state) or foreign, in a given sector.

[b] Percentage of assets held by "up to top three" firms irrespective of whether the firm is Chilean (state or private) or foreign; "up to three" because the number of top-111 industrials in a given sector may be fewer than three.

financial corporations, the top 37, shows that many of the principal shareholders-of-record (i.e. the official holders of the shares) in these corporations are institutions such as other corporations, banks, investment companies, and brokerage firms.[25] Following the practice of specialists who have analyzed the dispersion of corporate ownership in the United States and England, we analyzed the 20 largest (or "principal") shareholdings-of-record in each corporation. Of the 740 principal shareholdings in the top 37, just 424 are held in the names of individuals and another 17 via personal and family holding companies. On the average, then, between 11 and 12 of the 20 principal shareholdings are held by individuals. These principal individual shareholders combined held a majority (more than 50 percent) of the stock in 6 of the top 37; they held from 30 to 50 percent of the stock in 7, from 10 to 20 percent of the stock in 11, and less than 10 percent of the stock in 13 of the top 37. (Shareholding concentration is highest in manufacturing and lowest in utilities and other nonmanufacturing firms, in a pattern similar to that found by the studies of the Temporary National Economic Committee [TNEC] in the United States during the 1930s.)[26]

The median combined shareholding of the principal individual stockholders in the top 37 corporations is 13.6 percent. Among the top 10, the median is only 5.5 percent, while in the other ranges, it is as follows: top 11–20, 17.0 percent; top 21–30, 14.3 percent; top 31–37, 15.5 percent.

Most striking are the relatively minor shareholdings of management. The median aggregate holding of management, i.e. the combined shares held by the highest officers (president, vice-president, and general manager) and by the members of the board of directors, in the top 37 corporations is 1.9 percent. Studying the 176 largest nonfinancial corporations in the United States in 1939, Robert Gordon (one of the early proponents of the managerial thesis, for which his analysis was adduced in support) found that the median aggregate holding of management was 2.1 percent.[27] In 20 of the top 37, management's combined shareholdings come to less than 10 percent of the corporation's outstanding stock.

Thus, in summary, the top 37 corporations' principal individual

[25] See note 33 and Appendix A to this chapter for a description of the procedures used to select these top-37 nonfinancial corporations and of the sources and types of data obtained on them.

[26] Goldsmith and Parmelee 1940.

[27] Gordon 1966, p. 27.

shareholders only infrequently hold even a substantial minority, let alone a majority, of the outstanding stock. Few of the officers and directors of the top 37 are personally principal shareholders in the corporations they manage, and, even when they are, the typical executive owns only a slight percentage of his corporation's outstanding stock; in most of the top 37, even the combined shareholdings of management amount to only a small percentage of the stock in the corporation.

These findings on the distribution of stockownership in the top 37 corporations in Chile do not differ from the accepted generalizations reiterated over the past several decades concerning the dispersion of ownership of the largest corporations in the United States and England. The question, then, is whether the relative dispersion of ownership in Chile's largest corporations has "effected a radical separation of property and family" there—as is purported to have happened already in these advanced economies.[28]

Surely Chile has had powerful exponents of this doctrine, even in its most vulgarized variant: namely, "people's capitalism." This was a frequent refrain, from the 1950s on, of articles and editorials in leading newspapers and magazines representative of Chile's business community,[29] and it rose in pitch as the left's campaign against the "monopolies" and "financial clans" gained an increasing public hearing in the following years.[30] When reforms in the laws governing business corporations proposed by the Christian Democrats were being debated in congress during 1966, the influential daily *El Mercurio* returned again and again to the issues of "the stock exchange and economic development" and "people's capitalization." The newspaper noted, for example, that "the number of stockowners merely of the companies that sell their securities on the Stock Exchange is somewhere around 300,000. . . . This means that more than 10 percent of the country's 2.5 million economically active individuals are stockowners. This is especially flattering, because the United States, without doubt the most advanced in this direction, has about 19 million stockholders in a population of 190 million inhabitants, including both economically active and inactive individuals." Observing that "in the dec-

[28] The words are Bell's (1958, p. 246), describing the United States.

[29] For example, L.A.C. (pseudonym) 1950, p. 72ff.; Rodríguez Brieba 1955, p. 169ff.

[30] The 1961 work by Ricardo Lagos on the concentration of economic power was a best seller in Chile and the occasion of much public discussion in its congress and in the Chilean press.

ade 1950–1960 alone, the number of stockowners in the country rose 52.4 percent," *El Mercurio* editorialized that "contrary to the image drawn by the detractors of the corporation, it is not the preserve of small groups but an association of numerous investors. . . . The corporation is a great vehicle for popular capitalization." Another editorial, on the occasion of the establishment of a large forestry firm, remarked that it had been "financed through the system of people's capitalism." Similarly, the major business-economics journal *Economía y Finanzas* published an article in 1969 claiming that more than 5 percent of Chile's adult population were stockowners, concluding: "These figures categorically refute those who say that enterprise capital is in the hands of only a few. . . . It is thus worth observing that 'people's capitalism' has been successful in Chile despite tax obstacles and discriminatory competition by other sources of investment."[31]

What does a detailed analysis of the relationship between ownership and control in Chile's largest corporations reveal about such claims? Had "the established relations between the systems of property and family," i.e. the "kinship-property combination typical of classical capitalism," broken down in Chile by the mid-1960s?[32]

Types of Control

Our analysis of the top 37 nonfinancial corporations begins by following the original 1932 Berle and Means paradigm in their analysis of the 200 largest nonfinancial corporations in the United States, which has been emulated since, with scant modification, by other influential works.[33] Following their definitions and, insofar as possible, their pro-

[31] *El Mercurio* editorials, February 19, May 14, September 17, September 20, and July 7, 1966. Jorge Marty B., in *Economía y Finanzas* no. 389 (1969), p. 20, as quoted in Garretón and Cisternas 1970, p. 22.

[32] The words are Bell's (1958, p. 246) and Parsons and Smelser's (1957, p. 289), referring to the United States.

[33] Several works that delineate "economic groups" in Chile have appeared in the past quarter of a century, notably those by Lagos (1961), Cademartori (1968), Garretón and Cisternas (1970), and, most recently, Dahse (1979). None of these works attempts, however, to analyze the structure of the capitalist class or to probe systematically the connections between specific families or effective kinship units and corporate ownership and control among the top Chilean corporations. To the extent that they do attempt to identify the control groups of specific corporations, these studies rely almost entirely on a more or less intuitive (or arbitrary) grouping of several corporations as being under common control (or belonging to the same economic group), mainly because of the extensive interlocking among their directorates.

Dahse's analysis of "extreme wealth" attempts to delineate the "economic groups"

cedures, ensures the comparability of our findings and those of other such studies. It also enables us to compare the results obtained by using their methods with the results obtained by using our own alternative methods to analyze the same body of data. Utilizing our methods, in fact, not only discloses loci of control that their methods obscure, but also makes transparent the critical flaws in the Berle-Means analytical paradigm. Indirectly, moreover, revealing these flaws calls into question the validity of evidence presented in studies of ownership and control elsewhere, including the United States, that has been obtained by adhering to the Berle and Means analytical paradigm. As a guide to future work, therefore, we shall schematically present our own paradigm for the analysis of the locus of control in large corporations.

Following Berle and Means, "corporate control" generally has been defined as the "actual *power* to select the board of directors (or its majority)," although control also may "be exercised *not* through the *selec-*

(he finds 36) controlling "the 250 largest private enterprises" in Chile as of 1978. That he completed and published this work in Chile under its repressive right-wing dictatorship is, to say the least, a remarkable achievement—especially because his thesis (p. 13) is that during "the historical period beginning in September 1973 [when the military coup overthrew the constitutional government], there has been a strong process of concentration of property and control . . . in almost all sectors of the economy."

Dahse uses official information on these firms' directors and top-10 shareholdings. But he makes no attempt to identify the "beneficial" (real) owners of these shareholdings. As he notes (p. 26, italics added): "This makes it very difficult to determine the real control exercised over these enterprises by the various economic groups. Their stockownership is dispersed among numerous holding companies (*sociedades de responsabilidad limitada*), members of their families, and trusted executives, *most of whom do not appear on the list of the 10 major shareholdings*. The names of the real owners rarely appear either among the 10 major shareholdings or in the directorates of the corporations. [Elsewhere he added that 'dummies' (palos blancos) appear instead—or what are here more politely termed 'street names' or 'nominees'.] For this reason, it has to be emphasized that the control delineated for each corporation is evidently underestimated." Or, Dahse might well have added, his delineation of control groups may simply be wrong. For the failure to penetrate the nominee façade and identify the actual owners, as we discuss below, casts considerable doubt on the validity of any such designations of control, if it does not vitiate them entirely.

The analysis of corporate ownership and control in this chapter, in contrast to Dahse's and the other works mentioned earlier, is based on a systematic investigation of (a) the entire list of shareholders-of-record, (b) the specific business associations, and (c) the kinship relations among the shareholders, particularly the principal ones, both individual and institutional, of all of the top corporations analyzed, so as to identify their real principal stockowners and controlling interests. (This also applies to our analysis, in Chapter 3, of the ownership and control of the major commercial banks.) See Appendix A to this chapter.

tion of directors, but through *dictation* to the management, as where a bank determines the policy of a corporation seriously indebted to it." In the monumental studies by the TNEC, control was defined as "the *power* of determining the broad policies guiding a corporation and not . . . the actual influence on the day-to-day affairs of an enterprise."[34] Thus, control must be distinguished from business *management* and from what has been called "business leadership."[35] But if this is clear enough conceptually, the question is, How is this translated into practice in actual research? How is "control" adequately measured? In practice, Berle and Means and their followers have simply assumed, with no effort to demonstrate its validity, that if there is not an identifiable ownership interest (individual, familial, group of associates) having a specified minimum proportion of the stock (they used 20 percent in their study; their followers, in recent years, 10 percent), then the corporation has slipped imperceptibly (and inevitably) under "management control."[36] Unfortunately, this sort of analysis by operational definition merely assumes away critical analytical questions concerning the bases of control. Can control be exerted through the ownership of less than a standardized minimum proportion of the outstanding shares, and if so, how? What are the various *constellations of ownership interests* that can ensure control? Berle and Means surely know that these are critical questions, but their methods of analysis and research procedures neglect them in practice.

They distinguish five basic types of control, "though," they observe, "no sharp dividing line separates type from type": (1) private ownership, (2) majority control, (3) minority control, (4) management control, and (5) "control through a legal device without majority ownership." The latter three types are extra-legal types of control: they rest not on ownership of a majority of the stock, but rather on the specific constellation of power relationships in the corporation.

Under private ownership and control, of course, ownership and control are essentially identical. Berle and Means define this situation as one in which 80 percent or more of the stock is held by an individual or small group of associates. Majority control differs from private ownership in that a number of shareholders are already shorn of control (at least in part) because control is assured to the owner of the majority of the shares.

[34] Berle and Means 1967, p. 66, italics added; Goldsmith and Parmelee 1940, pp. 99–100, italics added.

[35] Gordon 1966, p. 150.

[36] See Zeitlin 1974a for a discussion of these studies.

Historically, it is with the exercise of minority control that the separation of ownership and control becomes significant in capitalist development. "Minority control" refers to a situation in which an individual or group of associates owns enough stock to ensure control in fact, though not in law. Minority control, Berle and Means note, ordinarily rests on a relatively even distribution of the remaining shares among many small stockowners, so that no rival has enough stock to challenge the controlling stockowners successfully. Of course, several minority shareholding interests can choose to cooperate in order to maintain "joint" (but still minority) control in their hands.

Minority stockowner control is a singularly significant fruition of the corporate form of capital ownership: it effectively allows a segment of the capitalist class consisting of the major stockowners of the large corporations to strip most other investors of control. That is to say, the *control* of capital is thereby extended far beyond the limits of the *ownership* of capital. This crucial development, the dissociation of ownership and control of capital, to which Rudolf Hilferding first gave systematic attention early in this century, is *not* the focus of analysis in the Berle-Means paradigm.[37] Rather, its focus is on an ostensibly emergent type of control of greater putative historical import, i.e. "management control": a situation, in their words, in which "ownership is so widely distributed that no individual or small group has even a minority interest large enough to dominate the affairs of the company."[38]

This raises two critical questions, to which, as we shall see, neither Berle and Means nor their many disciples have given satisfactory answers: (1) At what point does a block of shares in the hands of an individual or group of associates become too small to ensure minority control? (2) If that point is reached, whatever it may be, does this really mean the abrogation of corporate control by capitalists and its appropriation by a distinctive stratum of managers?[39] Berle and Means observe that "the dividing line between control by a minority interest and control by the management is not clear" in many corporations, but they assume anyway that such a line exists in reality, and draw it at "roughly 20 percent." Below that line, management generally can, they argue, be assumed to gain control of a corporation.[40]

The fifth type of control noted by Berle and Means is control through a "legal device"; the most important such device is "pyramid-

[37] Hilferding 1910.

[38] Berle and Means 1967, p. 78.

[39] See Chapter 2 for an analysis of the class situation of the managers.

[40] Berle and Means 1967, p. 85.

ing." Pyramiding is based on the fact that corporations can purchase and own shares in each other; intercorporate shareownership permits a congeries of corporations to be interconnected so that those at the apex of the pyramid are able to control those at the base, through a combination of majority and minority interests on each of its levels. Such pyramidal systems, as Means himself had pointed out in an earlier pioneering co-authored work on the "holding company," made possible the centralized control of capital and its concentration into larger and larger units. The holding company, Bonbright and Means emphasize, "is the most effective device . . . for combining under a single control and management the properties of two or more hitherto independent corporations."[41] So it is useful to precede our analysis of the locus of control in the top 37 corporations by providing a concise concrete example of pyramiding as a method of control.

Pyramiding

A relatively simple pyramidal system of control is exemplified by Tomé National Fabrics Company, one of the top 37 corporations. It is all but the epitome of control of a corporation at the bottom of a pyramid by an individual or group of associates having no direct ownership in it. The Furman family owns only the firm at the apex, National Oil Producing Company (in which they have 99.8 percent of the stock). But National Oil owns 98.7 percent of Andina Textiles, which, in turn, owns a dominant minority stock interest of 35.7 percent in Tomé National Fabrics. The Furman system also exemplifies a situation in which knowing the personal shareholdings of a corporation's officers and directors and of its individual principal shareholders does not necessarily disclose anything about the corporation's actual control. Tomé National Fabric's president and one director are principal shareholders, ranking ninth and eighth, respectively, each with about 1.25 percent of the company's outstanding shares, but neither of them is related to the controlling family. In fact, the one director of the firm from the controlling family (the son of Noy Furman Pocolillo, founder and president of National Oil and of Andina) owns *no* shares in Tomé National Fabrics in his own name, nor does any other Furman. This illustrates a general and far more complex set of relationships in which the actual connection between given officers and directors and a corporation's controlling interest cannot be disclosed by any simple

[41] Bonbright and Means 1932, p. 5.

enumeration of their proportionate holdings or ranks among principal shareholders. Thus, the only Furman family member on the board of directors simply would have been ignored in the sort of head count of "principal shareowners" among the higher executives that is typical of other studies of corporate control.[42]

Even this simple pyramidal system of control over Tomé National Fabrics indicates another general aspect of intercorporate control: namely, that the controlling firm, i.e. National Oil, which produces food oils, is in a different industry than the corporations it controls. It is neither part of a vertically integrated production system nor of a horizontally integrated marketing system designed to lessen competition. Rather, it is at the apex of a relatively simple conglomerate "interest group"—a mere hint of the greater complexity of interest groups and spheres of influence existing in Chile's corporate world. Whether the firms acting as holding companies are in the same industries as the corporations they control or are in unrelated industries, whether they are "pure holding companies" (which directly operate no part of their controlled properties) or are themselves operating companies, the pyramidal system serves the same basic purpose: no matter how intricate it may be, pyramiding unites a number of legally independent corporations under common factual control or maximum influence, with a minimum investment. Had the Furman pyramid depended on minority stockholdings at each level from National Oil through Andina Textiles to Tomé National Fabrics, this still would have permitted the Furmans to control it.

Pyramiding utilizes the capital of the controlled corporations to bring still more corporations under control, and thus drastically reduces the amount of the investment necessary to exert such control. This is a basic point: the web of intercorporate principal shareholdings is a method par excellence by which the same individual or small group of associates can expand the propertied realm under its control well beyond that provided by ordinary minority control. Berle and Means themselves, however, while noting the importance of the holding company and of pyramiding as a method of control, limited their analysis of control based on intercorporate relationships to cases in which one corporation controlled another through a "dominant minority stock interest." This, as we shall see, neglects a crucial feature of intercorporate control, i.e. the cumulative impact of several small

[42] Cf. Florence 1961, pp. 96–97, a study of the ownership and control of the large corporation in England.

pyramidal minority holdings in combination with each other and with individual, familial, and other institutional holdings. In fact, the very term "pyramiding" is misleading in some respects. For in the network of intercorporate holdings, a corporation at the base of the pyramid can, in fact, double back to take a principal shareholding in a corporation at the apex, or at any level of the pyramid, so that it has a principal shareholding in a corporation that also has a principal shareholding in it—and any number of intricate combinations of such intercorporate holdings of varying sizes is possible.

A simple illustration of this phenomenon appears in Figure 1.1, showing the minority control of the National Distributing Company (CODINA) by Bernardo Schmutzer Flemming and his son. They personally hold 25.6 percent of the shares of National Distributing, which owns 100 percent of Various Rents of Santiago (in combination with Huaquin Agricultural Company, which the Schmutzers own), which owns 96.4 percent of Real Estate and Forests, which owns 68.7 percent of Universal Insurance. But Real Estate and Forests also owns 4.2 percent of National Distributing, of which Universal Insurance owns another 2.8 percent (as well as 0.3 percent of Real Estate and Forests). This gives the Schmutzers a controlling block, when supplemented by these pyramided holdings, of 32.6 percent of National Distributing. In this way, corporations at the base of the pyramid, controlled by others at higher levels, themselves reinforce the original minority control of the corporation at the pyramid's apex. In National Distributing's case, this is of special importance since the Schmutzers share its control with those who control still another corporation, Viña del Mar Sugar Refining (CRAV), which itself ranks among the top 37. (In Berle and Means' terms, Viña del Mar Sugar would be classified under "management control," and National Distributing under "joint minority-management control, through pyramiding," an interesting hybrid form.) Such reciprocal holdings, as we shall see, can also be supplemented by and combined in varying degrees of complexity with still other holdings of varying sizes; although none of these holdings individually would be sufficient to ensure minority control, they would provide a stable base for control when combined. (Below, we examine a case of the control, through intercorporate relationships, of a corporation that at first appeared to be under management control.)

Control of the Top 37 Corporations

This brief discussion of pyramiding provides a glimpse of the complexity of the research process necessary to transform "information"

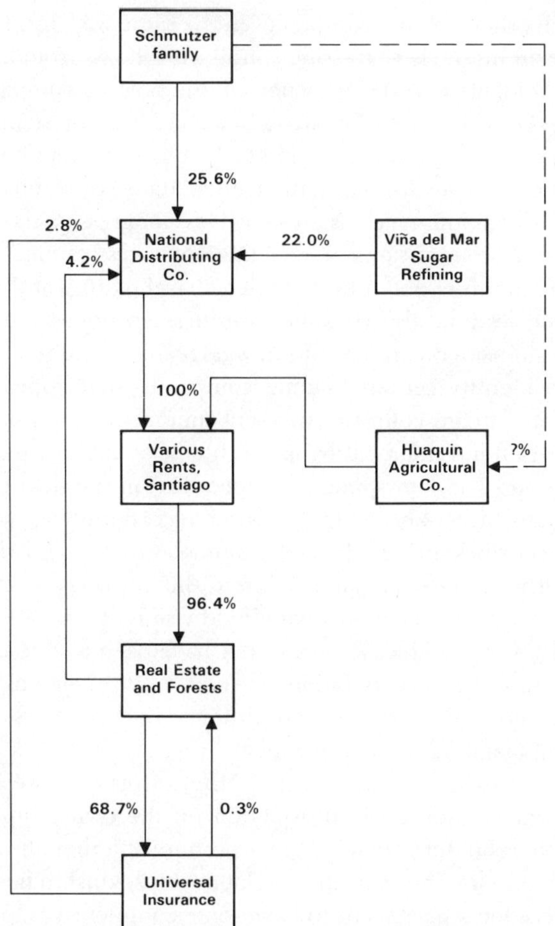

FIGURE 1.1. Pyramidal Control of the National Distributing Company by the Schmutzer Family and Associates in Viña del Mar Sugar Refining (CRAV)
⟵ Principal shareholding in firm, with percentage of stock held
⇠ Presumably controlling interest

into genuine "data." The basic sources of shareholding information utilized in our study, as noted earlier, were the annual report and list of stockholders filed by each corporation, as required by Chilean law, with the corporate regulatory commission. Although this gave us access to the full list of stockholders-of-record of each corporation, no law required public disclosure of their principal "beneficial owners" (the real owners). Many holding companies with important interests in the top 37 corporations had no records on file with the commission on corporations; and, even when they did, they often turned out to be held by still other holding companies in the same way, in what threatened to be an infinitely regressing spiral. To follow through was ordinarily unavoidable in order to penetrate the holding company façade and locate the real center of control. But there were no standard Chilean business reference sources (akin to Moody's manuals or Standard and Poor's *Corporation Records* in the United States) or results of official Chilean investigations (such as those by U.S. congressional committees and regulatory commissions) to facilitate our investigation.

We made inquiries about unidentified shareholdings at the relevant official agencies and also consulted business economists and several leading businessmen considered knowledgeable in these matters. To attempt to identify certain holding companies that appeared to be domiciled in foreign countries, we sent inquires to the financial sections of several international banks, to financial-page writers of leading British and U.S. newspapers, to specialists in the field known for their intimate "street knowledge" of foreign corporations, and to both the U.S. Securities and Exchange Commission (SEC) and the British Registry Office of Great Britain. Without the information supplied in confidence by the international banking division of one of the world's great banks, for example, we would not have been able to determine the ownership of two corporations in the top 37; their holding companies were domiciled in Panama, yet they were themselves controlled by a mining magnate resident in Chile.

Despite our exhaustive (and exhausting) efforts, we were still not able to obtain authoritative information on the ownership of a few principal shareholdings in several corporations, although other persuasive evidence on intercorporate relationships, kinship ties, and historical antecedents permits us to have some confidence as to the identity of their owners. These will be noted in the appropriate context. Unfortunately, no standard methodological technique in the social sciences has yet been devised (nor is there likely to be one) for penetrating the secrecy (or legal façade) that so often, when it comes to problems of power, surrounds and prevents access to "the facts."

Bearing these remarks in mind, what conclusions can be drawn concerning the locus of control in the top 37 nonfinancial corporations, *as analyzed and classified in accordance with Berle and Means' methods?* How far has the separation of ownership and control proceeded in the largest corporations in Chile, and how many have fallen under management control? Four of the top 37 are "privately owned," and 1 is "majority-owned"; 14 are under "immediate minority control" by dominant interests holding at least 20 percent of the stock (9 are controlled by a joint minority). (A cutoff of 20 percent for "minority control" was used by Berle and Means in their analysis of corporations that were far larger and had many more stockowners than the present top 37, and so it is probably appropriate here as well, rather than the 10 percent cutoff generally used in recent, similar studies of corporate control.) By this measure, i.e. a 20 percent minimum holding for minority control, 15 of the top 37 fall into the category of "immediate *management* control," because such a holding was not identified in any of them. But, in fact, in only 2 of these 15 corporations is there a minority ownership interest, identifiable by the Berle-Means methodology, as large as 10 percent. One top-37 corporation (Universo Printing) turned out to be a majority-owned subsidiary, through special class-B stock, of another in the top 37 (Zig-Zag Publishing). Two firms are in the special situation of being "mixed" corporations, having dominant-minority state shareholdings alongside those of their private investors (Pacific Steel Company and Tamaya Mining).

When Berle and Means found that a corporation was controlled by another through a dominant-minority stock interest, i.e. a holding large enough by itself to ensure minority control, but that the controlling corporation was itself management-controlled, they classified the first as minority in its "immediate" control but as management in its "ultimate" control. If the controlling corporation was "controlled otherwise than by its management," however, they classified the first under "immediate minority" but "pyramidal" in its ultimate control. Using these terms, then, 11 of the 14 firms classified under "immediate minority control" are ultimately controlled through pyramiding by another corporation that is itself "controlled otherwise than by its management." The 3 others remain under "ultimate minority control." None of the corporations under immediate minority control by another corporation shifts into the category of ultimate management control, since none of the controlling corporations was found to be under management control by Berle and Means' methods. Of the 15 corporations under immediate management control, none is controlled by another corporation through pyramiding. Thus, the proportions under immediate vs. ultimate management control are identical: of the 36 legally independent corporations, 15 (or 42 percent) would have been considered as under ultimate management control; these 15 management-controlled corporations held 56 percent of the aggregate assets of the top 36 corporations (see Table 1.3). This is apparently a major finding: the growth of the modern corporation—just as is supposed to have happened in the most advanced capitalist countries—has, so it seems, brought about the managerial demiurge in Chile.

TABLE 1.3. The Top 37 Nonfinancial Corporations in Chile, Classified by Types of Control, in Accordance with Berle-Means Definitions and Procedures, 1964/66

	% by Assets	*N*	% by Number
"Immediate" control			
private	11.1	4	11.1
majority	1.1	1	2.8
minority	5.9	5	13.9
joint minority	11.7	9	25.0
management	55.6	15	41.7
special situations[a]	14.6	2	5.6
TOTAL	100.0	36	100.0
"Ultimate" control			
private	11.1	4	11.1
majority	1.1	1	2.8
minority	4.3	3	8.3
pyramiding	13.3	11	30.6
management	55.6	15	41.7
special situations[a]	14.6	2	5.6
TOTAL	100.0	36	100.0

NOTE: One of the original top 37, a subsidiary of another, is not included here.
[a] Two corporations were "mixed," private- and government-owned.

By these methods, Chile, in the mid-1960s, has roughly the same proportion of her largest corporations classified under management control as did the United States and Great Britain in the 1930s, and Australia in 1955 (see Table 1.4). The 200 largest nonfinancial corporations in the United States included 42 railroads, while none were included in our study, because they were state-owned in Chile. There were also 52 public utilities in the top 200 corporations in the United States. Management control was found by Berle and Means to be far more frequent in railroading than among industrials; it is notable, therefore, that when we restrict our comparisons to manufacturing, these two countries still show a striking similarity in the proportion classified under management control, i.e. 38 percent in Chile in 1964 compared to 40 percent in the United States in 1929. Of course, these comparisons are merely suggestive, because the number of large corporations studied varied markedly from one country to the next. But what is most important is the similar pattern in all these countries. The very largest corporations were most likely to be classified under management control. Fully 8 of the 10 largest of the top 36 legally independent corporations appear to be under management control, com-

TABLE 1.4. The Top Nonfinancial Corporations in Chile (1964/66), the United States (1929), Great Britain (1936), and Australia (1955), Classified by Types of "Ultimate" Control, in Accordance with Berle-Means Definitions and Procedures (%)

	Chile	U.S.	Great Britain[a]	Australia[b]
Private	11.1	6.0	{ 6.2	2.7
Majority	2.8	5.0		8.2
Minority	8.3	23.3	26.2	45.2
Pyramiding	30.6	20.5	13.8	
Management	41.7	44.3	53.8	43.8
Special situations	5.6	1.0		
TOTAL	100(36)[c]	100(200)[c]	100(65)[c]	100(73)[c]

SOURCES: For U.S., Berle and Means 1967, pp. 86–102, 109; for Great Britain, Florence 1961, pp. 112–113; for Australia, Wheelwright 1957, chap. 3.

[a] "Top" in Great Britain refers to 67 corporations that had £3 million or more capital in 1936, 2 of which (excluded here) were, in fact, majority-owned foreign subsidiaries of Ford and Woolworth. We reclassified the 65 remaining corporations into Berle-Means types of control from the 42 logically possible types (of which 16 "cells" actually existed) presented by Florence, based on type of principal shareholder (personal, company, institutional, nominal, mixed, and "shareholdings all relatively small and not categorized") and on the proportion held by the largest holding (three size categories) and the 20 largest holdings (four size categories). We could not distinguish between private and majority control, and the figure of 6.2% in this column refers to the proportion in the combined categories of private and majority. The detailed types, for interested readers, are as follows: *private majority*, type 1(P); *minority*, types 2(P), 2(N), 3(P), 3(N), 3(M), 4(P), 4(N), 4(M); *management*, type 5, "shareholdings all relatively small and not categorized," 20 largest holdings have 20–29% of stock (if the 13 corporations in this category of doubtful shareowner control had been classified under "minority control," the proportion under "management control" would have been 33.8%), types 6 and 7 (as in type 5, except the 20 largest holdings have less than 20% of stock).

[b] Excluded here are 17 corporations that Wheelright classified as under foreign control.

[c] Number in parentheses is total number of firms.

pared to 5 of those ranking 11–20; 2 of those ranking 21–30; and none of those ranking 31–36. (The pattern among the 14 corporations under minority or pyramidal control is the reverse, being, in those same ranks, 0, 3, 6, and 5, respectively, though the 5 private- and majority-owned corporations were not distributed directly with corporate size: in those same ranked groups, the numbers are 1, 2, 2, and 0, respectively.)[43]

Intercorporate Control

Forty-two percent of the largest corporations were *classified* under management control, by following the definitions, methods, and pro-

[43] Two firms were classified as "special situations" (mixed private- and government-owned). See Table 1.5.

cedures of Berle and Means. Does this mean that these corporations are really under the control of their managements? Or is such classification the artifact of an inadequate methodology? Is the finding that these corporations are under management control, rather than under the control of proprietary interests, more apparent than real? Have their principal owners, in fact, been shorn of control by nonowning managements? Obviously, there are both methodological and theoretical issues involved. The very selection of such a percentage, at which the divide between control by a minority ownership interest and control by the management is supposed to occur, is not a trivial analytical act. On the contrary, here is an instance in which method and theory are transparently seen to be inseparable aspects of the same intellectual process. By defining as under management control a corporation in which a given minimum percentage of outstanding shares is *not* held by an individual or closely knit group, a hypothesis is "confirmed," as it were, by an act of definition.

In our conception, corporate control refers not to an attribute of an individual or control group as such, but rather of a *social relationship*. Corporate control—like social power, of which it is a specific historical form—is

> essentially relative and relational: how much power, with respect to whom. . . . When the concrete structure of ownership and of intercorporate relationships makes it probable that an identifiable group of proprietary interests will be able to realize their corporate objectives over time, despite resistance, then we may say that they have "control" of the corporation. . . . To estimate the probability that a given individual or group controls a corporation, then, we must know who the rivals or potential rivals for control are, and what assets they can bring to the struggle.
>
> This has two obvious implications concerning the study of corporate control: . . . a specific minority percentage of ownership in itself can tell us little about [its] potential for control. . . . We can discover this only by a case study of the pattern of ownership within the given corporation. However, it also means that confining our attention to the single corporation may, in fact, limit our ability to see the pattern of power relationships of which this corporation is merely one element; and it may restrict our understanding of the potential for control represented by a specific block of shares in a particular corporation. An individual or group's capacity for control increases correspondingly depending upon how many other

> large corporations (including banks and other financial institutions) in which it has a dominant, if not controlling, position. The very same quantitative proportion of stock may have a qualitatively different significance, depending on the system of intercorporate relationships in which the corporation is implicated.[44]

Thus, because minority control depends upon both a corporation's pattern of ownership *and* the constellation of intercorporate relationships in which it is involved, it is misleading simply to set a specified minimum shareholding percentage as necessary to ensure control. Although a given percentage may be *sufficient* to ensure control, it may not be *necessary* for control. Without explaining their reasons, Berle and Means themselves credited a holding smaller than 20 percent with control "in a few special instances."[45] In contrast, the TNEC investigators recognized this problem explicitly, and set no specified lower limit to what they called "small minority control," which could be exerted, they found, with *less than 10 percent* of the outstanding shares. Rather, their empirical analysis, proceeding from company to company, showed that "in particular companies a small percentage of ownership in a large issue may be sufficient to give dominance when the remainder of the stock is widely dispersed among disconnected holdings, each representing but a fraction of the size of those in the hands of the dominant group."

The TNEC investigators found that, though less stable than control based on large minority holdings, small minority control in the United States was usually reinforced by the disproportionate representation of the family in the management, "partly because of the absence of any other large block of stock."[46] To discover control by such a minority, whose holdings might otherwise not become visible to the investigator, close study of the identity of the officers and directors is essential; otherwise, appearances might be taken for reality, and a minority-controlled corporation might be relegated to the residual category of management control simply because of insufficient information. This was shown, for instance, in a fine systematic study by Phillip Burch of

44 Zeitlin 1974a, p. 1091.

45 Berle and Means 1967, p. 108.

46 Goldsmith and Parmelee 1940, pp. 113–114, 109. For example, the TNEC found that the Swift family owned only 5.2 percent of the common stock of Swift and Co., but all of its top officers and an overall total of six of the nine directors were members of the Swift family (Goldsmith and Parmelee 1940, pp. 113, 1491). Berle and Means (1967, p. 105) had classified Swift and Co. as "presumably" under management control, but presented no supporting evidence.

the control of the 300 largest U.S. industrial corporations as of the mid-1960s. Burch "searched carefully" through such magazines as *Fortune, Forbes,* and *Business Week* and through the business section of the *New York Times* over a period of some two decades (1950–1971); he also consulted standard reference works, such as Moody's and Standard and Poor's *Corporation Records.* He found that these sources showed "a marked difference in stockownership totals" compared with those in the SEC's official summaries, which provided far smaller estimates. Burch's company-by-company analysis led to an estimate of "probable family control" or "possible family control" of 60 percent of these 300 industrials, with at most 40 percent under management control (a figure he considers inflated).

Aside from this clear indication of how important it is to use appropriate sources to reveal who is in control, there is also the question of how to measure control. Rather than simply assuming that some specified minimum percentage in itself is necessary for control, Burch based his judgment on two criteria for "probable family control": (1) "that approximately 4 percent – 5 percent or more of the voting stock was held by a family, group of families, or some affluent individual," according to one of his sources, and (2) that the same individual or family was represented "on the board of directors of a company, generally over an extended period of time."[47] This would seem to be a far more reliable basis for identifying the control group, since these criteria, to some extent, take account of qualitative relationships in the firm. But the point is that the validity of an index of proprietary control cannot be determined apart from the actual research process itself. The question is, Which method of research and analysis in practice reveals more about the identity of the controlling individuals or families in a corporation? For there are no easily standardized criteria independent of such research by which control can somehow be measured. That research also involves following through on a host of clues and hints, aside from using documentary information, concerning the proprietary interests in a given corporation.

We are convinced by our own research that genuine disclosure of the control group ordinarily requires detailed investigations of the corporation's history and of the business associations and careers of its principal shareholders and higher executives. Particularly crucial, as we discovered, are the kinship relations among them. Only such thor-

[47] Burch 1972, pp. 29–30.

oughgoing research can begin to reveal the real controlling interests whose interconnections are otherwise invisible.

Fundamental, also, is analysis of the congeries of intercorporate relationships in which the corporation may be (and usually is) involved. It is generally recognized that many legally distinct personal holdings, investment companies, trusts, and estates, as well as such intermediaries as nominees and brokers, can form a single familial bloc for purposes of control. Aggregating such holdings (and penetrating their anonymity) is a primary research task in any adequate study of corporate control. But not so well understood is the fact that, hidden among the apparently independent small shareholdings of other corporations in a given corporation, may be a welter of interlocking and overlapping corporate and familial relationships that actually bind them together. Coordinated with individual or family holdings, these can serve as a base for control. Typically, as we shall see, the framework of the single corporation has to be broken out of in an effort to identify interconnections between it and other corporations, and through them to identify specific individuals, families, or other cohesive groups that might exert control; otherwise, the search for the locus of control is severely hampered, if not hopelessly hobbled at the outset. Indeed, after finding one's way through a complex maze of intercorporate relationships, a researcher may discover that a corporation that at first sight appears to be under management control, and then, as one looks closer, seems to be under small minority control, is in fact, on sufficiently close inspection, really under the control of a dominant-minority stock interest.

This was very much our own experience. Following through such manifold intercorporate relationships reveals that of the 15 corporations we originally classified under "management control," according to the methods, procedures, and definitions of Berle and Means, 14 are really controlled by minority ownership interests, generally by one or more interrelated families and their associates. Only 1 corporation continues to appear to us to be definitely under the control of its management. One corporation is controlled through a minority ownership interest of less than 5 percent of the stock; 4 by interests holding from 5 through 9.9 percent; 6 more by interests from 10 through 19.9 percent; and 3, as it turns out, by dominant-minority ownership interests having 20 percent or more of the stock. *These conclusions negate the findings presented earlier in this chapter*: i.e. that 42 percent of the 36 largest corporations are management-controlled. Table 1.5 lists each of the

TABLE 1.5. Control of the Top 37 Nonfinancial Corporations in Chile, 1964/66

		Classified by Berle-Means Methods				Classified by the Authors	
Rank	Corporation	Type of Control: Immediate	Type of Control: Ultimate	Largest Holding or Dominant Interest	Size of Holdings (%)	Controlling Proprietary Interests	Size of Holdings (%)[a]
1.	Pacific Steel Co. (CAP)	S.S.	S.S.[b]	CORFO and Amortization Institute	36.7	CORFO and Amortization Institute	36.7[b]
2.	Paper & Cardboard Mfg. Co.	Mgt.	Mgt.[c]	"El Melón"	4.1	Matte family and associates	9.0
3.	"El Melón" Industrial Enterprises	Mgt.	Mgt.[c]	Bank of London & South America	4.4	Cortés family and associates	12.7
4.	South America Steamship Co. (CSAV)	Mgt.	Mgt.[c]	Southern Pacific Industrial & Commercial Co.	3.8	Vial and MacAuliffe families and associates	12.3
5.	Sumar Products	Priv.	Priv.	Sumar family	83.8	Sumar family	83.8
6.	United Breweries Co.	Mgt.	Mgt.	Federico Sta. María Technical Univ.	7.5	Edwards family and associates	19.0
7.	General Industries Electricity Co.	Mgt.	Mgt.[c]	United Capital Investments	2.1	Claro family and associates	7.7
8.	Petroleum Company of Chile (COPEC)	Mgt.	Mgt.[c]	IBEC, Chile	1.3	None disclosed[d]	—
9.	Tierra del Fuego Cattle	Mgt.	Mgt.[c]	Bank of London & South America	4.5	Braun-Menéndez family and associates	13.6
10.	Lota-Schwager Coal	Mgt.	Mgt.	"El Melón"	7.6	Cousiño and Claude families with Cortés family	25.6
11.	Mantos Blancos Mining Enterprise	Joint minority	Pyr.	Marvis Corp. Consolidated S.A. Enterprises	46.0 23.2	Mauricio Hochschild and associates[e]	78.9
12.	Yarur Chilean Cotton Products	Joint minority	Pyr./Min.	Chase Manhatan Trust Yarur interests	24.5 14.1	Yarur Banna family and Grace (?) interests	43.2

13.	Hirmas Cottons	Priv.	Priv.	Hirmas family	100.0	Hirmas family	100.0
14.	The Industrial Co. (INDUS)	Mgt.	Mgt.[c]	Federico Sta. María Technical Univ.	17.2	Edwards family and associates	27.3
15.	Copper Products (MADECO)	Mgt.	Mgt.[c]	Bartolomé Mateo Castellvi	1.9	Simonetti family and associates	4.8
16.	Viña del Mar Sugar Refining Co. (CRAV)	Mgt.	Mgt.	Bank of Chile	6.0	Edwards and Claude families and associates	16.9
17.	Metal Mfg. (MADEMSA)	Min.	Min.	Simonetti family	31.6	Simonetti family and associates	34.5
18.	Santiago Gas Consumers Co. (GASCO)	Mgt.	Mgt.	Claudio Troncoso Fernández	5.0	Claudio Troncoso and associates	9.3
19.	*El Mercurio* Journalism Enterprises	Priv.	Priv.	Edwards family	100.0	Edwards family	100.0
20.	"Pasaje Matte" Urban Rental Association	Mgt.	Mgt. (Pyr.?)	CODICO	14.6	Matte family and associates	32.7
21.	Caupolicán Textiles	Joint minority	Pyr./Min.	Yarur Chilean Cotton Juan Yarur Enterprises	49.0 21.0	Yarur Banna and Grace interests	70.1
22.	Glassware of Chile	Joint minority	Pyr. (Foreign?)	Corning Glass Works PPG International	19.5 8.8	Corning-PPG "joint control" with Cousiño and Edwards interests	47.5[f]
23.	National Distributing Co. (CODINA)	Joint minority	Min./Mgt.	B. Schmutzer and Son CRAV	25.6 22.0	Schmutzer family with Edwards and Claude families	58.8
24.	Penco National Ceramics Factory (FANALOZA)	Mgt.	Mgt.[c]	United Capital Investments	4.3	Díaz family and associates	6.8
25.	Enamelware Factory (FENSA)	Mgt.	Mgt.	Hernán Briones and wife	8.9	Briones family and associates	15.7
26.	Zig-Zag Publishing Enterprises	Maj.	Maj.	Helfmann family	60.7	Helfmann family and associates	67.9
27.	Saíd Rayon and Chemicals Industries (RAYONSAID)	Priv.	Priv.	Saíd family	81.4	Saíd family	81.4

TABLE 1.5. Control of the Top 37 Nonfinancial Corporations in Chile, 1964/66 (*cont.*)

		Classified by Berle-Means Methods				Classified by the Authors	
		Type of Control					
Rank	Corporation	Immediate	Ultimate	Largest Holding or Dominant Interest	Size of Holdings (%)	Controlling Proprietary Interests	Size of Holdings (%)[a]
28.	BellaVista–Tomé Cloth Factory	Joint minority	Pyr.	FABRILANA Intl. Financial Consortium	34.3 12.6	Yarur Asfura and Grace (?) interests	47.8
29.	Tomé National Fabrics	Min.	Pyr.	Andina Textiles	35.7	Furman family and associates	37.1
30.	Petroleum Navigation Corp.	Joint minority	Pyr./Mgt.	Interoceanic Nav.[g] Interocean Gas CSAV Punta Arenas Ins.	100.0	Braun-Menéndez and Vial families	100.0
31.	Chile Interoceanic Navigation Co.	Min.	Min.	Braun-Menéndez family	43.2	Braun-Menéndez family	43.2
32.	Progreso Textiles	Joint minority	Pyr./Min.	Urban Progress Yarur Kazakía family	31.7 27.6	Yarur Kazakía family (with Grace?)	70.8
33.	Saavedra Bénard	Min.	Pyr.?[h]	Bank of Chile	49.9	Bank of Chile	49.9[h]
34.	Universo Printing & Lithography	Subsidiary of zig-zag		10.4% of A stock[i] 88.5% of B stock	—	Helfmann family and associates	24.1A 88.5B
35.	Oruro Mining Co.	Joint minority	Pyr.	Corona Mercantile Consolidated S.A. Enterprises	34.7 17.6	Mauricio Hochschild and associates[e]	69.2
36.	Tamaya Mining Co.	S.S.	S.S.	CORFO[e]	30.0	Jointly by CORFO and private interests[e]	—
37.	Coronel Shipping	Min.	Pyr.	Pacific Chilean Navigation	46.6	Cousiño and Claude families	51.0

NOTE: Maj. = majority ownership; Mgt. = management control; Min. = minority control; Priv. = private ownership; Pyr. = pyramiding; Min./Mgt., Pyr./Mgt., and Pyr./Min. = joint control (e.g. joint control by a minority interest and by management is indicated by Min./Mgt.); S.S. = special situation.

[a] Details on the actual controlling proprietary interests in the ostensibly management-controlled corporations are given in Table 1.6, Appendix B to this chapter.

[b] CORFO owns 32.5% of CAP's A (voting) stock, and the publicly owned Amortization Institute holds 4.2%. The B stock is held by private investors.

[c] A peculiar problem, never resolved satisfactorily, was posed by the shareholdings-of-record in the name of the Stock Exchange of Santiago, which appeared as a principal shareholder-of-record in 1964 in 27 of the top 37 corporations. Its median holding is 1.7%; its mean, 1.9%. In the corporations here designated by a superscript c, the Exchange holds one of the top 3 holdings-of-record. We had no way of knowing on whose behalf these shares are held, or who their beneficial (or voting) owners are. As in the United States, these shares could have been owned by the member firms of the Exchange and/or their customers. (According to U.S. Senator Lee Metcalf, for example, Cede and Co., a nominee partnership composed solely of employees of Stock Clearing Corporation, a wholly owned subsidiary of the New York Stock Exchange, "is a principal—sometimes the largest—security holder in major airlines, utilities, and other corporations, according to companies' reports to regulators" [Metcalf and Reinemer 1971, p. 301].)

[d] For details on COPEC, see the discussion in Chapter 2.

[e] Tamaya Mining may be jointly controlled by CORFO and a private minority interest, since the Stock Exchange of Santiago holds a block of 26.9% of the shares (see note c). An educated guess is that this is held on behalf of the Cuevas Mackenna interests, descendants of the Cuevas and Vicuña Mackenna nineteenth-century mining families. Francisco Cuevas Mackenna, a past minister of mines, holds Tamaya's largest individual shareholding of 2.0%; his wife holds the 20th largest, 0.3%. Another possibility is that the Exchange represents the Mauricio Hochschild interests, because Francisco Cuevas is also a director and principal shareholder (top 10) of Mauricio Hochschild, S.A., and, as of the mid-1960's, Dr. Hochschild's mining interests in Chile and elsewhere are extensive. (He owned the Hochschild tin mines that were expropriated in Bolivia during the 1952 revolution.)

[f] Given the sizable holding of 8.8% by Pittsburgh Plate Glass (PPG) International and of 19.5% by Corning Glass Works, and the fact (aside from the technological integration and dependence of the firm on these U.S.-based multinationals) that PPG and Corning have a long-standing association through the Pittsburgh Corning Corporation (PCC, organized in 1937), in which they are co-owners (fifty-fifty), Glassware of Chile represents a form of what we might term "pyramidal foreign control," by a combined 28.3% foreign interest. This firm, therefore, represents one significant way in which the interests of foreign and national capital (primarily Edwards and Cousiño interests) are fused, probably under the control of the former but managed by the latter. See Chapter 6.

[g] We could not ascertain the specific proportions of the stock owned by each of these companies in Petroleum Navigation, because no list of the 1964 shareholders was available. The above information on the combined 1966 holdings of these four companies comes from the commission on corporations' "Top 200 of 1966, Chile," which lists the 10 largest shareholdings (and provides their *combined* proportion of all shares) for each corporation.

[h] The 49.9% holding in Saavedra Bénard by the Bank of Chile all but legally qualifies the bank as the parent corporation and Saavedra Bénard as its subsidiary. For an analysis of the control of the Bank of Chile, see Chapter 3.

[i] Baquedano Investments also holds 22.5% of Universo's A stock. We were not able to find further information on Baquedano, which seems likely, though, to be a Zig-Zag nominee, since it also appears as Zig-Zag's 25th largest shareholder-of-record, but has no principal shareholdings in the other top-37 corporations.

top 37 corporations, classified both by Berle-Means types of control on the basis of their methods and by the identity of the real controlling proprietary interests disclosed through our own methods of analysis.

The detailed descriptions of the actual controlling proprietary interests discovered in the ostensibly management-controlled corporations show that these controlling interests typically consist of members whose interconnections are anything but readily apparent on the surface. (See Table 1.6, Appendix B to this chapter.) The real control structure beneath the appearance of management control of one of the largest corporations can serve as a general illustration of this point (see Figure 1.2). The pattern of ownership of this corporation, the United Breweries Company, is a veritable model of control through intercorporate relationships.

United Breweries ranks 6th among all nonfinancial corporations owned by Chilean private capital. It supplies about 97 percent of Chile's beer market, and is Chile's only licensed producer of Orange Crush and Pepsi-Cola.[48] Our research disclosed that it is controlled by the Edwards family and associates through an intricate network of nine interrelated institutional holdings, only two of which amounted to more than 2 percent of the corporation's outstanding shares. The single-largest holding, by the Federico Santa María Technical University, whose investment portfolio the Edwards interests control, amounts to 7.5 percent. None of the Edwards family members have personal shareholdings in United Breweries, except for the Estate of Agustín Edwards Budge, which has 0.3 percent and ranks 24th among all stockowners-of-record. Edwards interests in United Breweries, amounting to 14.4 percent of the shares, are distributed across the Edwards Budge Estate, two insurance companies, two investment companies, the Bank of Edwards, the Santa María University, and the Chilean subsidiary of the Rockefellers' international investment firm (International Basic Economy Corporation) in which the Edwards family holds a substantial minority stockholding. Although it has no direct holdings in United Breweries, *El Mercurio*, the daily newspaper owned by the Edwards family, as well as their publishing company, are crucial in the structure of control. (As is partially revealed by a perusal of Table 1.5, the Edwards interests among other top-37 corporations are also extensive.) Because of their size, none of these shareholdings in itself remotely qualifies as a dominant-minority stock interest, yet the nature of the interconnections among them makes it clear that,

[48] Bohan and Pomeranz 1960, p. 125.

together, they constitute a block that ensures the Edwards interests a working control of the corporation. To this block, moreover, must be added the second largest shareholding-of-record, amounting to 4.6 percent of the stock, held by the Bank of London and South America, with which the Edwards family has had long-standing associations. Thus, this gives them a coordinated interest of 19 percent of the stock of United Breweries.

Berle and Means discussed how "an intricate series of pyramided holding companies" could be used to create and retain control of a system of corporations. But they limited their *analysis* of intercorporate relationships to cases of pyramiding in which one corporation was immediately controlled by another through a dominant-minority stock interest; they explicitly "disregarded" what they termed (but did not explain) "a mild degree of pyramiding."[49] The problem with this procedure (followed by their many disciples in later years) is that precisely such "mild" pyramiding may be the critical element (or one of them) in a complex pattern of corporate control, involving a number of ostensibly independent but in fact closely related companies. In addition, the same intricate interweaving of interests is often repeated within those firms whose own stockholdings form part of the control system of the original corporations. The fact is, as we pointed out earlier, the term "pyramiding" is often inadequate as a short-hand descriptive term for the actual pattern of control (see Figure 1.2). Corporations in the "pyramid" often have reciprocal shareholdings or shareholdings in corporations at higher levels of the pyramid. Thus, the term "intercorporate control" is much more appropriate, if less striking in its imagery, for conceiving the web of connections among companies under common or coordinated control. Indeed, many of the top 37 corporations are themselves involved in "communities of interest" (as a careful reading of Table 1.5 reveals), and their control structure can be fully grasped only by viewing them as constituents of such extra-corporate communities of interest, spheres of influence, or interest groups.

The "Kinecon Group"

If the term "pyramiding" is often inadequate to grasp the complexities of a given structure of intercorporate control, the term "family" is also

[49] Berle and Means 1967, p. 108.

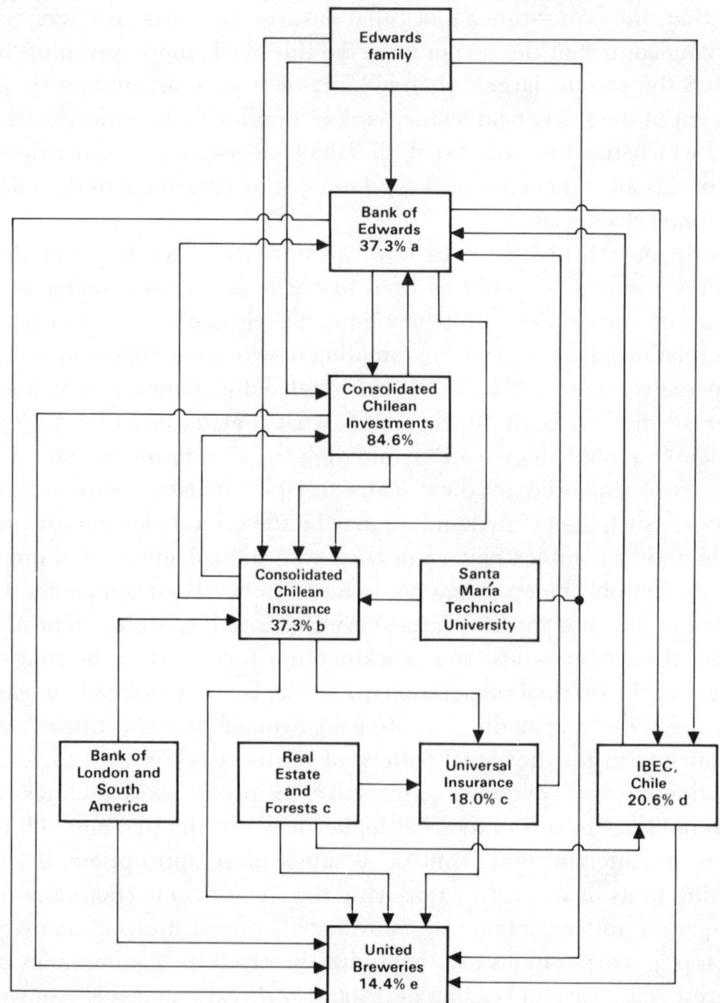

FIGURE 1.2. Intercorporate Control of the United Breweries Company by the Edwards Family and Associates

←—— Principal shareholding in firm, with percentage of stock held

[a] Includes shareholdings by the Lord Cochrane Publishing Co. and *El Mercurio* Journalism Enterprises, owned by the Edwards family but not shown in this chart. Does not include the 11.6% shareholding in the name of "Amolana," suspected to be a nominee of the Bank of London and South America.

[b] Coincidentally (?) the same proportion held in the Bank of Edwards. Does not include the 9.3% shareholding in the name of "Amolana" or the 3.9% shareholding of the Bank of London and South America; it

often unable to encompass the intricate kinship network binding a number of related officers, directors, and principal shareowners into a cohesive group or "effective kinship unit," to use Parsons's apt term.[50] This effective kinship unit can include close relatives and other kindred outside the immediate family who are also essential members of the extended and tightly organized kinship network that controls a given corporation.

So, for example, we have identified the Cousiños as one of the two controlling families in Lota-Schwager Coal Company, the single-firm monopoly of coal production resulting from a 1964 merger of the two previous competitors, the Lota and Schwager companies. Three of its principal shareowners, two of whom were also directors, are lineal and collateral descendants of Matías Cousiño Jorquera, who founded the Lota Coal and Industrial Company well over a century earlier, in 1852. None of them, however, is a member of the same immediate family.[51] Arturo Cousiño Lyon, a Lota-Schwager director, is the great-grandson of Matías Cousiño. The wife of Gilles de Heeckeren, also a director of Lota-Schwager, is Luz Lyon Cousiño, Arturo Cousiño's first cousin, while Arturo von Schroeders Cousiño is Mr. de Heeckeren's second cousin. Given their direct involvement and common interests in Lota and their descent from the founding family, they almost certainly are members of the same effective kinship unit. Further, Mr. de Heeckeren is president of the family investment company, Matías Cousiño Investments. He is vice-president and Arturo Cousiño is president of Colcura Agricultural and Forestry, Inc. Mr. de Heeckeren is also a director of Arauco Shipping; established by Lota Coal in 1954 as its coal carrier, it also shared its president, vice-president, and

[50] Parsons 1953.

[51] See Chapter 2 for an explication of the kinship terminology and a description of the kinship data. Briefly, "immediate family" and "primary relatives" refer interchangeably to persons in an individual's two nuclear families: parents and siblings in the "family of orientation," spouses and children in the "family of procreation." The primary relatives of one's primary relatives are secondary relatives, and their primary relatives, in turn, are one's tertiary relatives.

---

does, however, include the 3.8% shareholding by *El Mercurio* that is not shown in this chart.

[c] Controlled by the Schmutzer family through pyramiding. See Figure 1.1.

[d] Includes the 7% shareholding by El Mercurio that is not shown in this chart.

[e] Does not include the 4.6% shareholding by the Bank of London and South America.

another director with Lota until the 1964 merger with the Schwager company. Mr. de Heeckeren is president and Arturo Cousiño is a director of another Lota subsidiary, Lota Green Refractories. Thus, these close kindred share common concrete interests not only in the Lota-Schwager coal company, but in several interconnected and interlocked companies.

The effective kinship unit is not always quite so opaque in design. In "El Melón" Industrial Enterprises, for instance, Elena Cortés Brown, the widow of Adolfo Eastman Cox (El Melón's president for more than two decades, until his death) is a principal shareowner, as is Elena's sister Josefina. Their brother Scipión is also a principal shareowner, and his son Scipión Cortés Bryan is a director. Another principal share-owner is Addie Hall, the widowed first cousin of Mary Bryan Hall, the wife of Scipión Cortés Brown. In addition, a principal shareholding is held by the estate of María Teresa Brown, the latter's (Scipión's) aunt. Here, at least, is a solid core of primary relatives to whom others are related, who, in turn, bring in more distant relatives.

The Cousiño and Cortés families are merely instances of a recurrent and characteristic pattern among the kinship groups that own and control the top 37 corporations.[52] To refer to such a group as an "extended family" would be misleading, because this term has its own technical usage in anthropological studies of nonliterate peoples.[53] Also, a term is needed not merely for a group of interrelated kindred, but in particular for one forming *a more complex social unit in which economic interests and kinship bonds are inextricably intertwined.* We thus use the term "kinecon group" to designate the type of effective kinship units controlling the top corporations. The concept of the kinecon group is class-specific; that is to say, it applies only where the owner-

[52] Our analysis of "El Melón" Industrial Enterprises led us to the conclusion that it was controlled by the Cortés Brown family. So it is interesting to note that, after we had reached this conclusion, our research concerning the largest landed estates in the country (see Chapter 4) revealed that the Cortés Brown family held an estate in common ("Comunidad Cortés Brown") named, appropriately enough, "El Melón"! It was located in Nogales, Valparaíso, and ranked among the 25 largest in Chile's Central Valley (ICIRA 1966).

[53] The "extended family" refers to a composite family that unites several nuclear families through consanguineal rather than affinal kinship bonds; it ordinarily has a common residence and consists of three or more generations, according to Murdock (1949, pp. 23–24, 32–33). Firth (1964) has persuasively argued for restricting usage of the term "extended family" to such "corporate lineal kinship groups," as has Adams (1968).

ship of stock in the large corporation is the characteristic and preponderant form of capital ownership and where the connection between stock ownership and corporate control has become attenuated, if not historically problematic. The corporation is the characteristic juridical unit of ownership of the means of production under contemporary capitalism, and the set of interrelated kindred who control it through their combined ownership interests and strategic representation in management constitutes the kinecon group. Ordinarily, the kinecon group consists of the primary, secondary, and other relatives among the officers, directors, and principal shareowners, whose combined individual and indirect (institutional) shareholdings constitute the dominant proprietary interest in the corporation.[54]

The concepts of "kinecon group" and "intercorporate control," as the preceding analysis of the actual loci of control in ostensibly management-controlled corporations should have made clear, are thus closely connected. They are both integral to our specific methods for investigating the relationship between ownership and control of the large corporations. As our investigation has revealed, the large corporation in Chile is—appearances to the contrary notwithstanding—ordinarily controlled by a kinecon group through an intricate system of intercorporate relationships.[55]

A Paradigm for Investigating Corporate Control

To discover whether this proposition applies in advanced capitalist economies requires the same sort of detailed, rigorous, and systematic investigation as we have carried out concerning the top 37 corporations in Chile. For this reason, the following paradigm is presented as a succinct guide to research on corporate ownership and control. But many kinds of information (especially those crucial clues and hints given by a concrete juxtaposition of apparently unrelated bits of data) cannot be summarized here, for they are not easily categorized, item-

[54] A kinecon group can, of course, control more than one corporation. Consequently, any single corporation under its control may not have all or even most of the members of the kinecon group among its higher executives and principal shareowners. Two unrelated kinecon groups may also jointly control a corporation, as was true, for example, of the Cousiños and the Schwager heirs in Lota-Schwager Coal.

[55] The place of kinship relations in corporate control, and the centrality of the kinecon group (following our earlier statement of the present paradigm), has been shown in several excellent detailed investigations of the top corporations in England (Scott 1979, 1985) and the United States (Dunn 1980; Schuby 1974, 1975). Also see White 1978.

ized, or counted. Withal, this paradigm provides specialists with a useful basis for taking inventory of their data, filling in information gaps, and assessing the validity and reliability of the evidence for their own interpretations of the connection between ownership and control of the large corporation. Not least, this paradigm also facilitates the comparability of the findings of various studies:

1. *Who were the founders (organizers, promoters) of the given corporation?*[56] *What identifiable kinship ties, if any, are there among these founders?*
   a. How many of the original individual founders have traceable descendants among the corporation's present higher executives (top officers and directors) or principal shareowners?
   b. When the corporation was founded, in what other firms were any of the original founders involved? What other close business associations did any of the original founders have at that time?
   c. Do any of these other firms (or their successors through mergers, acquisitions, takeovers, etc.) show up among the present principal institutional shareowners of the corporation? Do any of the original founders' business associates in other companies have traceable descendants among the corporation's higher executives or principal shareowners?
2. *What are the identifiable kinship ties among the present higher executives and principal shareowners of the corporation? Is there a specific family or set of immediate relatives at its core? Can other shareowners, ranking below its principal shareowners (i.e. below the top 20), be identified who also belong to the same effective kinship unit?*
   a. Which of the higher executives and principal shareowners are identifiable members of the same effective kinship unit?
   b. What rank among all shareholders-of-record and among individual stockowners does each of these relatives have?
   c. What percentage of stock in the corporation is held by each identifiable relative, and what is the combined percentage they all hold? What percentage of the aggregate stock held *only* by the principal shareowners is in the hands of members of the same effective kinship unit? Does the available evidence so far permit

[56] "The history of every corporation," as Sweezy remarks (1953, p. 160), "has certain critical phases: organization and promotion, expansion, and possibly bankruptcy and reorganization [or merger]. The role . . . certain individuals or groups play during these periods commonly determines their importance in more normal times. It is for this reason that it is so important to have a knowledge of historical facts."

the provisional identification of an identifiable set of relatives as the kinecon group in control of the corporation?

3. *Which of the corporation's higher executives and principal shareowners also occupy management posts or own stock in other companies, including other nonfinancial corporations, as well as in banks, investment firms, insurance companies, and other financial institutions? What companies? What amount of stock? What positions in management?*
   a. Which of these interlocking individuals are identifiable as members of the kinecon group in the original corporation?
   b. What kinship ties can be identified among the higher executives and principal shareowners of the original corporation and their counterparts in the other companies in which they occupy management positions or own stock?
   c. What are the career patterns of the higher executives and principal shareowners of the original corporation, particularly of those in the management or among the principal shareowners of other companies? Have any of them had long-standing associations with the other companies in which they are also principal shareowners or higher executives?
   d. What are the career patterns of the higher executives and principal shareowners of the other companies that are directly interlocked with or have principal shareowners in common with the original corporation? Have any of them been associated with the original corporation in any capacity in the past?
4. *What companies have principal shareholdings (in their own names or through nominees) in the corporation?*
   a. Are any of the higher executives and principal shareowners of the latter shareholding companies also higher executives or stockowners of the original corporation?
   b. Have any of the higher executives or principal shareowners of the companies that have principal shareholdings in the original corporation been associated in any capacity with that corporation? In what capacity?
   c. Have any of the higher executives or principal shareowners of the original corporation been associated with any of its principal shareholding companies? In what capacity?
   d. What kinship ties can be identified among the higher executives or principal shareowners of the original corporation and their counterparts in the companies that are among its principal shareholders?

5. *Recapitulate the immediately preceding series of questions for other companies of which the original corporation itself can be identified as a principal shareholder.*
6. *In the steps so far, we have, minimally, the following analytical types of companies*: (i) companies that directly interlock with the original corporation; (ii) companies whose principal shareowners are higher executives of the original corporation; and/or (iii) companies whose higher executives are principal shareowners of the original corporation; and/or (iv) companies that have principal individual shareowners and/or institutional shareholders in common with the original corporation; and/or (v) companies whose higher executives or principal shareowners are identifiable close relatives of those in the original corporation's provisional kinecon group; and/or (vi) companies that have principal shareholdings in the original corporation; and/or (vii) companies of which the original corporation is itself a principal shareholder.
   a. For these seven types of companies, are any of their higher executives or principal shareowners also higher executives or principal shareowners of any of the other companies?
   b. Do any of these companies have overlapping institutional principal shareholders?
   c. Do any of these companies have higher executives or principal shareowners who are close relatives of the higher executives or principal shareowners of any of the other companies?
   d. Are any of these companies' principal shareholders also principal shareholders of any of the other companies?
7. *For each of the companies that appear in types i–vii, recapitulate, mutatis mutandis, all relevant questions (i.e. where information on critical interconnections is still insufficient).*

This paradigm for the investigation and analysis of the locus of control in the large corporation is no mere logical exercise. It is the concise embodiment, in schematic outline, of the complex research process (painstaking, tedious, detailed, time-consuming, and exhausting) that we were compelled to undertake if we were to reveal the controlling interests in most of the top corporations originally appearing to be under management control.

The difficulties of such research are compounded, of course, when (as has been the situation in the United States) the following conditions obtain: (a) the list of shareholdings-of-record (and surely of beneficial shareowners) is not publicly available; (b) the number of shareholdings in each large corporation is far greater than in Chile's corporations; (c) the law prohibits interlocks between competitors; (d) an efficient internal revenue service enforces statutorily progressive personal income tax, so that the wealthy make even greater use of nominees, street names, agents, and other front men; (e) the number of principal capital-owning families and the size of the business community is much larger; and (f) systematic genealogical sources are less adequate than in Chile.

This paradigm is also, alas, unquestionably incomplete. Many of the designated phases of the research process are necessarily interrelated and can have still other prerequisites. It must be emphasized, too, that there is no substitute for close study of the critical periods in the history of the corporation—its establishment, consolidation, mergers, etc.—and that even this may fail to disclose such important information on the companies and individuals involved as, for instance, the informal (extra-bureaucratic or extra-legal) relations between business associates. Nonetheless, this paradigm succinctly focuses attention on the main business associations and familial entanglements that may have to be investigated in order to ferret out the actual locus of control in a large corporation. We are confident that, at the very least, research guided by this paradigm for investigating corporate control will provide far more valid and reliable data on the question than has been gathered in research guided by the Berle-Means paradigm.

APPENDIX A

SOURCES AND METHODS

In 1966, when Zeitlin began the research for this book, no official data had yet been compiled systematically on the largest corporations in Chile; there was no official list of the largest corporations ranked by assets or sales for any recent years. The cost of reviewing the annual reports of all registered corporations in order to obtain assets figures, and thus to be able to select a group of the largest ones for study, was prohibitive—especially because of the disorganized condition then prevailing in the commission on corporations' files, some of which were missing and many of which were incomplete.

Therefore, the procedures for selecting the top corporations were as follows. From the 290 large corporations listed in the various "economic groups" described by Lagos (1961), the 50 largest were selected and ranked by their 1964 assets (the most recent data then available). Subsequently, it was discovered that two of these corporations went out of business after 1964, so they were replaced to bring the number up to 50 again. Research disclosed that the necessary stockholder information was not available in the commission's files for 4 of these 50 companies, so they were dropped from this study. The commission on corporations was thoroughly reorganized under the Frei administration, and its official compilation of data on the 200 largest firms in Chile was made available to us in late 1969 (see note 14, Chapter 1). At that time, we reincorporated 2 of the 4 (Petroleum Navigation and Cadena Industrial Fibres Company) that had been dropped earlier. Of these 48 firms, we found that 11 were foreign-owned. (At the outset, the wholly owned subsidiaries of Anaconda and Kennecott mining companies had been excluded from this study.)

A comparison of our "sample" of 37 of the largest 1964 corporations with the official list of the top 200 of 1966 shows that the top 15 of 1964 are identical with the top 15 of 1966; of those ranked 16–20 in 1966, our 1964 sample omits 2. So the top 37 of 1964 includes all but 3 of the top 25 of 1966. Of the 12 others in the top 37 of 1966, 6 are not in our 1964 sample. In sum, the top 37 of 1964 includes 30 of the top 37 on the official 1966 list. Of the 7 in the top 37 of 1964 that are not in the top 37 of 1966, 3 rank among the top 50 of 1966, 1 ranks 113th, and 3 are not listed in the top 200 of 1966. The top 37 are ranked by their official 1966 net capital assets because these estimates are presumably more accurate than the 1964 figures; most important, using the 1966 figures allowed us to calculate the percentage of the assets held by the top 37 in (a) their various three-digit industrial categories and (b) among all corporations, domestic and foreign. These calculations could not have been made with the poor and incomplete 1964 data originally available in the files of the commission on corporations.

Twenty-three SIC three-digit industrial groups are represented among the top 37 corporations; in only two of these industries (metal mining and electric power) is the top-37 corporation outranked by a foreign corporation; 18 of the top 37 corporations are the single-largest private (i.e. nonstate) enterprise in their industry; several of the top 37 are in the same industry, and all are among the 3 or 4 largest in their industry, except in textiles, where the top 37 includes the 8 largest in that industry. Ten of the top 37 hold more than half of the assets in their industry; 7 hold between a quarter and half of the assets; and another 7 hold at least a tenth but less than a quarter of their industry's assets. Whether measured by their aggregate share of Chilean-owned assets or their share of all assets (Chilean and foreign) in their specific industry, the top 37 are surely among the small number of dominant nonfinancial corporations in Chile. The top 37 hold, in the aggregate, 40.1 percent of the net capital assets of all 1,611 domestic nonfinancial corporations. The top 10 alone hold 24.8 percent; the top 20, 34.3 percent; and the top 30, 38.9 percent of the total.

Systematic data were obtained on the number and market value of the shares held by the officers (president, vice-president, general manager) and directors of the top 37 corporations, the 11 foreign-owned firms, and the 16 largest Chilean-owned commercial banks, and on their 20 largest shareholdings-of-record; on a number of standard biographical and demographic attributes of each of the higher executives (officers and directors); and on the bilateral (primary through tertiary, and often more distant) relatives of the higher executives. Data on landholdings and public offices of the higher executives were also obtained for the analyses presented in Chapters 4–6, and are described in the appropriate notes.

Biographical information came largely from various editions (1948–1966) of the *Diccionario biográfico de Chile* and from informants. Kinship information came, first, from this *Diccionario* and then, with this information as a basis, from several genealogical works (Domínguez Barros 1968; Cuadra Gormaz 1950) and two major historico-biographical dictionaries (P. Figueroa 1889; V. Figueroa 1925–1931). Responsibility for the kinship research, conducted over some five years or more, was borne principally by Richard Earl Ratcliff, as well as by Lynda Ann Ewen. Aside from references in the *Diccionario biográfico*, information on the positions held by the top 37's higher executives in other firms was obtained from *Anuario ejecutivos de sociedades anónimas . . . 1963*, which was the most complete publicly available listing of corporate executives in Chile, and (to our knowledge) the only such publication in the 1960s.

APPENDIX B

CONTROLLING INTERESTS IN THE OSTENSIBLY MANAGEMENT-CONTROLLED CORPORATIONS

TABLE 1.6 Descriptions of the Controlling Proprietary Interests in the Ostensibly Management-Controlled Top 37 Corporations in Chile, 1964/66

2. Paper and Cardboard Manufacturing Company (P&C)

The Matte family and associates:

Composition of Group	*Stock Owned* %	*Rank*
Rosa Elvira Matte de Prieto	0.3	17
Jorge Alessandri Rodríguez, "former" P&C president	0.3	26
Jaime Larraín García-Moreno	0.4	13
Combined holdings of Mattes who are executives but not principal shareowners	0.1	—
Cordillera Insurance Co.	0.3	16
"La Rosa de Sofruco" Agricultural Company	0.3	15
Covarrubias Educational Foundation	0.3	18
Distribution and Trade Co. (CODICO)	1.3	5
SUBTOTAL	3.3	
"El Melón" Industrial Enterprises	4.1	2
Mines and Fertilizers	1.6	4
PROBABLE WORKING BLOC	9.0	

The firm was founded through a merger of Ebbinghaus, Haensel, and Co. and the Maipú Box Factory in 1920. The latter had been established two years earlier by Luis Matte Larraín, elder brother of two of P&C's board members as of 1964/66.

The president and four directors are Mattes or close relatives; a fifth director is a distant relative. The sister of Jorge Alessandri Rodríguez is the wife of Arturo Matte Larraín. Mr. Alessandri was president of P&C until he became president of Chile itself in 1958; in 1965, after his presidential term ended, he again became P&C's president.

Cordillera Insurance Co. is owned (99 percent) by Pasaje Matte, and its directors are all Mattes.

The family of Manuel Ossa Covarrubias, president of P&C, controls the Educational Foundation, and has the controlling interest of 31.8 percent in Sofruco. Mr. Ossa's sister is the aunt of P&C director Arturo Matte Larraín. (Another sister may be Eliodoro Matte Ossa's mother; or, at least, Eliodoro was Arturo's first-cousin's son.) Mr. Ossa Covarrubias was on the original board of P&C in 1920.

On the Distribution and Trade Co., see under "Pasaje Matte" below, in which it is the largest shareholder. It is also the largest shareholder in Mines and Fertilizers, with a holding of 25.0 percent, alongside the presumably Matte-controlled O'Higgins Agricultural and Commercial Co., with 14.5 percent, and "El Melón," with 18.8 percent. On O'Higgins, see under "Pasaje Matte."

3. "El Melón" Industrial Enterprises

The Cortés family, in association with the Bank of London and South America:

Composition of Group	*Stock Owned* %	*Rank*
Mary Bryan de Cortés	0.5	16
Scipión Cortés Brown	0.6	10
Elena Cortés vda. de Eastman	0.8	8
Josefina Cortés vda. de Eastman	1.9	5
Addie Hall vda. de Barton	0.3	23
Estate of María Teresa Brown vda. de Ariztia	2.0	4
Mines and Fertilizers	2.2	3
Subtotal	8.3	
Bank of London and South America	4.4	1
Working Bloc	12.7	

One Cortés family member (the son of Scipión Cortés) is on the board. The president, for more than two decades until his death, had been Adolfo Eastman Cox, whose widow is Elena Cortés. He was succeeded by Eliodoro Matte Ossa, with whose family the Cortés family are close associates in Mines and Fertilizers, and indirectly, therefore, in Paper and Cardboard Manufacturing Co.

The Bank of London is apparently represented by one director, Tomás Douds, of Williamson, Balfour. Mr. Douds himself is an investor in El Melón. (The bank and Williamson, Balfour merged in 1964.)

El Melón is one of three controlling corporations (with Distribution and Trade Co. and O'Higgins) in Mines and Fertilizers, in which it ranks 2nd with 18.2 percent. Elena Cortés also ranks 21st among the principal shareholders in the latter, with 0.24 percent.

4. South American Steamship Company (CSAV)

The Vial and MacAuliffe families, and associates:

Composition of Group	*Stock Owned* %	*Rank*
Ana Castillo de Vial	0.5	15
Carlos Vial Correa	0.7	14
Alfonso Vial Errázuriz	0.3	24
Hernán Concha Garcés	0.7	13
Bernardo Larraín Vial	0.2	—

4. South American Steamship Company (CSAV) (*cont.*)

The Vial and MacAuliffe families, and associates:

Composition of Group	*Stock Owned* %	*Rank*
Combined holdings of Vials who are executives but not principal shareowners	0.4	—
South American Bank	2.2	4
"La Marítima" Insurance Co.	0.3	32
SUM OF VIAL INTERESTS	5.3	
Vitalicia Cooperative Life Insurance Co.	2.8	3
Vitalicia Continental Life Insurance Co.	0.3	27
Brian MacAuliffe Martínez, director	0.1	—
SUM OF PRESUMED MACAULIFFE INTERESTS	3.2	
Southern Pacific Industrial and Commercial Co.	3.8	2
WORKING BLOCK	12.3	

Vials and close relatives hold the presidency and four directorships; a distant cousin has a fifth directorship.

CSAV controls the South American Bank through a dominant minority interest of 20.4 percent. Carlos Vial Infante, CSAV's president, is a director of the bank; Francisco Subercaseaux Aldunate, related through marriage to two CSAV directors and the president, is also a director of the bank; a third CSAV director, nonkin, is also a South American Bank director.

CSAV has 20.4 percent and the South American Bank 1.1 percent of "La Marítima" Insurance Co.

Vitalicia Cooperative controls Vitalicia Continental through a 43.4 percent holding, while the MacAuliffe family has 14.6 percent. The MacAuliffes presumably control Vitalicia Cooperative. The only bank close to ranking among Continental's principal shareholders is the South American Bank, ranking 25th, with 0.5 percent. Further, Mr. MacAuliffe's nephew began his career, at age 18, working in the Trade Department of the South American Bank; three years later, he was transferred to CSAV. Mr. MacAuliffe is a director of Vitalicia Continental.

The Southern Pacific Industrial and Commercial Co. is a majority-owned (54 percent) subsidiary of "El Melón" Industrial Enterprises, whose president, Eliodoro Matte Ossa, is a director of the South American Bank.

Carlos Vial Infante is Bernardo Larraín Vial's great-uncle's son.

6. United Breweries Company

The Edwards family and associates:

Composition of Group	*Stock Owned* %	*Rank*
Estate of Agustín Edwards Budge	0.3	24
Consolidated Chilean Investment Co.	2.0	3

6. United Breweries Company (*cont.*)

The Edwards family and associates:

Composition of Group	Stock Owned %	Rank
Consolidated Chilean Fire Insurance Co.	0.3	18
Bank of Edwards	1.7	6
SUBTOTAL	4.3	
IBEC, Chile	1.7	5
Federico Santa María Technical University	7.5	1
SUBTOTAL	9.2	
Universal Insurance Co.	0.3	20
Real Estate and Forests	0.6	14
SUBTOTAL	0.9	
SUM OF EDWARDS AND SCHMUTZER INTERESTS	14.4	
Bank of London and South America	4.6	2
WORKING BLOC	19.0	

The president and two directors are Edwards kindred. Two more directors are career associates of Edwards: Nicanor Señoret Silva, who began with the Bank of Edwards in 1905, and Gustavo Olivares Cosulich, who joined the bank the next year, and both of whom are directors of the bank as of 1964/66. In all, there are five direct interlocks between the Bank of Edwards and United Breweries, including the bank's president, who is a United Breweries director.

The Bank of Edwards, founded in 1846 by Agustín Edwards Ossandón, is firmly controlled by Edwards interests, which hold at least 42.75 percent, not including the single-largest holding of 11.6 percent by an unidentified firm called "Amolana," which we suspect is a nominee of the Bank of London and South America (see below). Edwards family members personally hold 22.6 percent; another 0.75 percent is held by a family estate; Lord Cochrane Publishing Co., owned by the Edwards family, holds 10.0 percent; *El Mercurio*, also owned (69.0 percent) by the Edwards family, holds 3.8 percent; and Consolidated Chilean Fire Insurance, Universal Insurance, and IBEC, Chile, hold 2.1 percent, 2.6 percent, and 0.9 percent, respectively.

The president of Consolidated Chilean Investment Co., is Agustín Edwards Eastman, who is also the vice-president of the Bank of Edwards. His first cousin once-removed, Arturo Lyon Edwards, president of the bank, is also a director, as is Jorge Bande Weiss, a career Edwards associate. Mr. Bande began with Consolidated Chilean Fire Insurance in 1941, rising successively through assistant manager, manager, and (after 1957) managing director. The top 10 shareholders are known to hold a combined 84.6 percent of the shares. Represented among them are Agustín Edwards and Mr. Bande, the Bank of Edwards, and Consolidated Chilean Fire Insurance.

Consolidated Chilean Fire Insurance was founded in 1853 by Agustín Edwards Ossandón, who orchestrated a merger of several insurance companies in order to survive in competition with British companies. Edwards interests in Consolidated control at least 37.3 percent (including their indirect control of the single-largest shareholding of 12.5 percent by the Santa María Technical University).

Federico Santa María was long a business associate of Agustín Edwards Ossandón, father of Agustín Edwards Ross, the great-grandfather of Agustín Edwards Eastman, and was also the great-uncle of Jorge Ross Ossa, an Edwards cousin and director of the Bank of Edwards and United Breweries. Agustín Edwards MacClure organized the university, as ordained in Santa María's will at his death in 1925. Part of Mr. Santa María's personal fortune also was bequeathed to Mr. Ross's grandmother. Agustín Edwards Eastman is president of the university, as of 1964/66, and his father and grandfather before him had also been president. Nicanor Señoret Silva has been its vice-president, and G. Olivares Cosulich its general administrator for more than three decades. Carlos Ceruti Gardeazabal is a partner of Agustín Edwards Eastman's second cousin, Carlos Edwards Mackenna (Arturo Lyon Edwards' first cousin). Edwards' control of the university's investments (60 percent of whose financing comes from the government), therefore, seems certain.

Mr. Santa María was himself "one of the main clients and a large shareholder" of Anglo–South American Bank, which was later taken over in 1935 by the Bank of London and South America. Mr. Santa María appointed Andrew Geddes, the bank's manager in Valparaíso, as executor of his will directing the establishment of the university, along with Agustín Edwards MacClure. John Thomas North and Agustín Edwards Ross were close business associates, as well as conspirators and financiers of the successful overthrow of President José Manuel Balmaceda in 1891. North was the founder of the Bank of Tarapacá and London, the precursor of the Anglo–South American Bank. Agustín Edwards MacClure, son of Agustín Edwards Ross, became a director of the Anglo–South American Bank in 1920, when he retired "from his distinguished tenure" as the Chilean ambassador in London. That same year, at the urging of Andrew Geddes, the Anglo–South American Bank bought 60 percent of the shares (paying a high price) of the Bank of Edwards, which thereafter regularly paid a 16 percent dividend to its new parent. The largest shareholder (11.6 percent) in the Bank of Edwards in 1964 is a firm called "Amolana," which we could not identify; but, given its literal meaning ("I love wool"), the fact that the Anglo–South American Bank was once an Edwards Bank majority shareholder and also had major interests in wool production in Magallanes, and that Amolana also owns 9.3 percent of the stock of Consolidated Chilean Fire Insurance, it may be a nominee of the Bank of London and South America. In any case, the foregoing confirms the close association of the two banks. (See Joslin 1963.)

IBEC, Chile is a 66-percent owned subsidiary of the Rockefeller parent, IBEC. The Bank of Edwards holds 7.0 percent; *El Mercurio*, 7.0 percent; Real Estate and Forests, 5.2 percent; and Jorge Ross Ossa, 1.4 percent—for a total of 20.6 percent Edwards interests. Agustín Edwards Eastman is IBEC's president; Jorge Ross Ossa, a director.

Consolidated Chilean Fire Insurance holds 18.0 percent of Universal Insurance, which is owned 68.7 percent by Real Estate and Forests, an investment company, which, as we noted earlier, is associated with the Edwards family in IBEC and also in Viña del Mar Sugar Refining (CRAV). (See the description of CRAV below.) Real Estate and Forests is controlled through pyramiding by the Schmutzer family.

7. General Industrial Electricity Co.

The Claro family and associates:

Composition of Group	Stock Owned %	Rank
Héctor Claro Salas, president	1.9	4
Teresa Vial de Claro	0.7	8
Francisco Subercaseaux Aldunate, director	0.4	21
Fernando Subercaseaux Amenabar	0.4	24
Manuel Claro Vial, director	0.1	—
SUBTOTAL	3.5	
United Capital Investments Co. (UCI)	2.1	2
Osvaldo Pérez Valdés, vice-president	2.1	1
WORKING BLOC	7.7	

The firm was founded in 1904 by the Claro brothers, Raúl and Luis, with their partner, Francisco Huneeus Gana. The president, Héctor Claro Salas, and two directors (one the son of Héctor, the other his brother-in-law) are direct and collateral descendants, respectively, of the founding partners. The manager is a collateral descendant of Huneeus and related through marriage to the president.

The wife of United Capital Investment's president, Gastón Cruzat Paul, is a second cousin of Manuel Claro Vial. Mr. Cruzat and his brother, a director of UCI, are also among UCI's 25 partners (holding all its stock). Another UCI director, Jenaro Prieto Vial, is related to four of General Industrial's executives and five of its principal shareowners. His sister is the wife of Francisco Subercaseaux Aldunate's son, and he is thereby a distant (quaternary) relative of the Claros.

Osvaldo Pérez Valdés, a distant relative of the Claros through marriage, formerly was manager and director of the Stock Exchange of Santiago, holding a seat on the Exchange since 1920. We presume that the shareholding of the Exchange is held on his behalf or that he represents its beneficial owner.

Three other families, with no apparent representation on the board, but with principal shareholdings in the hands of eight different individuals, may be considered associates of the Claros: the Marín Larraíns, the Rolleris, and the Terrazas, with 1.2 percent, 1.7 percent, and 2.0 percent, respectively, of the shares. They are the only individuals, as a group, whose holdings put them in a position to challenge the Claros. If they are associates of the Claros, the bloc's holdings would come to 12.6 percent. Otherwise, the firm can be considered as under joint small-minority control, in the sense that different interests are in a position, depending on agreement between them, to control the firm.

9. Tierra del Fuego Cattle

The Braun-Menéndez family and associates, with the Bank of London and South America, and Duncan, Fox, Ltd.:

	Stock Owned	
Composition of Group	*%*	*Rank*
The Oscar and Elsa Braun Foundation	0.6	9
Herminia Menéndez de Gómez	0.4	17
Fanny Gazitua Brown de Oyuela	0.3	27
Combined shareholdings ranking below the top 20 (excluding Gazitua's) held by other Braun-Menéndez family members	1.2	—
Combined holdings of Braun-Menéndez family members who are executives but not principal shareowners	0.5	—
Francine Arnaud vda. de Mari	0.5	14
René Mari Arnaud	0.4	19
SUM OF BRAUN-MENÉNDEZ FAMILY AND ASSOCIATES	3.9	
Bank of London and South America	4.8	1
Duncan, Fox, Ltd.	1.7	5
WORKING BLOC	10.4	
Bank of Chile	3.2	
PROBABLE WORKING BLOC	13.6	

The president, vice-president, manager, and two directors are Braun-Menéndez family members or close kin.

The Maris are also associated with the Braun-Menéndez family in Laguna Blanca Cattle, another Punta Arenas sheep firm, in which the Braun-Menéndez family holds 25.0 percent and the Maris family 3.0 percent. The Mari family also owns extensive lands surrounded by Braun-Menéndez ranchlands in Punta Arenas.

The Bank of London and Duncan, Fox became associated with Tierra del Fuego Cattle at its organization in 1890, providing capital for the exploitation of the concessions obtained by José Nogueira, his wife Sara Braun, and his brother-in-law Mauricio Braun. They and other British interests supplied 50.3 percent of the initial financing (Segall 1953, pp. 193–194). Family members have had close business associations with the Bank of London and Duncan, Fox ever since; several have served with them as agents and officers and directors in London and Chile. In addition, a nonfamily director, Alexander Bertie Donaldson, is a career representative of Duncan, Fox, having begun with them at age 16 in Manchester, England, then emigrating to Chile five years later (in 1930) and serving in Duncan, Fox offices successively in Peru, Bolivia, and Chile. He became a director and general manager of Duncan, Fox in 1956.

The additional holding of 3.2 percent, ranking 4th, in Tierra del Fuego Cattle, in the name of the Bank of Chile, may be held for the Braun-Menéndez family. Two members of the Braun-Menéndez family sit on the bank's national board of directors; two more are on the board of its Punta Arenas branch, where the family's interests are centered and dominant; Enrique Chirgwin Coo, nonkin, who has been with Tierra del Fuego since 1938, when he became general manager and a director, is on the national board of the Bank of Chile also. With this holding, the Braun-Menéndez interests would amount to 7.2 percent. Whether or not the family is, in fact, the bank's beneficial owner, the bank, by virtue of the family's close ties with it, is probably part of the working bloc, for a total holding of 13.6 percent.

10. Lota-Schwager Coal

The Cousiño and Claude families, in association with the Cortés family:

Composition of Group	*Stock Owned* %	*Rank*
Arturo Cousiño Lyon, director	1.5	13
Gilles de Heeckeren Schaunberg, director	1.5	14
Arturo von Schroeders Cousiño	1.8	12
SUBTOTAL	4.8	
Fernando Gmo. Claude Squire	3.9	5
Jane Carolyn Sharman Claude	1.1	17
Percy MacDonald MacGraw	1.2	15
SUBTOTAL	6.2	
Arauco Shipping	5.0	2
Pacific Chilean Shipping (NACHIPA)	2.0	10
SUM OF COUSIÑO AND CLAUDE INTERESTS	18.0	
"El Melón" Industrial Enterprises	7.6	
WORKING BLOC	25.6	

The Cousiños are lineal and collateral descendants of the founder of Lota Coal and Industrial Company in 1852, Matías Cousiño Jorquera. Gilles de Heeckeren is married to Arturo Cousiño's first cousin, Luz Lyon Cousiño, and is the president of Matías Cousiño Investments, as well as officer or director of at least three other Cousiño firms.

The Claudes and MacDonalds are collateral descendants of Federico W. Schwager, who in 1858 established the coal company that would bear his name. A director, F. I. Sharman Monk, married Mr. Schwager's great-niece, whose daughter is Jane Carolyn Sharman Claude.

Lota-Schwager Coal resulted from a merger, between Lota Coal and Schwager Coal and Smelting Co., in early 1964.

Arauco Shipping was established in 1954 by Lota Coal, as its coal carrier, a decade before the merger with Schwager, and shared its president, vice-president, and two directors with Lota until the merger (Bohan and Pomeranz 1960, p. 190).

Pacific Chilean Shipping was organized in 1947, probably as a Schwager subsidiary, by Lota-Schwager's vice-president, Arturo Fernández Zegers. It shares five directors with Quiñenco Forestry, a subsidiary (84 percent) of Lota-Schwager.

"El Melón" is represented on Lota-Schwager's board by at least two directors: Salustio Prieto Calvo, El Melón's general manager, and Manuel Mardones Restat, who since 1947 has managed El Melón affiliates Juan Soldado Cement Co. and Mines and Fertilizers.

14. The Industrial Company (INDUS)

The Edwards and Claude families, and associates:

Composition of Group	*Stock Owned* %	*Rank*
María Isabel Eastman vda. de Edwards	1.7	4
Arturo Lyon Besa	0.4	24
Arturo Lyon Edwards, vice-president	0.6	17
Estate of Agustín Edwards Budge	0.7	16
Bank of Edwards	1.5	6
Nicanor Señoret Silva, director	1.0	10
Santa María Technical University	17.2	1
IBEC, Chile	1.5	7
SUM OF EDWARDS INTEREST	24.6	
Federico W. Schwager Foundation	1.2	8
Quiñenco Forestry	0.8	14
Federico Gmo. Claude Squire	0.7	15
SUM OF CLAUDE INTEREST	2.7	
WORKING BLOC	27.3	

The president and vice-president are Edwards kindred; four directors are also Bank of Edwards directors, making a total of six direct interlocks between the bank and INDUS. See description of United Breweries (above) for Santa María University, IBEC, and Mr. Señoret. On the Claudes, see descriptions of Lota-Schwager (above) and CRAV (below).

15. Copper Products (MADECO)

The Simonetti family and associates:

Composition of Group	*Stock Owned* %	*Rank*
Américo Simonetti Fiorentini, general manager–director	1.4	5
Aurelio Simonetti Fiorentini, director	0.4	37
Aida Guadaroli vda. de Magnani	1.1	7
Mateo Castellvi Bartolomé	1.9	2
SUM OF SIMONETTI AND ASSOCIATED INTERESTS	4.8	

Américo Simonetti is general manager and director of MADECO; his brother Aurelio, production manager and director. Aida Guadaroli is Américo's widowed sister-in-law. Mateo Castellvi also has the 7th ranking shareholding (2.9 percent) in MADEMSA, which the Simonettis control through a predominant minority interest of 31.6 percent. Both Castellvi's New York City firm and Aurelio Simonetti are among the 10 top shareholders in another major metals firm, Steel Products Co. (COMPAC). Aurelio and another MADECO director, Germán Picó Cañas, are also directors of COMPAC.

MADECO heavily interlocks with MADEMSA: the brothers occupy the same posts there, as do the president, vice-president, and two other directors.

16. Viña del Mar Sugar Refining Co. (CRAV)

The Edwards and Claude families, and associates:

Composition of Group	*Stock Owned* %	*Rank*
Santa María Technical University	3.70	4
Bank of Edwards	0.75	11
Nicanor Señoret Silva, vice-president	0.30	25
SUM OF EDWARDS INTERESTS	4.75	
Inéz García de Claude	0.60	16
Percy MacDonald MacGraw	0.50	21
Quiñenco Forestry	4.20	3
SUM OF CLAUDE INTERESTS	5.30	
Real Estate and Forests	1.70	7
Bank of London and South America	5.10	2
WORKING BOC	16.85	

For the Santa María University, Bank of Edwards, and Mr. Señoret, and Real Estate and Forests, see the description of United Breweries Company above.

Inéz García married a collateral descendant of Federico W. Schwager. Mr. MacDonald himself is a collateral descendant of Mr. Schwager. Quiñenco Forestry is controlled by Lota-Schwager Coal, the result of a merger of Schwager Coal and Lota Coal in 1964. The Claudes controlled Schwager before its merger, and now share control of the merged company. See the description of Lota-Schwager above.

Aside from their common interests here, the Edwards kinecon group and the Claudes also share interests in INDUS, where the Claudes have 2.7 percent, the Edwardses 24.5 percent.

Jorge Ross Ossa, CRAV's president, aside from being a director of the Bank of Edwards, is a distant cousin of both the Edwards family and the Claudes. (Inéz García Lyon may also be a first cousin of Arturo Lyon Edwards, president of the Bank of Edwards.) With Mr. Señoret, the Edwards family has two members on the board. Two other board members are tentatively identified as Claude representatives, by virtue of their positions in what appear to be Schwager-controlled firms in Concepción. Another director, Ernesto Ayala Oliva, sits on the board both of Real Estate and Forests and of National Distributing (CODINA), in which CRAV shares control together with the Edwards-controlled United Breweries.

For the long-standing community of interest between the Edwards family and the Bank of London, see the description of United Breweries.

18. Santiago Gas Consumers Co. (GASCO)

Claudio Troncoso Fernández and associates:

Composition of Group	Stock Owned %	Stock Owned Rank
Ricardo Labarca Benítez, president	0.4	18
Renato Sánchez Errázuriz, director	2.3	3
Julio Subercaseaux Aldunate, director	0.7	11
Claudio Troncoso Fernández, director	5.0	1
Other GASCO executives' combined holdings	0.4	—
GASCO Commercial Department	0.5	16
WORKING BOCK	9.3	

Mr. Troncoso apparently has no relatives among the officers and directors of any of the top 37 corporations or 6 largest banks in our study. However, Mr. Sánchez Errázuriz has two second cousins who are partners in 2 different firms of which Mr. Troncoso is president: Leonidas Larraín Vial and his brother Bernardo are both directors of SANICOM, a pharmaceutical and chemicals firm, and Leonidas is a director of Mineral Water and Health Springs. Three of the directors of GASCO as well as its manager and vice-president are distantly related. Pedro García de la Huerta Matte, for example, probably is Mr. Sánchez's second cousin, and the wife of Mr. García's first cousin is the sister of the Larraín brothers. Thus, close business association is buttressed by distant kinship ties among the executives.

20. "Pasaje Matte" Urban Rental Association

The Matte family:

Composition of Group	Stock Owned %	Stock Owned Rank
Rosa Elvira Matte de Prieto	2.1	7
Domingo Tocornal Matte, director	0.6	22
Domingo Matte Messia Foundation	2.8	6
Perpetua Freire de Valdés	0.4	25
Pasaje Matte itself	1.6	11
American Life Insurance Co.	1.9	8
SUBTOTAL	9.4	

20. "Pasaje Matte" Urban Rental Association (*cont.*)

The Matte family:

Composition of Group	Stock Owned %	Rank
Distribution and Trade Co. (CODICO)	14.6	1
O'Higgins Agricultural and Commercial Co.	4.5	2
"El Melón" Industrial Enterprises	4.2	3
WORKING BLOC	32.7	

The Mattes and immediate relatives through marriage hold the presidency and six of the seven directorships; a distant relative has the seventh.

American Life Insurance is owned (99.5 percent) by "Pasaje Matte."

Distribution and Trade Co.'s general manager Patricio Grez Matte is the nephew of Domingo and Arturo Matte Larraín, both of whom are directors of Pasaje Matte. He is also general manager of Mines and Fertilizers, of which Eliodoro Matte Ossa is president, and in which Distribution and Trade is the single-largest shareholder, with 25.0 percent, alongside O'Higgins (presumably under Matte control, and whose president, from 1948 on, is Eliodoro Matte) with 14.5 percent, and "El Melón" with 18.8 percent. Eliodoro Matte is a director both of Distribution and Trade and of Pasaje Matte. Eliodoro Matte's brother and other close relatives are on the board of Distribution and Trade; and five Matte close relatives, including Eliodoro, with 8.3 percent himself, hold a combined 9.1 percent of its shares. The largest shareholder (72.2 percent) of Distribution and Trade is O'Higgins Agricultural and Commercial Co., whose general manager also is Mr. Grez; his brother Manuel is on the board; Eliodoro Matte is president, and his brother Eduardo is a board member. Another close relative sits on both Distribution and Trade's and O'Higgins' board. We were not able to discover the principal shareowners in O'Higgins. It should be noted, also, that O'Higgins has a 15 percent interest in Quiñenco Forestry, which is owned (84 percent) by Lota-Schwager; and the wife of Mr. Grez is the daughter of Gilles de Heeckeren, one of the members of the controlling family in Lota-Schwager, in which "El Melón" also has a major interest. Thus, "El Melón" and the Mattes have a close community of interest. Eliodoro Matte's directorship in Paper and Cardboard and in Pasaje Matte, and his presidency of "El Melón," Mines and Fertilizers, and O'Higgins is one visible indicator of this.

24. Penco National Ceramics Factory (FANALOZA)

The Díaz family and associates:

Composition of Group	Stock Owned %	Rank
Angelina Roni de Díaz	1.2	10
Raúl Díaz Boneau, director	1.2	13
Gregorio Díaz Boneau, director	1.0	15

24. Penco National Ceramics Factory (FANALOZA) (*cont.*)

The Díaz family and associates:

Composition of Group	Stock Owned %	Rank
Eliana Díaz Roni	0.7	21
Reginald Díaz Batchelor	1.0	16
José Díaz Carlin	0.7	20
François Langlois Vidal, president; his son; and his son's brother-in-law, a director	0.6	—
Anfión Varela Moure, director	0.4	—
WORKING BLOC	6.8	

The son of Gregorio Díaz is finance manager.

Langlois Vidal's daughter-in-law's brother Gustavo Vicuña Salas is also the son of a former Penco National director.

Anfión Varela joined Penco National in 1920.

25. Enamelware Factory (FENSA)

Hernán Briones and associates:

Composition of Group	Stock Owned %	Rank
Hernán Briones Gorostiaga, president	7.2	1
Silvia Goich Aviani de Briones	1.6	7
Georgiana Balbontín vda. de Mitrovic	0.7	20
Ernesto Ayala Oliva, director	0.7	23
Guillermo Purcell Winter, director	0.5	31
Purcell and Co.	0.5	32
Vitalicia Cooperative Life Insurance	3.7	2
Vitalicia Continental Life Insurance	0.8	25
WORKING BLOC	15.7	

Mr. Briones and his wife Silvia hold 8.8 percent.

Georgiana Balbontín is the mother of Luis Mitrovic Balbontín, vice-president.

Ernesto Ayala joined FENSA in 1945, and served as general manager before becoming a director in 1957.

Guillermo Purcell is a partner in Purcell and Co.

The Vitalicia interests are apparently represented on the board by Patricio García Vela, director of Vitalicia Cooperative, which controls Vitalicia Continental through a 43.4 percent dominant interest.

NOTE: The Petroleum Company of Chile's description appears in the text of Chapter 2, because it is the only management-controlled firm in which we identified no specific controlling proprietary group.

CHAPTER TWO

"New Princes" for Old?

THE BASIC PREMISE of managerialism—and of its close variant, the functionalist theory of social stratification—is that the ascendance of the large corporation has meant a "revolution" in "the relations between power and class position in modern society."[1] The "old unity that was private enterprise"—the "kinship-property combination typical of classical capitalism"—has been split asunder, and thus the very "social cement of the bourgeois class system" has been irrevocably broken-up.[2] The dissolution of the ownership and control of capital has meant the dissolution of the capitalist class itself: "capital—and thereby capitalism—has *dissolved*," as Ralf Dahrendorf avers, "and [has] given way, in the economic sphere, to a plurality of partly agreed, partly competing, and partly simply different groups."[3] The result, in turn, has been the "breakup of the 'ruling class' ": "a power-holding group which has both an established *community* of interest and a *continuity* of interest" no longer exists in the societies wrought by the rise of the large corporation.[4] For, as Adolf Berle, Jr. and Gardiner C. Means put it, the split in the atom of property, the separation of ownership and control in the large corporation, makes it "evident that we are dealing not only with *distinct but often with opposing groups*, ownership on the one side, control on the other—a control which tends to move further and further away from ownership and ultimately to lie in the hands of management itself, a management capable of perpetuating its own position. The concentration of economic power separate from ownership has, in fact, created . . . a new form of absolutism, relegating 'owners' to the position of those who supply the means whereby the new princes may exercise their power."[5] Or, as John Kenneth Galbraith sums it up in a recent representative formulation, "The

[1] Bell 1958, p. 248.

[2] Berle and Means 1967, p. 116; Parsons and Smelser 1957, p. 254; Bell 1958, p. 247.

[3] Dahrendorf 1959, p. 47; italics added.

[4] Bell 1958, p. 248; italics in original.

[5] Berle and Means 1967, p. 116; italics added.

decisive power in modern industrial society is exercised not by capital but by organization, not by the capitalist but by the industrial bureaucrat."[6]

"Bureaucrats" and "Capitalists"

Thus, aside from the issue already addressed in Chapter 1—"whether the large corporations continue to be controlled by ownership interests despite their management by functionaries who may themselves be propertyless"—managerialism implicitly raises a second issue: "whether the undisputed rise of managerial functions means the rise of the functionaries themselves. Do they constitute a separate and cohesive stratum, with identifiable interests, ideas, and policies . . . opposed to those of the extant owning families? Are the consequences of their actions, whatever their intentions, to bring into being social relationships which undermine capitalism? How, with their rise, is the 'incidence of economic power' changed?"[7] The question, in short, is, Who are the "new princes" of the managerial realm? What relationship is there between the "capitalists" and the "industrial bureaucrats"? Or, to put it more prosaically and precisely, What is the "class situation," in Max Weber's terminology, of the "managers"?[8]

This is the leading empirical question of our analysis in the present chapter. And it can well begin with an examination of a particular "management-controlled" corporation. We saw in the previous chapter that all but one of the 15 ostensibly management-controlled corporations among the top 37 turn out, upon close inspection of their constellation of ownership relations and intercorporate connections, to be controlled by identifiable proprietary interests. But the Petroleum Company of Chile (COPEC), the eighth largest corporation in the mid-1960s (which has risen to the number-one position in recent years), is not, insofar as our data reveal, definitely controlled by an identifiable family or cohesive group of major stockholding associ-

[6] Galbraith 1971, p. xix.

[7] Zeitlin 1974a, p. 1078; the internal quote is from Bendix 1952, p. 119.

[8] See Weber 1946, pp. 181–186, 301, for his concept of "class situation." Although Weber usually focuses on the "mode of distribution"—in contrast to Marx's emphasis on production and appropriation of the social product in a "mode of production" constituted by contradictory/exploitative class relations—the content of the concept of "class situation" in his substantive sociological analyses is quite similar to Marx's sense of "class location" (or "class position"). See also note 21, Chapter 3.

ates.[9] Does this mean that the company's "managers," its top officers and directors, indeed possess a distinctive social identity "utterly different than their capitalist predecessors"?[10]

The Petroleum Company of Chile is in many respects the management-controlled corporation par excellence: its shares are held by some 20,000 stockholders, and the company's biggest individual shareowner holds only 0.9 percent of the stock; the biggest institutional shareholding comes to only 1.3 percent of the company's stock. The *combined* shareholdings of its nine officers and directors amount to only 1.2 percent of the stock, and their composition is highly technical and professional: four of the seven directors and the vice-president are civil engineers; the president and two directors are lawyers; and another director worked his way up the rungs of the administrative hierarchy over a decades-long career with the company.

But the corporation's officers and directors, despite their genuine professional credentials, are scarcely mere "professional managers." Although their combined stock is small in proportion to the company's total shares outstanding, which are widely dispersed, several executives have quite substantial shareholdings in absolute terms, i.e. in their stock market worth: three executives have stock in the company worth well over E°100,000, and two others have stock worth over E°75,000.[11] The three largest executive shareholdings rank 12, 23, and 29 among all shareholdings in the corporation.

[9] As of 1978, COPEC was ranked number one by assets among all corporations, according to government figures. See Dahse 1979, p. 140.

[10] Dahrendorf 1959, p. 46.

[11] In 1964, E°100,000 was the equivalent (at the average trading rate that year of E°2.70 = U.S.$1.00) of roughly $37,000. Even in the United States, this represents a rather sizable sum. In 1962, the most comparable year for which systematic information is available, roughly 90 percent of all consumer units in the population of the United States had a *total wealth* of less than $37,000, including *all* liquid assets, checking and savings accounts, and investments, such as real estate, stocks, and bonds. See Projector and Weiss 1966. No comparable figures on wealth distribution are available for Chile. The value of the escudo on international currency markets is not an accurate measure of its domestic purchasing power, or especially of the market worth of stocks in a period of slow trading in the stock market, since paper fortunes in stockownership fluctuate greatly with the level of active trading. Some sense of the orders of magnitude involved, however, may be grasped from the following: the minimum legal *daily* wage in industry in 1964 was E°2.4; in agriculture, depending on the zone, it ranged from E°1.7 to E°3.2, averaging E°1.9 *daily* (CORFO 1966, p. 105). Simple arithmetic shows that if an industrial worker regularly earned precisely the minimum wage, worked every day of the year, lived on air, and saved every cent he earned, it would take him about 115 years to save E°100,000 (not allowing for inflation). It would take a peasant somewhat longer. To be less facetious, the median fam-

Their aggregate stock comes to only 1.1 percent of the company's stock; and, with the minor shares being held by the other four executives, the management as a whole holds only 1.2 percent of the company's stock. But this gives management a combined shareholding, if they choose to vote as a bloc, that is outranked only by the 1.3 percent shareholding of the Rockefellers' International Basic Economy Corporation, Chile (IBEC). In addition, one of the directors, Carlos Vial Infante, is the first cousin of the 21st ranking shareholder, whose holding amounts to 0.3 percent of the company's stock. Mr. Vial is also the director (and former president) of Chile's South American Bank, the nation's fourth largest commercial bank, in which his family (see Chapter 3) shares control. The bank itself holds the 10th largest shareholding, amounting to 0.5 percent of the stock. The brother of general manager Manuel Zañartu Campiño has the 28th largest shareholding, with 0.2 percent of the company's stock (though he himself has only a token holding in the company). So, if they cooperate, COPEC's "managers" can vote 2.2 percent of its outstanding shares, which constitute the biggest block of stock in the company. In this limited sense, then, this "management" of a "management-controlled" corporation can scarcely be characterized properly as "opposed to ownership."

But, aside from their share ownership in the Petroleum Company of Chile, several of the executives are either major owners of capital or are closely related to principal shareowners in other top corporations or leading commercial banks. Mr. Vial, for example, has identifiable stockholdings in other corporations worth nearly E°200,000.[12] Besides being the former president of the South American Bank, as just noted, Mr. Vial is also the president of the South American Steamship Company, which ranks 4th in the top 37, and in which his family also has the controlling interest.

ily income in 1964 was roughly E°225 monthly; assuming no work days lost, and the same monthly income throughout the year, the median *annual family income* would have been about E°2,700 in 1964. Readers are invited to make their own calculations as to how long it would take this "typical family" to *earn* (not save) the sum of E°100,000. In 1964 (according to CORFO 1966, p. 108), only 6.1 percent of all *families* earned a monthly income exceeding E°1,000; only 1.5 percent earned even as little as E°1,500 monthly.

[12] This sum, a higher executive's "total stock worth," covers only stock held personally, and only in one or more of the top 37 nonfinancial corporations, top 11 foreign firms, and 16 major domestic commercial banks. Stock held by family holding companies, trusts, estates, foundations or other such intermediaries is not included in the sum of an individual's "total stock worth."

The president of COPEC, Francisco Bulnes Correa, has modest holdings in it worth only E°85,657, and his identifiable stockholdings elsewhere are worth a mere E°13,202. But he also owns one of Chile's 25 largest landed estates, the *tax-assessed* valuation of which—set far below market value—was E°305,656 in *1961* (the only year for which such information was available to us). By 1964, at a conservative estimate, inflation would have tripled the estate's worth. Mr. Bulnes is also a director of the Mortgage Bank (Santiago), Chile's largest private long-term agricultural credit institution. In addition, he sits on the boards of W. R. Grace of Chile and two other important Grace subsidiaries, and has served as legal counsel and representative of Grace for at least two decades. Carlos Alessandri Altamirano, a director whose stock in COPEC is worth only E°8,717 and whose total identifiable personal stockholdings amount to only E°27,700, has five relatives who rank among the country's 500 wealthiest individual stockowners, or "top investors."[13] Julio Durán Neumann, a director, is the company's 12th largest shareowner, but he has no identifiable relatives among the principal shareowners elsewhere. All told, therefore, six of the company's nine managers have clear-cut and significant personal ties to principal owners of capital.

In addition, the president and three directors are, as our investigation disclosed, part of the same overlapping and intertwining set of propertied kin: Mr. Vial's niece is married to the son of director Walter Müller Hess; Mr. Vial's son-in-law is a first cousin, once-removed, of the president, Mr. Bulnes, as well as the brother-in-law of a first cousin of Mr. Alessandri. That Mr. Vial, apparently the most powerful COPEC director, stands at the center of this entangling web of kinship among the company's executives, is probably not coincidental.

It should also be stressed that the interests of specific large institutional investors necessarily impinge upon the conduct of these managers: three of Chile's Big Five commercial banks, plus two domestic investment companies, one foreign investment company, and a major foreign bank, rank among COPEC's 10 biggest shareowners. Its executives surely must perform their managerial functions creditably and profitably on behalf of the common immediate interests of these financial institutions (despite these same institutions' competing interests elsewhere), or they will be replaced. Under such circumstances, the *conduct* of the company's managers, whatever their own class situation or personal motives, is not likely to differ fundamentally from

[13] The procedures for selecting the "top investors" are described below.

that of their counterparts in owner-controlled corporations. In short, close examination of an ostensibly management-controlled corporation in the top 37, the one that our research did not reveal to be controlled by an identifiable family or other minority-ownership interest, has in fact shown that its managers and owners are not distinct, let alone opposed, groups.

Of course, it is *possible* that a point can be reached at which an individual, family, or small group of business associates cannot typically dominate the affairs of immense corporations. But the question is whether, as managerial theory assumes, control of the means of production by the *class* of principal owners of capital would also thereby be abrogated. Our detailed investigation of the concrete relationships among the Petroleum Company of Chile's higher executives and major shareholders, and the principal owners of capital in other top corporations and big banks, suggests instead that the managers and owners of large corporations may well be closely bound together by intimate kinship ties as well as overlapping and common economic interests. Thus, without a systematic in-depth investigation of the social attributes, associations, and interests of the "new princes," there is no way to know whether they *are* "new," or—even if they are—whether they have merely become new members of an old, but reorganized, "business nobility."[14]

In the prevailing view, of course, the answer is not in doubt. Andrew Hacker, for one, sums it up sharply, referring to the putative situation in the United States: the higher executives of the large corporations "have little in the way of property and their influence lasts only so long as they sit at a particular desk." Mere bureaucrats or "anonymous administrators," he says, "most [U. S.] executives . . . do not overlap to any great extent with the world of inherited wealth."[15]

In contrast, a number of social scientists, although they accept the factuality of a separation of ownership and control in the large corporation, nonetheless reject the implication that with it has come the "decomposition of capital" or the dissolution of the capitalist class. These "plain marxists" argue that, whatever the situation within the large corporation as the decisive historical form of capital ownership, the owners and managers of large corporations, taken as a whole, merely constitute different strata—when, indeed, the managers are not simply agents of ownership—of the same more or less unified so-

[14] See Baltzell 1966.

[15] Hacker 1975, p. 368; also see Hacker 1961.

cial class.[16] What is remarkable, of course, is that systematic research on the social location of the higher executives of large corporations in the advanced economies is rare; and even the most thorough studies have not (as yet) investigated the concrete ensemble of social relations, particularly the entangling bonds of kinship, among the higher executives and principal owners of capital.[17]

The relative dispersion of ownership in the higher managerial realms of the advanced economies and of Chile is, as we noted earlier, very similar. For instance, Robert A. Gordon found (using TNEC data) that in the 176 top nonfinancial corporations in the United States, as of 1939, the median aggregate stockholding for the entire management was 2.1 percent; for the officers, it was 0.3 percent; and for the directors, 1.1 percent.[18] In the top 37 of Chile, the medians are 1.9 percent for management as a whole, 0.6 percent for the officers, and 1.1 percent for the directors. (Comparable contemporary U.S. data on the median holdings are not available.) Figures on stockownership in their firms by the officers and directors on the boards of the top nonfinancial corporations in the United States, in 1939 and 1975, and in Chile during the mid-1960s, reveal a strikingly similar pattern among them. Thus, for instance, as Table 2.1 shows, in roughly half of these top corporations, in both periods in the United States, and in Chile during 1964/66, the directors own less than 1 percent of the common stock in "their" company; similarly, in roughly another three out of ten of these corporations, the directors' combined holdings amount to

[16] "Plain marxists" (lower case) is C. Wright Mills' term (1962, p. 98) for thinkers to whom Marx's "general model and . . . ways of thinking are central to their own intellectual history and remain relevant to their attempts to grasp present-day social worlds." He lists such varied thinkers, aside from himself, as Jean Paul Sartre, Joan Robinson, and Paul M. Sweezy in that category. Among the "plain marxists" who accept the alleged split between ownership and control as real are Baran and Sweezy (1966, chap. 2), Miliband (1969, chap. 2), Nichols (1969, pp. 140–141), Playford (1972, pp. 116–118), Herman (1981), and Useem 1984; while others, such as Domhoff (1967, pp. 47–62) and Kolko (1962, pp. 60–69) both deny that this alleged split is real and argue that "managers" and "owners" are in the same social class. Also see, in particular, Lundberg (1946, 1968), who lays stress on the need to study the kinship relationships among the owners and higher executives of large corporations. For a more detailed discussion of these points, see Zeitlin 1974a, pp. 1078–1079.

[17] See Useem 1980, for a review of relevant studies, as well as Domhoff 1967, 1970, 1983; Soref 1980; and Soref and Zeitlin 1988. Domhoff's studies investigate a variety of social relations other than kinship tying together managers and owners. Also see note 55, Chapter 1, for several studies that detail the kinecon groups controlling specific top corporations in Great Britain and the United States.

[18] Gordon 1966, p. 27.

TABLE 2.1. Distribution of the Top Nonfinancial Corporations in the United States (1939 and 1975) and Chile (1964/66), According to the Percentage of Common Stock Owned by Management

% of Stock Outstanding	% of Top Corporations in Stockownership Category								
	Officers			Directors			All Management		
	U.S.		Chile	U.S.		Chile	U.S.		Chile
	1939	1975	1964/66	1939	1975	1964/66	1939	1975[a]	1964/66
0–0.9	68.2	81.0	67.6	48.9	46.0	51.3	35.8	—	40.5
1–4.9	18.8	10.5	10.8	29.5	28.0	27.0	32.4	—	29.7
5–9.9	5.7	1.5	2.7	9.7	10.0	10.8	11.4	—	10.8
10–19.9	3.4	1.5	8.1	7.4	5.5	2.7	11.4	—	2.7
20–29.9	1.1	5.5[b]	10.8	2.8	10.5[b]	8.1	4.0	—	8.1
30–39.9	0	—	0	0.6	—	0	1.1	—	0
40–49.9	0.6	—	0	0	—	0	0.6	—	5.4
50 and over	2.3	—	0	1.1	—	0	3.4	—	2.7
Number of companies	176	200	37	176	200	37	176	200	37
Median %	0.3	—	0.6	1.1	—	1.1	2.1	—	1.9

SOURCE: U.S. figures for 1939 compiled by Gordon (1966, p. 27) from data in TNEC monograph no. 29 (Goldsmith and Parmelee 1940). U.S. figures for 1975 compiled by Herman (1981, pp. 93, 89).

[a] Not presented in Herman 1981.

[b] Twenty percent and over; Herman 1981 presents only "20 percent and over" figures.

at least 1 percent, but less than 5 percent, of the outstanding stock. (Incidentally, to the extent that the U.S. data for the two periods are comparable, they reveal, at the other end of the spectrum, an *increase* from 1939 to 1975 in the percentage of companies whose board members—officers and directors alike—hold 20 percent or more of the stock. For instance, during these years, the percentage of top U.S. corporations in which the directors hold at least 20 percent of the stock rises from 4.5 percent to 10.5 percent.) Gordon's observation concerning his 1939 findings thus applies as well both to the United States in 1975 and to Chile in the mid-1960s: these findings "emphasize the relatively small ownership by officers and directors in the very large firm. . . . In general . . . management ownership does not constitute even a substantial minority of the voting common stock issued by the giant concerns."[19]

But whatever the combined stockownership of management, individual officers and directors can still be among their firm's principal shareowners—especially to the extent that the firm's shares are highly dispersed among very small stockholdings. Ownership of a small *proportion* of the stock outstanding can, under such circumstances, *rank* that stockholding among the firm's *biggest* stockholdings. We know of no study that has examined this relationship in the United States; even the classic TNEC studies do not present the relevant data. In England, however, P. Sargant Florence found that one-fourth of the directorships in the top 98 nonfinancial corporations of 1936 were held by men who were principal shareowners in "their own" firms. Among Chile's top 37 corporations the figure is far smaller: 17 percent of the directorships are filled by men who are principal shareowners in their own company.[20] As we might expect, the probability that a director is also a principal shareowner in his company varies inversely with the size of the company—as Florence also found in England. In our top 10 corporations, only 10 percent of the directorships are filled by principal shareowners; in those ranking 11–20, 15 percent; in those ranking 21–30, 20 percent; and in those ranking 31–37, 25 percent. So it is clear that, even in the smallest of the top 37 corporations, the over-

[19] Gordon 1966, pp. 25, 28. Herman's figures on directors' stockownership include "represented holdings," i.e. "all identifiable ownership interests in the companies by institutions represented on the board, with sole voting power held by the institution. The main institutions involved are commercial banks, insurance companies, and investment companies" (1981, p. 89).

[20] Florence 1961, p. 91.

whelming majority of the directorships are not occupied by their own principal shareowners.

The question, though, is whether these findings—which are consistent with managerial theory, and which reveal a similar pattern among the managements of the top corporations of England, the United States, and Chile—distort the real class situation of higher corporate management. Do these data adequately gauge the depth of the relationship between the top corporations' managers and the principal shareowners? The answer is no, they do not, for two main reasons. First of all, these findings (Gordon's and Florence's) are based only on an analysis of a management's or board's shareholdings in "its own" corporation; that is to say, these findings disregard the higher executives' shareholdings in other corporations (whether these be other "top corporations" or smaller ones), as well as in banks and other financial institutions in which they do not participate in management. Second, these findings are based on examinations of *directorships*, i.e. the offices held, not the individuals who are the directors. Because one man often serves on several boards simultaneously, however, this focus on the directorship understates the extent of the overlap between directors and principal shareowners.

The problem is compounded, of course, if both the first *and* the second situation occur simultaneously for the same executive (e.g. a man who sits on the boards of several corporations in which he owns no substantial stock, but who is a principal stockowner in another top corporation in whose management he does not participate). This situation would yield a finding that none of the directorships is filled by a man who is also a principal shareowner in "his own" corporation (i.e. where he is on the board), even though every one of the men filling each of these directorships is a principal shareowner elsewhere. From the standpoint of *class* analysis, of course, such a measure thereby understates considerably the extent of the real overlap between managers and owners. In any higher corporate world where interlocking among directorates is extensive because the same men sit in the managements of many different corporations, this is a critical error in the method of assessing the real class situation of the managers.

How, then, does the picture change when we correct for these errors—when we focus on the individual rather than the office, not only on principal shareholdings in "his own" top corporation, but on those in other top corporations as well? The 231 directorships in Chile's top 37 corporations are filled by just 165 men, and whereas only 17 percent of these 231 directorships are held by men who are also principal shareowners in their own top corporations, 27 percent of the directors are principal shareowners in at least one of the top 37 corporations, whether or not they serve in its management. (Of these 44 directors who are also principal shareowners, 7 are principal shareowners in at least two top-37 corporations.)

Taking account of *principal* shareholdings in all of the top 37 corporations, however, may still neglect other stockholdings that, although not ranking among the principal ones in a given top corporation, are nonetheless quite valuable—and may put their owners among the corporate world's small number of major investors. A man, for instance, whose blocks of stock in several different corporations were, in the aggregate, worth more than any single principal shareholding, would have been omitted from our count so far. And, of course, a "small" shareholding that does not rank as a "principal" shareholding in one corporation may well be worth far more on the market than a principal shareholding in another corporation. In addition, as we mentioned earlier, a man might own sizable amounts of stock in other firms not ranking among the top corporations, as well as in banks and other financial institutions. For all of these reasons, focusing only on the higher executives' principal shareholdings in the top corporations probably does not provide an adequate measure of their relative place among the wealthiest individual owners of capital.

The Principal Owners of Capital

There are roughly 173,000 shareholdings in Chile's top 37 corporations and 16 major commercial banks. To examine all of them in order to identify the biggest total stock portfolios held by individual shareowners was not feasible. So we proceeded as follows. In each of the top 37 corporations and 16 major commercial banks controlled by domestic capital, as well as in the top 11 foreign firms (those appearing on our original list of Chile's top 50 corporations), we calculated what amount of stock was worth at least E°50,000 at the stock's selling price on the Santiago Stock Exchange as of the final quarter of 1964. We then located the roughly 6,600 shareholdings in these 48 firms worth E°50,000 or more, identified their individual owners, and aggregated all such blocks of stock to arrive at the market worth of these individuals' stock porfolios. We also identified all the principal individual shareowners in these 48 nonfinancial firms and 16 banks (i.e. individuals whose shareholdings rank them among the 20 biggest stockowners in any firm) and aggregated all of their principal shareholdings, as well as any holdings worth E°50,000 or more, to arrive at the "total market worth" of their stock portfolios.

By these criteria, we identified 502 individuals whose stock portfolios are worth *over* E°100,000, defining them as the "top investors" in the country's leading banks and top corporations. Many of them doubtless own other, uncounted smaller shareholdings in these same firms and banks; and they probably also own substantial stock in other smaller corporations (both financial and nonfinancial) not included in our study. Also, of course, there may well be individuals whose portfolios are worth as much as or more than those owned by these 502 individuals, but who were missed because their major shareholdings are in firms other than these 16 banks and top-48 corporations. Finally, uncounted also were shares held on behalf of individuals by various nominees, brokers, foundations, trusts, estates, eleemosynary institutions, or other intermediaries (or "palos blancos" [dummies] as they are known in Chile). Withal, these 502 "top investors" are surely among the wealthiest individual owners of capital in the country.

So, taking into account not only whether an executive is a principal shareowner in any top-37 corporation, but also whether he is a top investor, we find that 42 percent of the officers and 31 percent of the directors fall into this category; all told, 35 percent of these "managers" are, in fact—as we shall call this group for short—"principal owners of capital" or "principal capitalists." That such a substantial proportion—more than one in three—of managers are also personally principal capitalists is not consistent with the notion that managers of top corporations are a separate breed from (or "utterly unlike") owners. Nonetheless, a large majority of these higher executive are, in fact, apparently "propertyless." Much as his counterpart in England or in the United States, the typical manager of the large corporation in Chile, so it appears, is also a mere "business administrator—a bureaucrat," in Mabel Newcomer's words, rather than a "capitalist."[21]

But focusing only on their ownership of stock in the top banks and corporations understates the higher executives' personal stake in the system of private enterprise. A host of "small" companies, both financial and nonfinancial, are the repositories and base of immense family and individual private wealth and often are the source of commensurate power among the nation's top corporations. Such smaller com-

[21] Newcomer 1955, p. 149.

panies, as we saw in the previous chapter, can be crucial in the actual control structure of a far larger and seemingly management-controlled corporation. Most important, in the present context, they can also be the base on which an apparently "propertyless" manager's position in a top corporation rests: he may represent or himself be among the major stockowners of such smaller companies that have important business relations (as suppliers, customers, creditors, and so forth) with that corporation, or that own sizable stock in it. Such crucial ownership connections have, to our knowledge, not been probed at all in studies purporting to find mere bureaucrats at the helms of the largest corporations in the "modern industrial societies" of the West.[22] Alas, given an already overburdened research agenda, neither did we systematically investigate such lesser business connections of Chile's higher managers.

Capital, Kinship, and Class

But what especially obscures the real class situation of the managers—and what has been entirely neglected in empirical analyses purporting to characterize these "business leaders" in the top corporations of the advanced economies—is the failure to investigate their relations with the wealthiest families. By focusing on individuals, the class itself gets ignored. For, as Joseph Schumpeter rightly argues, "class membership . . . is not individual at all. . . . The family, not the physical person, is the true unit of class and class theory."[23] Not only, as is obvious, are "individuals born into a given class situation," but the family is the center of the ensemble of social relations in which an individual's experience is mediated and the particularity of his personality and character shaped. Even when one shifts from one class to another through "social mobility," the new class membership is secured and certified socially by "appropriate" marriage for oneself and one's offspring. Thus, "families and their mutual relations are the stuff of a class system."[24] Freely intermarrying families sharing a common location in production relations constitute and reproduce the "social classes" rooted in those relations.

[22] "Of the West" because, to our knowledge, managerialists have never made the same claim about "the breakdown of family capitalism" in, for instance, Japan's largest corporations, where family spheres of influence, or *zaibatsu*, are recognized as having continuing preeminence.

[23] Schumpeter 1955, p. 113.

[24] Sweezy 1953, p. 124.

The significance of the family in the integration and historical continuity of classes is recognized in principle—even emphasized, as we noted at the outset—by functionalist stratification theorists and managerialists. For they claim that, in fact, the *fusion* "between the systems of property and family . . . , which has been the social cement of the bourgeois class system," has *broken down*, as the supposed rise of the managerial demiurge has created the new classless division of labor of "postcapitalist society."[25] But this notion that the large corporation has "effected a radical separation of property and family," or abolished "the kinship-property combination" underpinning capitalism's class relations, is not supported by any appropriate empirical research. Again, this false notion survives despite the finding of sociologists studying the family that so-called upper classes everywhere (including, for all its vastness and mobility, the United States) tend to have an extensive and tightly knit network of intraclass kinship relations.[26] The families "at the top of the social class hierarchy" in the United States, as E. Digby Baltzell reminds us, "are brought up together, are friends, and are intermarried one with another. . . . The tap root of any upper class, that which nourishes each contemporary generation with a sense of tradition and historical continuity, is a small group of families who were born to that class, and whose ancestors have been 'to the manor born' for several generations."[27]

A variety of institutions specific to such dominant classes, "from debutante balls to select social clubs, resorts, and assorted watering places, as well as the 'proper' schools, colleges (fraternities, sororities, and 'living groups'), assure their comingling and psychological compatibility—and, therefore, differential propensity to intermarry. Protection of the family's property (and 'good name'), which injects a further note of caution in the selection of proper marriage partners, merely increases this 'natural' social tendency."[28] On those rare occasions when wealth does not marry wealth, as Ferdinand Lundberg remarks of the United States, "it is front-page news."[29] Extensive intermarriage among propertied families not only results from close mutual interaction, but also serves (whether intentionally or not) to establish reciprocal obligations and loyalties and to buttress and reinforce the economic basis of class unity.

[25] Bell 1958, pp. 246–249; see, also, Dahrendorf 1959.
[26] See Goode 1963, Goode et al. 1971; Cavan 1963.
[27] Baltzell 1958, pp. 7, 9.
[28] Zeitlin 1974a, p. 1109.
[29] Lundberg 1968, p. 25.

Particularly among the higher classes, individual and family status are virtually inseparable. Aside from the variety of legal devices (bank and brokerage holdings, and various eleemosynary arrangements) that formalize the proprietary community linking together individual and family members, individuals often own real property and capital only insofar as they belong to a given family. Even where ownership, rather than being concentrated in family trusts and estates, is legally dispersed among persons, these individual family members who are in "good standing" benefit from the family fortune as a whole, receive income from it, and are the potential heirs of one another's holdings, each of which is "a slice from a single source."[30] By necessity, individual members of a family have a common stake in its combined proprietary interests; the emotional ties that already exist among its members are given rather "pragmatic nourishment" by the intertwining of interests and controls within the propertied family.[31]

The boundaries of the "family" within a dominant class extend far beyond the immediate family itself, and may not be altogether visible even to its own "members." This is evident from the precision with which inheritance rights are defined and codified in the legal systems of capitalist societies: the members of "the family" characteristically include, by consanguinity and affinity, quinary relatives and beyond.[32] Thus, as Lundberg rightly observes, it is "quite arbitrary in many cases to speak of a person as representing a single fortune"; and it is also inaccurate to conceptualize the nuclear family as the effective kinship unit at the higher levels of the class structure.[33] Writing of this "upper-upper class family" in the United States, for instance, Ruth Cavan has made this clear, in an acute passage worth quoting at length:

> The upper-upper class family has not only historical continuity but also functioning lateral relationships. It consists of nuclear units closely interconnected by blood ties, marriage, the past history, and present joint ownership of property. The great family thus includes uncles, aunts, and cousins of various degrees of closeness, organized into conventional nuclear units but functioning also as *a large kinship family*. Moreover, the tendency of members of the small upper-upper class to marry within the class—even within the larger family, as cousin with cousin—has created a complicated sys-

[30] Lundberg 1968, p. 163.
[31] McKinley 1964, p. 24.
[32] Rheinstein 1967.
[33] Lundberg 1968, p. 163.

> tem of relationships, so that it often may be truthfully said that the entire upper-upper class in a given community tends to be a related kinship group. . . . In the kinship family, the ties of loyalty are very strong. *One is a member of the kinship family first, of the small-family unit second.* Family organization therefore tends to be on a kinship rather than a marital basis, with the headship resting in the oldest person or in a group of collateral elders. . . . The elders wield great power over both adult and youthful descendants, often determining such matters as type and place of education, occupation, and selection of the spouse. If, as often happens, they hold the joint family property and wealth, they possess an enormous authority since they may control the amount of income of younger members. The middle-aged men who, in other social classes, would be independent heads of their small families and control their own social and economic destinies, in the upper-upper class may still play the role of dependent sons to their old parents.[34]

Or, as Lundberg argued decades ago: "The wealthiest Americans, with a few exceptions, are already joined by a multiplicity of family ties, just as they are joined by interlocking directorates and mutual participation in economic and social undertakings. The 'community of interest' of the rich . . . has become . . . a joint family interest."[35]

Indeed, writing as an early critic of the then emerging managerialist doctrine, Lundberg suggested that "most of the desirable jobs throughout the biggest corporations and banks . . . are filled to an astonishing extent by men who are either collateral descendants of the wealthy families, married to direct or collateral descendants, or connected by blood relationship with persons directly or indirectly related. . . . *Scratch any big corporation executive and the chances are even that one will find a close relative of the wealthiest families.*"[36]

Lundberg's crucial observations about the role of kinship relations in integrating the American "upper-upper class," and, in particular, in incorporating the higher executives of the large corporations into that class, have not been followed up by any systematic empirical research although, as we know, many social scientists have nonetheless permitted themselves to assure us that the capitalist class has either disintegrated or been "lopped off" in an "unseen revolution" in the United States, England, and other such advanced economies. One reason for

[34] Cavan 1963, pp. 96–97; italics added.

[35] Lundberg 1946, p. 9.

[36] Lundberg 1946, p. 19; italics added.

the absence of the necessary empirical research is clear: to carry it out would be enormously difficult, tedious, and time-consuming. As Lundberg remarks, kinship relationships among wealthy families "are so numerous, and intertwine at so many points with one another, that to survey them all would turn this into a genealogical study."[37]

Kinship Analysis

Indeed, in an effort to provide an unambiguous measure of the class situation of the managers, and to gauge the extent to which they and the owners belong to the same social class, we did find it necessary in part to "turn this into a genealogical study." Surely Schumpeter is right to insist that genealogical research is essential to the analysis of processes of class formation and that "under capitalism, the lack of genealogical material becomes even more keenly felt" than in the analysis of precapitalist societies. He is also right to lament "the lack of zeal with which social scientists gather and evaluate this material [despite] . . . the fact that it alone can provide a reliable knowledge of the structure and life processes of capitalist society."[38] But, unfortunately, this "lack of zeal" becomes quite easy to understand as soon as one has experienced the consequences of taking this injunction seriously!

Whether or not a manager has a capitalist in the family is a question easier asked than answered. For the data are not there for simple gathering, but have to be carefully ferreted, teased, and squeezed out of diverse reference sources, in a long, hard, and tedious, if often intriguing, research process. We investigated, traced, and reconstructed the kinship relationships in which each of the 229 higher executives of our top 37 nonfinancial corporations, their 68 counterparts in the Big Six commercial banks, the 132 top landowners, and the 502 top investors are involved. (For the top investors, however, we investigated "only" whether any of them showed up among the 6,000 or so relatives of the higher corporate and banking executives and top landowners.) As might be expected, these 6,000 relatives are very unevenly distributed among the individuals in these three universes. Some individuals have many identified relatives; others have only their parents, wife, children, or some brothers and sisters identified; still others have none of their relatives identified. We found basic kinship data on

[37] Lundberg 1946, p. 12. But see a partial effort in Soref and Zeitlin 1988.

[38] Schumpeter 1955, p. 129.

207 of the 229 corporate executives (90 percent), 66 of the 68 bankers (97 percent), and 111 of the 132 top landowners (84 percent).

After completing the identification of the relatives, we then investigated *their* stockholdings in the top 37 corporations and *16* national commercial banks, as well as the 11 top foreign firms, and also determined the offices they hold in these companies. We also tried to find and record their large landholdings. The results of these latter investigations are reported in the following chapters. For the moment, however, the question is the extent to which the kinship analysis reveals an otherwise hidden depth of intimate interconnections between the higher executives of the top corporations and the wealthiest capital-owning families.

In order to make precise comparisons among analytically relevant categories of individuals, we also devised a quantitative method for measuring the "kinship distance" between an individual and specific types of relatives. This method is based on the observation that an individual in Western society belongs simultaneously to two "nuclear families": the "family of orientation," in which one is born and reared, consisting of one's parents and siblings; and the "family of procreation," established by marriage, consisting of one's spouse and children. These are defined as an individual's "primary relatives," and together they comprise an individual's "immediate family." Thus, an individual forms a link between these two nuclear families; and "a ramifying series of such links," as George P. Murdock explains, "binds numbers of individuals to one another through kinship ties."[39]

An individual, whom we might call "Ego" for convenience, can thus be thought of as standing at the center of a web of kinship relations, with a measurable distance in "kinship links" between Ego and each of Ego's relatives, and among the relatives themselves. In many cases, given the marital maze, any two individuals may be united by kinship relations through several different individuals, so that the number of kinship links between them varies, depending on the path traced. Therefore, the kinship distance between any two individuals in this study has been stated as the number of kinship links corresponding to their closest relationship.

The terms "primary relatives" and "immediate family" are used interchangeably. The kinship distance between Ego and any primary relative (parents, siblings, spouse, children) is, of course, one link. By this method of measurement, therefore, relationships established

[39] Murdock 1949, p. 94.

through marriage are equated with relationships based on common descent. Each primary relative of Ego also has primary relatives, most of whom are not Ego's primary relatives (only unmarried siblings have the identical set of primary relatives). These are Ego's "secondary relatives," at a distance of two kinship links: grandparents, aunts and uncles, nephews and nieces, in-laws, and grandchildren. Each secondary relative, in turn, has primary relatives who are neither primary nor secondary relatives of Ego, and whom we term "tertiary relatives," at a distance of three kinship links: first cousins; great-grandparents; great-grandchildren; great-aunts and great-uncles; the parents of the spouses of Ego's children; the spouses of uncles, aunts, nieces and nephews, etc. This measure of kinship distance can be continued systematically to distinguish quaternary relatives (e.g. first cousins once-removed) and quinary relatives (e.g. second cousins). We use the term "close relatives" or "close family" to designate all relatives within three kinship links and, following Murdock, refer to "all who are more remote than tertiary relatives as distant relatives."[40]

How the kinship and economic data can be combined is shown in

[40] Murdock 1949, p. 95. Several investigators devoted themselves to kinship research during an interrupted series of investigations over a five-year period. The early phase of the research, in which Lynda Ann Ewen participated fully, relied heavily on two published sources: mainly the seventh (1948–1949) and eleventh (1959–1961) but also various other editions of the *Diccionario biográfico de Chile* and the privately printed upper-class genealogical reference work by Guillermo de la Cuadra Gormaz (1950). The *Diccionario* is a Chilean rough equivalent of *Who's Who*, and de la Cuadra's work has considerably more historical information than genealogical information on major upper-class families. To supplement these sources, Zeitlin also interviewed informants who have close ties to the higher circles of the Chilean upper class. The third major reference work used was the five-volume work of Virgilio Figueroa, a.k.a. Virgilio Talquino (1925–1931). This work contains a vast amount of historical and biographical data, including a careful detailing of kinship information on many important families in Chile from 1800 to 1930. It also has richly detailed histories for many of these families. The fourth reference used, discovered late in our research and located in the library of the University of California at Santa Barbara, was the privately published work by Arturo Domínguez Barros (1968). While focusing on the many branches of the Domínguez family, this work also contains individual genealogies of 20 of the most prominent Chilean families that have married into the Domínguez line during the 150 years since Don Francisco arrived in Chile in 1818 from Spain. This book, while having little family history, is more rigorously complete in its kinship data than any of the other sources utilized. It not only gives the full names of all brides and grooms, but often gives the same information for the in-laws, too. It should be noted that by "full names" we refer to the Spanish surname system, which combines both the father's patronymic surname and mother's patronymic surname; thus, for example, as we have seen, Carlos Vial Infante is "Mr. Vial."

Figure 2.1. The focus here is on one male member of the family, "Ego." The number within the symbol of each relative (e.g. a 3 or a 2) indicates the number of kinship links *most closely* (i.e. with respect to the "shortest distance") binding that person to Ego.

Using these terms, it is not only stylistically convenient but also analytically precise to speak of the individual and the family, and of the attributes of each, interchangeably. Thus, for example, if any of a manager's primary relatives is a principal owner of capital, whether or not he himself is, he thereby belongs to a "capitalist family." Similarly, his wife and children are considered members of a capitalist family if he is a principal capitalist; and the same is true of him if any one of them, or a parent or sibling, is personally a principal owner of capital, even if he himself is not. *Each individual takes on the family's proprietary attribute, and each also endows it with that attribute.* This method, we might add, allows us not only to discover and delineate what might otherwise be invisible—the common class membership of apparently quite different social types of individuals—but also to measure the concentration and centralization of ownership of the means of production within given families. (See Chapter 4.)

All in the Family

What, then, does analysis of these kinship data reveal concerning the level of intimate social relations tying together the managers and principal owners of capital? First, there is a substantial overall increase in the proportion of those who are principal capitalists. Overall, 45 percent of the higher executives of the top 37 corporations are principal owners of capital, either personally or via someone in their immediate family. Second, when the stockownership of their immediate family members is taken into account, although there is scarcely any change among the officers, there is a substantial increase in the proportion of directors who are principal capitalists. In fact, the previous finding of a sizable difference in the proportions of principal capitalists among officers and directors disappears: among both types of executives, 45 percent are in an immediate capitalist family.

But multiple strands of intertwining consanguineal and affinal bonds, extending far beyond the immediate family, knit these apparently disparate managerial and capitalist elements tightly together into the same social class. In fact, the chances are even or better that a higher executive is in a close capitalist family: precisely one-half are

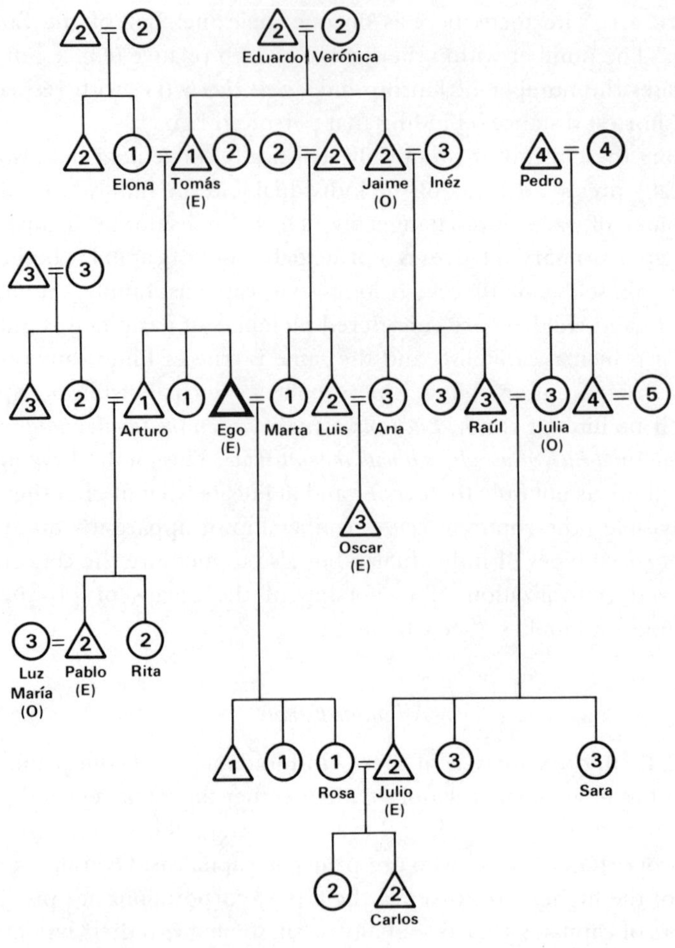

FIGURE 2.1. Kinship Relations among Hypothetical Higher Executives and Principal Owners of Capital

personally principal capitalists or have secondary relatives who are, and slightly over half are in a close capitalist family (see Table 2.2). So, at each analytical phase of measuring the strength of the "kinship-property combination" in the managerial realm, it is not a "radical separation of property and family" but rather an indivisible interconnection between them that has been revealed, and the hitherto-hidden common class membership of the managers of the top corporations and the principal owners of capital has become increasingly transparent.

Yet, the intricacy of the kinship web binding them together has been *under*stated so far. For to avoid burdening these already heavily table-laden pages with still more (and more complex) tables, we have merely asked whether or not an officer or director has a close relative who is a principal owner of capital. But, in fact, as Table 2.3 shows, 28 percent of the officers and 26 percent of the directors, for an average of 27 percent of all higher executives, have three or more close capitalist relatives. The vast majority of the higher executives who have a close capital-owning relative actually have several: 18 of the 30 officers (or 60 percent) and 43 of the 72 directors (also 60 percent) with one or more close capitalist relatives have, in fact, three or more of them.

We also want to emphasize that too narrow a focus on the measured percentage of officers and directors who are either principal owners of capital or closely related to them might unwittingly lead to an

TABLE 2.2. Percentage of Higher Executives of the Top 37 Nonfinancial Corporations in Chile Who Are in a Principal Capital-Owning Family, 1964/66

	Personally Principal Shareowners[a]	Personally Principal Capitalists[b]	Principal Capitalists in: Immediate Family[c]	Secondary Family[d]	Close Family[e]	(*N*)
Officers[f]	42	42	45	52	56	(64)
Directors	27	31	45	49	53	(165)
All higher executives	31	35	45	50	54	(229)

[a] Men who are personally among the 20 largest shareholders in one or more of the top 37 corportions.

[b] Men who are personally principal shareowners or top investors.

[c] Men who are personally principal capitalists or in whose immediate family there is a principal capitalist.

[d] Men who are personally principal capitalists or in whose immediate family or among whose secondary relatives there is a principal capitalist.

[e] Men who are personally principal capitalists or in whose immediate or secondary family or among whose tertiary relatives there is a principal capitalist.

[f] Nondirector officers; among the 165 directors are 11 men who serve as officers in two top corporations and 8 who so serve in three.

TABLE 2.3. Percentage of Higher Executives of the Top 37 Nonfinancial Corporations in Chile Who Have a Specified Number of Close, Principal Capital-Owning Relatives, 1964/66

	None	One	Two	Three-plus	(*N*)
Officers	53	17	2	28	(64)
Directors	56	13	5	26	(165)
All higher executives	55	14	4	27	(229)

NOTE: "Close relatives" include members of the immediate family as well as secondary and tertiary relatives. We do not consider here whether the executive is himself a principal owner of capital.

underestimation of the strength and complexity of the kinship web holding them together. The tabular presentation does not adequately convey the nature of these entangling alliances. For around each of the close capitalist relatives of an officer or director, there is typically another set of close relatives who, by that same criterion, are also members of a principal capitalist family. Thus, even the statement that a manager has three or more close relatives who personally are principal owners of capital understates how many of his relatives actually have a stake in the protection and advancement of their common class interest. By limiting to tertiary links the kinship distance actually measured, many other capital-owning relatives among the higher executives' kindred remain uncounted.

In fact, as we know, any number of both close and distant relatives can constitute the group of kindred controlling a given corporation: their combined capital is necessary to retain their common corporate control and its attendant advantages. This kinecon group, the effective intraclass unit of capital ownership and corporate control, can and often does include relatives who are far more distant from each other, or from the core nuclear family, than three "links." (For example, two well-documented cases of such kinecon groups in the United States involve the Dows and Duponts. Dow Chemical Company was controlled, in 1964, by "78 dependents [plus spouses] of H. W. Dow [who] owned 12.6 percent of the [company's] outstanding common stock." Similarly, the U.S. government, in its 1964 antitrust case against General Motors, held that the Duponts were a cohesive group of at least 75 persons, and named 184 Dupont relatives in its complaint.[41])

As of 1964/66, the situation in many of Chile's top 37 corporations is qualitatively the same. The Edwards "family" is an apt illustration of

[41] Larner 1970, p. 75; Lundberg 1968, p. 171.

the capital-kindred interrelationship. This kinecon group controls 3 and shares control of another 3 of the top 37 corporations, plus the Bank of Edwards (the fifth largest bank), 2 major insurance companies, and several other important financial, commercial, and industrial enterprises. The president of all 3 of the top 37 firms controlled by the Edwards kinecon group is Agustín Edwards Eastman, who is not personally a principal shareowner in any of the 3. (Had the family not enjoyed considerable notoriety, Mr. Edwards probably would have been counted, in a standard sort of managerial study, as a propertyless "bureaucrat.") Mr. Edwards' first cousin once-removed, Arturo Lyon Edwards, who is himself a principal owner of capital, is in the management of 2 of the same top-37 corporations of which Mr. Edwards is president. Another director of the biggest Edwards firm, United Breweries Company, is Jorge Ross Ossa, a principal shareowner both in that firm and in the Bank of Edwards. Mr. Ross's great-aunt is the grandmother of Mr. Edwards' great-grandfather as well as the great-grandmother of Mr. Lyon. Mr. Ross also sits on the board of several other corporations in which the Edwards kindred has substantial investments or shares control with other interests. As is obvious, the kinship distance between these identifiable members of the same kinecon group is much farther than the distance considered in our systematic quantitative analysis of linkages among the higher executives and the principal capital-owning families. Mr. Edwards is separated from Mr. Lyon by four kinship links and from Mr. Ross by seven, while the distance separating Mr. Ross and Mr. Lyon is six links.

The fact is that our method of computing kinship distance is more restrictive than the method ordinarily used in Western common or canon law. While our unit of measurement, the "link," coincides with the "degree" in lineal relationships, the two units do *not* coincide in collateral relationships. A first cousin, for example, is *three* links from Ego in our system of measurement, but only *two* degrees from Ego in both common and canon law. A second cousin is *five* links from Ego in our system (and, as a result, is not included in our quantitative analysis of the kinship-property nexus), but is only *three* degrees distant in both common and canon law. Thus, collateral relatives who are ordinarily considered "close" in these formal Western codifications, for purposes of determining the proper lines of inheritance and of intermarriage proscriptions (or of nepotism), are defined by our system of measurement as "distant" relatives.[42] In short, our finding that more than half

[42] For example, the constitution of the State of Missouri provides that "any public

of the officers and directors of Chile's top 37 nonfinancial corporations belong to a close capitalist family is a minimum estimate of the mutual social integration and common class membership of the nation's "managers" and "owners."

The "Inner Group"

Of course, there is no a priori "scientific" criterion (aside from the "simple majority" rule) by which to decide how much of an overlap there must be between these allegedly "distinct" or "opposed" groups before we can correctly regard them as *essentially* having the same class location. It happens that, in the case of Chile's top 37 corporations, our analysis has revealed that a simple majority of their higher executives are closely related to at least one (and often more) of the wealthiest capital-owning families. But the question is not really what manner of man the "average executive" is; for, as in the analysis so far, this implicitly assumes that all higher executives are roughly equal men of power, more or less equally sharing in basic decisionmaking about "corporate objectives, strategies, and broad policies."[43]

In practice, however, there is little doubt that some executives are more equal than others. And we are concerned precisely with the men who, as *Business Week* puts it, *are* able to "call the shots," who *can* make the decisions that matter in shaping the conduct of the top corporations and, consequently, the nation's economic life. Of course, it has to be stressed repeatedly that management itself does not necessarily hold the decisive power in the large corporation, and that control can be exerted without actual membership in management and "without participating in the formation of many, perhaps most policies."[44] Other mechanisms of long-term influence or of actual power can be

---

officer or employee in this state who by virtue of his office or employment names or appoints to public office or employment *any relative within the fourth degree, by consanguinity or affinity*, shall thereby forfeit his office or employment" (italics added).

[43] *Business Week* 1971, p. 51, in denying that such decisions are actually made by directors; also see Mace 1971, chap. 3. Both claim that such basic decisions are the prerogative, in practice, of "self-perpetuating" chief officers. In contrast, others argue that "the Board is indisputably the core of the management of the company" (C. Hartley Grattlan, quoted in Newcomer 1955, p. 24). Vance, however, is probably closest to the mark when he concludes (1964, p. 2), after a detailed study of the managements of large corporations in the United States, that only with intensive case studies is it possible to discover (and still without certainty) who are the most influential policymakers in a specific management.

[44] Gordon 1966, p. 173.

utilized when necessary by major lenders and creditors, as well as by principal owners and leading competitors, to set limits on the discretionary authority of the higher executives. As Robert A. Gordon, though himself an early managerial theorist, rightly recognizes, a wealthy family

> may *choose* to take a direct interest in the controlled company. They may, however, choose to be relatively passive or perhaps take a hand in decision-making only sporadically. . . . [In either case] we must not minimize their power, [which] . . . cannot help but be an important conditioning influence operating on management. . . . Wealth automatically carries with it some degree of economic power and influence. Wealthy [individuals and families] can enlist the support of bankers and other financial leaders, and they can use the power of these associates to reinforce their own power if they desire to become active. Out of these financial interrelations and business associations comes a strong set of influences which can condition the direction of business leadership."[45]

The question, then, is where in management the leading owning families choose to place their members or representatives. Do some positions in the higher levels of the corporate hierarchy or intercorporate apparatus carry such authority and responsibility that they are likely to be disproportionately reserved for these families? Are there certain "command posts" in which their "sporadic" or indirect participation may be risky—or in which placing mere "witty or eccentrically knowledgeable fellows [who] perk up otherwise dull meetings of essentially stodgy men" or those "willing to act as directors in a purely ornamental capacity" would, to say the least, be imprudent?[46]

Among such high-level positions in the corporate world, we suggest, are those which are central to the elaborate network—if not "endless chain"—of interlocking directorates tying together the top corporations.[47] The interlocking directorate, as C. Wright Mills correctly remarks, "is no mere phrase: it points to a solid feature of the facts of business life, and to a sociological anchor of the community of interest, the unification of outlook and policy, that prevails among the propertied class." The men who sit at the interlocking managerial helms,

[45] Gordon 1966, pp. 186–188; italics added.

[46] Lundberg (1968, p. 534) goes on to say that such wit is the only reason that some directors ("a few") are invited on boards, while Sweezy (1953, p. 162) notes that some directors are merely high-status "ornaments."

[47] Brandeis 1913.

then, are, in a very concrete sense, the leading organizers of the corporate system of what Mills calls "operating classwide property."[48] Compared with other higher executives, the authority of the men in this "inner group" of interlocking officers and directors ranges farther, and their responsibility is far broader—whether in attempting to protect and enhance the common interests of the principal capital-owning families dispersed among the interlocked corporations or to reconcile the opposed interests of the contending major investors involved in them.[49] The inner group may constitute the formal link among those top corporations having overlapping and interpenetrating ownership, as well as among those having no ownership connections, which must, because they are sufficiently powerful competitors (potential or actual) in a highly concentrated economy, work out a form of "co-respective behavior" that is least damaging to all of them and their principal shareowners and major investors.[50] In short, the men in this inner group bear a special class burden: they have a disproportionate responsibility for managing the common affairs of the entire business community.

For, even more than other higher executives, those who sit at the center of the web of interlocking directorates must embrace an outlook and a strategy that serve not only the particular and narrow interests of "specific firms and industries and families," but also "the broader economic and political interest," to borrow Mills' phrase, "of a more genuinely class type."[51] Such an outlook can, of course, be assimilated, and such a strategy can be designed and implemented by men who are not themselves from wealthy families. Those selected to

[48] Mills 1956, pp. 123, 122.

[49] The term "inner group" has been around for decades in the United States, and recurs, for instance, throughout U.S. Congress 1965. But it was first conceptualized and elaborated in a theory of the internal social relations of the capitalist class by Zeitlin and his students. See Zeitlin, Ewen, and Ratcliff 1974b; Zeitlin, Neuman, Ratcliff, and Ewen 1974; Zeitlin 1976, pp. 900–901. Since then, Useem (1978, 1979, 1980, 1984) has taken our theory of the inner group as the basis of his own fine work. G. William Domhoff (1983, pp. 70–72) (who mistakenly attributes the concept and ideas concerning it to Useem) also provides evidence concerning the centrality of the inner group in top corporations in the United States.

[50] See Baran and Sweezy (1966, pp. 50–51) on "co-respective behavior" (a term borrowed from Joseph Schumpeter) as the form of competition among giant corporations.

[51] Mills (1956, p. 147) sees the translation of "narrow" into "broader" class interests as the role of "the chief executives of the major corporations," rather than, as we have suggested here, as the specific role of the executives in the inner group (and, as we discuss in the next chapter, of the finance capitalists).

ascend to the pinnacles of corporate authority and responsibility will be those men whose code of conduct, social allegiance, and overriding commitments fit them to be "the protectors and spokesmen for all large-scale property," whatever their own social origins or personal wealth.[52] Nonetheless, however fitted or gifted they might be, mere business administrators are not as likely to be entrusted with such classwide responsibility, we suggest, as members of the wealthiest families, whose own privileges and prerogatives rest on their common ownership of the large corporations, and who will want, therefore, to occupy the key positions in their interlocking directorates. If we are correct, then the men in this inner group typically will be wealthier than other higher executives and also more likely to be principal owners of capital personally or to belong to the principal capital-owning families. In short, the inner group should stand out as occupying, in comparison with other executives, a distinctive intraclass location.

This is, in fact, what one finds. First, it is clearly the pattern that the more top-37 managements in which an executive serves, the greater his stockowning wealth. Also, the inner group consists not only disproportionately but overwhelmingly of the wealthiest men, as compared with the executives outside it, and this is true among officers and directors alike. When the stock owned by an executive's close family is considered, the contrast between the wealth of those men in the inner group and that of other executives is even sharper. Consistently, the individual and family wealth of the men in the inner group places them disproportionately in the highest wealth-owning brackets. This is especially so for the small group of men (16 directors) who serve in the managements of three or more top corporations: well over half of them belong to a close family owning E°500,000 or more in stock (see Tables 2.4 and 2.5).

Second, the men of the inner group are not only wealthier than their fellow executives, in terms of the value of their personal as well as familial stockholdings, but they are also far more likely to belong to Chile's major owning families—i.e. they stand out with respect to the extent of their intimate integration into the capitalist class. Both among officers and directors, the men holding two or more management seats are far likelier to belong to a principal capital-owning family than those with a single seat. And again, the contrast is sharpest

[52] Baran and Sweezy (1966, p. 35) also, like Mills, see this as the role of managers in general, but make no reference to the class implications of interlocking directorships.

TABLE 2.4. Percentage of Higher Executives of the Top 37 Nonfinancial Corporations in Chile Who Own Stock of Specified Market Worth, by the Number of Top-37 Management Seats Held, 1964/66

	Stockholdings (E°1,000s)					
	Under 50	50–99	100–149	150–199	200-plus	(*N*)
Officers						
one seat	60	2	6	4	28	(53)
two seats (only)	45	0	0	9	45	(11)
all officers	58	2	5	5	31	(64)
Directors						
one seat	60	11	8	3	19	(113)
two seats	42	25	5	8	19	(36)
three-plus seats	25	19	19	13	25	(16)
all directors	53	15	8	5	19	(165)
All higher executives						
one seat	60	8	7	3	22	(166)
two seats	43	19	4	9	25	(47)
three-plus seats	25	19	19	13	25	(16)
all executives	54	11	7	5	23	(229)

between what we might call the "inner group within the inner group" and the rest of the higher executives. Those men who are higher executives of three or more top corporations are not only disproportionately but overwhelmingly drawn from the country's principal capitalist families: 69 percent of them, as compared with 39 percent of the men holding a single management seat, belong to an immediate capitalist family; and 75 percent of them, compared with 47 percent of those holding a single seat, belong to a close capitalist family (see Table 2.6).

Finally, the same pattern tends to appear when we count a manager's actual number of close capital-owning relatives. Although no difference shows up among officers, the directors in the inner group—and, again, particularly in the "inner group within the inner group"—typically have more close relatives who are principal capitalists than do the directors sitting on one board only. Half of the men who hold three or more directorships, but only a third of those who hold two directorships and a fifth of those who hold a single directorship have three or more close relatives who are principal capitalists (see Table 2.7).

Conclusion

Our systematic empirical analysis of the linkage of family and property systems under the domain of the large corporation in Chile has

TABLE 2.5. Percentage of Higher Executives of the Top 37 Nonfinancial Corporations in Chile Whose Families Own Stock of Specified Market Worth, by the Number of Top-37 Management Seats Held, 1964/66

	Family Stockholdings (E°1,000s)									
	Immediate			Secondary			Close			
	100–249	250–499	500-plus	100–249	250–499	500-plus	100–249	250–499	500-plus	(*N*)
Officers										
one seat	13	2	25	17	0	28	15	2	34	(53)
two seats (only)	9	18	27	9	18	27	0	27	27	(11)
all officers	13	5	25	16	3	28	13	6	33	(64)
Directors										
one seat	11	8	16	11	9	20	10	6	18	(113)
two seats	11	14	19	14	14	22	11	11	36	(36)
three-plus seats	37	6	31	19	13	44	19	13	56	(16)
all directors	36	9	18	12	6	24	11	8	25	(165)
All higher executives										
one seat	12	6	19	13	6	23	11	5	30	(166)
two seats	11	15	21	13	15	23	9	15	34	(47)
three-plus seats	37	6	31	19	13	44	19	13	56	(16)
all executives	13	8	20	13	8	25	11	7	33	(229)

TABLE 2.6. Percentage of Higher Executives of the Top 37 Nonfinancial Corporations in Chile Who Are in a Principal Capital-Owning Family, by the Number of Top-37 Management Seats Held, 1964/66

	Personally Principal Capitalists	Principal Capitalists in: Immediate Family	Secondary Family	Close Family	(*N*)
Officers					
one seat	40	43	49	55	(53)
two seats (only)	55	55	64	64	(11)
all officers	42	45	52	56	(64)
Directors					
one seat	27	39	43	47	(113)
two seats	42	55	58	61	(36)
three-plus seats	37	69	69	75	(16)
all directors	31	45	49	53	(165)
All higher executives					
one seat	31	40	45	49	(166)
two seats	45	55	60	62	(47)
three-plus seats	37	69	69	75	(16)
all executives	35	45	50	54	(229)

TABLE 2.7. Percentage of Higher Executives of the Top 37 Nonfinancial Corporations in Chile Who Have a Specified Number of Close, Principal Capital-Owning Relatives, by the Number of Top-37 Management Seats Held, 1964/66

	Relatives Who Are Principal Capitalists: None	One	Two	Three-plus	(*N*)
Officers					
one seat	53	17	2	28	(53)
two seats (only)	55	18	0	27	(11)
all officers	53	17	2	28	(64)
Directors					
one seat	60	14	5	20	(113)
two seats	55	8	3	33	(36)
three-plus seats	31	13	6	50	(16)
all directors	56	13	5	26	(165)
All higher executives					
one seat	57	15	4	23	(166)
two seats	55	11	2	32	(47)
three-plus seats	31	13	6	50	(16)
all executives	55	14	4	27	(229)

revealed, then, not that owners and managers are distinct and often opposed groups, but—on the contrary—that those groups have extensive and close kinship relations tying them intimately into the same class. Moreover, it is precisely those men in the inner group of interlocking officers and directors, bearing the broadest classwide responsibility, whose assimilation by the principal capital-owning families is greatest—thereby disclosing the inseparability of class power and so-called bureaucratic authority in the higher managerial realm of the corporate world.[53]

[53] Cf. Zeitlin 1974a, p. 1110.

CHAPTER THREE

Finance Capital

A HANDFUL of immense banks, concentrating within their coffers the bulk of the assets and deposits of the entire banking system and providing much of the loans and credits for industry, are the decisive units in the circulation of capital in contemporary capitalist economies.[1] With this consolidation of oligopoly in banking itself, the amount of loans and credits granted by the leading banks actually determines the amount of money deposited with them, because what they lend flows back to them as deposits. They can, within rather wide limits, "vary at will the supply of credit or short-term capital available at any given time" and thus determine the price of (or rate of interest on) loan capital.[2] As C. Wright Mills aptly remarks, "not violence, but credit may be a rather ultimate seat of control within modern societies."[3]

The leading banks are also structurally interconnected—through

[1] As of 1964, the 100 largest commercial banks in the United States held 46 percent of all the deposits of the 13,775 commercial banks in the country. The 14 largest alone held 24 percent of all commercial bank deposits. See U.S. Congress 1968, p. 804. Germany's dominant Big Three, the Deutsche, the Dresdner, and the Commerz, have long dominated its banking system. In England, the same was true of the Big Five (when there still were five): Lloyds, Westminster, Midland, Barclays, and National Provincial; they already controlled three-fourths of all funds deposited in British banks by the end of the Second World War (Eaton 1949, p. 143). The merger of Westminster and National Provincial to become National Westminster left only the Big Four. The United States, despite its concentration, is unusual in the *number* of competing banks. England has 11 clearing banks and 24 joint stock banks, and Canada has 8 chartered banks, for instance, compared to the nearly 14,000 in the United States (Nadler 1968, p. 167). Also see Auburn 1960, Sayers 1962.

[2] Strachey 1956, pp. 273–275, referring to the theory of John M. Keynes. Research on the relationship between banking concentration and interest rates in the United States shows that when regional and local market conditions, and differences in loan characteristics, are held constant, there is a significant relationship between banking concentration in metropolitan areas and loan rates. The Chicago Federal Reserve Board's own studies have shown that "the greater the number of banks or the lower the percentage of deposits held by the largest bank in the study, the lower were effective interest rates charged on loans. . . . Higher banking concentration was also associated with greater pre-tax earnings on assets" (Fischer 1968, p. 369).

[3] Mills 1963, p. 46.

longstanding business associations, financial arrangements, interlocking directorates, and overlapping and interpenetrating ownership—with the top nonfinancial corporations. Thus, if our originating question here is how this affects the dynamics of contemporary capitalism, the present chapter focuses on the inner structure of the capitalist class and asks the following questions: Who owns and controls the major banks, and do the banks' interconnections with large corporations constitute an institutional means of intraclass power? Do the men who sit simultaneously in the managements of banks and corporations play a distinctive role in the corporate world? Are they, in a phrase, "a special social type, in contrast to the other officers and directors of the largest corporations and banks?"[4]

The Contending Theories

"Historically," as a U.S. congressional antitrust subcommittee notes, "*interlocking relationships between bank managements and the directors of other corporations have been of special significance* [because of the potential] . . . misuse of the power to control money and credit from financial institutions."[5] In recent years, several sociologists and economists have conducted informative, albeit essentially descriptive, studies and "network analyses" of interlocking directorates.[6] But the critical theoretical issues and empirical questions in this chapter have been all but entirely neglected—primarily, perhaps, because they cannot be posed within the academic paradigms regnant in the social sciences.[7]

Remarkably, despite its explicit focus on the large corporation's impact on contemporary society, even managerial theory simply discounts, when it does not ignore, the major bank as a decisive locus of economic power, and its adherents dismiss the bankers themselves with witticisms concerning their ostensible "dwindling social magnet-

[4] Zeitlin 1974a, pp. 1103, 1110; also see Zeitlin 1976, pp. 900–901. On the interconnections between commercial banks and nonfinancial corporations in the United States, see U.S. Congress 1967, 1968; also see Kotz 1978.

[5] U.S. Congress 1965, p. 164, italics added; see, also, FTC 1951, U.S. Congress 1978.

[6] For a review of the issues and evidence from several of the most influential studies, see Glasberg and Schwartz 1983.

[7] Earlier formulations of these questions and several hypotheses on the inner group and finance capitalists in the United States appear in Zeitlin 1974a, 1976. Analyzing data for the United States, Soref (1976, 1979, and 1980) and Soref and Zeitlin (1988) test Zeitlin's hypotheses concerning finance capitalists. Cf. Mintz and Schwartz 1985; Ratcliff 1980a, 1980b.

ism."[8] For although banking functions persist, these functions are supposedly no longer vital in the "new industrial state" or "postcapitalist society." Rather, in managerial theory, because the large corporation exists in a state of splendid—and self-perpetuating—autonomy, generating earnings "wholly under its own control," and running "on its own economic steam," it no longer depends on "financial capital."[9] Thus, management "becomes, in an odd sort of way, the uncontrolled administrator of a kind of trust, having the privilege of perpetual accumulation."[10] Freed from the dictates of capital and the control of its major shareowners, and thereby of the imperatives of profit maximization, the large corporation is thus, in managerial doctrine, the embodiment of economic rationality. The large corporation's management (or "technostructure"), deriving its "decisive power" not from capital but from *organization*, is said to administer social investment much as if it had become a "purely neutral technocracy," allocating "the income stream on the basis of public policy rather than private cupidity."[11]

Sociological analyses of the large corporation, whether or not they explicitly accept such managerialist notions, tend to have the same implicit premises. In the "interorganizational paradigm," for instance, the large corporation is also conceptualized essentially as merely one sort of complex organization operating "within a larger environment comprised of other organizations."[12] In this paradigm, too, neither the imperatives of capital accumulation nor the private ownership of capital is considered of decisive relevance. Instead, what impels the interaction of the large corporations is an "interorganizational" dynamic based on their efforts to "avert threats to their stability or existence" as autonomous organizations and to anticipate and control "environmental contingencies."[13] This same dynamic accounts for the interlocking pattern among the large corporations and major banks.[14]

[8] Galbraith 1967, p. 68.

[9] Galbraith 1967, p. 92; Berle and Means 1967, pp. xiv–xv. Berle's phrase was "financial capital," which he used as a synonym for "loan capital," *not* with the conceptual content we elaborate below concerning "finance capital."

[10] Berle and Means 1967, pp. xiv–xv.

[11] Galbraith 1971, p. xix; Berle and Means 1967, p. 313. Galbraith's concept of "technostructure" was adumbrated three decades earlier by Berle and Means' "technocracy."

[12] Allen 1974, pp. 393, 403 et passim; also see Allen 1976.

[13] Thompson 1967, p. 35; Allen 1974, p. 393; also Pennings 1980, pp. 7–10.

[14] Allen 1976; Pfeffer 1972; Pennings 1980, pp. 67, 107ff., although these are rather vague about the meaning and implications of "financial interlocks." Pennings

Thus, although managerialism dismisses or ignores interlocking directorates, and the men who fill them, both among large corporations and between them and the major banks, while interorganizational theory actually focuses on these interlocks, the paradox is that the two theories share a basic paradigmatic presupposition: the major banks and large corporations are assumed to be, as Ratcliff has put it elsewhere, more or less "distinct islands of self-interest."[15] Neither theory attaches any significance to the so-called outside interests (let alone the controlling interests) of ownership, or considers the possibility that the so-called outside directors who interlock the big banks and the top corporations are bearers of decisive *extra-organizational powers*. Both theories assume that the management of the large corporation or leading bank is "invulnerable to external authority" and "selects itself and its successors as an autonomous and self-perpetuating oligarchy."[16] For both theories, the basic unit of analysis is the "firm," i.e. the corporate *organization* itself, as it interacts with other organizations to maximize its security and minimize its uncertainty.

In our conception of class theory, however, the top nonfinancial corporations and leading banks are considered "units in a class-controlled apparatus of appropriation; and the whole gamut of functionaries and owners of capital participate in varying degrees, and as members of the same social class, in its direction." This means that the relevant analytical unit in an adequate explanation of the significance of the interlocking directorate is not merely the corporation or the bank as

---

(1980, p. 67, italics added) finds, for instance, an "ubiquity of financial directors in nonfinancial organizations" and even remarks that "financial directors belong to *a distinct class*." But his only "analytical" comment on this finding is that "their large share of multiple board membership naturally tempts one to attribute a huge amount of influence to them. However, while interdirector relationships might be interesting—for example, for investigating 'who rules America'—the present study is primarily concerned with relationships between organizations."

[15] Ratcliff 1980b, p. 557. Gordon (1966, p. x), for instance, simply notes, in a new preface to his study of U.S. corporations in the late 1930s, that there is extensive interlocking between banks and corporations, and says that this is a "far cry from what was once meant by 'financial control' " but suggests no possible implications. Interorganizational theorists often make reference to the "interorganizational context" as well as the "characteristics of the organization," but the "unit of study . . . [is] construed as an individual organization," and the "context" as other organizations. See Pennings 1980, pp. 9–10. The so-called interorganizational context never involves even the concrete interests of principal shareowners and major investors, let alone the class and intraclass relations within which these organizations—the major corporations—operate.

[16] Galbraith 1967, pp. 88, 409.

an "organization," or even as a "firm," but rather the internal structure of the *class* that owns and controls them both. Our central proposition, then, is that it is not a process of autonomous self-selection or of "interorganizational elite cooptation" that underlies the pattern of interlocks and the selection of the interlocking directors, but rather a process of intraclass integration, coordination, and control.[17]

For, if managerialism poses a false problem and provides a false solution, the ascendancy of the large corporation surely has altered the structure of the capitalist class to the extent that, within the large corporation itself, the ownership of capital has become partly dissociated from the control of production. "With the dispersion of shares," as Rudolf Hilferding observed as long ago as 1910, "capitalist property has been converted increasingly into a limited form of property which merely gives its owners a simple claim to surplus value, without in itself allowing them to decisively intervene in the productive process. . . . Effective control of productive capital is in the hands of individuals who actually have provided only a part of it. The owners of the means of production no longer exist in isolation, but rather form an association [*Gesellschaft*] in which the individual has a claim only to a proportionate share of the total profits."[18]

The critical theoretical issue, then, is how the dissociation of these once-unified functions of capital affects the inner structure of the capitalist class. This, in turn, necessitates recognizing and specifying the different locations occupied in the accumulation (and appropriation) process by various types of owners and managers, and analyzing their implications. In fact, the so-called managers themselves do not constitute a homogeneous category of functionaries identically situated in the accumulation process or in the capitalist class. The crucial empirical question, then, is how the various types of higher executives—these leading functionaries of capital—are related to the principal owners of capital in the actual ensemble of intraclass social relations.

If the large corporation has partly dissociated the functions of capital ownership and corporate control, it has also unified functions of capital that were dissociated until its ascendancy—functions that once constituted "a qualitative division" both of the "total capital" and the "entire class of capitalists." As Marx argued a century ago, "interest-

[17] Zeitlin 1974a, p. 1079. Cf. Palmer (1983), who construes, "the 'interorganizational' and the 'intraclass' approaches" to the analysis of interlocking directorates as "different but *compatible*" (our italics)—a notion we reject.

[18] Hilferding 1910, chap. 7, pp. 155–156.

bearing capital as such has, not wage-labour, but productive capital for its opposite." The "money capitalist" confronts the "industrial capitalist . . . as a special kind of capitalist"; that is, they confront each other "not just as legally different persons but as *persons playing entirely different roles in the reproduction process*." In their hands, "the same capital really performs a two-fold and wholly different movement. The one merely loans it, the other employs it productively." The "capitalist working on borrowed capital" ends up with only a "portion of profit," i.e. "profit minus interest."[19] Thus, in Marx's time, as he saw it, "money capitalists" and "industrial capitalists" constituted, as did "merchant capitalists" also, "rival fractions . . . of the appropriating class."[20] They were, in our conceptual terms, separate and opposed "class segments" occupying—despite their common ownership of the means of production—relatively distinct locations in the process of accumulation of capital, and, consequently, having inherently contradictory interests.[21]

Under the domain of the large corporation and major banks, and the consequent interpenetration of industrial, commercial, and loan capital, however, there emerges a new form of capital and, with it, a new, coalesced class segment: "finance capital" and the "finance capitalist." The big banks and top nonfinancial corporations, as we have noted, enjoy both proprietary and organizational interconnections. Not only are the big banks major creditors of the top corporations, but they also simultaneously own or administer some of the principal corporate shareholdings. And the top corporations (which in the United States are being transformed into "conglomerates" spanning all economic sectors) tend, in turn, to own substantial blocks of stock in the leading banks.

Aside from such reciprocal institutional shareholdings and financial connections, however, the big banks and top nonfinancial corporations also tend to have the very same individuals and families among their

[19] Marx 1967, III, pp. 379, 372–378; italics added.

[20] Marx 1952, p. 86.

[21] Weber's concept of "class situation" in his concrete historical and comparative analyses is similar to Marx's concept of "class location" or "class position," as we noted earlier, despite Weber's emphasis on "market relations" rather than "production relations." Further, Weber differentiates the propertied according to the specific form in which they appropriate their portions of the social product, and underlines the contradictions between the industrialist, on the one side, and "the rentier . . . and the banker," on the other; the latter's "cash boxes," writes Weber, are filled with " 'unearned' gains" taken from "the pockets of the manufacturers" (Weber 1946, pp. 181–186, 301).

principal owners. In the United States, for example, such prominent wealthy families as the Mellons, Rockefellers, Stillmans, Duponts, Fishers, Weyerhausers, Rosenwalds, Motts, Fords, and Hannas have identifiable principal ownership interests in some of the largest industrial corporations *and* leading commercial banks.[22] But, in all likelihood, these wealthy families are merely well-documented instances of a general tendency of the principal capital-owning families to have interests that overlap finance, industry, and commerce. They thus illustrate the critical theoretical question of to what extent it is at all valid to think of the various firms to which these families are attached as independent organizations, whatever their formal or legal status. Rather, these firms tend to be "interconnected points of decision-making within larger networks of class interests."[23] The big banks, other financial institutions, and top nonfinancial corporations tend, in other words, to be "units in, and instrumentalities of, the whole system of propertied interests controlled by these major capitalist families" and their entire class.[24]

Under these circumstances, the interlocking directorates tying together the major banks and the top nonfinancial corporations take on a crucial political-economic role in integrating the simultaneous and potentially contradictory financial, industrial, and commercial interests of the wealthiest families, whose various investments span these ostensibly separate sectors. Those who sit at the conjoined managerial helms of the big banks and the top industrial corporations as functionaries of "finance capital" are, to this extent and in this limited sense—by virtue of their simultaneous administration of loan and productive capital—themselves "finance capitalists." In short, we suggest that the interlocking of the leading banks and the top nonfinancial corporations is an organizational expression of the inner transformation of the capitalist class: "neither 'financiers' extracting interest at the expense of industrial profits nor 'bankers' controlling corporations, but finance capitalists on the boards of the largest banks *and* corporations preside over the banks' investments as creditors *and* shareholders, organizing production, sales, and financing, and appropriating the profits of their integrated activities."[25]

With this coalescence of banking and industrial capital, however, the

[22] Zeitlin 1974a, p. 1102; Domhoff 1983, pp. 60–63; Dunn 1980; White 1978.

[23] Ratcliff 1980b, p. 557.

[24] Zeitlin 1976, p. 901.

[25] Zeitlin 1974a, p. 1102; italics in original.

contradictions between them are not eliminated; nor are the claims of the former to a share of the profits extracted by the latter. Rather, this form of capital, i.e., finance capital, now contains as "constitutive contradictions" the contradictory interests once dividing qualitatively different, coexisting segments within the capitalist class. In Hilferding's ironic imagery: "Industrial capital is the Father that sired commercial and banking capital as its Son, and money as the Holy Spirit. They are three but only one in finance capital."[26] Put more mundanely, in the words of a leading econometrician, the "financial policies of industrial enterprises should be meshed with their investment behavior, but exactly how remains an open question."[27] "Meshing" these potentially contradictory investments, then, is the special double role of the finance capitalist, who, as James O'Connor observes, "combines and synthesizes the motives [and functions] of the merchant, industrialist, and banker."[28] As a representative of the nonfinancial corporation's lenders and bondholders, the finance capitalist must favor higher interest rates, but as a representative of its principal shareowners, he must strive to ensure maximum industrial profits. In other words, the coalescence of banking and industrial capital produces a *self-contradictory intraclass location*. Thus, the higher executives who personify this coalescence must continually try, in practice, to reconcile the irreconcilable—these contradictory interests of loan and productive capital. If this reconciliation cannot be ensured, interlocking directorates between the leading banks and the top nonfinancial corporations are the singular "interorganizational means of administration" with which to attempt it.

To the extent that propertied individuals and families have major investments and principal shareholdings in financial, industrial, and

[26] Cf. Poulantzas 1975, p. 130; Hilferding 1910, p. 299.

[27] Kuh 1963, p. 16.

[28] O'Connor (1968, p. 31), referring to "corporate capital," which he substitutes for the term "finance capital," because, he says, it is often confused with "bank capital," or the notion that the banks control the corporations or dominate the economy. Hilferding occasionally seems to have lapsed into this, perhaps because of the specific situation at the time in Germany, when the ascendancy of the big banks seemed indisputable. Yet, notwithstanding his occasional tendency to speak of industry as under bank control, this is not the overall theoretical thrust of *Das Finanzkapital*. Lenin's formulation of the concept of finance capital was borrowed explicitly, with slight modification, from Hilferding (Lenin 1967, I, p. 711). We think that referring, as O'Connor does, to the decisionmakers in simultaneous charge of the leading banks and the large nonfinancial corporations as "corporate capitalists" deflects attention from the theoretical focus on contradictions inherent in the coalescence of loan and productive capital.

merchandising companies, they have a special, and heavy, stake in trying to harmonize their broad policies and reconcile the contending interests involved. And to the extent that actual participation in management is necessary (and it may not be) for them to try to shape a business strategy best accommodating their own specific self-contradictory interests, they should also seek (and be sought out) to sit simultaneously on the boards of big banks *and* top nonfinancial corporations. Faced with having to coordinate the business strategies of the various firms in which they have substantial interests—in order to maximize the entire system's profits, irrespective of the profits earned by each of its separate financial, industrial, and commercial units—these men of property may well wish to provide an added measure of insurance that such coordination actually occurs, by sitting personally on the boards of these companies.

For these reasons, the "finance capitalists," defined here in a limited sense as those higher executives who sit simultaneously in the management of a major bank and of a large nonfinancial corporation, should tend (a) to have a more extensive role in coordinating the policies of the top nonfinancial corporations, by sitting on several of their boards, and (b) to be more likely than other higher executives to be drawn from among the nation's principal capital-owning families. These are the two main hypotheses of the present empirical analysis. For, in accord with our theory of the self-contradictory intraclass situation inherent in the coalescence of loan and productive capital, it is not mere "bureaucrats" or "purely neutral technocrats" who should occupy the strategic seats, but, on the contrary, members of the principal capital-owning families themselves.

The Big Banks

Chile possesses, as we know, a highly concentrated economy, dominated by the large corporation; and, like its more advanced counterparts, that country has also witnessed a parallel process of concentration in banking. For more than a century, Chile has possessed the basic elements of a capitalist credit system. By the early 1900s, it had already developed a modern financial system, characterized by the existence of private banks of issue and deposit, a central bank, savings-and-loan associations, brokerage houses, and a thriving stock exchange, utilizing the full range of standard financial instruments, and was involved in international as well as domestic financial activities.[29]

[29] Cf. Goldsmith 1969, p. 44.

Chile had 24 domestic, privately owned commercial banks as of the mid-1960s: 13 of them were nationwide banks, with their head offices in Santiago or the port city of Valparaíso and 113 branches located throughout the country; 11 were regional banks.[30] Another 4 banks were foreign subsidiaries (of Citibank, the Bank of London and South America, the Bank of Brazil, and the Franco-Italian Bank of South America), but none of these had assets or deposits exceeding those of any of the 6 largest privately owned Chilean banks. The Big Five consisted of the top 5 nationwide commercial banks; a major regional bank ranked 6th. In the aggregate, these 6 banks (Bank of Chile, Spanish Bank of Chile, Bank of Credit and Investments, South American Bank, Bank of Edwards, and Bank of Osorno) held 77.6 percent of the deposits. They controlled more than two-thirds of all private commercial bank branches, provided more than four-fifths of the private commercial banking credit, and held some two-fifths of all negotiable paper in the country.[31] Chile also had 22 savings-and-loan associations, 5 major investment companies (ranking among the top 200 corporations), 173 insurance companies, and 2 mortgage credit banks providing private financing. But the commercial banks (mainly the Big Five) were virtually the only source of short-term funds in the country.[32] In long-term financing, they were buttressed by the state development agency, CORFO, which accounted for some 30 percent of all investment in machinery and equipment and as much as 18 percent of gross domestic investment in the late 1950s and early 1960s.[33]

[30] Superintendencia de Bancos 1964.

[31] Superintendencia de Bancos 1964, pp. 11 and 15, balances as of December 31, 1964; Tarasov 1966, p. 66.

[32] Stunzi 1968, p. 68.

[33] Mamalakis 1965, p. 19. The state bank, which operates both as a commercial bank and as an agent of the government, was established in 1953. It provides loans and credits for private industry in areas the government seeks to foster. By the mid-1960s, it accounted for some 40 percent of commercial banking loans (Stunzi 1968, p. 68). Its role is akin to that of France's semipublic bank, the Credít National. In both France and Italy, public banking authority, as of the 1960s, played an even more decisive role in overall investment than in Chile. Similarly, the stock exchange in Chile is governed privately, whereas in France and Italy, government financial institutions have long been decisive in the bond market. See Shonfield 1965, pp. 166–171, 180–184. Chile's central bank, established in 1925, is similar in most respects to the Federal Reserve in the United States. It has the exclusive right of note issue, acts as the depository and fiscal agent of the government, and establishes credit policy for the private commercial banks by fixing interest rates and reserve requirements. Despite its official status, however, it "is mostly privately-owned with the Government holding a minority position." Shares are divided among the private banks in proportion to their paid-in capital, and among other private shareholders as well. See Moody's 1970, p. 1786; Stunzi 1968, p. 68; Bohan and Pomeranz 1960, p. 223.

The present analysis of the ownership and control of Chile's major banks focuses on the Big Five and the largest regional bank, which ranks 6th nationally. In fact, however, we obtained the shareholding lists and the names and positions of the higher executives, i.e. officers and directors, of all of the 16 largest commercial banks in the country, and these data are used in the following analysis. Systematic analysis of the finance capitalists themselves is limited to the higher executives of the 6 leading banks and the top 37 nonfinancial corporations. As we discovered, however, and as we discuss in detail below, this is not really a significant limitation, since, in fact, the "bankers" of the Big Five and the "finance capitalists" of Chile's top 37 nonfinancial corporations turn out to be almost synonymous.

The ownership of the 6 leading banks, like that of their top-37 corporate counterparts, is relatively dispersed. In the aggregate, the principal individual shareowners (i.e. those ranking in the 20 largest) hold a substantial minority of the shares in only 2 of these 6 banks, and a majority in none. By this measure, the concentration of stockownership is inversely related to the size of the bank. When we divide the 16 largest commercial banks, on which we have the relevant data, into three ranked assets-groups—i.e. first, the leading 6, and then the next ranking 10 divided into two groups of five—the median aggregate amount of stock held by the principal individual shareowners comes to 14.2 percent in the leading 6 banks, 24.0 percent in the middle-ranking group of banks, and 30.7 percent in the lowest-ranking group. Few of the officers and directors of the leading 6 banks are themselves among their bank's principal shareowners, and, even when they are, they typically own but a slight percentage of the stock. Of the 18 officers with the leading 6 banks, only 2 are personally principal shareowners in "their own" banks; of the 50 directors, only 4. Even the aggregate stockholding of the entire bank management is typically insubstantial: management's median aggregate stockholding comes to 2.9 percent of the stock in the 6 leading banks. This indicates, of course, that there is a rather sharp separation between the ownership and the management of Chile's largest banks.

As to their *control,* however, the situation is, in fact, markedly different. Without recapitulating here what has already been discussed in detail in Chapter 1, we can note that, based on the standard procedures and criteria—drawn from Berle and Means—usually used to define the locus of control in large corporations, 4 of these 6 banks would have been considered "management controlled." But, when analyzed in depth, in accordance with our paradigm of intercorporate ownership and entangling kinship relations among principal stockowners and managers, each of these big banks turns out, in fact, to be under the control of a specific kinecon group or set of business associates (see Table 3.1). Only with respect to the locus of control of the Bank of Chile is that conclusion somewhat tentative.

At mid-century, the Bank of Chile had long been without peer among the country's private commercial banks. As of 1964, its coffers hold 29.5 percent of the *deposits* in all 24 domestic commercial banks, but its share of the *assets* of these banks is far greater: 43.5 percent of the total, or an amount almost equal to the combined assets of the next 9 ranking banks. Its assets are more than five times those of the 2nd-ranking bank and eight times those of the smallest of the leading 6.

Its stock is highly dispersed. The single-largest block of shares is held by the Stock Exchange of Santiago, amounting to 2.7 percent of the bank's outstanding stock.[34] None of the bank's officers or directors is personally among its principal shareowners, and the executives' combined stock comes to only 0.63 percent of the total. According to some authorities, such a "diffusion of capital" in this Chilean "prototype of capitalism" is nothing less than a "true foundation for a democratized economy." Even some socialist economists who thoroughly reject this characterization, however, have also argued that the Bank of Chile's "higher executives are autonomous policy makers," constituting a "banking bureaucracy . . . with a certain power of its own."[35]

The Bank of Chile was established in 1894 as the result of the merger of three of the oldest banks existing at the time, the National Bank of Chile, the Bank of Valparaíso, and the Agrarian Bank.[36] Thus, from its inception it has acted as an institutional center not only of the coalescence of financial, commercial, and industrial capital, on the one hand, but of them and of large landed property, on the other. By 1964, the bank had branches from one tip of Chile to the other, serving each of the major regional economic centers (northern nitrates

[34] See note c, Table 1.5, on the holdings of the Stock Exchange of Santiago. As of 1978, the Bank of Chile was still, by far, the nation's dominant commercial bank, with assets nearly three times the 2nd-ranking Bank of Credit and Investment (Dahse 1979, p. 140).

[35] "The Bank of Chile, this prototype of capitalism, is in the hands of women and charitable foundations that put their savings there. . . . This constitutes a true foundation for the democratized economy" (L.A.C. 1950, p. 73). On the autonomy of the Bank of Chile's "banking bureaucracy," see Garretón and Cisternas 1970, p. 45; Garretón 1971, pp. 147–148.

[36] Bohan and Pomeranz 1960, p. 224.

TABLE 3.1. Control of the Big Six Commercial Banks in Chile, 1964/66

		Classified by Berle-Means Methods				Classified by the Authors	
		Type of Control					
Rank	Bank	Immediate	Ultimate	Largest Holding or Dominant Interest	Size of Holdings (%)	Controlling Proprietary Interests[a]	Size of Probable Working Block (%)[a]
1.	Bank of Chile	Mgt.	Mgt.	Stock Exchange[b]	2.7	Cortés and Cousiño families, and associates	5.4
2.	Spanish Bank of Chile	Mgt.	Mgt.	COPESA (newspaper consortium)	3.9	García and Picó families, and associates	11.2
3.	Bank of Credit and Investments	Joint minority	Pyr./Min.	Yarur interests J. F. Ladley	36.0 11.1	Yarur Banna family, Grace (U.S.) interests (?), and Prieto family	55.8
4.	South American Bank	Min.	Mgt.	South American Steamship Co.	24.4	Vial and MacAuliffe families	23.0
5.	Bank of Edwards	Joint minority	Joint minority	Edwards interests "Amolana" Investments	26.1 11.6	Edwards and Lyon families (with Bank of London and South America?)	54.3
6.	Bank of Osorno and the Union	Mgt.	Mgt.	Sotta interests	6.0	Sotta Barros family and associates	7.7

NOTE: Mgt. = management control; Min. = minority control; Pyr. = pyramiding; Pyr./Min. = joint control.

[a] See Table 3.11, appended to this chapter for details on the actual controlling proprietary interests in these banks.

[b] See Table 1.5, note c, on the holdings of the Stock Exchange of Santiago.

and trade, Central Valley agriculture and industry, near-south coal mining, and far-south cattle and sheep ranching). Indeed, the Bank of Chile seems to epitomize "bank control" of industry: in its own name, the bank holds principal stockholdings in 13 of the top 37 nonfinancial corporations, as well as several smaller substantial blocks of stock; it interlocks with 7 of these same top 37 firms, as well as with another 8 in which it is not a principal shareholder. Thus, with principal ownership interests or interlocking directorates connecting it to well over half of the top 37 nonfinancial corporations, the Bank of Chile had, by the mid-1960s, become a powerful centralizing institution of private capital, if not a unifying force for the entire capitalist class.

But this is surely *not* an instance of the "democratization of capital," the "bank control" of industry, or even a neutral bureaucratic arbitration of the financial interests of an entire class. Rather, the actual control of the Bank of Chile is, our investigation reveals, probably jointly held by two of the most powerful industrial families in the nation, the associated Cortés and Cousiño families. The Cortés family controls Chile's 3rd largest nonfinancial corporation, El Melón Industrial Enterprises (see Table 1.5). An "El Melón" subsidiary, the South Pacific Commercial and Industrial Co., is the Bank of Chile's 2nd largest stockholder, and El Melón itself is the third largest. Another Cortés family affiliate, the Maipo Canal Society (the canal was built by the nineteenth-century mining and milling magnate José Tomás Urmeneta, with whom much of the Cortés fortune originated), holds the bank's 6th largest block of shares. Together with personal minor stockholdings by two of the family members (one of whom, María Teresa Brown de Ariztia, widow of a lineal Urmeneta descendant, is also the 4th largest stockholder in El Melón), the Cortés family's block comes to 2.7 percent of the Bank of Chile's outstanding stock. The Cortés interests are probably represented on the bank's board by Arturo Cousiño Lyon, in whose family-controlled firm, Lota-Schwager Coal, the biggest stockholder is El Melón. The Cousiños' Arauco Shipping Company holds the 14th largest stockholding in the bank, and, with Mr. Cousiño's own stock, the probable working control of the Cortés and Cousiño families is based on 3.3 percent of the bank's stock (see Figure 3.1).

Also prominent among the Bank of Chile's stockowners, and represented by two directors on its board, is a set of related landlord and capitalist families who are (as we shall show in Chapter 5) at the very

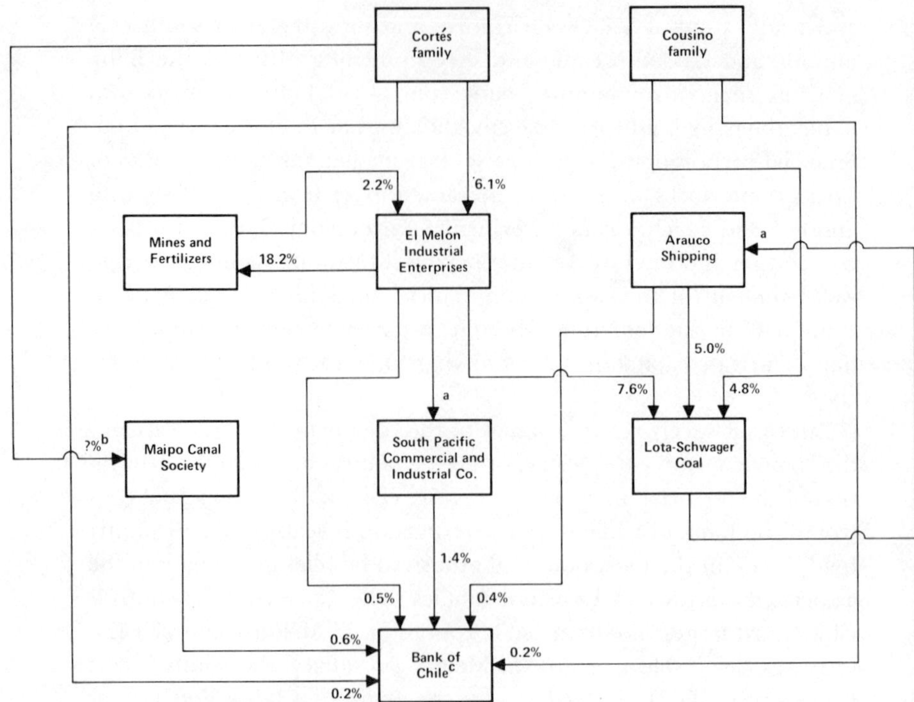

FIGURE 3.1. Intercorporate Control of the Bank of Chile by the Cortés and Cousiño Families

⟵ Principal shareholding in firm, with percentage of stock held

[a] Subsidiary of the parent firm; actual percentage of ownership not ascertained.

[b] Known to be under Cortés control; actual percentage of ownership not ascertained.

[c] Percentages are rounded.

"core" of the entire dominant class: the Larraín, Matte, and Valdés families, among whom are the descendants of the founders of the three original banks that merged to form the Bank of Chile. Dispersed among 19 closely related individuals, the combined holdings of these three families come to 2.2 percent of the bank's outstanding stock. In collaboration with the Cortés and Cousiño families, with whom they also have close kinship ties, the combined bloc controls 5.4 percent. Given the relative dispersion and small size of the remaining stockholdings in the bank, this probably ensures the Cortés and Cousiño families and their associates working control. Thus, although at first the Bank of Chile appeared to be under management control, and then—with its vast range of institutional holdings and interlocking directorates throughout the top 37 corporations, as well as the singularity of its financial power and peerless status among the country's most powerful banks—appeared to epitomize "bank control" of industry, the reality is quite different. The Bank of Chile, our analysis reveals, is under the joint control of several dominant owning families, whose diverse economic interests transcend industry, commerce, agriculture, and banking. These families, indeed, are "finance capital" personified.

The families controlling the other big banks also have extensive interests in the largest industrial and commercial corporations. In fact, 3 of the Big Five, not including the Bank of Chile, are controlled by specific kinecon groups that are also dominant in several of the top 37 nonfinancial corporations. The Bank of Credit and Investments is controlled by the Yarur Banna interests, who also control 2 of the largest textile firms, Yarur Chilean Cotton Products and Caupolicán Textiles. The South American Bank is controlled by the Vial and MacAuliffe families, through a simple dominant-minority holding by their jointly controlled South American Steamship Co.; the Vials also share control of Petroleum Navigation. The Bank of Edwards is controlled by the inseparable Edwards and Lyon families, who also control, or share control in, 6 of the top 37 corporations (see and compare Tables 3.1 and 1.5). Thus, in all 6 leading banks, the interests of the dominant or controlling families span banking, industry, and commerce. (For details, see Table 3.11, appended to this chapter.)

Further, the banks they control also have extensive institutional shareholdings throughout the top 37 nonfinancials, and the latter, in turn, have principal shareholdings in these banks. But our analysis shows that the Big Five nationwide banks stand above and beyond the rest of the banks in the extent and density of their interconnections—both through reciprocal institutional stockownership and interlocking directorates—with the top 37 nonfinancial corporations. These Big Five are the *only* banks, of all 24 Chilean-owned commercial banks, that have multiple institutional stockholdings in several top-37 firms.[37]

[37] The Bank of London and South America, descendant of the Bank of Tarapacá founded by the "Nitrate King" John Thomas North, also has multiple holdings in the top 37 corporations, and probably forms an integral part of the Edwards control group in several of them. There are enduring connections between the Edwards family and North associates, dating from the nitrate era and their collaboration in the overthrow of President José Manuel Balmaceda in 1891. In particular, the South American Bank (which was later taken over by the Bank of London and South America) purchased 60 percent of the shares of the Bank of Edwards in 1920, and the lat-

And these stockholdings are concentrated heavily in the very largest of the top 37. Of the 46 principal blocks of top-37 stock held by the Big Five banks, 19 are in the top 10 corporations, 10 are in the corporations ranked 11–20, 11 more are in those ranked 21–30, and the remaining 6 stockholdings are in the corporations ranked 31–37.

In turn, the principal blocks of stock that top-37 nonfinancial corporations hold in commercial banks are similarly concentrated in the Big Five banks. Analysis of the stockownership of the 16 largest commercial banks reveals that top-37 corporations have five separate principal stockholdings in the Big Five banks, but just four in the next 11 smaller banks. In sum, intercorporate stockholdings and the institutional coalescence of banking, industrial, and commercial capital provide a base for control of the leading banks by specific capitalist families, which have extensive and substantial investments throughout the entire economy.

Aside from their extensive interpenetrating ownership, the Big Five banks and the top-37 nonfinancials are also bound together by an elaborate network of interlocking directorates. In fact, 12 of the top-37 nonfinancials interlock directly with 2 of the Big Five banks, and another 2 top-37 nonfinancials interlock with 3 of the Big Five.[38] What is crucial, in the present context, about the interlocking between the big banks and the top corporations is how it has shaped the ensemble of social relations in which the bankers are located. Among the officers and directors of the Big Five banks, a slight majority also sit in the management of 1 or more top-37 nonfinancial corporations, whereas among their counterparts in the lesser banks, only a small fraction also hold top-37 seats: one-tenth of the latter, compared to slightly over half of the former, are what we have called "finance capitalists" (see Table 3.2). In fact, the Big Five bankers all but monopolize the crucial interlocking bank-corporation positions. Of all of the higher executives of the 16 major commercial banks who are also higher executives in 1 or more top-37 corporations, the overwhelming majority, i.e. 30 out of 42 (or 71 percent), are higher executives of the Big Five banks. Thus, the milieu of the finance capitalist is the management of the Big

ter regularly paid a 16 percent dividend over the following years to its parent bank-holding company. See Joslin 1963, p. 261; Moody's 1970a, p. 1789. In 1964, the only probable foreign holding in the Bank of Edwards was the 16 percent holding by "Amolana."

[38] The Bank of Osorno is not directly interlocked with any of the top 37 nonfinancials.

TABLE 3.2. Percentage of Officers and Directors of the 16 Largest Commercial Banks in Chile Who Are Also in the Management of One or More Top-37 Nonfinancial Corporations, 1964/66

	Officers	(*N*)	Directors	(*N*)	All Bank Executives	(*N*)
Big Five banks	47	(15)	53	(43)	52	(58)
Other banks	12	(33)	9	(84)	10	(117)
All 16 banks	23	(48)	24	(127)	24	(175)

Five bank, just as the milieu of the Big Five banker is the milieu of the finance capitalist.

The Finance Capitalists

But the milieu of the finance capitalist is also, of course, though in a distinctive way, the management of the large corporation. For it is, as we shall see, the specific milieu of the "inner group" (see Chapter 2), i.e. the interlocking officers and directors who unite the managerial apexes of the top nonfinancial corporations.

Among the men who sit simultaneously in the managements of a major bank and of 1 or more of the top 37 nonfinancials, we have identified three types of "finance capitalists," defined both by the assets rank of their bank and by their relative location in its managerial hierarchy. The first type of finance capitalist is a higher executive in a top-37 nonfinancial corporation who is also a higher executive in 1 of the Big Five banks. (There are no direct interlocks between any commercial banks, because this is prohibited by Chilean law; thus no finance capitalist is an officer or director of more than 1 commercial bank.) Given the relative ascendancy of the Big Five banks in the entire banking system, we have designated men of this type "primary finance capitalists." The second type of finance capitalist holds a position as a higher executive in 1 or more top-37 nonfinancials and in 1 of the 16 largest commercial banks other than the Big Five. (In fact, remember, we actually began our analysis with the executives of the 6 leading banks, but, as it turned out, none of the men in the management of the regional 6th-ranking Bank of Osorno holds any top-37 management position.) The third type of finance capitalist, although not in the higher *national* management of a bank, holds a position as an officer, director, or member of the "executive board" (*consejo*) of a *major branch* of 1 of the Big Five banks (e.g. the Valparaíso or Punta Arenas branch, or even the main branch in Santiago). The latter two types have been merged in the following analysis because there are too few of each type to allow discrete quantitative analysis; we refer to them as "secondary finance capitalists."

The first empirical question, then, is whether finance capitalists, while presiding over the confluence of loan, productive, and commercial capital, also play a special role in coordinating and integrating the classwide interests embodied in the top nonfinancial corporations. Insofar as their structural relationship to the inner group is a valid indicator, the answer is an emphatic yes. Compared with the "ordinary corporate executives," none of whom holds a formal bank management position, both the primary and secondary finance capitalists are more likely to sit in the managements of 2 or more top-37 corporations. But the primary finance capitalists especially stand out: the proportion of them having seats in the management of 2 or more top-37 firms is more than two and a half times that of the secondary finance capitalists and more than four times that of the ordinary corporate executives. Moreover, not only are the primary finance capitalists the most *likely* of all corporate higher executives to hold multiple top-37 seats, but the *vast majority* of them (66 percent) actually do. In contrast, both among the secondary finance capitalists and the ordinary corporate executives, the vast majority (70 percent and 81 percent, respectively) hold a seat in the management of *only 1* top-37 corporation. Thus, most primary finance capitalists are within the inner group, but most other corporate executives, regardless of whether or not they have a formal banking connection, are not (see Table 3.3).

But what if we examine the converse of this relationship? What are the chances that the men who hold single vs. multiple top-37 seats are finance capitalists? Here, again, the primary finance capitalists stand out: the more top-37 management seats an executive holds, the more likely he is a primary finance capitalist. Similarly, the fewer seats he holds, the more likely he is an ordinary corporate executive having no formal banking connection. As a gauge of their real social weight, however, it bears emphasizing that primary and secondary finance capitalists combined amount to about half of the entire inner group. The primary finance capitalists alone actually constitute roughly two-thirds of the small subset of men in the "inner group within the inner group" who hold seats in 3 or more top-37 managements (see Table 3.4). Thus, the finance capitalists, particularly the primary finance capitalists, have not only established a form of "personal union," as Hilferding terms it, between the leading banks and the top nonfinan-

TABLE 3.3. Percentage of Finance Capitalists and Other Higher Executives of the Top 37 Nonfinancial Corporations in Chile Who Serve in a Specified Number of Top-37 Managements, 1964/66

	Top-37 Seats Held			
	One	Two	Three-plus	(*N*)
Primary finance capitalists	23	43	33	(30)
Secondary finance capitalists	70	22	7	(27)
Ordinary executives	81	16	2	(172)
All executives	72	20	8	(229)

NOTE: No distinction is made here between officers and directors. To have shown all the relationships separately would have meant repeating each relationship shown—in this and most of the following tables—for bank officers, bank directors, top-37 officers, and top-37 directors. We do not consider the distinction theoretically relevant in the present analytical context. Nonetheless, to be sure that we had not unwittingly neglected anomalous relationships, we ran the full tables; no relevant differences from the present tables were found.

TABLE 3.4. Percentage of Higher Executives of the Top 37 Nonfinancial Corporations in Chile Who Are Finance Capitalists, by the Number of Top-37 Management Seats Held, 1964/66

	Primary Finance Capitalists	Secondary Finance Capitalists	Ordinary Executives	(*N*)
One seat	4	11	84	(166)
Two seats	28	13	60	(47)
Three-plus seats	63	12	25	(16)
All executives	13	12	75	(229)

cial corporations, but are also the preeminent embodiment of the interlocking community of interest formed among the top nonfinancial corporations themselves.[39]

Indeed, the finance capitalists are especially well placed at the helms of the very largest of the top 37 corporations, just as they are placed overwhelmingly at the helms of one or another of the Big Five banks. To see this clearly, we have to focus for the moment not on the individuals themselves, but on the management *seats*, or positions, they

[39] Hilferding 1910. Zeitlin's analysis of the directors of the top 500 U.S. industrial corporations of 1968 reveals the same pattern: "commercial and investment bankers are disproportionately overrepresented among the occupants of multiple corporate directorships. . . . Indeed, the proportion of bankers who are outside directors rises directly with the number of corporate posts held. . . . Viewing the same relationship differently, commercial and investment bankers stand out in marked contrast to other outside directors in the top 500 corporations: a far higher proportion of them have multiple corporation posts than do outside directors from other top 500 corporations" (1974a, p. 1104).

occupy in the top 37 nonfinancials. Because the occupants of multiple top-37 seats are more likely to be primary finance capitalists than they are to be some other type of executive, this means, of course, that they hold a disproportionate number of all top-37 management seats. Our 30 primary finance capitalists constitute 13 percent of the 229 men in the managements of the top 37, but they occupy 23 percent, nearly double their share, of the 320 management seats in these 37 corporations.

The question, then, is how the proportion of top-37 seats held by primary finance capitalists varies with the size of the corporation—and how this compares with the proportions held by the secondary finance capitalists and ordinary corporate executives. Are the seats in the largest of the top 37 corporations more likely to be occupied by primary finance capitalists than the seats in the smaller ones? The answer is clear: the larger the corporation, the higher the proportion of its management seats that are filled by primary finance capitalists. They hold, for example, 31 percent of the management seats in the 10 largest, but only 14 percent in the 7 smallest, of the top 37.[40] In contrast, management seats in the smallest corporations are somewhat more likely than those in the largest to be occupied by ordinary corporate executives. The same is true for the secondary finance capitalists. Drawn from the management of a smaller bank or from a branch office of a Big Five bank, the secondary finance capitalist is also more likely to hold a management seat in a smaller top-37 nonfinancial than in a larger one (see Table 3.5).

Our analysis so far has shown that their location in the apparatus of operating classwide property gives the finance capitalists unique access to the means of coordinating and harmonizing the policies of the big banks and top nonfinancial corporations, with the aim of maximizing the net return of the entire system of large-scale investment and production under their command. But who are they in sociological terms? Leaving aside their personal predilections, individual character, tal-

[40] Research by Soref and Zeitlin (1988) reveals the same pattern in the United States among the biggest financial institutions and top industrial corporations of 1964: a finance capitalist (on the board of one of the top 50 commercial banks, top 50 insurance companies, or any major financial company, or a partner in a leading investment bank *and* a director of a top-200 industrial) is far more likely than an ordinary director to hold multiple industrial directorships; conversely, the more boards on which he sits in the top 200 industrials, the more likely a director is to be a finance capitalist. The same pattern repeats itself if we take into account the relative assets-size of the industrial corporation—paralleling, on both counts, the findings presented here on Chile's finance capitalists.

TABLE 3.5. Percentage of Management Seats in the Top 37 Nonfinancial Corporations in Chile, Ranked by Assets, Held by Finance Capitalists and Other Higher Executives, 1964/66

	Primary Finance Capitalists	Secondary Finance Capitalists	Ordinary Executives	(*N*)
Rank				
1–10	31	9	60	(97)
11–20	24	9	67	(88)
21–30	18	17	65	(72)
31–37	14	13	73	(63)
All seats	23	12	66	(320)

ents, and skills, what sort of men are socially selected and recruited to exercise decisive power in the interlocking higher managerial realms of banking, industrial, and commerical capital? Do these finance capitalists, as we have suggested elsewhere, represent "a special social type in contrast to the other officers and directors of the largest corporations and banks"? No single indicator is sufficient to answer this question, but what is critical in class terms, we suggest, is "information concerning their own propertied interests, their relative wealth, [and] their kinship relations."[41]

Wealth, Capital, Kinship, and Bureaucracy

So, are these finance capitalists men of wealth, especially in comparison to the "mere bureaucrats" with whom they sit at the managerial helms of the top corporations? Based on a survey of their stockownership in the top 37 nonfinancial corporations, 16 largest commercial banks, and 11 top foreign firms,[42] the answer is clear: our finance capitalists stand out in high relief from other corporate higher executives. Counting the market worth of their bank and nonfinancial stockholdings separately and combined, proportionately far more primary and secondary finance capitalists than other executives are in the wealthiest brackets. Indeed, roughly twice as many primary finance capitalists as ordinary corporate executives are in the two highest stockowning brackets: 43 percent of the former but only 23 percent of the latter, for instance, owned E°150,000 or more in stock (see Table 3.6).

That the finance capitalists are typically far wealthier than ordinary corporate executives sets them apart as having a greater stake in the

[41] Zeitlin 1974a, pp. 1103, 1110.

[42] See Chapter 2 for a description of the sources of these data.

TABLE 3.6. Percentage of Finance Capitalists and Other Higher Executives of the Top 37 Nonfinancial Corporations in Chile Who Own a Specified Amount of Stock in the Largest Banks and Top Nonfinancial Corporations, 1964/66

	Stockholdings (E°1,000s)												
	16 Largest Commercial Banks				Nonfinancial Corporations				Banks and Corporations				
	Under 50	50–99	100–149	150-plus	Under 50	50–99	100–149	150-plus	Under 50	50–99	100–149	150-plus	(*N*)
Primary finance capitalists	80	7	0	14	43	13	7	37	26	17	13	43	(30)
Secondary finance capitalists	81	7	0	11	37	26	11	26	37	19	7	37	(27)
Ordinary executives	93	2	2	3	65	8	8	20	62	9	6	23	(172)
All executives	90	3	1	6	59	10	8	23	55	11	7	27	(229)

protection and expansion of corporate capital. Surely they are not "propertyless." But being wealthier than other executives does not indicate what their relationship is to the very rich or to the principal owners of capital. The question is, Do they also stand out in the extent of their ties with the richest capital-owning families? And the answer is that no matter how one measures the extent of their integration into the capitalist class (or their intraclass location), the finance capitalists are distinctive: roughly half of the finance capitalists as a whole are personally principal owners of capital, compared to less than a third of the ordinary corporate executives.

Most important, the more deeply we probe the integument of the class, the more transparent the distinctive intraclass location of the finance capitalists becomes: they are the veritable embodiment of the fusion of the systems of family and property in the corporate world. As was shown in the previous chapter, probing the linkage between kinship and capital ownership, from the immediate family through secondary and close relatives, reveals that the proportion of all managers—these so-called bureaucrats—who actually belong to principal capital-owning families increases at each distance, until a simple majority of them are seen to belong to a close capitalist family. Now we see that, at each kinship distance from the immediate through the close family, not only are proportionately more finance capitalists than other executives drawn from a principal capital-owning family, but the vast majority of them are so drawn. Nearly 70 percent of *all* (primary and secondary) finance capitalists, compared to 49 percent of the other higher executives, are in a close capitalist family. But it should also be noted that, even when we just consider the immediate family, two-thirds of the primary finance capitalists belong to a capitalist family, compared to "only" 40 percent of ordinary corporate executives (see Table 3.7). As we hypothesized, then, the finance capitalist unquestionably constitutes a "special social type," a specifically *class* type that interlocks the managerial helms of the biggest banks and the top nonfinancial corporations.[43]

[43] Soref and Zeitlin (1988) have investigated this relationship in the United States and find a similar pattern. They identify directors of the top 200 industrials who belong to a leading propertied family (from information either on their capital ownership in a sample of 40 industrials analyzed or from their membership in the national status-community of the very rich) and find that the finance capitalists (see note 40, above) consistently stand out, compared with other industrial directors, as belonging to a leading propertied family. Also see the fine analysis of family, kin-

TABLE 3.7. Percentage of Finance Capitalists and Other Higher Executives of the Top 37 Nonfinancial Corporations in Chile Who Are in a Principal Capital-Owning Family, 1964/66

	Personally Principal Capitalists	Principal Capitalists in: Immediate Family	Secondary Family	Close Family	(*N*)
Primary finance capitalists	47	67	70	70	(30)
Secondary finance capitalists	52	56	56	67	(27)
Ordinary executives	30	40	45	49	(172)
All executives	35	45	50	54	(229)

NOTE: See Table 2.2, notes, for explanation of terms.

The Inner Group and the Finance Capitalists

We saw earlier, however, that alongside the finance capitalists, who form a "personal union" between the banks and the top corporations, is the inner group of men who form such a union among the top nonfinancial corporations; and we have just seen that the finance capitalists tend to absorb the inner group, and to predominate in the "inner group within the inner group." For this reason alone, the finance capitalists and the inner group must be examined simultaneously in order to gauge the comparative extent of their integration into the world of the wealthiest capitalist families. In other words, the relationship between familial ownership of capital and type of higher executive (finance capitalists vs. others) has to be examined while holding constant the number of top-37 seats held.

For it may be that it is not the location of the finance capitalists at the confluence of loan and productive capital, but merely their long corporate reach—through the interlocking managements of the top nonfinancial corporations—that accounts for their apparent distinctiveness. Thus, the "null hypothesis": it is not that they are finance capitalists, but rather that they are in the inner group which explains their difference from ordinary higher executives. If this reasoning is correct, then when we hold constant the number of management seats in the top 37 corporations, the family capital ownership of finance capitalists should become indistinguishable from that of ordinary executives, while the inner-group members should continue to stand

ship, and finance capitalists in Britain, by Scott and Griff (1984). Their findings, to the extent that they are comparable, also parallel our own.

out, as drawn disproportionately from a principal capital-owning family.

Aside from this straightforward "analytical" reason for holding inner-group membership constant, it also addresses a specific theoretical question. For we have suggested that it is not only the special role of the finance capitalists in managing the affairs of the interlocked top nonfinancial corporations which explains why the finance capitalists must tend to constitute a distinctive class segment: it is also their specifically *self-contradictory intraclass situation*—both as financiers and industrialists, and as creditors and owners, embodied in their simultaneous managerial role in the biggest banks and top nonfinancials. The principal capital-owning families, in order to harmonize these self-contradictory interests in their own behalf, must strive to place their members at the helms both of the banks and the corporations. As much as they might seek seats interlocking top nonfinancial corporations, they must especially work to reserve a place for themselves in the management of a big bank as well. If this hypothesis is correct, then we should find that, with the number of top-37 seats held constant, the intraclass distinctiveness of the finance capitalists endures or may even be accentuated while that of the inner group tends to disappear. Such a finding would be consistent with our theory of how the constitutive contradictions inherent in finance capital are expressed both interorganizationally and in the inner structure of the capitalist class itself.

So, then, controlling for the number of top-37 seats reveals that the difference between the inner group and the outsiders tends to disappear among ordinary higher executives. To examine this relationship, we have had to merge the primary and secondary finance capitalists, because there are too few of each type to allow separate analysis of their kinship connections to capital while also holding constant their membership in the inner group. There is no significant difference in capital ownership, at any phase of our deepening probe of the capital-kinship nexus, between ordinary executives who hold multiple seats and those who hold a seat in the management of only 1 top-37 corporation. Among these ordinary executives, the men outside the inner group are as likely as those within it to belong to a principal capitalist family: in each group, half belong to a close capitalist family. Also, although the differences are small, those finance capitalists holding single top-corporation seats are still more likely than their counterparts among ordinary executives to be principal owners of capital personally and to belong to a close capital-owning family.

Finally—and most important theoretically—among finance capitalists, those in the inner group not only stand out from the others, but those finance capitalists in the inner group are *nearly all* from principal capital-owning families: 81 percent of the finance capitalists who sit in 2 or more top-37 managements, and 92 percent who sit in 3 or more, belong to a close capitalist family, compared to "only" 54 percent of the finance capitalists who sit in 1 top-37 management. Thus, precisely the most important command posts in both the intercorporate and the bank–corporation interorganizational apparatuses are filled overwhelmingly by men from leading capital-owning families whose investments span finance and industry. Not only do the finance capitalists represent, but they virtually personify, finance capital[44] (see Table 3.8).

Bank Control or Finance Capital?

A theoretically crucial empirical question remains. So far, our findings tend to confirm that the finance capitalists are a special class type, if

[44] Michael Useem, as we noted earlier, has utilized our theory (and earlier findings in Chile) concerning the inner group in the corporate world to guide his own fine empirical studies in the United States (esp. 1978, 1984). In Zeitlin's original formulation, the crucial connection between the inner group and the finance capitalists is emphasized as follows: "To the extent that the largest banks and corporations constitute a new form of class property—of social ownership of the means of production by a single social class—the 'inner group' of interlocking officers and directors, *and particularly the finance capitalists*, become the leading organizers of this system of class-wide property. . . . They should be far more likely than ordinary corporate executives to be drawn from the 'upper' or 'dominant' or 'capitalist' class—the social class formed around the core of interrelated principal owners of capital" (Zeitlin 1976, p. 901, italics added). Now, we have seen that, among ordinary higher executives in Chile's top 37 nonfinancial corporations, the men occupying multiple management seats do *not* differ socially from those holding just a single seat. Only among the finance capitalists is membership in the inner group relevant with respect to distinguishing their place in the corporate world and the capitalist class. The question, then, is whether Useem's extensive findings on the special role and distinctiveness of the inner group would be similarly affected if finance capitalists were considered simultaneously, as we have done here. Would the differences between the inner group within the U.S. capitalist class, on the one hand, and outsiders, on the other, tend to disappear among ordinary corporate executives, but become even sharper (as we have found here) among finance capitalists? If so, of course, this would require considerable qualification of Useem's findings concerning the inner group, insofar as the relevance of the finance capitalists has been neglected in his analyses. Domhoff (1983, p. 72) does note that "members of the inner group are very often bankers . . . or top corporate executives who sit on bank boards," but neither he nor the work he cites concerning "bank centrality" in the "networks formed by interlocking directors" analyzes the interrelations between the inner group, the finance capitalists, and their intraclass location.

TABLE 3.8. Percentage of Finance Capitalists and Other Higher Executives of the Top 37 Nonfinancial Corporations in Chile Who Are in a Principal Capital-Owning Family, by the Number of Top-37 Management Seats Held, 1964/66

	Personally Principal Capitalists	Principal Capitalists in: Immediate Family	Secondary Family	Close Family	(*N*)
Finance capitalists					
one seat	38	42	42	54	(26)
two seats	63	74	79	79	(19)
	58	77	81	81	
three-plus seats	50	83	83	92	(12)
all finance capitalists	49	61	63	68	(57)
Ordinary executives					
one seat	30	40	46	49	(140)
two seats	32	43	46	50	(28)
	28	41	44	50	
three-plus seats	0	25	25	50	(4)
all ordinary executives	30	40	45	49	(172)

not, indeed, a distinctive class segment. The question, however, is whether their preponderant tendency to be drawn from principal capitalist families reflects an as yet hidden reality underlying their apparent distinctiveness?

Is it possible that, in reality, what matters is not that they are finance capitalists, but merely, alas, that they are bankers? Can it be that what accounts for the apparently distinctive intraclass location of the finance capitalists is their position as helmsmen of the big banks? The bankers, in general, might well be men of wealth and property, drawn from the great banking families, *irrespective of* their managerial positions in the top corporations. Thus, perhaps, if some bankers (namely, the finance capitalists) are active in representing a bank's investments in the top corporations by actually participating in corporate management also, while others attend only to managing the bank's immediate affairs, their intraclass situations should, if this hypothesis is correct, be otherwise identical.

Such a finding would not only tend to confute the specific intraclass theory of finance capital that guides our empirical analysis, but it would also lend credence to the notion of "bank control" of industry. Rather than the biggest banks of Chile, as the evidence presented here thus far seems to confirm, merely being "units in, and instrumentalities of, the whole system of propertied interests controlled by . . . major capitalist families,"[45] such a finding about the distinctiveness of the bankers as a whole would support the view that the banks are the "real owners of capital" and the real loci of control of the top corporations.[46] Such a finding, at least, would be consistent with the notion that *bankers*, representing interest-bearing capital and acting at the expense of industrial capital, are the real men of power in Chile's top corporations, and that their investment objectives and policies are aimed at benefiting the interests of the *banks* rather than the interests of the principal capitalist families, whose holdings span the industrial, commercial, and banking sectors.

That, however, is not what our evidence reveals. Rather, the wealth and principal capital ownership of the bankers, relative to that of the finance capitalists, is consistent with our intraclass theory of finance capital and with the other findings that have been presented so far in its support. First of all, the wealth of the finance capitalists is much greater than that of other bankers. The "bankers," i.e. the ordinary bank executives who do not sit in any top-37 management, are less likely than the finance capitalists to own substantial blocks even of *bank* stock. Although among both types of bank executives only small proportions own substantial amounts of bank stock, proportionately three times as many finance capitalists are in the wealthiest bracket of bank stock ownership, i.e. of E°150,000 or more. Perhaps most crucial from the standpoint of our intraclass theory of finance capital, very few of the ordinary bankers (not even a tenth) own substantial amounts of stock in the top nonfinancial corporations. In fact, the vast majority of the "bankers" have top-37 stock valued below E°50,000, but well over half of the finance capitalists have top-37 stockholdings that put them above that same mark. When we consider combined stockholdings both in the major banks and the top nonfinancial corporations, the wealth of the finance capitalists is far greater than that of the ordinary bank executives. The vast majority of the ordinary bankers, roughly 80 percent, own only negligible amounts of stock. But most finance capitalists fall within the two wealthiest stockholding brackets; indeed, the modal finance capitalist is in the wealthiest bracket (see Table 3.9).

[45] Zeitlin 1974a, p. 1102.

[46] This thesis has been widely held by the Chilean left. See, for instance, Cademartori 1963, p. 32; Lagos Escobar 1961, esp. pt. 2, passim. In the United States, Fitch and Oppenheimer (1970) and Kotz (1978) have been the most recent exponents of this thesis, focusing on the supposed parasitic role of "the banks" vis-à-vis "industry." See, also, Mariolis 1975, 1978. For a critique of this notion, see Herman 1973 and 1981.

TABLE 3.9. Percentage of Finance Capitalists and Other Higher Executives of the Big Six Commercial Banks in Chile Who Own a Specified Amount of Stock in the Largest Banks and Top Nonfinancial Corporations, 1964/66

	Stockholdings (E°1,000s)												
	16 Largest Commercial Banks				Nonfinancial Corporations				Banks and Corporations				
	Under 50	50–99	100–149	150-plus	Under 50	50–99	100–149	150-plus	Under 50	50–99	100–149	150-plus	(*N*)
Finance capitalists	80	7	0	14	43	13	7	37	26	17	13	43	(30)
Ordinary bank executives	87	5	3	5	89	0	3	8	79	5	3	13	(38)
All bank executives	84	6	1	9	69	6	4	21	54	10	7	28	(68)

Second, the same striking differences appear when we consider kinship connections to principal owners of capital. At each kinship distance, the finance capitalists stand out: they are far more likely personally to be principal owners of capital and to belong to a principal capitalist family. Even at the level of individual capital ownership, the difference between the ordinary bankers and the finance capitalists is striking; in fact, a much greater gap in both individual and family capital ownership separates them than separates the finance capitalists and the ordinary corporate executives. Only 13 percent of the ordinary bank executives, compared to 30 percent of the ordinary corporate executives and 47 percent of the primary finance capitalists, are personally principal owners of capital. The pattern, moreover, is about the same at each level of the kinship-capital nexus, from the immediate through the secondary and close family. The gap in the extent of integration into the wealthiest capitalist families is even wider between the primary finance capitalists and the ordinary bank executives than it is between the ordinary bankers and the ordinary corporate executives: whereas 70 percent of the finance capitalists belong to a close capitalist family, only 39 percent of ordinary bank executives but 49 percent of ordinary corporate executives belong to such a family. Thus, it is clear that finance capitalists—particularly those in the inner group among the higher executives of the top nonfinancial corporations—do not merely "represent" but are also members par excellence of the nation's preeminent capital-owning families (see Tables 3.10 and 3.7).

Conclusion

The empirical analysis in this chapter has been guided by our theory of the internal class relations that link various types of managers of

TABLE 3.10. Percentage of Finance Capitalists and Other Higher Executives of the Big Six Commercial Banks in Chile Who Are in a Principal Capital-Owning Family, 1964/66

	Personally Principal Capitalists	Principal Capitalists in: Immediate Family	Secondary Family	Close Family	(*N*)
Finance capitalists	47	67	70	70	(30)
Ordinary bank executives	13	26	32	39	(38)
All bank executives	28	44	48	53	(68)

NOTE: See Table 2.2, notes, for explanation of terms.

big banks and top corporations with their owners, under conditions of high concentration and coalescence of loan capital and productive capital. Together with the consequent historical emergence of a new self-contradictory form of capital, i.e. finance capital, a specific class type or distinctive class segment also emerges: namely, the finance capitalist, representing and embodying finance capital simultaneously in the managements both of big banks and top nonfinancial corporations.

In Chile, as in other highly concentrated capitalist economies, a few big commercial banks command the flow of loan capital. Chile's Big Five banks and top 37 nonfinancial corporations, as our empirical analysis has revealed, are interwoven both by interpenetrating ownership and interlocking directorates, and they are controlled by major capitalist families whose interests cut across the financial, industrial, and commercial sectors. Presiding at the helms of the Big Five banks, in marked contrast even to the managers of the other major commercial banks, are higher executives who also typically sit in the interlocking managements of the top 37 nonfinancial corporations, particularly the very largest of them. As we probed systematically into the comparative intraclass situations of the various types of bankers and corporate executives, we found that finance capitalists do, indeed, play a special role and constitute a genuine social type within the corporate world and the capitalist class. These "finance capitalists" and the "inner group" of higher executives interlocking the top nonfinancial corporations are, in reality, all but synonymous.

These leading organizers of Chile's corporate system of classwide property and private appropriation—presiding over the coalescence of financial and industrial capital, and bearing the specific intraclass burden of coordinating and attempting to reconcile the self-contradictory interests inherent in the interpenetrating ownership and interlocking directorates of the leading banks and top nonfinancial corporations—are drawn preponderantly, unlike other bank and corporate managers, from among the nation's leading capitalist families. Indeed, they virtually personify the fusion of family and property within the so-called bureaucratic and interorganizational managerial realm of the large corporation.[47]

[47] Mintz and Schwartz analyze the role of financial institutions in intercorporate relationships, but do not consider the role of the capitalist class itself or of the place of specific segments within it. They argue, however, that "class can be introduced into this analysis" by focusing both on the "inner group" and the "finance capitalists" and integrating such an "analysis of individuals with the theory of finance capital" (1985,

From the standpoint of managerial theory in general, and of interorganizational theory in particular, the findings in this chapter are inexplicable, directly contradicting some of the most basic assumptions and central propositions of those theories. In both, the large corporation appears as nothing more than another complex organization in an uncertain environment made up of other organizations; and the corporations are administered by propertyless "managers" who even take on a semblance of being a "purely neutral technocracy" or "technostructure." Neither the private ownership of capital nor the imperatives of capital accumulation determines these managers' conduct or the dynamics of the large corporation and its interrelations with other corporations, banks, and financial institutions. In short, neither theory predicts the systematic findings presented here, and neither theory can account for them. For we have shown conclusively that it is not "organization" but capital, and not the "mere administrator" but the finance capitalist—representing and personifying the coalescence of financial and industrial capital—that exercise the decisive power in Chile's top nonfinancial corporations. Not a process of supposed "interorganizational elite cooptation" but discrete, specific intraclass relations and concrete propertied interests explain the selection and recruitment of the men who fill the strategic positions of power interlocking the managerial helms of the biggest banks and top corporations.

---

p. 253). Based on Zeitlin's elaboration of that theory for analysis of the internal structure of the capitalist class, and on related empirical analyses (Zeitlin 1974a, 1976; Zeitlin, Neuman, and Ratcliff 1976; and Ratcliff 1980a and 1980b), Mintz and Schwartz go on to suggest, "combining . . . inner-group analysis with the theory of finance capital, that business leadership accrues to a special social type: a cohesive group of multiple directors . . . who sit on bank boards as representatives of capital in general. . . . [D]ecisions on capital allocation are affected by the needs of this inner group of finance capitalists . . . and [are] conditioned by the class networks they create and inhabit." Thus, if finance capitalists are constrained and limited in their conduct by the imperatives of capital accumulation and by the centrality of banks in this process, "they must also make real choices about which investment options to pursue [as Ratcliff (1980a, 1980b) has stressed]. . . . Without their input, capital would be allocated in different ways and in response to different pressures. Like everyone else, the capitalist class makes decisions but not under conditions of its own choosing" (Mintz and Schwartz 1985, pp. 253–254).

APPENDIX

CONTROLLING INTERESTS IN THE LEADING COMMERCIAL BANKS

TABLE 3.11. Descriptions of the Controlling Proprietary Interests in the Leading Commercial Banks in Chile, 1964/66

1. Bank of Chile

The Bank of Chile, because it is by far Chile's largest commercial bank, and widely considered an exemplar of the "democratization of capital," is discussed in the text of Chapter 3.

2. Spanish Bank of Chile

The García and Picó families, and associates:

Composition of Group	*Stock Owned* %	*Stock Owned* Rank
"La Española" Insurance Co.	1.12	5
Territorial Insurance Co.	0.75	10
Vasconia Consolidated Insurance Co.	0.75	11
Iberia Insurance Co.	0.65	18
SUBTOTAL	3.27	
COPESA (Newspaper consortium)	3.93	1
José Picó Miró, former vice-president	0.61	21
Raúl Jaras Barros and Co.	0.54	24
SUBTOTAL	5.08	
Jaime Artigas Valls, vice-president	0.69	15
Lorenzo Reus Martí, director	2.14	3
PROBABLE WORKING BLOC	11.18	

The four insurance companies are controlled (or control is shared) by the family of Patricio García Vela, a director of the bank, as follows: 29.58 percent of "La Española," 10 percent of Territorial, 20.34 percent of Vasconia, and 32.4 percent of Iberia.

José Picó Miró, a former vice-president of the bank and a principal shareowner, is the father both of the president of COPESA and of a COPESA director. Raúl Jaras, a director of the bank, is the manager of COPESA.

Patricio García Vela and Germán Picó Cañas, son of José Picó Miró, are married to sisters, whose brother Emilio Domínguez Rielo is a director of the bank.

3. Bank of Credit and Investments

The Yarur Banna family, Grace (U.S.) interests (?), and the Prieto family:

Composition of Group	Stock Owned %	Rank
Yarur Chilean Cotton Products	9.8	2
Amador Yarur Banna, director	8.5	3
Juan Yarur Enterprises	7.0	4
Jorge Yarur Banna	4.9	6
Carlos Yarur Banna	4.2	7
Caupolicán Textiles	1.6	11
SUBTOTAL	36.0	
John F. Ladley	11.1	1
Memphis and Chattanooga Investment Corporation	5.4	5
SUBTOTAL	16.5	
Sergio Larraín Prieto, director	2.7	9
Luis Prieto Vial	0.6	18
Alberto Larraín Prieto	0.5	22
Jaime Prieto Vial	0.5	23
SUBTOTAL	4.3	
PROBABLE WORKING BLOC	55.8	

Yarur Chilean Cotton Products, we think, is controlled jointly by the Yarur family and Grace (?) interests. See the discussion of Grace-Yarur interconnections below. Amador Yarur is managing director of Juan Yarur Enterprises, which he and his brothers, Jorge and Carlos, own, with the shares equally divided among them.

Caupolicán Textiles, in which Yarur Chilean Cotton owns 49.0 percent and Juan Yarur Enterprises 21.1 percent, is controlled by the Yarurs. However, its board is dominated by W. R. Grace and Co. representatives; that is to say, it has six directors in common with each of two Grace subsidiaries, Grace and Co. of Chile and Industries and Sugar Co. (COIA), while Yarurs are neither on the board nor officers of Caupolicán. The Chase Manhattan Trust Department holds the single-largest shareholding (24.5 percent) in Yarur Chilean Cotton, and Memphis and Chattanooga Investment has a much smaller shareholding, ranking 11th (1.24 percent). Because of the tight interlocking between Grace firms and Caupolicán, as well as two interlocks between them and the Bella Vista–Tomé Cloth Factory, in which the Yarur Asfura family is dominant, we think it likely that Chase Manhattan and Memphis and Chattanooga are, in fact, Grace nominees. In any case, the appearance of Memphis and Chattanooga only in a corporation and a bank in which Yarur interests are dominant indicates it is probably part of the working bloc. Of course, rather than being a Grace holding, it may be simply a nominee for the Yarur family. However, the presence of John F. Ladley here, as the single-largest shareholder, suggests otherwise.

Bernardo Larraín Vial, who is the bank's president, the two Larraín brothers, one of whom is a bank director, and the two Prieto brothers are first cousins.

4. South American Bank

The Vial and MacAuliffe families:

Composition of Group	*Stock Owned* %	*Rank*
South American Steamship Co. (CSAV)	20.4	1
Vitalicia Cooperative Life Insurance Co.	1.9	2
Lidia Martínez Oyarzún	0.7	9
WORKING BLOC	23.0	

The Vial and MacAuliffe families hold working control of South American Steamship (see Table 1.6). The MacAuliffes presumably control Vitalicia Cooperative, which also has the third largest shareholding in South American Steamship; Lidia Martínez is the aunt of Brian MacAuliffe Martínez, a South American Steamship director. Carlos Vial Infante, who is the shipping company's president, and Francisco Subercaseaux Aldunate, another of the latter's directors, are related through marriage to Mr. Vial (as well as to two other shipping company directors) and are both directors of the bank.

5. Bank of Edwards

The Edwards and Lyon families (with the Bank of London and South America?):

Composition of Group	*Stock Owned* %	*Rank*
Lord Cochrane Publishing Co.	10.0	2
Arturo Lyon Edwards, president	5.1	3
El Mercurio Journalism Enterprises	3.8	4
María Lyon de Covarrubias	3.7	5
Universal Insurance Co.	2.6	6
María Isabel Eastman vda. de Edwards	2.4	8
María Luisa Edwards de Lyon	2.2	9
Juan Braun Lyon	2.1	10
Chilean Consolidated Insurance Co.	2.1	11
Jorge Ross Ossa, director	2.1	12
Monica Hurtado Edwards	1.9	13
Verónica Braun Lyon	1.1	15

5. Bank of Edwards (*cont.*)

The Edwards and Lyon families (with the Bank of London and South America?):

Composition of Group	*Stock Owned* %	*Rank*
María Edwards vda. de Errázuriz	1.1	16
IBEC (Fondo Crecinco de Sociedad Financiera y de Administración, IBEC, Chile, S.A.)	0.9	19
Sonia Edwards Eastman de Berthet	0.9	20
Estate of Marisol Edwards de Lyon	0.75	25
FAMILY BLOC	42.75	
"Amolana" Investment Co.	11.6	1
WORKING BLOC	54.35	

Lord Cochrane is wholly owned by Edwards interests, distributed among *El Mercurio*, the estate of Agustín Edwards Budge, his widow María Isabel Eastman and their sons Roberto and Agustín, the latter's brother-in-law Santiago Lyon Giralt, and Santiago Lyon Edwards, who is a first cousin once-removed of the Edwards Eastman brothers.

El Mercurio is controlled by the Edwards family through the estate of Agustín Edwards Budge, which holds 69.0 percent of the stock.

Edwards control of Universal Insurance Co. and Consolidated Chilean is described in Table 1.6. Edwards interests in IBEC are also detailed there.

The individuals listed here are all closely interrelated members of the Edwards kindred.

"Amolana" 's probable status as a nominee for the Bank of London and South America, with which the Edwardses have a long-standing association going back to the late nineteenth-century senior partners of both banks, is detailed in Table 1.6.

6. Bank of Osorno and the Union

The Sotta Barros family and associates:

Composition of Group	*Stock Owned* %	*Rank*
Daniel Sotta Barros	1.9	2
Daniel Sotta Novoa	1.7	3
Victor Sotta Novoa	1.6	4
Juan Pablo Sotta Novoa	0.8	16
SUBTOTAL	6.0	
Pedro Despouy Rescart	1.0	12
Ernesto Hott Siebert	0.7	17
PROBABLE WORKING BLOC	7.7	

Mr. Sotta Barros is a director of Zig-Zag Publishing Enterprises, and his brother-in-law Raúl Infante Biggs is a former president, while Mr. Infante's brother Arturo is a principal shareowner of Zig-Zag and president of its subsidiary, Universo Printing and Lithography. These connections are important because two cousins of Mr. Despouy are, respectively, also principal shareowners of Zig-Zag and Universo, thus indicating that they are probably close business associates. Mr. Sotta Barros, though not on the board of the bank in 1964, was named its president in 1966.

Mr. Hott's son is the bank's director, Ernesto Hott Schwalm.

CHAPTER FOUR

Landlords and Capitalists

CAPITALISM is profoundly conditioned by the historical forms of landed property and the types of agrarian classes it confronts in its development, and this shapes the most basic features of a country's concrete "social formation." The latter is thus not only split into the constituent classes unique to capitalism, but also incorporates "strata of society which, though belonging to the antiquated mode of production, continue to exist side by side with it in gradual decay."[1]

More than a century ago, Karl Marx wrote that "wage-laborers, capitalists and landlords constitute the three great social classes," which "together and in their mutual opposition, form the framework of modern society." The British dominant class of the time was, in his words, an "antiquated compromise" between landed aristocracy and bourgeoisie, and that of Prussia one that, by subordinating itself to the "representatives of ancient society, the monarchy and the nobility, . . . had degenerated into a kind of estate."[2] But comparative analysis of the development of capitalism also reveals the decisive presence of landowners in other industrial countries. Japan and Germany are merely the best-known instances of the generic place of large landowners in the formative process of contemporary dominant classes. Even in France, where the lords of the soil had been formally abolished as an "estate" in the revolution of 1789, they continued to be at the core of the dominant class throughout the subsequent century. Similarly, in the United States, despite its lack of a feudal past, capitalism was compelled to absorb an agrarian slaveholding aristocracy, whose descendants left their own peculiar stamp on the dominant class. Thus, if the manifold process through which "economic" classes become "social" classes is a central issue in the theory of class, the relationships between, and the interpenetration of, landlords and capitalists is a critical problem in any analysis of the internal structure of the dominant class of contemporary capitalist countries.

[1] Marx 1967, III, p. 765.

[2] Marx 1967, III, pp. 886, 618; Marx and Engels 1953, p. 410; Marx and Engels 1958, I, p. 69.

Such an analysis also bears directly on another set of complex theoretical issues and substantive questions. For in the course of development of capitalism, the "agrarian question," and the specific nature of its resolution, particularly the cleavages and contradictions, coalitions and conflicts that have arisen among and between landlords and capitalists, has been of far-reaching historical importance. Varying in duration and timing from one country to another, there was a period during which these contending classes engaged in more or less continual struggle for social and political supremacy. They represented, as Max Weber remarks, "two social tendencies resting upon entirely heterogeneous bases . . . [wrestling] with each other."[3] Depending on the concrete historical conditions in each country—i.e. the particular pace, timing, and phase of capitalist development and its impact on the specific historical forms of landed property and on the types of agrarian relations, and how this coincided with the level of organization and political consciousness attained by workers and peasants in a given international situation—the resolution of the struggle of these contending classes for social hegemony has had differing, but always profound, significance. It has simultaneously shaped the pattern of capitalist development and the form, authoritarian or democratic, taken by the state.[4] The advent of military dictatorship and fascism in Chile in late 1973 was only the most recent verification of the fateful significance for democracy of an alliance between landlords and capitalists against workers and peasants.

Theories of Development

Contending theories of development in Latin America, in varying degrees and differing phraseology, largely derive from their own specific imagery of this historical process. For until quite recently, the thesis has prevailed among Communist, *Aprista*, and Social Democratic parties, as well as among liberal academic social scientists, that Latin America needs an "agrarian, antifeudal and national revolution." As Victor Alba, a Social Democratic proponent of the thesis, has put it: "What the Latin American who speaks of revolution would like to do is to establish a regime that is fundamentally *capitalistic* (that is, *opposed to the feudal regime of the landholding oligarchy*), politically democratic,

[3] Weber 1946, p. 373.

[4] See, for instance, Bendix 1964, chap. 6; Hilferding 1910, chap. 23; Moore 1966; Neumann 1944; Norman 1940; Smith 1961; Zeitlin 1984.

economically mixed (with both public and private investment, and state planning), and socially capable of integrating the inhabitants of each country into a national entity."[5] Communist theoreticians in Latin America have argued that eliminating "the remnants (or predominance) of feudal relations of production in the majority of the countries of Latin America" is a critical revolutionary objective. "The struggle against feudal survivals," it is explained, "is taken on by the proletariat from the standpoint of its own revolutionary aims, and this attitude explains why the national bourgeoisie must become an ally of the proletariat and not the reverse." Consequently, the struggle is not against "the bourgeoisie in general," as certain "ultra-leftists" maintain, but against *"the fundamental enemy*—imperialism and the *large landowning oligarchy*."[6]

Liberal theoreticians and academic social scientists have their own variants of this thesis, based on the underlying assumption, in Jacques Lambert's representative formulation, that "because of the dualistic nature of society, in the great majority of Latin American countries there are two hierarchies of classes [one in 'urban society,' the other in 'rural society'] which are completely separate from one another." Typically, however, they find that the urge toward "development" or "modernization" comes from unspecified "modern" groups or "sectors," or from so-called marginal or new "elites"; real social groups or collectivities are referred to in only the vaguest terms. Walt Whitman Rostow's formulation is typical: "the takeoff usually witnesses a definitive social, political, and cultural victory of those who would mobilize the economy over those who would either cling to the traditional society or seek other goals. . . . The victory can assume forms of mutual accommodation, rather than the destruction of the traditional groups by the more modern."[7]

This at least vague reference to real social actors often becomes transmogrified entirely into an opposition between disembodied forms of traditionality *vs.* modernity, normal *vs.* deviant psychological states, or ascriptive *vs.* achievement motivations.[8] Rarely, however, some reference is made to an identifiable group: "a new elite—a new leadership—must emerge and be given scope to begin the building of a modern industrial society. . . . Sociologically, this *new* elite must—to

[5] Alba 1969, p. 314, italics added; also see pp. 141, 151–152, 191.

[6] Mora 1966, p. 45; Giudici 1966, pp. 30, 41, italics added.

[7] Lambert 1967, p. 145; Rostow 1971, p. 58.

[8] Hoselitz 1960; Nash 1963; Hagen 1962; McLelland 1961.

a degree—supersede in social and political authority the *old land-based elite*."[9] In a standard formulation, academic social scientists have argued that the "middle sectors" must challenge the landed oligarchy and seek to reorganize the social and economic structure in accordance with their modern values.[10] Celso Furtado has expressed one variant of the thesis in the following words: "The leading elements of industrial capitalism have not realized that the parasitism of the semi-feudal agrarian sector tends to hamper the industrialization process. . . . Since the industrial class has failed to become aware of its conflicts with the agrarian class, it has no reason to judge this class on an independent scale of values."[11]

Similarly, John Gillin refers to a "social revolution underway in Latin America," in which a decisive role is played "in most countries [by] two upper classes. . . . One of these comprises the members of the old landowning aristocracy or its remnants. . . . The other is what may be called a new upper class, composed mainly of self-made men and their families and descendants . . . [which] runs or owns most of the larger business enterprises not controlled by foreign corporations. . . . The landed and the monied upper classes are often opposed in many of their interests. . . . In general, the new upper class is much more innovative from the outside world than is the landed upper class."[12] Federico Gil specifically applies this characterization to Chile's class structure: coexisting alongside the landowning class, he argues, is a "new upper class, not nearly so tightly closed as the landowners," and many of their interests are opposed. In his view, this new class favors "higher living standards and the increase of the population's ability to consume" and is "much more receptive to innovations and appreciative of technology than the old aristocracy," which "is chiefly concerned with preservation of the semi-feudalistic *latifundio* system."[13]

The same idea is expressed by José Cademartori (then a leading

[9] Rostow 1971, p. 26; italics added.

[10] J. Johnson 1958; Whitaker 1964.

[11] Furtado 1965, p. 118.

[12] Gillin 1958, pp. 14, 22–23. Cardoso's view on this issue is somewhat unclear. Although he notes (1966, p. 156) that Chile has "an active entrepreneurial elite," he also argues that Chile's industrialization requires "profound changes in the power pattern, but without the exclusion of the old entrepreneurial classes." He does insist, though, for countries lacking such an "entrepreneurial class," that "successful industrialization [requires] the formation of entrepreneurial elites with social origins different from those of the old dominant class," which may also depend "on a previous revolution."

[13] Gil 1966, p. 24.

theoretician of Chile's Communist party and a member of congress): "the working masses, the new middle strata, the *national bourgeoisie*, the *oligarchy*, and imperialism" constitute "the most adequate social categories" for the analysis of Chilean society. To the question "What type of revolution is necessary (*se plantea*) in Chile?" Cademartori's answer is: "an antifeudal, antioligarchic, and anti-imperialist revolution."[14] The Communists continued to hold this theory throughout Salvador Allende's aborted presidency. In November 1972, for instance, Miereya Baltra, then on the Communist party's central committee, declared that the *Unidad Popular* program "marks an anti-imperialist, antioligarchic, antifeudal transitional state."[15]

These otherwise apparently antagonistic theories of development in Latin America thus frequently share similar, if not identical, premises concerning the class structure. In particular, their common assumption is that there are, in reality, two distinguishable upper or dominant classes, variously called, on the one hand, "semifeudal," "agrarian," "landowning oligarchy," or "land-based elite," or, on the other, "national bourgeoisie," "middle sectors," " new elite," "industrial class," "new upper class," or "monied upper class."

In contrast, some theorists, principally non-Communist Marxists, have argued almost precisely the opposite. For instance, Luis Vitale, of the left wing of Chile's Socialist party, argues:

> the Latin American bourgeoisie was associated from the beginning with landholders. . . . Latin America is not a copy of nineteenth-century Europe, in which the new rising middle class had to overthrow feudalism to initiate the cycle of bourgeois democratic revolutions. . . . The Latin America that gained its independence from Spain was governed, not by a feudal oligarchy but by a bourgeoisie that, through its dependence on the world market, has contributed to the backwardness of the continent. This bourgeoisie is incapable of fulfilling the aims of democracy. . . . It is neither able nor desirous of achieving agrarian reform because all of the dominant classes are committed to the holding of land.[16]

[14] Cademartori 1968, pp. 277, 292; italics added. Writing of the "more well-to-do Latin American countries," Seymour Martin Lipset makes the same argument, though referring to a split not between a "new upper class" or an "antifeudal national bourgeoisie" and traditional landowners, but between a "growing middle class" and "anticapitalist traditionalists." "The growing middle class in these countries, like its nineteenth-century European counterpart, supports a democratic society by attempting to reduce the influence of the anticapitalist traditionalists" (1960, p. 138).

[15] Baltra 1973, p. 2073, as quoted in Plotke 1973.

[16] Vitale 1968, pp. 42–43.

Rodolfo Stavenhagen writes that "although the latifundist aristocracy was eliminated by revolutionary means in some Latin American countries (however, always by the people, never by the bourgeoisie), there does not seem to be a conflict of interests between the bourgeoisie and the oligarchy in the other countries. On the contrary, the agricultural, financial, and industrial interests are often found in the same economic groups, in the same companies, and even in the same families."[17]

To the question "What . . . is the class structure in Latin America and how is the anti-colonial and class struggle to proceed to socialism?" André Gunder Frank replies: "Far from asking how isolated and 'feudal' this rural 'oligarchy' is, we must inquire . . . to what extent in fact landed monopoly is owned by the same persons, families, or corporations as commercial and industrial monopoly."[18] This is roughly the leading empirical question of the present chapter; and we shall attempt to provide a reasonably precise answer, based on a systematic, quantitative analysis of the relationships, as of the mid-1960s, between landlords and capitalists in Chile.

Quantitative Analysis and Historical Specificity

Quantitative analysis of the social relations between landlords and capitalists tends to freeze them, so to speak, in abstraction from the actual historical processes of their formation. If not aesthetically pleasing, this is nonetheless analytically necessary in order to isolate specific and essential aspects of the class structure for empirical investigation. The present inquiry is, moreover, a venture in *discovery*, as well as in explanation. What is reliably known of the concrete relationships and inter-

[17] Stavenhagen 1968, p. 22. Some leading members of the Christian Democratic (PDC) left wing also shared this critique—as did, for instance, Manuel Valdés Solar, national director of the PDC's "peasant department," who was also a member of congress. In late 1966, he wrote: "It is often said that there is an accentuated conflict of interests between the new 'elite,' represented by the industrialists and modern entrepreneurs, and the traditional 'elite,' represented by the great landowners. But this conflict does not take place in Latin America, where, indeed, agricultural, industrial, and financial interests are almost always bound together in the same economic groups, in the same companies, and even in the same families. There is no reason why the 'national bourgeoisie' and the latifundist oligarchy should not understand each other; on the contrary, they complement each other well. And in those instances where possible conflicts of interests might arise (for instance, with respect to some legislation that benefits one class and harms another), the bourgeois State . . . can provide the injured sectors ample compensation" (Valdés Solar 1966, p. 7).

[18] Frank 1969, pp. 393–394, 399.

nal forms of differentiation of dominant classes under contemporary capitalism is so scant as to warrant every effort to grasp them empirically and quantitatively, especially because so much nonsense has been written about them.

Yet, making correct inferences from a quantitative analysis such as ours depends also on having detailed knowledge of the specific society and its history. So Barrington Moore is certainly right to observe, for instance, that a quantitative measure of the coalescence of landlords and capitalists by itself "tells us little about social anatomy and its workings." As he notes:

> In nineteenth-century Prussia the members of the bourgeoisie who became connected with the aristocracy generally absorbed the latter's habits and outlook. Rather the opposite relationship held in England. Thus if we did have a technically perfect measure of mobility that gave an identical numerical reading for the amount of fusion in England and Prussia, we would make a disastrous mistake in saying that the two countries were alike on this score. Statistics are misleading traps for the unwary reader when they abstract from the essence of the situation of the whole structural context in which social osmosis takes place.[19]

This is an important admonition.

Obviously, not merely the number of ties, but their substance, is crucial to understanding their meaning for "social anatomy and its workings." If, for instance, we found that capitalist families typically own large landed estates, any inference about the meaning of that fact would depend on our knowledge of the place of such landed estates in the political economy. The meaning of such landownership would scarcely be the same if landed estates were merely status-yielding rural retreats, rather than, as they are in Chile, enduring and profitable enterprises at the base of both economic and political power. But, even given this qualification, assessing the importance of given structural relationships also depends on knowing how prevalent they are. Instances of structural ties between landlords and capitalists will have

[19] Moore 1966, p. 37. Moore's own meaning is not entirely unambiguous; his discussion might also be read as an objection not merely to the misuse of statistics, but to their use per se in historical investigation. Whenever he finds it necessary to dispute historical interpretations that rest on quantitative evidence, however, Moore also brings his own quantitative evidence to bear or reinterprets the data presented by others. See, particularly, his discussion (1966, p. 509ff.) of statistics and conservative historiography.

quite different implications if they are marginal, rare, and exceptional rather than typical, extensive, and central.

Of course, to grasp their meaning fully, it is necessary to know not merely how a constellation of class relations is structured, but *how it came to be that way*. For class relations are shaped and reshaped in struggle, and not merely by their so-called objective place in the productive process. These struggles are no less "objective" realities, and they may be decisive in the formation of class and intraclass relations and in the demise or ascendance of classes and class segments. In Chile, two civil wars in the mid- and late nineteenth century were crucial in shaping the subsequent process of coalescence between landlords and capitalists, and in determining the present configuration of their relations. A separate work, Zeitlin's *The Civil Wars in Chile*, has been devoted to their analysis; but a few points bear emphasis here.

The accelerated accumulation of capital from the second third of the nineteenth century onward led to immense fortunes both for the emergent capitalists, in banking, trade, and especially mining (copper, silver, and coal), and for the great landed families who also prospered in the nation's vibrant export economy. But this also led to contradictions between them and, despite the intimacy of their social ties, led to now hidden, now open, and finally violent political struggles between them, which profoundly shaped the pattern of capitalist development in Chile and the formation of its dominant class. These struggles between landlords and capitalists in Chile, however, were never the result of a collision between feudalism and capitalism.

For Chile's agrarian relations were neither feudal nor capitalist but, rather, constituted a specific historical form of seignorial commodity production in agriculture that emerged when a "world-embracing commerce and a world-embracing market" already existed and when industrial capital was already ascendant in England, which stood astride world commerce. So, from the colonial period onward, agriculture produced for national, regional, and international markets. But the productive process was based neither on the employment of wage labor nor, to the contrary, on the coercive appropriation of the surplus product of petty producers possessing their own means of production. Even where the exploitative process in Chilean agriculture had the *appearance* of a "feudal" peasant-lord relationship, it was by no means a "survival." On the contrary, the peculiar historical form of seignorial exploitation of agrarian labor in the landed estate (*fundo*)—which involved production by tenants (*inquilinos*), who used the tools, machinery, equipment, supplies, as well as the land belonging to the landlord, in exchange for a parcel, dwelling, and minimal subsistence—was not the relic of a feudal past, but *the product of capitalist development.*

The landowners encroached on the lands of an earlier, relatively independent class of small cultivators and successfully converted them into a subordinate, landless tenantry producing on the great estates, in response to rising land values during the rapid growth in the production of wheat, cereals, and other foodstuffs for Chile's burgeoning metal-mining and nitrate areas and for transoceanic (mainly English) markets in the mid- to late nineteenth century. To consolidate this new manorial system of agrarian relations, armed revolutionary warfare threatening the domain of the owners of the Central Valley's vast estates had to be twice defeated in the 1850s.[20] To maintain and reinforce this system has been an unavoidable and enduring social objective of the great landed families and their allies ever since. They successfully maintained the social and political isolation of agrarian labor, secured state financial subsidies for agriculture, exempted their resident tenants and other workers from labor legislation and prevented them from securing the right to organize, even after the labor movement had become a major political force in mining and industry, and, above all, stymied all efforts at agrarian reform. Not until a century after the abortive revolutionary struggles of the 1850s did the landlords experience significant political setbacks or suffer any erosion of their hold on agrarian labor.

This deterioration in the political power of the dominant landed families came after a half century or more of deepening stagnation in agricultural production (for the copper-mining and then the nitrate-mining zones had declined drastically as major internal markets, and the industrial capitalist countries were now regularly supplying their own vast needs). Nonetheless, the landowners' secure base in agriculture, resting on their monopoly of most arable and irrigated land, guaranteed them continuing political power, even as they were increasingly challenged by reform elements, some drawn from their own ranks, and by the emergence, first, of a unified working-class movement led preponderantly by Communists and Socialists and, later, of allied peasant organizations.

But, as of the mid-1960s, the dominion of the large landed estate in Chile—a country then having one of the world's highest recorded lev-

[20] See Zeitlin 1984.

els of concentrated landownership[21]—was still relatively secure. This is the point at which we intercept Chile's landlords and capitalists, and attempt to analyze their qualitative structural interrelations in quantitative terms.

The Landlords

Our analysis of Chile's large landowners (*terratenientes*) is based on two official sources of data. First is a list, compiled by the agrarian reform institute (ICIRA), of the 968 legally independent proprietors-of-record of the 1,067 "great landed estates" in the Central Valley (running through the nine provinces from Aconcagua to Ñuble). After a detailed aerial-photographic survey of the Central Valley from 1960 to 1963, all landholdings had been classified area by area into seven categories of cultivable and nonarable land, and each holding or "parcel" (*predio*) had been converted into a sum of equivalent units of "basic irrigated hectares." The 1,067 estates each containing the equivalent of at least 150 hectares (1 hectare = 2.47 acres) of first-class agricultural land were identified as "fundos de gran potencial." These 1,067 "estates of great potential" (or "great estates" for short) amounted to 1.7 percent of all agricultural "holdings" in the Central Valley but held 46.9 percent of the 714,405 "basic irrigated hectares" contained by these holdings. The Central Valley, with only 29 percent of all of Chile's agricultural land and 39 percent of its arable land, held 76 percent of all irrigated landholdings. Second, aside from this extraordinarily rich source of data on the great-estate owners, we also utilized a list, compiled by the Department of Internal Revenue, that revealed the legal owners and *tax-assessed valuations* of all 1,848 agricultural properties in Chile that were worth E°40,000 or more as of *1961* (the only such data available for the 1960s).[22] These two lists were merged to provide one compilation of the nation's "landlords." Of the 1,848 large landholdings, 78.2 percent were in the Central Valley.

We assigned any estate owned as family "community property" (*comunidad*) to the individual whom our research identified as the dominant "partner" in the family. Using the precise estimates of first-class agricultural land held by each legal proprietor of the 1,067 great estates, we compiled sums for each individual and, in accord with our kinship research, also aggregated these sums for the various great

[21] Sternberg 1962, p. 34; CIDA 1966, p. 337.

[22] CIDA 1966, p. 44; ICIRA 1966; Dpto. de Impuestos Internos 1963.

landed families. We chose not to use the Department of Internal Revenue list of assessed valuations because of the notorious unreliability everywhere of such estimates. In fact, our random comparisons between the tax-assessed valuations and the estimates of first-class land in specific holdings showed many discrepancies and inconsistencies in these valuations; so, while the tax department's list of the largest landholdings was probably accurate, it did not provide reliable estimates of land values either in market terms or in comparison with other properties in the same jurisdictions.[23]

In the following tables on landownership, the individual's ownership of an estate on the tax list is indicated separately from the ownership of a "great estate," and the land value is measured in "basic irrigated hectares" (BIH). Readers should thus bear in mind that these sums are not measures of land *area*, but of relative *value*, and that the greater the proportion of an estate's land that is in lower categories, the greater the disparity between land value in BIH and the actual area of that estate. Indeed, typically, the number of basic irrigated hectares is considerably less than the actual area covered by an estate. Chile's agrarian reform institute, which calculated equivalent BIH units based on seven categories of land, completely excluded from its calculations all land not considered to be of agricultural use. Vast marginal dry lands and hilly regions, which constitute an important aspect of the land monopoly underlying the social domination of the landlords, were not included in the calculations. (Take, for example, the estate of Francisco Bulnes Correa, whom we met earlier as an officer or director in several of the top 37 nonfinancial corporations. Mr. Bulnes's landed estate in the municipality of Panquehue, in Aconcagua province, covered 3,948 hectares [or 14.7 square miles], of which 639 were irrigated.[24] On the agrarian reform institute's list, however, his estate contained only 312 BIH.) The mean size of the 1,067 great estates was, according to the agrarian reform institute, 302.5 BIH, with an average population of 227.5 inhabitants per estate. In all, 28 percent of the entire rural population of the Central Valley lived on these 1,067 great estates.

The universe of large landowners contained on our merged list closely approximates the actual population of large landowners; certainly the vast majority of its leading individuals are included. For purposes of this analysis, however, we selected a subuniverse of 132 "top

[23] Fellmeth 1973; Feder 1960; Sternberg 1962.
[24] Sternberg 1962, p. 182ff.

landowners" for systematic comparison with our two universes of officers and directors of the top 37 nonfinancials and Big Six banks. These 132 top landowners were the product of a combination of the original sampling steps and of refinements to the list as new information became available to us through our continuing research. Basically, though, the 132 top landowners were selected as follows. The 100 top *holdings* on the ICIRA list and the 100 top holdings on the internal revenue list were identified and compiled, and from these 200 holdings a random sample of 100 was selected, to which were also added any holdings among the top 50 on each list that had not already been drawn in the sample of 100. Some holdings, of course, appeared on both top-100 lists, and some holdings shown on two lists were owned by the same individual. After taking account of these anomalies, and making other refinements based on our investigation of the entire list of 1,067 great estates, we ended up with our ranked list of 132 "top landowners."[25]

What, then, do these data reveal of the structural connections between landlords and capitalists in Chile? Are the nation's leading businessmen—whom the International Committee of Chambers of Commerce of the United States called "members of the select company of men who are part of the mainstream of twentieth-century capitalism"—and its great landlords related? How and to what extent are Chile's supposedly benighted landed oligarchs related to these "representatives of enlightened Latin American capitalism"?[26]

In order to answer this question, our analysis proceeds through a series of successive approximations attempting to grasp the inner relations of Chile's dominant class, both to convey their richly complex structure and to measure them quantitatively. Conceptually, the empirical question is whether Chile's landlords and capitalists are, as is widely assumed, separate and contending *classes* or, as we suggest, *segments* of the same internally differentiated, yet peculiarly cohesive, class. Such "class segments," as we call them, while owning the means of production—land and capital—in common, are differently located in the productive process as a whole. Marked off by "specific conditions of production" and by ownership of "different kinds of property," segments of the dominant class must nonetheless strive to protect and advance "the common class interest without giving up their

[25] For more procedural details, see Appendix to this chapter.

[26] Nehemkis 1964, p. 220.

mutual rivalry."[27] Class segments consequently have the inherent potential of developing their own specific variants of "intraclass consciousness" and common action vis-á-vis each other as well as against other contending classes. But how and to what extent their varying intraclass situations actually become manifest politically depends on the particular combination of concrete interests, specific historical circumstances, and structural relations—especially those differentiating or integrating the various class segments. In this chapter, we explore and reveal the structural relations between landlords and capitalists in detail; in the next, we try to gauge their political relevance.

Bankers, Corporate Executives, and Landowners

Our analysis of the structural relations between landlords and capitalists proceeds in two steps. As a first approximation to "capitalists," we focus on the higher functionaries of capital, i.e. the leading bankers and the higher executives of the top nonfinancial corporations, and explore their landowning relations and actual landed wealth. We then assess the bearing of capital ownership on these landowning relations; that is to say, we analyze the interconnections among the principal owners of capital, the higher functionaries of capital, and the great landowners.

Our analysis begins with a "simple" empirical question: How many of the higher executives of the 6 biggest commercial banks and the top 37 nonfinancial corporations are personally top landowners? Of the 68 "bankers," as we call them for short, only 7 are top landowners, and of the 229 corporate executives, only 13 are; or, conversely, of the 132 top landowners, only 16 of them are also bankers or corporate executives. When we consider, however, not merely the "top" landowners, but all owners of large estates, the proportion of bankers and corporate executives who are personally landlords more than doubles: 16 bankers (nearly 24 percent) and 29 of the corporate executives (13 percent) personally own large estates. In Table 4.1, the ownership of a large estate included on the all-Chile tax list is indicated separately from the ownership of a "great estate" in the Central Valley (of a given size, or number of basic irrigated hectares).

Of course, for reasons discussed in detail in Chapter 2, the crucial question in an analysis of class integration is the relationship between the property and kinship systems: i.e. not merely what individuals in

[27] See Marx 1948, pp. 100–110; 1963, pp. 27, 47; 1965, pp. 21–42; pp. 8–9, n. 6, above.

TABLE 4.1. Percentage of Higher Executives of the Big Six Commercial Banks and the Top 37 Nonfinancial Corporations in Chile Who Own a Specified Amount of Land in Great Estates, 1964/66

			BIH Owned[b]			
	No Land	Other Estates[a]	150–499	500–999	1,000-plus	(*N*)
Bankers	76	7	10	4	1	(68)
Corporate executives	87	3	7	1	2	(229)

NOTE: The "great estates" are the 1,067 "fundos de gran potencial" from the agrarian reform institute's list of Central Valley landholdings (ICIRA 1966).

[a] These estates, on the all-Chile internal revenue list (Dpto. de Impuestos Internos 1963), do not appear on the Central Valley list of "great estates."

[b] All agricultural lands on each "great estate" have been converted into "basic irrigated hectares" (BIH). See text.

decisive locations in the economy own personally, but what their families own as well. Are the leading bankers and the higher executives of the top 37 corporations members of landed families? For, as we noted earlier, quoting Lundberg, it is "quite arbitrary in many cases to speak of a person as representing a single fortune," when, in fact, each owns "a slice from a single source."[28] Kinship analysis makes it possible both to delineate the class situation of individuals with some precision and to measure the concentration of land ownership and capital ownership within specific families and within the owning class as a whole. Because our method of measuring kinship distance allows us to specify the center and boundary of each effective kinship unit, the extent of concentration of ownership can be measured for the immediate, secondary, close, and even more distant family. If the known relatives of several persons were counted irrespective of the distance between them and their relatives, the resulting "families" of these persons would not be comparable, and the findings based on such a count would be uninformative if not seriously misleading. "Bigger" family groups (i.e. those with many identified relatives at unknown distances from each other) would tend, ipso facto, to have more property even if, in fact (once precise comparisons were possible), they turn out to have less property than genuinely comparable kinship units.[29] So, to measure

[28] Lundberg 1968, p. 163.

[29] This, for example, is the problem with the analysis of the 82 "family groups" identified by José Luis de Imaz (1970) among Argentina's major landowners. These are not comparable kinship units, as he himself acknowledges. Imaz identified them only by their shared "basic surnames," so there is no way of knowing how closely or distantly related they are, which relatives are included in or excluded from a "family

the concrete interests and ensemble of social relations linking the bankers, corporate executives, and landowners, we constructed two sets of indicators: (1) the individual's total number of relatives, in the immediate, secondary, and close family, who are among the 968 owners-of-record of the 1,067 great estates of central Chile; and (2) the aggregate number of basic irrigated hectares owned by the individual and these relatives at the same three kinship distances.[30]

Taking into account land in the family results in a substantial increase in the measurable mutual integration between bankers and corporate executives, on the one hand, and large landowners, on the other. This is especially clear when all close relatives are considered: among the bankers, precisely one-third, and among the corporate executives nearly one-third, have close relatives who are personally on the list of 968 owners of the nation's great landed estates. All told, 43 percent of the bankers and 36 percent of the corporate executives either own a "large" or a "great" estate or have close relatives—often several—who personally own one. And of those whose family owns a great estate, the majority own one of the most valuable estates: for instance, 26 of the 68 bankers belong to a close family that owns one or more great estates, of whom 15 (58 percent) have a combined total of 1,000 or more BIH; and among the 229 corporate executives, 81 are in a close landed family, of whom 42 (52 percent) are in that same category. (See Tables 4.2 and 4.3.)

That as many as a sixth of the corporate executives and a fifth of the bankers have three or more close relatives who own great landed estates is merely a minimum measure of the extent and density of the

group," or even if they are really related at all. While acknowledging the imprecision of his methods ("members of the groups may be only distantly related"), Imaz nevertheless uses these "basic family groups" as a means to analyze the integration of the ownership of agricultural and nonagricultural enterprises. In the United States, Ferdinand Lundberg's pathbreaking study of "America's 60 families" (1946) was not systematic; that is to say, he did not compile the same data on each person or family and attempt to analyze those data and generalize from them. And, as C. Wright Mills notes in detail (1956, p. 377), "Lundberg's list . . . is not uniformly made up of families or individuals or companies, but is a miscellany."

[30] There are several individuals who jointly own a single landed estate or a group of estates with their siblings or other immediate relatives. In such cases, each of the individuals has been credited with owning the *total amount of land* included in these estates, but the co-owners of the estates are *not* counted as immediate landowning relatives. In this way, each of these individuals appears as the owner of an estate, but as having no immediate estate-owning relatives—unless, of course, he actually has *other* immediate relatives who own other estates. Where two or more close relatives of a banker or corporate executive jointly own a great estate, it has been assigned to the owner most closely related to him.

TABLE 4.2. Percentage of Higher Executives of the Big Six Commercial Banks and the Top 37 Nonfinancial Corporations in Chile with a Specified Number of Great-Estate Owners in the Family, 1964/66

		Landowners in Immediate Family			
	No Land	1–2	3–4	5-plus	(*N*)
Bankers	72	28	0	0	(68)
Corporate executives	81	18	1	0	(229)
		Landowners in Secondary Family			
	No Land	1–2	3–4	5-plus	(*N*)
Bankers	65	28	7	0	(68)
Corporate executives	74	21	5	0	(229)
		Landowners in Close Family			
	No Land	1–2	3–4	5-plus	(*N*)
Bankers	57	23	10	10	(68)
Corporate executives	64	20	11	5	(229)

NOTE: See Table 4.1 for definition of "great estates." Estates on the all-Chile internal revenue list (Dpto. de Impuestos Internos 1963) owned personally by bankers or corporate executives are also included here (see Table 4.3).

entangling kinship alliances between them and the great landowners. For around each of the close landed relatives of a banker or a corporate executive there is also ordinarily another set of intimate landowning kindred, constituting a cohesive and enduring community of landed privilege and power. Because we have limited the kinship distance considered to the "close family," however, this integral propertied community has barely been touched upon by our quantitative analysis so far. It will be remembered that collateral relatives far more distant than those within three "links" in our system of measuring kinship distance are considered to be close relatives in Western canon and common law. A first cousin, for instance, is three links away from Ego in our system, but only two degrees away from Ego in common and canon law; a second cousin is five links from Ego, but only three degrees in common and canon law. So far, therefore, we have not counted many collateral relatives—and their landed property—that are considered "close" by Western law and custom.

The "Maximum Kinship Group"

As the cumulative result of our actual kinship investigations, we were struck by how thoroughly Chile's bankers and corporate executives are surrounded by close lineal and collateral landowning relatives, and

TABLE 4.3. Percentage of Higher Executives of the Big Six Commercial Banks and the Top 37 Nonfinancial Corporations[a] in Chile Whose Families Own a Specified Amount of Land in Great Estates, 1964/66

	No Land	Individuals Own Other Estates[b]	BIH Owned in Immediate Family[c] 150–999	1,000–1,999	2,000-plus	(N)
Bankers	72	7	16	3	1	(68)
Corporate executives	81	3	12	4	0	(229)

	No Land	Individuals Own Other Estates[b]	BIH Owned in Secondary Family[c] 150–999	1,000–1,999	2,000-plus	(N)
Bankers	65	6	21	4	4	(68)
Corporate executives	74	2	15	6	4	(229)

	No Land	Individuals Own Other Estates[b]	BIH Owned in Close Family[c] 150–999	1,000–1,999	2,000-plus	(N)
Bankers	57	4	16	9	13	(68)
Corporate executives	64	1	17	9	9	(229)

[a] Referred to in following tables as "bankers" and "corporate executives," respectively.

[b] These estates, on the all-Chile internal revenue list (Dpto. de Impuestos Internos 1963), do not appear on the Central Valley list of "great estates."

[c] "Basic irrigated hectares" (BIH) of all "great estates" owned by individuals or by their families at the specified kinship distance.

we realized that the preceding indicators and tables do not adequately convey that complex fusion of kinship and property relations. In a sense, there is a sort of hidden exponential kinship function; for, as the number of an individual's close landholding relatives increases, even to two or three, then many other landowners closely related to the latter appear. Yet, as we have emphasized, our criteria for close kinship have excluded and left them uncounted thus far, even though they are undoubtedly integral members of the individual banker's or corporate executive's propertied kindred.

So, if one is to grasp the actual *structure* of that ensemble of kinship relations in which bankers, corporate executives, and landowners are located, even a focus on the individual's family is inadequate. What one needs is a method that can get at the *integral structure of intimate interrelationships formed among freely intermarrying propertied families*. We have therefore conceptualized a cluster of intermarried families located at the "commanding heights" of the economy as a "maximum kinship group," and defined it operationally in the present analysis as consisting of at least two families that are closely related through one or more individuals in any of the three universes of leading bankers, higher corporate executives, and top landowners. All maximum kinship groups are, by definition, unrelated to each other; i.e. they are mutually exclusive clusters of closely interrelated *families*, even though all the *individuals* in a cluster are not necessarily closely related.

Our procedures for establishing the boundaries and composition of specific maximum kinship groups were as follows. First, a given maximum kinship group includes all individuals among the bankers, corporate executives, and top landowners who are either a "close relative" of at least one other individual in any of these three universes or a relative of at least one, within *four* links. Second, also included in that same maximum kinship group are all individuals in these universes who share any relative, within four links distance of each of them. Obviously, by these criteria it is possible for concrete maximum kinship groups to vary greatly both in size and internal structure, i.e. in the actual number of individual members and in the types of relationships tying them together. Of course, it is also possible for a banker, corporate executive, or top landowner to have no relatives or relatives in common (within four links) among the other bankers, corporate executives, or top landowners. If so, such an individual belongs, by definition, to an "unrelated family" rather than to a "maximum kinship group," which, as we said earlier, must consist of at least two interrelated families.

The size (number of individuals) and composition (specific member families) of the 24 maximum kinship groups that our investigations disclosed are given in Tables 4.4 and 4.5. We found that a substantial proportion of the bankers, corporate executives, and top landowners (varying between two-fifths and one-half) are in "unrelated families." But what is now immediately evident is the existence of what we shall call the "central core": a single maximum kinship group comprising close to 40 percent of the individuals *in each universe*. In marked contrast, only 1 other maximum kinship group contains more than 5 percent of the individuals in any universe, namely the Yarur-Hirmas-Saíd group of interrelated Arab-Chilean families, which includes 8 percent of the corporate executives (but only 3 percent of the top landowners and 1 percent of the bankers).

Some individuals, as we know, appear simultaneously at the commanding heights of more than one of our economic sectors, so that there are actually only 383 individuals in the three overlapping universes, of whom 172 are in unrelated families and 211 are in the 24 maximum kinship groups. Table 4.5 shows how they are distributed across the "pure types" of subuniverses: 137 of the 383, or 36 percent,

TABLE 4.4. Percentage of Chilean Bankers, Corporate Executives, and Top Landowners Who Are in the Central Core, Unrelated Families, and Specific Maximum Kinship Groups, 1964/66

	Bankers	Corporate Executives	Top Landowners[a]
Individuals in unrelated families	49	44	37
Central core	38	36	39
Azócar Álvarez–Bustamante Pinto	0	0	2
Cattan Davique	0	0	2
Correa Armanet–Encina Armanet	0	0	2
Díaz Boneu	0	1	0
Donoso–Vicuña Correa[b]	0	0	2
Fernández Zegers	0	0	1
García Vela–Picó Cañas–Domínguez Rielo	3	1	0
Hott–Hoelck Buhler	4	0	0
Lira Vergara–Ruiz Tagle de Conrads[b]	0	0	2
Mardones Restat[b]	1	1	0
Marín Larraín–Estevez	0	0	2
Meller Gram	1	0	0
Murillo-Nebel-Soffia	0	1	0
Petrinovic Wadsworth	0	0	2
Riesco[b]	0	0	2
Ruiz	0	0	2
Schmutzer	0	1	0
Serrano Mahns–Mahns Choupay–Gildemeister Becherel[b]	0	2	0
Simonetti-Barbaglia	0	2	0
Sotta Barros–Rodríguez de la Sotta	1	0	0
Sumar	0	2	0
Urrutia	0	0	2
Yarur-Hirmas-Saíd	1	8	3
N	(68)	(229)	(132)

[a] Some of these "top landowners" are not owners of "great estates" (see Table 4.1), but do own estates on the all-Chile internal revenue list (Dpto. de Impuestos Internos 1963).

[b] Inconclusive data suggest that the families constituting these maximum kinship groups are, in fact, also members of the central core.

turn out to belong to the huge central core itself. All other maximum kinship groups, except the Yarur-Hirmas-Saíd group, which consists of 18 men, have no more than 4 members, and most (14 of the 24) have only 2.

The "Central Core" of the Dominant Class

The "central core," we have discovered, is a cluster of interrelated families among whom the ownership of much of Chile's land is con-

TABLE 4.5. Number of Individuals in "Pure Types" of Subuniverses of Chilean Bankers, Corporate Executives, and Top Landowners Who Are in the Central Core, Unrelated Families, and Specific Maximum Kinship Groups, 1964/66

	Total Individuals in Group	Bankers Only	Corporate Executives Only	Top Landowners[a] Only	Bankers and Top Landowners	Corporate Executives and Top Landowners	Bankers and Corporate Executives	Bankers, Corporate Executives, and Top Landowners
Individuals in unrelated families	172	20	91	48	2		10	1
Central core	137	9	61	45	1	5	13	3
Azócar Álvarez–Bustamante Pinto	2	0	0	2	0	0	0	0
Cattan Davique	2	0	0	2	0	0	0	0
Correa Armanet–Encina Armanet	2	0	0	2	0	0	0	0
Díaz Boneu	2	0	2	0	0	0	0	0
Donoso–Vicuña Correa[b]	4	0	1	3	0	0	0	0
Fernández Zegers	2	0	1	1	0	0	0	0
García Vela–Picó Cañas–Domínguez Rielo	3	1	1	0	0	0	1	0
Hott–Hoelck Buhler	3	3	0	0	0	0	0	0
Lira Vergara–Ruiz Tagle de Conrads[b]	2	0	0	2	0	0	0	0
Mardones Restat[b]	2	0	1	0	0	0	1	0
Marín Larraín–Estévez	3	0	0	3	0	0	0	0
Meller Gram	2	1	1	0	0	0	0	0
Murillo–Nebel–Soffia	3	0	3	0	0	0	0	0
Petrinovic Wadsworth	2	0	0	2	0	0	0	0
Riesco[b]	2	0	0	2	0	0	0	0
Ruiz	2	0	0	2	0	0	0	0
Schmutzer	2	0	2	0	0	0	0	0

TABLE 4.5. Number of Individuals in "Pure Types" of Subuniverses of Chilean Bankers, Corporate Executives, and Top Landowners Who Are in the Central Core, Unrelated Families, and Specific Maximum Kinship Groups, 1964/66 (*cont.*)

	Total Individuals in Group	Bankers Only	Corporate Executives Only	Top Landowners[a] Only	Bankers and Top Landowners	Corporate Executives and Top Landowners	Bankers and Corporate Executives	Bankers, Corporate Executives, and Top Landowners
Serrano Mahns–Mahns Choupay–Gildemeister Becherel[b]	4	0	4	0	0	0	0	0
Simonetti–Barbaglia	4	0	4	0	0	0	0	0
Sotta Barros–Rodríguez de la Sotta	2	1	1	0	0	0	0	0
Sumar	4	0	4	0	0	0	0	0
Urrutia	2	0	0	2	0	0	0	0
Yarur–Hirmas–Saíd	18	0	13	0	0	4	1	0
N	(383)	(35)	(190)	(116)	(3)	(9)	(26)	(4)

[a] Some of these "top landowners" are not owners of "great estates" (see Table 4.1), but do own estates on the all-Chile internal revenue list (Dpto. de Impuestos Internos 1963).

[b] Inconclusive data suggest that the families constituting these maximum kinship groups are, in fact, also members of the central core.

centrated. No other maximum kinship group has even one-tenth as many of the top landowners. And, of course, we wish to emphasize that, as the earlier detailed description of our methods makes clear, the methods used to select the top landowners (as well as the bankers and corporate executives) and to determine the kinship relations among individuals in each universe were entirely independent of each other.

For descriptive historical purposes, and in order to document the centrality of the central core within Chile's dominant class as a whole, we have listed in Table 4.6 detailed information on the landownership of the specific maximum kinship groups that own at least 1,000 BIH in the great estates of the Central Valley. The landholdings included in Table 4.6 are owned by bankers, corporate executives, or top landowners or by a relative (or relatives) belonging to the maximum kinship group. Nearly all of the land belonging to these 20 great-landowning maximum kinship groups lies within estates owned by the banker's, executive's, or top landowner's close family. (Only 4,788 BIH of the 140,893 BIH, i.e. 3.4 percent, in Table 4.6 are owned by 15 "distant" relatives who are *exactly* four kinship links away from 1 or more of the bankers, corporate executives, or top landowners, and the latter all belong to the central core.)

These 20 great-landowning maximum kinship groups own 117,989 BIH—a sum amounting to 35.7 percent of *all* BIH owned by the great estates. But the central core of interrelated banking, corporate, and top landowning families alone owns 81,418 BIH, or 24.3 percent of all BIH in the great estates (see Table 4.6, cols. X and XI).

This latter sum also amounts to 58 percent of the total BIH owned by the 20 great-landowning maximum kinship groups and by the other, lesser landowning maximum kinship groups and unrelated families—although the 137 individual bankers, corporate executives, and top landowners belonging to central core families constitute, as noted earlier (see Table 4.5), "only" 36 percent of all 383 such individuals.

A significant structural feature of landownership in the central core, however, is the finding that much of its land is held by owners of great estates who do not rank among the "top landowners." Thus, of the 137 bankers, corporate executives, and top landowners in the central core, 52 are top landowners (see Table 4.6, cols. I and III); in addition, 9 more of them own great estates (though not "top" ones) (see col. IV), as do 131 of their close family members and other relatives (see col. VII). In comparison, the other great-landowning

TABLE 4.6. Maximum Kinship Groups in Chile That Own 1,000 Basic Irrigated Hectares (BIH) or More in Great Estates, 1964/66

	(I) Number of Bankers, Corporate Executives, and Top Landowners in Kinship Group	(II) Universes Represented in Kinship Group[a]	(III) Number of Top Landowners Owning Great Estates[b]	(IV) BIH Held by Top Landowners	(V) Number Of Other Bankers and Corporate Executives Owning Great Estates[c]	(VI) BIH Held by Other Bankers and Corporate Executives	(VII) Number of Other Family Members Owning Great Estates[d]	(VIII) BIH Held by Other Family Members	(IX) Total Great-Estate Owners in Kinship Group	(X) Total BIH Held by Kinship Group	(XI) Kinship Group BIH as % of All BIH in Great Estates[e]	(XII) Kinship Group BIH as % of All BIH in Central Valley Estates[f]
Central Core	137	L-B-C	52	39,192	9	2,104	131	40,122	192	81,418	24.3	11.4
Marin Larraín–Estévez	3	L	3	3,718	0	0	0	0	3	3,718	1.1	.5
Urrutia	2	L	2	964	0	0	8	2,368	10	3,332	1.0	.5
Donoso–Vicuña Correa[g]	4	L-C	3	2,064	0	0	4	1,022	7	3,086	.9	.4
Lira Vergara–Ruiz Tagle[g]	2	L	1	676	0	0	6	1,984	7	2,660	.8	.4
Riesco[g]	2	L	2	939	0	0	5	1,436	7	2,375	.7	.3
López López, A.	1	L	1	2,303	0	0	0	0	1	2,303	.7	.3
Palma Eguiguren, E.[g]	1	L	1	2,121	0	0	0	0	1	2,121	.6	.3
Correa Armanet–Encina Armanet	2	L	2	1,778	0	0	1	304	3	2,082	.6	.3
Correa Larraín, E.[g]	1	L-B	1	1,373	0	0	2	470	3	1,843	.5	.2
Cattan Davique	2	L	2	1,490	0	0	1	196	3	1,686	.5	.2

Infante Valdés, S.[g]	1	L	1	734	0	0	3	950	4	1,684	.5	.2
Ruiz Tagle	2	L	2	1,545	0	0	0	0	2	1,545	.5	.2
Azócar Álvarez–Bustamante Pinto	2	L	2	1,357	0	0	0	0	2	1,357	.4	.2
Campos Valenzuela, E.	1	L	1	971	0	0	1	301	2	1,272	.4	.2
Prado de Infante, J.	1	L	1	1,236	0	0	0	0	1	1,236	.4	.2
Yarur–Hirmas–Saíd	18	L-B-C	4	1,146	0	0	0	0	4	1,146	.3	.1
Mujica López, H.	1	L	1	705	0	0	1	376	2	1,081	.3	.1
Pizarro Espínola, J.	1	L	1	1,041	0	0	0	0	1	1,041	.3	.1
Nuñez Casanova, M.	1	L	1	520	0	0	1	483	2	1,003	.3	.1
Other families and maximum kinship groups, owning fewer than 1,000 BIH			39	20,594	3	784	6	1,526	48	22,904	6.3	3.0
TOTAL	185		123	86,467	12	2,888	170	51,538	305	140,893	42.0[h]	19.0[h]

[a] This column shows whether the kinship group includes top landowners (L), bankers (B), corporate executives (C), or any combination of these universes.

[b] Some "top landowners" are not owners of "great estates" (See Table 4.1) but do own estates on the all-Chile internal revenue list (Dpto. de Impuestos Internos 1963).

[c] "Other bankers and corporate executives" refers to bankers and corporate executives in the kinship group who are not top landowners.

[d] "Other family members" are not themselves in any of the three universes, but are within four kinship links of at least one banker, corporate executive, or top landowner. Of the 170 individuals included here, only 15 are outside the close family of at least one top landowner, banker, or corporate executive.

[e] The percentage of all 335,056 BIH owned by the great estates in the Central Valley.

[f] The percentage of all 714,405 BIH owned by all agricultural "holdings" in the Central Valley.

[g] Inconclusive data suggest that these families are, in fact, also members of the central core kinship group.

[h] Percentages in this column do not quite add up to the total percentage because of rounding.

maximum kinship groups typically have few great estates aside from the "top" ones that originally put one or more of their members in the "top landowner" universe. Of the 305 great-estate owners represented among the great-landowning maximum kinship groups and the other, lesser landowning maximum kinship groups and unrelated families, 192, or 63 percent, are in the central core itself (see col. IX).

What is the internal structure of the central core? The methods used to discover and delineate the maximum kinship groups allowed for immense variation in their actual composition. Conceivably, in the first place, what we have been calling the "central core" could, in fact, be merely an aggregate of distantly related individuals, rather than a cluster of closely intermarried families having multiple kinship bonds with each other. Secondly, even if the families in this core are closely related, they might be demarcated from each other by the types of property they own, rather than typically owning, as is the issue here, both land and capital. Given its immense size, the central core might, that is, still have a considerable distance between the "landowning" and "landless" families within it. If either, let alone both, of these features—a loose aggregate of related individuals, some of whom are landowners and some of whom are not—is true of our central core, then it is not really central in the economy or at the core of the dominant class.

Within the central core, then, how closely intertwined are the families of the bankers and corporate executives, on the one hand, and the landowning families, on the other? And what is the distribution of landed wealth within it in comparison to that in the other maximum kinship groups and in the unrelated families? (In the following tables, the various maximum kinship groups outside the central core are grouped within a single category, because they are too small to be analyzed separately. Tables 4.8 and 4.9 are in several parts, allowing landownership comparisons at increasing kinship distances, ranging from the immediate family to the entire close family.)

Many more of the bankers and corporate executives in the central core personally own landed estates than do their peers in other maximum kinship groups and in unrelated families. In the central core, 39 percent of the bankers and 25 percent of the corporate executives own landed estates; among those in other kinship groups, however, the figures on landownership are zero for the bankers and 9 percent for the executives; and among unrelated families the respective figures are 18 percent and 5 percent (see Table 4.7).

What is a crucial discovery, however, is that great landowners are pervasive among the families of the bankers and corporate executives in the central core; outside the core, in marked contrast, there are comparatively few close family ties among the bankers, corporate executives, and landlords. The overwhelming majority of the banking and corporate families in the central core, in fact, are also great landowning families, while outside the core only a small fraction of them are. Thus, for instance, in the maximum kinship groups outside the central core, only 13 percent of the corporate executives are in a close landed family, and none includes more than two landowners; among those in unrelated families, the comparable figure is 9 percent, and, again, none has more than two close landed relatives. Among the bankers in the non-core maximum kinship groups, none owns a landed estate and none has a landowner within his close family. Nearly a fifth of the bankers in unrelated families have someone in the close family who owns a great estate; usually, however, that landowner is the banker himself.

The pattern is vastly different, however, in the central core: 50 percent of the bankers, and 39 percent of the corporate executives, have landowners in their *immediate* family; the figures increase to 69 percent and 58 percent, respectively, for the secondary family, and to 89 percent and 81 percent, respectively, for the entire close family. Furthermore, unlike the bankers and corporate executives in other maximum kinship groups and unrelated families, those in the central core typi-

TABLE 4.7. Percentage of Chilean Bankers and Corporate Executives in the Central Core, Other Maximum Kinship Groups, and Unrelated Families Who Own a Specified Amount of Land in Great Estates, 1964/66

			BIH Owned		
	No Land	Other Estates	150–999	1,000-plus	(*N*)
Central core					
bankers	62	8	31	0	(26)
corporate executives	74	6	18	1	(82)
Other kinship groups					
bankers	100	0	0	0	(9)
corporate executives	91	0	0	9	(45)
Unrelated families					
bankers	81	9	6	3	(33)
corporate executives	95	2	3	0	(102)

BIH = "basic irrigated hectares."

cally have *many* close landowning relatives: nearly half of the corporate executives (45 percent) and well over half of the bankers (54 percent) in the central core have three or more close relatives who are great landowners. (See Tables 4.8a, 4.8b, and 4.8c.)

The concentration of land is also unsurpassed in the central core, where 54 percent of the bankers and 45 percent of the corporate executives belong to a close family owning 1,000 or more BIH, in contrast

TABLE 4.8a. Percentage of Chilean Bankers and Corporate Executives in the Central Core, Other Maximum Kinship Groups, and Unrelated Families Who Have a Specified Number of Great-Estate Owners in the Immediate Family, 1964/66

		Landowners in Family		
	No Land	1–2	3-plus	(*N*)
Central core				
bankers	50	50	0	(26)
corporate executives	61	37	2	(82)
Other kinship groups				
bankers	100	0	0	(9)
corporate executives	89	11	0	(45)
Unrelated families				
bankers	82	18	0	(33)
corporate executives	94	6	0	(102)

NOTE: Estates on the all-Chile internal revenue list (Dpto. de Impuestos Internos 1963) owned personally by bankers or corporate executives are also included here (see Table 4.3).

TABLE 4.8b. Percentage of Chilean Bankers and Corporate Executives in the Central Core, Other Maximum Kinship Groups, and Unrelated Families Who Have a Specified Number of Great-Estate Owners in the Secondary Family, 1964/66

		Landowners in Family		
	No Land	1–2	3-plus	(*N*)
Central core				
bankers	31	50	19	(26)
corporate executives	42	44	14	(82)
Other kinship groups				
bankers	100	0	0	(9)
corporate executives	89	11	0	(45)
Unrelated families				
bankers	82	18	0	(33)
corporate executives	93	7	0	(102)

NOTE: See Table 4.8a, note.

TABLE 4.8c. Percentage of Chilean Bankers and Corporate Executives in the Central Core, Other Maximum Kinship Groups, and Unrelated Families Who Have a Specified Number of Great-Estate Owners in the Close Family, 1964/66

	No Land	Landowners in Family			(*N*)
		1–2	3–4	5-plus	
Central core					
bankers	11	35	27	27	(26)
corporate executives	19	36	30	15	(82)
Other kinship groups					
bankers	100	0	0	0	(9)
corporate executives	87	13	0	0	(45)
Unrelated families					
bankers	82	18	0	0	(33)
corporate executives	91	9	0	0	(102)

NOTE: See Table 4.8a, note.

with barely 3 percent of all 189 other bankers and corporate executives. So, this is, indeed, a discovery of great import: an incomparably large effective kinship unit, formed of multiply intermarried banking, industrial, and landowning families, erases any ostensible social cleavages between supposedly contending landowning vs. capitalist "upper" classes in these economic sectors; further, within the central core are the nation's preponderant landed families, possessing among them unparalleled concentrations of the most valuable agricultural land encompassed by the great estates. (For detailed comparisons of the amount of land in great estates owned within the immediate through close family by persons in the central core, other kinship groups, and unrelated families, see Tables 4.9a, 4.9b, and 4.9c.)

What remains to be examined, however, is the extent to which the nation's capitalists and landlords are one; for, in our analysis thus far, with its exploration of the complex relationships between the leading banking and corporate families, on the one hand, and the great landed families, on the other, the relevance of the ownership (rather than the management) of capital has not yet been considered. The careers, interests, and overriding commitments of the bankers and higher executives of the top 37 nonfinancial corporations are bound to the expansion of corporate capital; in this sense, they are surely "capitalists." Further, as our earlier analysis has revealed, they and the principal owners of capital are also tied together by an intricate web of entangling kinship alliances, and, by this clear-cut index and surest

TABLE 4.9a. Percentage of Chilean Bankers and Corporate Executives in the Central Core, Other Maximum Kinship Groups, and Unrelated Families Whose Immediate Families Own a Specified Amount of Land in Great Estates, 1964/66

			BIH Owned		
	No Land	Other Estates	150–999	1,000-plus	(*N*)
Central core					
bankers	50	8	35	8	(26)
corporate executives	61	5	27	7	(82)
Other kinship groups					
bankers	100	0	0	0	(9)
corporate executives	89	2	9	0	(45)
Unrelated families					
bankers	82	9	6	3	(33)
corporate executives	94	2	4	0	(102)

BIH = "basic irrigated hectares."

TABLE 4.9b. Percentage of Chilean Bankers and Corporate Executives in the Central Core, Other Maximum Kinship Groups, and Unrelated Families Whose Secondary Families Own a Specified Amount of Land in Great Estates, 1964/66

			BIH Owned			
	No Land	Other Estates	150–999	1,000–1,999	2,000-plus	(*N*)
Central core						
bankers	31	4	46	8	11	(26)
corporate executives	42	2	35	11	10	(82)
Other kinship groups						
bankers	100	0	0	0	0	(9)
corporate executives	89	2	9	0	0	(45)
Unrelated families						
bankers	82	9	6	3	0	(33)
corporate executives	93	2	5	0	0	(102)

BIH = "basic irrigated hectares."

determinant, belong to the same social class. Nonetheless, the empirical question remains: How and to what extent are those who are unambiguously among Chile's preeminent capitalists—those higher executives of the top 37 nonfinancial corporations who also belong to principal capital-owning families—interconnected with the nation's great landowners?

To answer this question properly, the connection between familial landownership and several aspects of capital ownership and intraclass

TABLE 4.9C. Percentage of Chilean Bankers and Corporate Executives in the Central Core, Other Maximum Kinship Groups, and Unrelated Families Whose Close Families Own a Specified Amount of Land in Great Estates, 1964/66

			BIH Owned			
	No Land	Other Estates	150–999	1,000–1,999	2,000-plus	(*N*)
Central core						
bankers	12	0	35	19	35	(26)
corporate executives	18	0	37	21	24	(82)
Other kinship groups						
bankers	100	0	0	0	0	(9)
corporate executives	87	0	4	9	0	(45)
Unrelated families						
bankers	82	9	6	3	0	(33)
corporate executives	91	2	7	0	0	(102)

BIH = "basic irrigated hectares."

differentiation need to be considered simultaneously: whether or not the higher executives' families are principal owners of capital; how many close relatives they have who are principal capitalists; how great is their wealth, measured by the market value of their stockholdings; and whether they are in the central core or in other kinship groups and unrelated families. (To avoid misplaced precision and unnecessary complexity, not to mention tedium, we shall collapse the non-core families into a single category, considering only the ownership of land and capital by secondary relatives and the close family as a whole.)[31]

Within the central core, as Tables 4.10a and 4.10b show, the principal capital-owning families are also simultaneously landed families. Remarkably, not only are the capitalist families far more likely to be landed than the "propertyless" corporate executive families, but as the number of principal owners of capital in the family increases, so does the number of great landowners; and, among those close families having three or more principal capitalists, virtually all of them are also landed. Still, even among the central core's "propertyless" executives (having no principal owners of capital in the close family), 62 percent have at least one great landowner in the close family; of those central core executives with one or two principal capitalists in the close family,

[31] The full complex of relationships would include ownership of capital at each distance, from the immediate through the close family; ownership of land at each of these distances; and all the combinations among them. We did examine these relationships, and they are fully consistent with those shown in Tables 4.10 and 4.11.

TABLE 4.10a. Percentage of Chilean Corporate Executives in the Central Core and in All Other Families with a Specified Number of Great-Estate Owners in the Secondary Family, by the Number of Principal Capitalists in the Secondary Family, 1964/66

		Landowners in Family		
	No Land	1–2	3-plus	(*N*)
Central core				
no capitalists	54	42	4	(26)
1–2 capitalists	38	29	33	(42)
3-plus capitalists	29	64	7	(14)
all central-core executives	42	39	20	(82)
Other families				
no capitalists	93	7	0	(88)
1–2 capitalists	94	6	0	(33)
3-plus capitalists	85	15	0	(26)
all other executives	92	8	0	(147)
All families				
no capitalists	84	15	1	(114)
1–2 capitalists	63	19	19	(75)
3-plus capitalists	65	32	2	(40)
all executives	74	19	7	(229)

NOTE: Estates on the all-Chile internal revenue list (Dpto. de Impuestos Internos 1963) owned personally by corporate executives are also included here.

75 percent also have at least one great-landowning close relative; and among those who have three or more principal capitalists in the close family, that figure is 97 percent (!).

The pattern is the same when we consider the *number* of great landowners that the central core executives have in their close families. "Only" 15 percent of the "propertyless" corporate executives have at least three great landowners in the close family; however, of the executives with one or two close relatives who are principal capitalists, 54 percent also have at least three close relatives who are landowners; and of those having at least three principal capitalists in the close family, 63 percent also have at least three landowners in their close families. Within the central core families, then, the ownership of land and capital is indissoluble; and the more concentrated the close family's ownership of capital, the more concentrated is its ownership of land.

Outside the central core, on the other hand, the ownership of both capital and land within the same family is not prevalent. While it is true that an executive in a close capitalist family is slightly more likely than an executive in a noncapitalist family to have great landowners

TABLE 4.10b. Percentage of Chilean Corporate Executives in the Central Core and in All Other Families with a Specified Number of Great-Estate Owners in the Close Family, by the Number of Principal Capitalists in the Close Family, 1964/66

	No Land	Landowners in Family			(*N*)
		1–2	3–4	5-plus	
Central core					
no capitalists	37	47	5	10	(19)
1–2 capitalists	25	21	36	18	(28)
3-plus capitalists	3	34	40	23	(35)
all central-core executives	18	33	30	18	(82)
Other families					
no capitalists	91	9	0	0	(86)
1–2 capitalists	91	9	0	0	(32)
3-plus capitalists	86	14	0	0	(29)
all other executives	90	10	0	0	(147)
All families					
no capitalists	81	16	1	2	(105)
1–2 capitalists	60	15	17	8	(60)
3-plus capitalists	41	25	22	12	(64)
all executives	64	18	11	7	(229)

NOTE: See Table 4.10a, note.

in the family, the vast majority of the non-core families (whether or not they include principal capitalists) are *not* landowning families. For instance, a mere 14 percent of the non-core executives who belong to a close family having three or more principal capitalist members also have at least one landowner in the family, as contrasted with the already noted 97 percent (!) of their central core counterparts (see Tables 4.10a and 4.10b).

Within the central core, it is the wealthiest capitalist families (measured by the market value of their stockholdings in the 16 leading banks, the top 37 nonfinancial corporations, and the 11 major foreign firms) that are also the greatest landowners. While the close families of 15 percent of the "propertyless" corporate executives each have three or more great landed members, for example, this is true of 75 percent of the wealthiest close capitalist families (owning E°1 million or more in stock). The vast majority (62 percent) of even the central core corporate executives who belong to a noncapitalist close family have at least one landed family member; but the close family of *all* of the central core executives who belong to one of the *wealthiest* capitalist families has at least one landowner in it.

Outside the central core, however, there is no such pattern: even among the wealthiest close capitalist families, for instance, only a small fraction (14 percent) have one or two landed members (and none have more). Whatever their wealth in stock, the non-core families are overwhelmingly landless (see Tables 4.11a and 4.11b). This distinction between central core and other families is obviously important in the internal structure of the dominant class, for it reveals that a significant part of that class is not closely integrated with the owners of the great estates. It should be clear, nonetheless, that in the class as a whole, it is precisely the principal capitalist families that are also typically great landed families, and that among the wealthiest capitalists, the majority are. Overall (see Table 4.11b, "All Families"), barely one-fifth of the

TABLE 4.11a. Percentage of Chilean Corporate Executives in the Central Core and in All Other Families with a Specified Number of Great-Estate Owners in the Secondary Family, by the Market Worth (E°1,000s) of Stock Owned by Principal Capitalists in the Secondary Family, 1964/66

		Landowners in Family		
	No Land	1–2	3-plus	(*N*)
Central core				
none	54	42	4	(26)
under 100	46	27	27	(11)
100–499	37	26	36	(19)
500–999	40	27	33	(15)
1,000-plus	18	82	0	(11)
all central-core executives	42	39	20	(82)
Other families				
none	93	7	0	(88)
under 100	100	0	0	(11)
100–499	89	11	0	(18)
500–999	100	0	0	(4)
1,000-plus	85	15	0	(26)
all other executives	92	8	0	(147)
All families				
none	84	15	1	(114)
under 100	73	14	14	(22)
100–499	62	19	19	(37)
500–999	53	21	26	(19)
1,000-plus	65	35	0	(37)
all executives	74	19	7	(229)

NOTE: Estates on the all-Chile internal revenue list (Dpto. de Impuestos Internos 1963) owned personally by corporate executives are also included here.

TABLE 4.11b. Percentage of Chilean Corporate Executives in the Central Core and in All Other Families with a Specified Number of Great-Estate Owners in the Close Family, by the Market Worth (E°1,000s) of Stock Owned by Principal Capitalists in the Close Family, 1964/66

	No Land	Landowners in Family			(N)
		1–2	3–4	5-plus	
Central core					
none	37	47	5	10	(19)
under 100	43	0	57	0	(7)
100–499	18	29	35	18	(17)
500–999	13	47	13	27	(15)
1,000-plus	0	25	50	25	(24)
all central-core executives	18	33	30	18	(82)
Other families					
none	91	9	0	0	(86)
under 100	100	0	0	0	(10)
100–499	88	12	0	0	(16)
500–999	86	14	0	0	(7)
1,000-plus	86	14	0	0	(28)
all other executives	90	10	0	0	(147)
All families					
none	81	16	1	2	(105)
under 100	76	0	24	0	(17)
100–499	52	21	18	9	(33)
500–999	36	36	9	18	(22)
1,000-plus	46	19	23	12	(52)
all executives	64	18	11	7	(229)

NOTE: See Table 4.11a, note.

noncapitalist executives have landowning members in the close family (and merely 3 percent have three or more), contrasting with well over half of the executives who belong to a capitalist family in the top stock-owning bracket (E°1 million or more). In fact, in the dominant class as a whole, the wealthier (in stockownership) the capitalist close family is, the more likely it is to have three or more landed members.

As to the relevance of the interpenetration of land and capital ownership in the central core, that phenomenon, of course, is the consummate basis of the dominant class's integration *as a class*, whereby the landed and capitalist families are thoroughly intermarried and monopolize, in town and countryside alike, the ownership and control of the decisive means of production. *We wish to emphasize that not only is the central core the specific locus of the dominant class's integration, but it is also within the central core that both the principal capitalist and the great landed families are concentrated.* Among the 105 executives whose close families own no substantial capital, 86 men (or 82 percent) are outside the central core; in contrast, among the 124 executives who belong to a principal capitalist family, 63 men (or 51 percent) are within the central core.

Similarly, and far more striking, among the 82 executives who belong to a great landed family, 67 men (or 82 percent) are within the central core, whereas of the 147 executives who belong to a landless family, 132 men (or 90 percent) are outside it. Most important, of the 85 executives whose close families own neither land nor capital, whom we call "propertyless managers," 92 percent are outside the central core; but among the 62 executives whose close families are simultaneously landlord and capitalist, whom we call "landed capitalists," 89 percent are within the central core (see Table 4.12).

Thus, contrary to the social imagery prevailing in liberal as well as socialist political circles, and among theorists of "modernization" as well as "development," Chile's principal capitalist families and great landed families are all but indivisible.[32] A huge central core of multiply

TABLE 4.12. Percentage of Chilean Corporate Executives in the Central Core and in All Other Families, by the Ownership of Landed Property or Capital in the Close Family, 1964/66

	Central Core	All Other Families	(*N*)
Landed capitalists	89	11	(62)
Landless capitalists	13	87	(62)
Landed managers	60	40	(20)
Propertyless managers	8	92	(85)
All executives	36	64	(229)

NOTE: "Landed capitalists," for instance, includes those executives having both a great-estate owner and a principal capitalist in the close family, whereas "propertyless managers" includes those executives having neither a great-estate owner nor a principal capitalist in the close family.

[32] Analyzing "the relations between the industrial bourgeoisie and the established upper classes" in Chile in the mid-1960s, the same period encompassed here, Dale Johnson also rejects "the 'struggle for supremacy' thesis flowing from Marxian and traditional sociological doctrines." Nonetheless, he does claim (1968–1969, p. 175) that these *are* distinct classes: "Nor is what might be termed the 'fusion thesis' correct. . . . Industrialists have not fused with the established economic elite to form a new oligarchy or ruling class. . . . Industrialists apparently do not invest extensively in land or marry their daughters to the sons of oligarchical families." In neither of the published reports of Johnson's study (1967–1968, 1968–1969), however, is any evi-

intermarried families indissolubly unifies them as segments of the same dominant class. Of course, our analysis has focused on the most intimate social relations, those formed by consanguineal and affinal kinship bonds: freely intermarrying families constitute the most precise and unambiguous criterion of common class "membership." But around such close family relationships, certainly, are a host of unifying experiences, common interests, and overriding commitments that unite them. The complex pattern of extensive intermarriage among the dominant landowning and capitalist families results from, and in turn reinforces and extends, their web of primary social interaction and of mutual obligations and loyalties.

We are thus led to conclude that even conceptualizing Chile's "landlords" and "capitalists" as distinctive "class segments" must tend to distort our perception of their inner connections, if not reify our two categories, so that they appear to be coexisting, rather than indissoluble, elements of one coalesced class. The contradictions between landed property and capital—and the clashes over state policies affecting them, where these have led to political rivalries within the dominant class in Chile *in recent decades*—have not arisen between separate, ontologically "real" class segments of "landlords" and "capitalists." For contradictory interests and social cleavages within Chile's dominant class have *not coincided*; rather, the dominant agrarian and capitalist elements have been internally related, if not "fused," in so complex a pattern that *neither of them possesses a specific autonomy or dis-*

dence presented either on investments in land or on intermarriage patterns with which to support his claim. (The one index of social interaction between the industrial managers and "agriculturalists" that is shown [1968–1969, p. 198] indicates that 55 of the 138 managers interviewed were asked whether they had "good friends" in any of several "occupational groups"; and of those 55, 27 stated that they did have "good friends" among "agriculturalists"—a finding that suggests significant social ties between them, but one that Johnson ignores analytically. Further, Johnson's respondents were the general managers of 69 manufacturing firms employing 50 to 99 workers and 69 such firms employing 200 or more. So his respondents were supervisory officials, rather than higher corporate executives, in firms (even the latter 69 "large" ones) that were ranked well below the top corporations we analyze here. Although Johnson refers to his managers as "industrialists," they seem more appropriately to fit the still quite relevant category of "middle sectors," "middle strata," or "small and medium industrial entrepreneurs," who purportedly hold progressive views and are wont to support liberal social reform or even a "popular anti-imperialist and antioligarchic government"—as the secretary general of the Chilean Communist party hoped (Corvalán 1971, pp. 197, 227, 324; also see J. Johnson 1958). Instead, Dale Johnson reports (1968–1969, p. 196) that the thinking of most of the industrial managers he interviewed "simply mirrors the value premises of the staid and conservative, the class prejudices current in the upper ranks of society."

tinctive social identity.[33] Any theory of traditionalism vs. modernity (or of contradictions between ostensibly feudal vs. capitalist modes of production) that posits the existence of two "upper" classes (or of a landed "oligarchy" and a "national bourgeoisie"), in conflict over the destiny of the nation, has no basis in *recent* Chilean reality.[34]

[33] Cf. Poulantzas 1973b, pp. 237–238n.

[34] We have used italics in the phrases "*recent decades*" and "*recent* Chilean reality" to emphasize that our findings concerning the internal relations unifying Chile's dominant landed and capitalist families cannot accurately be projected backward into prior and quite different historical periods. In the mid- and late nineteenth century, for instance, there *was* a certain tendency for contradictory interests and social cleavages to coincide: specific types of productive capitalists, in particular the great copper-, silver-, and coal-mining families of the Norte Chico, did tend to have a distinctive social existence. Indeed, they fought two bloody civil wars (first from "below" and then from "above") against other segments of their class. "These nineteenth-century civil wars . . . were historically crucial in the making of the dominant class, in the shaping of its internal relations, and in the entire process of class formation," Zeitlin argues. It was only with the defeat of José Manuel Balmaceda, a dissident aristocratic president intent upon nationalist development policies—whose intraclass allies as the struggle sharpened were the great mineowners—that "a 'coalesced bourgeoisie' of landlords and capitalists consolidated their historical reign . . . until the present" (1984, p. xi). For this reason, it is not correct to infer from the findings of the present chapter (some of which we reported in an earlier article [1975], as has Ian Roxborough (1984, p. 21), for instance, that "conflicts among dominant groups" were irrelevant in Chile's development because its "dominant class . . . was remarkably homogeneous." On the contrary, Zeitlin's historical analysis unveils and illuminates nineteenth-century intraclass conflicts that have been ignored or misunderstood in previous studies and shows that they were "crucial . . . not only in the making of the dominant class but also for the very development of capitalism and democracy in Chile" (1984, p. xi).

APPENDIX

REFINING THE LIST AND RANKINGS OF THE TOP LANDOWNERS

One part of our investigation to determine the identity of the "top landowners" involved an examination of all landed estates listed as held in the family as "community property" (*comunidad*). In such cases, we searched in biographical dictionaries and other sources to determine, when possible, which part of a given family, and which individuals within the family, claim ownership of the landed estates listed as being owned as "community property." Because of the prestige of landownership, such information is frequently provided in the brief biographical entries. In cases where we obtained this information, we assigned ownership of an estate held *en comunidad* to the individual or several individuals (always either siblings or a parent and his children) who claim ownership.

We made no attempt to assign ownership to individuals when the owners of the landed estates were listed as corporations. The exclusion of corporation-owned estates, as well as those held by other institutional owners, does have an effect on our list of top landowners because some of the largest estates are owned by corporations. The main problem that resulted, however, is one of ranking rather than of the omission of major landowning families. In our analysis of the stock lists of corporations that own landed estates, we found that most are controlled through either majority or dominant-minority stockownership by the families already included here as great landowners.

Another step in the refinement of the preliminary top landowner universe involved, first, determining which large corporations own more than one "great estate" on the agrarian reform institute list (ICIRA 1966) and, second, making a sum of the number of "basic irrigated hectares" (BIH) of those estates. The original sample of 125 top landowners was based on a rank listing by the size of single estates. Consequently, this further research increased the size of the landholdings of some of the top landowners.

Once the estates owned under family names had been assigned to individuals, and once all estates owned by an individual had been identified and combined in a sum total of landholdings for that individual, the need for other changes in the top landowner universe became apparent. First of all, some individuals, originally included among our top landowners only because they own top estates on the tax list, were found to have land totals in BIH exceeding the landholdings of the 100th-ranking landowner on the original ICIRA top-100 list; these individuals were re-ranked based on the sums of their BIH. Second, we found 7 individuals in the banking and corporate executive universes whose actual ICIRA land totals are large enough to rank them above the original 100th-ranking top landowner (although they had not been on that list originally); therefore, we added them to the top landowner sample. With these refinements and additions, the final top landowner list came to 132 individuals. All top landowners with Central Valley holdings, without regard to the list from which they were actually drawn, were re-ranked according to the total number of BIH on all of their "great estates." Thus ranked, the sample now contained 105 landowners with total holdings larger than the 100th-ranking, individually owned single estate on the original ICIRA top-100 list. In addition, there were 27 top landowners who had originally been selected because they own estates among the largest on the tax list (Dpto. de Impuestos Internos 1963), but for whom we found no "great estates," or estates large enough to rank them among the preceding top 105. Only 5 of these 27 actually own estates outside the Central Valley. Of the 22 who own estates in the Central Valley, we found that 18 have "great estates" of sizes ranking them below the original 100th-ranking landowner. We found no "great estates" for the remaining 4, even though the location of each of their estates on the tax list was the Central Valley.

Subsequent study of the ICIRA list also revealed the names of a group of 32 landowners with land totals, often based on more than one estate, greater than the lowest on the original top-100 list, but who had not been included on that list, and who, therefore, had not been selected as "top landowners." In most instances these landowners had been overlooked either because their holdings are listed as owned by a family partnership (*comunidad*) or because they own two or more smaller estates that were not combined (and could not have been without our subsequent research) when the original top-100 list was created. Although the omission of these landowners from the universe of top landowners is unfortunate, we do not think it affects the findings of the present study. For one thing, almost half (15 out of the 32) were eventually included in our study because they were found to be close relatives of the original respondents. Thus, their land totals and their positions in the kinship structure of the landowners have been incorporated into the analysis. In addition, the landowners selected as "top landowners" certainly include an overwhelming majority of those who, after all phases of this research were completed, were found to be the very largest landowners in Chile. We compiled a final list of the 100 largest landowners, based on the BIH of all estates owned by an individual and on all information available through our research, and it includes 81 of the present top landowners and 12 close relatives of individuals in the study, but only 7 persons who had not already been included in the data set either as members of one of our three universes or as relatives of those members.

CHAPTER FIVE

Land, Capital, and Political Hegemony

THE PROTRACTED presence and eventual incorporation of agrarian elements in the dominant classes of Western capitalist countries is nowhere accurately portrayed by "the simple picture of a declining aristocracy and a rising bourgeoisie." Rather, as Reinhard Bendix rightly remarks, "in most European countries, the social and political pre-eminence of the pre-industrial groups continued even when their economic fortunes declined."[1] This anomaly of the continuing "political dominion" of large landed property, despite the "economic supremacy" of capital is a problem wrestled with by many theorists, though with little satisfying resolution. Karl Marx, for instance, often spoke of the state in Great Britain as an "archaic, timeworn and antiquated compromise between the landed aristocracy, which *rules officially*, and the bourgeoisie, which in fact dominates in all the various spheres of civil society but *not officially*."[2] Friedrich Engels even went so far as to suggest that "the bourgeoisie has not the stuff in it for ruling directly itself"; therefore, it requires an "oligarchy, as there is here in England, to take over, in exchange for good pay, the management of state and society in the interests of the bourgeoisie."[3] Similarly, although from a rather different theoretical standpoint, Joseph Schumpeter has made essentially the same observation. He suggests that there was "an active symbiosis of the two social strata, one of which no doubt supported the other politically." Not only did the "aristocratic element . . . rule the roost right to the end of the period of intact and vital capitalism," Schumpeter argues, but it also "made itself the representative of bourgeois interests and fought the battles of the bourgeoisie. . . . For ends no longer its own, it continued to man the political engine, to manage the state, to govern."[4]

[1] Bendix 1970, p. 302.

[2] As quoted in Giddens 1971, p. 40, italics in original; also see Marx and Engels 1953, p. 419.

[3] Marx and Engels 1942, pp. 205–206.

[4] Schumpeter 1962, pp. 136–137.

Although we cannot examine the reasons why the great landlords of England and Europe successfully retained "political dominion" when the development of capitalism had already transformed the preexisting historical forms of landed property upon which their earlier power had rested, we can address a closely related and singularly important political sociological question here: namely, the political relevance of the ownership of large landed property within the dominant classes of contemporary capitalist countries. This is a particular formulation of the general theoretical question, What aspects of the internal differentiation and integration of the dominant class are politically relevant? Although one of the principal foci of academic political sociology is "the social correlates of political participation,"[5] systematic research on such correlates within contemporary dominant (or "upper") classes scarcely exists.

This is not to be confused with another quite different, though related, analytical issue: i.e. "the social composition of political decision-makers." Abundant investigations have documented the significant level of direct participation of "business elites," the "wealthy," the "upper classes," etc. in the formal institutions of governance in contemporary capitalist democracies. Such social elements have provided a disproportionate, if not predominant, share of the governing officials throughout the various components of the state system—in the executive, in the cabinets of presidents and prime ministers and among other appointive officials, as well as in parliament and other national and regional legislative bodies.

Class Segments and State Policy

In contrast, our analysis in this chapter attempts to grasp this sociopolitical relationship "from the inside," so to speak, by viewing it from *within the dominant class itself*. How does the internal structure of that class make possible, or even probable, the relative "political hegemony" (i.e. leadership or overriding influence, if not dominance) of one or another of its segments, *within that class itself*? What relationship is there between the structure of intraclass relations and the capacity of specific class segments to impose their own particular interests on the class as a whole?[6] In particular, how does the possession of large landed estates bear on the exercise of intraclass political hegemony?

[5] Janowitz 1968, p. 300.

[6] Marx (1973c, p. 13; cf. 1948, p. 40) refers to the "fraction" of the bourgeoisie that

These questions, quite obviously, assume that to understand the actual and potential uses of state power in existing (rather than abstractly conceived) capitalist societies—particularly in capitalist democracies—it is necessary to take full account both of the "self-activity" of classes and of the structures that limit and make it possible in various forms. And this includes answering such questions as, Which segments of the dominant class "actually [make] the laws, [are] at the head of the administration of the state, [and have] command of all the organized public authorities," and which ones are relatively excluded from the direct exercise of political power? Answering these questions helps illuminate the real workings of "the state," and the relationship between the formal process of governing and the realization of the "general class interests" of the dominant class.[7]

No doubt, the imperatives of capital accumulation and profitable investment, as well as the structure of class relations on which they rest, set limits on and impose their own demands on the conduct of public authorities and political officials, irrespective of their class location or social origins, their material interests or personal predilections. So long as certain canons of administrative behavior and political practice, as well as prevailing class relations, are presupposed, the range of "rational policy alternatives" or what is considered "realistic" for any government to attempt to carry out will be limited, in practice, by what is considered "rational" for the more "efficient" workings of the so-called economy, in which specific forms of social domination are, in

---

"dominates the bourgeoisie itself" as "the dominant bourgeois fraction" (*der herrschenden Bourgeoisfraktion*). It is in this fraction that others see "their natural mainstays and commanders," and it is this fraction that represents the class interest "in its vastest outlines, that represents it as a whole" (Marx 1948, p. 139; 1973c, p. 78). Poulantzas (1973a, p. 44), following Gramsci, adopts the term "hegemonic" (rather than "dominant") fraction; the various fractions of the dominant class, he writes, "function regularly under the leadership of . . . the hegemonic fraction," which may or may not be "dominant . . . in the economy." His conception of a class "fraction," however, is somewhat confusing analytically: he brings two quite different meanings under the same conceptual rubric. Thus he says that the "fractions of classes . . . constitute the substratum of eventual social forces . . . located at the level of the relations of production"—a conceptual specification close to our own. But he also refers to "fractions dependent on the political level alone" or "located solely at the political level" (1973b, pp. 84–85; also see 1973a). Not only is this formulation conceptually confusing, but it also tends to obscure or ignore precisely that which requires investigation and empirical analysis: namely, the relationship between intraclass structural differentiation and the "political level." That of course, is the main focus of this chapter.

7 These quotes and formulations are from Marx 1948, pp. 37–42, and 1973c, pp. 13–15. Also see Marx 1952, p. 86, and 1973b, p. 337.

fact, inherent. Thus, objective limits to policy exist precisely because certain options cannot be considered, for their implementation would touch—if not profoundly threaten—the essentials of the social order itself. But if this must be a major emphasis of any adequate analysis of the state, it is also necessary to grasp the specific connections between classes and class segments and their real political activities—including, of course, those of the dominant class—under actually existing capitalism.

Not only is it a sort of complicated structural reductionism, but it is also plain wrong to claim that for the so-called capitalist state, "the participation, whether direct or indirect, of the dominant class in government *in no way changes things*."[8] On the contrary, the immediate and even long-run interests of contending segments of the dominant class, and their conception of those interests and of the state policies deemed appropriate to their realization, often differ sharply. And how and to what extent they actually succeed in dominating their own class politically, as well as directly participating in government, can be crucial if not decisive in the outcome, depending on the specific historical circumstances and on how other, subordinate and exploited, classes align vis-à-vis these intra-dominant-class rivalries.

The proximate—perhaps even the ultimate—limits on the activities of the state are not pre-given; nor is the state an object whose functions inhere in and self-determine its structure (or vice versa?), or whose "relative autonomy" exists as if by definition but is untouched by the relative autonomy of real political activity (and struggle). Rather, what the state is, and what it can do, shifts in response to changes in the balance of forces, not only between but within classes, perhaps especially within the dominant class itself.

Whether or not such self-organization within the dominant class and the active effort to shape state policy go together—either indirectly, through "peak associations" or other voluntary class groups that formulate, advocate, and organize political strategy on a closely linked set of issues; or directly, through active intervention in the electoral arena, in party struggles, and in actual participation in government—varies with what is at issue (and at stake) in a specific historical situation. Intraclass struggles and their specific resolution can have far-reaching effects, and no adequate theory of the state under capitalism today can ignore or dismiss such political activity by elements of the dominant class as a mere "effect" or epiphenomeon of structures.

[8] Poulantzas 1973c, p. 246; italics in original.

Nor is it sensible to assert that any attempt to grasp the meaning of that activity somehow reduces the state to an "instrument," or diminishes "the role of the state to the conduct and 'behavior' of the members of the state apparatus."[9] The question, rather, is, *Who* is there, what they are *doing* there, and what the real *consequences* are of their conduct within the state.[10] The initiatives taken by the dominant class through its politically active representatives are always significant, and can be decisive, determinants of state policy, as the recent history of Chile itself attests.

Thus, the leading empirical questions of this chapter may be put as follows: Is there a specific segment of Chile's dominant class from which its reigning political cadre—its leaders and representatives—tend to be drawn? Do its members tend, more than other class segments, to serve in congress and as cabinet ministers and to participate in the leadership of the political parties of their class? What, in short, is the connection between the internal structure of the dominant class, in particular the ownership of landed property and capital, and the attainment of political hegemony within it?

Agrarian Production Relations and Political Power

Unless agricultural production has not only been subordinated to the "market," but is also based on the large-scale employment of wage labor and capital, landlords and capitalists occupy distinctive locations in the productive process. Even when landed property and capital have long since coalesced within the same class, ownership of the large landed estate rests on a specific historically determined class relationship between the immediate agricultural producer, whether peasant or landless laborer, and the landowner. Thus, large landownership constitutes the basis of a specific dominant-class segment even when capitalism is firmly established in the country as a whole.

In Chile, as of the mid-1960s, the great landed estates' monopoly of most arable and irrigated land still provided the landowners with a

[9] Poulantzas 1973c, p. 246.

[10] See Brady 1943; Domhoff 1978, 1983. Also see Zeitlin 1980, a collection that includes several systematic empirical analyses showing how critical the self-organization and political activity of various segments of the capitalist class, in the United States and elsewhere, have been in the defeat of rival interests within that class (as well as in the actual organization of specific agencies and departments of government). As a consequence of the latter activity, specific intraclass interests are institutionalized or "routinized" within the official forms of democratic public authority. See Yago 1980 and DiTomaso 1980; cf. Roy 1981.

continuing political, as well as economic, base. Not until recent years had the landowners experienced any serious challenge to their hold on agrarian labor, as peasant organizations increasingly penetrated the countryside, some led by Socialists and Communists, others by Christian Democrats, and as "agrarian reform" emerged as a serious item on the historical agenda. Until the 1960s, every effort at even modest land redistribution had been stymied.[11]

Indeed relations on the land were extraordinarily stable until the post–World War II period. On the eve of the war, the great estates still rested on "paternal," i.e. authoritarian and hierarchical, relations between the *patrón* and the resident laborers (*inquilinos*), who received a plot of land, a dwelling, and food allotments in exchange for labor services. The landowners organized the religious *fiestas*, the amusements, and the "civil jurisdiction" on their estates, which usually had a chapel where the *patrón*, the *inquilinos*, and their families heard Mass; and "the resident priest who gamed and supped with the landowner could be counted on to inveigh against disloyalty and immorality from the pulpit."[12] The apparatus of control and violence was regulated by the landowners, and alternative sources of information and voluntary associations were forbidden. Union organization, legal in the cities, was prohibited by law in the countryside, even among the landless laborers or "outsiders" (*afuerinos*) who, not attached to the land or resident on the estates, were consequently less subject to landlord dominance. In general, both the vote of the rural population as well as their labor power were in the hands of the great landowners, and this was the sine qua non of their continuing political power.[13]

Increasing mechanization and greater reliance on wage labor in the postwar period, by changing the external environment and internal relations of the landed estates, contributed to the decline of agrarian stability. This change was combined with the effects of increased migration of displaced tenants and small proprietors into the cities. The migrants maintained contact with their friends and relatives in the countryside, and their experiences, including organization and agitation by the left, became part of the cumulative sources of change in the peasants' conceptions of self and society. Rural electrification and

[11] In 1917, according to Bauer (1975, p. 129), 0.4 percent of the landowners owned 46.6 percent of the land; in 1935, 0.2 percent held 43.2 percent. In the mid-1960s, as noted earlier, 1.7 percent of all agricultural "holdings" in the Central Valley controlled 46.9 percent of the valley's first-class agricultural land.

[12] Bauer 1975, p. 166.

[13] Bauer 1975, p. 223; Loveman 1973, p. 292. Also see Petras and Zeitlin 1968.

improved means of transportation and communication made it possible to reach peasants in different areas, conveying new interpretations of their conditions of existence and exhortations to change them. In 1958, a new system of voting, utilizing a single ballot that listed the candidates of all parties, rather than separate, easily recognized ballots for each party, was pushed through parliament by an alliance of the center and the left. This made it easier for the rural poor to vote for these parties—especially, at first, for the Christian Democratic party, which had now become a serious political force in the countryside. The Christian Democrats brought issues to the peasants' attention that had not been legitimate (or safe) subjects of public discussion or debate on the *fundos* of the recent past. This in turn facilitated Socialist and Communist political access to the peasantry, even in the most remote and isolated zones. Thus, by the late 1950s, the solid rural political base of the great landlords was rapidly disintegrating. In fact, it was precisely the *afuerinos* (who worked on the estates but lived outside them), that segment of the peasantry which now voted most heavily for the left, that was also growing most rapidly. From 1955 to 1965 alone, this segment doubled in size as a proportion of the rural labor force, rising to roughly a fifth, while the proportion of *inquilinos* and small holders in the countryside declined considerably, many of them now compelled to seek jobs in the towns and cities.[14]

Under President Eduardo Frei's Christian Democratic government, inaugurated in 1964, there was continuing and sharp public debate about agrarian reform. The number of agricultural workers involved in strikes trebled in Frei's first year in office alone, while his government proceeded, though slowly and reluctantly, with the expropriation of several large *fundos*. Frei had promised in his campaign to distribute land to 100,000 families, and although only 30,000 were settled on new land during the six years of his presidency (while $100 million was spent to compensate former landowners), this, too, continued to shake up the countryside and threaten rural "social peace."[15]

Nonetheless, in comparison with the sharp struggle—against a militant, highly self-conscious, and politically radical working class in Chile's nitrate fields, mines, and factories—that their capitalist peers had faced for well over a half century, the great landowners had long enjoyed (and still held) a secure political base. Surely their chances of

[14] Petras and Zeitlin 1968, esp. pp. 256–257.

[15] For details on agrarian reform under Frei and Allende, see Barraclough 1973; Chinchilla and Sternberg 1974; Kay 1974; Loveman 1976; Swift 1971.

electoral victory had long been incomparably superior to others in the dominant class, given their social control of the peasantry and the economic dependence of much of the rest of the rural population; and precisely because of the support they could mobilize when necessary for favored candidates and established political figures, the great landowning families were also able to press with great success for the appointment of their own or their representatives to cabinet-level and other executive positions in government. To this must be added the peculiar social deference and prestige enjoyed by the great landed families, even among those not subject to their will. In part, this was because they actually had governed, as well as "ruled," the nation for so long in the past.[16] So, even assuming that the calling for politics had been evenly distributed in the dominant class, the landowners probably would have been more likely than other men of property to succeed in their quest for public office. In addition, if, as we have reason to suspect, the expectation was bred into men from landed families in this historical context that they were going to serve in government at some time in their lives, this would have inclined them, in particular, to hear and to heed the calling of politics.

The political calling, to be sure, was not restricted to the landed, for in Chile's relatively durable parliamentary system, the propertied in general displayed a marked propensity to participate actively in party politics, to run for elective office, and to enter government service. Men of ability and energy, even from the most privileged social origins, "looked on politics as a respectable career and, often after serving an apprenticeship in private affairs that provided them with a fund of common experiences and values, took to politics as a vocation."[17] There is no doubt an element of overstatement in one leading historian's biting observation that representative democracy in Chile "has amounted to little more than a system in which a small, privileged class has been gentlemanly in determining through very limited electoral processes which of its members would rule the country."[18] It is an essential truth, nonetheless, that, until Chile's representative government was smashed in late 1973 by a violent right-wing military coup, the recognized political leadership of the dominant class did, in

[16] In 1854, for instance, 41 percent of the deputies and senators were personally owners of a "large rural estate"; in 1874, 50 percent; in 1902, 57 percent; in 1918, 46 percent, according to the detailed studies by Bauer (1975, p. 216).

[17] Zeitlin 1968, p. 231.

[18] Pike 1963, p. 231.

fact, tend to reside in its congressional representatives, government ministers, and party leaders.

Especially because the Socialist and Communist parties had gained a mass base in the working class electorate in the past several decades, the political parties and the parliamentary representatives of the dominant class played a crucial role in translating their class domination into political power. As is true of their European counterparts, these political parties facilitated the articulation of general policies and programs that were acceptable to the class constituency as a whole, reconciling the various particular and parochial interests within it. They also facilitated the common action of their class, organizing it around the political line and specific demands those policies and programs required. To the extent that it became necessary for the dominant class to appeal to an electorate that extended far beyond its own ranks, and over whom its ability to exert direct political controls was increasingly being eroded, its political parties and congressional representatives had the unavoidable ideological task of presenting its class interest as the general interest. Thus, those parties and representatives played a decisive role in posing the issues and setting the limits of acceptable political controversy *within* the dominant class. In recent decades, in particular, challenged from the late 1950s on by the increasingly broad-based electoral coalition of the left, parties of the dominant class have played a relatively independent organizational role, and their leadership was crucial in formulating the political strategy of their class and making tactical initiatives in the sharpening political struggles.[19]

During most of this century, the Liberal, Conservative, and Radical parties have been the major parties of the propertied. By the late 1950s, "no significant political difference remained between the Conservatives and Liberals . . . [who] united with the Radical Party in a center-right bloc," called the Democratic Front.[20] "Although these parties sometimes differed on marginal questions," writes Robert Kaufman, "the major rivalries between them had long been settled." In mid-1966, in the face of the ascendant mass electoral coalition of the left, and after the "crushing electoral defeats suffered by the two rightist political parties in 1964 and 1965," the Liberal and Conservative parties officially merged to form the National party, which also incorporated most of the former so-called Radicals.[21]

[19] Cf. Miliband 1973, pp. 88–89.
[20] ICSPS 1963, p. 24.
[21] Kaufman 1972, pp. 53, 166.

Landownership and the Political Family

The first question, then, has to do with the measurable relevance of landownership as a source of representative political activity or intraclass hegemony. What bearing does landownership have on the political careers of the higher executives of the top corporations—on the likelihood that they will hold national political office, whether in congress and government ministries or in the political parties representing their class?[22]

What is remarkable, and worth noting at the outset as a simple but

[22] Information on the political careers of our "respondents" and their close relatives was drawn from various editions (from the mid-1950s through the mid-1960s) of the *Diccionario biográfico de Chile*. We also checked the *Anales de la República de Chile* (Valencia 1951), which lists the names and the terms of all incumbents of governmental executive and legislative offices from the foundation of the republic through 1950, for possible public offices held. For subsequent years, we obtained information from official registries and from a guide to public administration in Chile (Manteola 1966), as well as from a political dictionary listing the most prominent political figures in Chile's history and offering brief sketches of their careers (Fuentes and Cortés 1967). We were able to obtain sufficiently complete and reliable information on the incumbents of the offices of senator, deputy, and cabinet minister, and we report on each of these offices separately. We also utilized data on any other national political offices held, and these were included in the aggregate variable, the "number of national political offices held." Among the most important of such offices (on which systematic information was not available) are those within the autonomous government agencies whose functionaries are appointed by the president or selected to represent private employers' associations. These semipublic agencies, such as the state development corporation (CORFO), quite commonly have representatives of private associations on their boards. There are also diplomats, ambassadors, and so forth among our respondents, but complete and reliable information was not available to us on the incumbents of these offices; unsystematic information on this latter group had to be extracted from the often inadequate biographical entries in the *Diccionario biográfico*. We pointedly did *not* use the office of the presidency of the republic: it could scarcely be used as a dependent variable, for only a few respondents could possibly have occupied it. (In fact, one of our respondents, Gabriel González Videla, who sat on the board of 3 of the top 37 corporations, as well as on that of the regional Bank of Curico, had been Chile's president from 1946 to 1952.) We considered all national political offices held during each individual's career, not only the ones held during the 1960s. As detailed study of the biographical data reveals, the typical career did not follow a straight line from the commanding heights of the economy to political office, but involved frequent shifts back and forth over a lifetime. For reasons explained earlier, concerning the crucial political role played by the Liberal and Conservative parties within the dominant class, we have also included—as major positions of explicit intraclass political leadership—the chairmanship and vice-chairmanship of these parties. By the mid-1950s, remember, any significant political difference between these parties had disappeared, and they merged in mid-1966 to become the National party. It was therefore not necessary to distinguish party affiliations. We did analyze the limited data available on political affiliations, but found no significant differences between the various subgroups analyzed below.

crucial historical fact, is that almost one in three (28 percent) of the higher executives of the top 37 nonfinancial corporations have held, sometime during their careers, national political office. This suggests an extraordinary level of political consciousness and activism, for far more of them must have participated actively in politics than actually won and held national office.

The ownership of large landed property, as we anticipated, has a significant bearing on officeholding. Proportionately almost twice as many landowning (close to half in all) as nonlandowning executives have held political office at some time in their lives; the differences are even sharper when multiple officeholding is considered. The "top landowners" among the executives, moreover, are the most likely by far to hold more than two public offices during their careers (see Table 5.1). If we examine the specific office held, the differences are even more striking: three to four times as many landed as nonlanded corporate executives have been senators, deputies, or government ministers, while twice as many have been party leaders. All told, we must emphasize the historical importance of the fact that not only has the typical landed executive held public office, but almost a quarter of the landed executives have held two or more offices (see Table 5.2).

Conversely, if we ask what proportion of the political officeholders among our corporate executives own land, we find (calculating our data in the opposite direction) that the vast majority who have held office as senator, deputy, minister, or party official are *not* landowners, even though the landed *are* vastly overrepresented among them: just one-tenth of the corporate executives who have not held public office,

TABLE 5.1. Percentage of Higher Executives of the Top 37 Nonfinancial Corporations in Chile Who Have Held Political Office, by Landownership, 1964/66

	Offices Held			
	None	One	Two-plus	(*N*)
No land	75	16	9	(199)
Great estates	47	35	18	(17)
	53	23	23	
Top estates	61	8	31	(13)
All executives	72	17	11	(229)

NOTE: The "great estates," it will be remembered, are the 1,067 "fundos de gran potencial" from the agrarian reform institute's list of Central Valley landholdings (ICIRA 1966); the "top estates" are great estates that are owned by one or more of the nation's 132 "top" landowners. If an executive owns an estate appearing on the all-Chile list, but not appearing on the Central Valley list, that holding is counted under "great estates." For details on the great landowners, see Chapter 4.

TABLE 5.2. Percentage of Higher Executives of the Top 37 Nonfinancial Corporations in Chile Who Have Held a Specific Political Office, by Landownership, 1964/66

	Deputy		Senator		Minister		Party Official		(*N*)
No land	8		5		7		9		(199)
Great estates	24	23	18	23	18	20	18	20	(17)
Top estates	23		31		23		23		(113)
All executives	10		7		9		10		(229)

NOTE: See Table 5.1 for definition of "great estates" and "top estates."

TABLE 5.3. Percentage of Higher Executives of the Top 37 Nonfinancial Corporations in Chile Who Own Landed Property, by the Specific Political Office Held, 1964/66

	No Land	Great Estates	Top Estates	(*N*)
Deputy	70	17	13	(23)
Senator	59	18	23	(17)
Minister	70	15	15	(20)
Party official	74	13	13	(23)
No office	90	5	5	(165)

NOTE: See Table 5.1 for definition of "great estates" and "top estates."

but from one-quarter to two-fifths of the men who have served in congress or a government ministry or who have led one of their class's political parties, own land. It is also worth underscoring that among those who have been a senator (an eight-year term of office, compared with a deputy's four years, as well as a position of greater political influence), landownership is most prevalent: 41 percent are landowners (and 23 percent, "top landowners"). (See Table 5.3.)

We noted earlier that the expectation of, if not the desire for, "government service" has probably been instilled in men from landed families. Indeed, many have been born into a "political family" with a long tradition of government service. In England, it has been remarked, "membership of political families [was] . . . naturally and logically connected with the territorial predominance of so many landed families in their country or in parts of it."[23] The same has been true in Chile, where parliamentary seats frequently descended as if held in title, with sons succeeding fathers as representatives of their districts. Correa, Echenique, Errázuriz, and Bulnes are only a few of the great landed families whose names have been prominent in Chilean national poli-

[23] Guttsman 1965, p. 160.

tics for many generations. "Frequently one son inherited the estate," the historian Arnold J. Bauer notes, "while others studied law and entered politics."[24]

If this is a generalized phenomenon, then our corporate executives who are large landowners should not only be more likely than others to hold political office, but they should also be more likely to have a father, or brother or son, who has pursued a political career. Our findings amply confirm this suggestion. Among our corporate executives who are large landowners, 37 percent are the sons of present or former officeholders, compared to only 14 percent (or far less than half that proportion) among their landless counterparts. The pattern is the same when the officeholding of a man's brothers and sons, as well as that of his father, is taken into account: in fact, nearly two-thirds (60 percent) of the corporate executives who own large estates have at least one immediate family member who has held national political office, compared to one-quarter of the nonlandowning executives (see Table 5.4).

Implicit in this finding and in the preceding discussion is the hypothesis that membership in a political family ought to enhance the chances of a man's successful pursuit of a political career. As Wilhelm Guttsman, writing of England, suggests: "The tradition of political activity in a man's family affects his career in two ways. It facilitates his advancement in the political arena, because an illustrious name enhances his reputation and influential members of his family can assist him in climbing the rungs of the political ladder. But it also helps to determine a man's career on the subjective plane. The political activity and prominent position of an ancestor [or older sibling] influence the

TABLE 5.4. Percentage of Higher Executives of the Top 37 Nonfinancial Corporations in Chile Whose Immediate Families Include Political Officeholders, by Landownership, 1964/66

	Father		Someone in Family[a]		(*N*)
No land	14		25		(199)
Great estates	41	37	65	60	(17)
Top estates	31		54		(13)
All executives	17		30		(229)

NOTE: See Table 5.1 for definition of "great estates" and "top estates."

[a] An executive's father, brother(s), or son(s) has/have held political office.

[24] Bauer 1975, p. 217.

entry into politics of the young descendant by raising the level of his aspiration, or by turning it into politics."[25]

For these reasons, we suggest that those of our corporate executives who are members of a political family should also be more likely to hold political office themselves than those having no officeholder in the immediate family. This is, in fact, what we find. Among our corporate executives with an officeholder in the immediate family, proportionately twice as many (43 percent) have also held public office, compared with their counterparts who are not from a political family (22 percent). The pattern is even more pronounced when we compare the proportions of multiple officeholders in these groups: 22 percent of the former versus 6 percent of the latter have held at least two political offices (see Table 5.5). This same pattern holds true when one compares the specific types of political office occupied. Membership in a political family is closely linked to a man's own chances of becoming a member of congress, a government minister, or a party leader (see Table 5.6).

Given these two preceding sets of findings concerning the relevance both of large landownership and membership in a political family to a corporate executive's chances of holding political office, the question is how the combination of these attributes, or the absence of either one or both of them, affects his political chances. As might be expected, we found that landed executives who come from a political family are most likely to hold public office themselves, while their peers who neither have an immediate-family political relative nor own a landed estate are least likely to hold office: 61 percent of the first type have held

TABLE 5.5. Percentage of Higher Executives of the Top 37 Nonfinancial Corporations in Chile Who Have Held Political Office, by Political Officeholding in the Immediate Family, 1964/66

	Offices Held Personally			
	None	One	Two-plus	(*N*)
Someone in family has held office	57	21	22	(68)
No family member has held office	78	16	6	(161)
All executives	72	17	11	(229)

[25] Guttsman 1965, p. 162. Johnson (1973) finds that the "political family" is of special importance in the Conservative party of England. Clubok et al. (1969) find that among the members of the 90th Congress of the United States, 54 percent have one or more relatives in some *elective* office at the state, local, or national level.

TABLE 5.6. Percentage of Higher Executives of the Top 37 Nonfinancial Corporations in Chile Who Have Held a Specific Political Office, by Political Officeholding in the Immediate Family, 1964/66

	Offices Held Personally				
	Deputy	Senator	Minister	Party Official	(*N*)
Someone in family has held office	21	16	13	21	(68)
No family member has held office	6	4	7	6	(161)
All executives	10	7	9	10	(229)

TABLE 5.7. Percentage of Higher Executives of the Top 37 Nonfinancial Corporations in Chile Who Have Held Political Office, by Landownership and Political Officeholding in the Immediate Family, 1964/66

	Offices Held Personally Where Someone in Family Has Held Office				Offices Held Personally Where No Family Member Has Held Office			
	None	One	Two-plus	(*N*)	None	One	Two-plus	(*N*)
No land	64	18	18	(50)	79	15	6	(149)
Great estates	39	28	33	(18)	75	17	8	(12)
All executives	57	21	22	(68)	78	16	6	(161)

political office, compared to 21 percent of the second type. What is particularly noteworthy, however, is the finding that while landownership very much enhances the chances of a man's own political officeholding *if he comes from a political family*, landownership has scarcely any relevance if he does not. Among the corporate executives having no officeholder in the immediate family, landownership hardly makes a measurable difference in a man's own political future (see Table 5.7).

When we look at the specific political offices held, the pattern is similar, but not identical. Generally, the contrast between landowning and nonlandowning executives is sharper among those who are from a political family than among those who are not (ministers excepted). Also, as we anticipated, the number of landed executives who have been a deputy, senator, or party official is proportionately far greater among those from a political family than among their fellows from a nonpolitical family. Even among the executives from a nonpolitical family, however, the relationship between landownership and political officeholding persists, deputies excepted (although, because the actual proportions involved are so small, their relative *social* significance is minimal). (See Table 5.8.)

The Landed Capitalists

What, then, about the ownership of *capital*? What bearing does family ownership of both landed property *and* capital have on the political chances of Chile's higher corporate executives? In the previous chapter, we saw that the "landed capitalists," those executives whose families are both landlord and capitalist, are the most thoroughly integrated into their class's "central core." The question now is whether or not the relative centrality of their social location is matched by the relative weight of their political leadership within the dominant class. Do they play a disproportionate role in its highest party councils, and in its representation within the legislative and executive branches of the state? In short, are the landed capitalists the hegemonic segment of Chile's dominant class?

We begin by considering the political relevance of the ownership of both capital and landed property by the executives' immediate family. When this is taken into account, how are their political chances affected?

First of all, both the landed capitalists and the landed managers (those whose families own land but not capital) stand out as roughly

TABLE 5.8. Percentage of Higher Executives of the Top 37 Nonfinancial Corporations in Chile Who Have Held a Specific Political Office, by Landownership and Political Officeholding in the Immediate Family, 1964/66

	Deputy	Senator	Minister	Party Official	(*N*)
Someone in Family Has Held Office					
No land in family	14	10	10	18	(50)
Great estates in family	39	33	22	28	(18)
All executives in political-officeholding families	21	16	13	21	(68)
No Family Member Has Held Office					
No land in family	6	3	6	5	(149)
Great estates in family	0	8	17	8	(12)
All executives not in political-officeholding families	6	4	7	6	(161)

twice as likely as their landless counterparts to hold political office and three times as likely to hold multiple offices. On this level (*personal* political officeholding), the landed managers are even more likely than the landed capitalists to hold political office. As soon, however, as the officeholding of other family members is considered, as will be seen in a moment, the landed capitalists stand out. Also, on this level, there is no sharp contrast between the number of political offices held by landless capitalists (whose family owns capital but not land) and the number of those held by propertyless managers (whose family owns neither). The pattern is about the same when we examine the specific offices held. Proportionately, about three times as many landed capitalists as landless capitalists have served in congress or as a cabinet minister or as a leader in one of the political parties of the right. About the same is true when one compares the specific offices held by landed and propertyless managers. Among the landed capitalists, for instance, 20 percent have been senators, but only 6 percent of the landless capitalists have; for the landed managers, the figure is 30 percent as contrasted with a mere 4 percent for the propertyless managers (see Tables 5.9 and 5.10).

Conversely, the more political offices a man has held, the more likely he is to be from a landed capitalist family; the pattern is again more or less the same for the men from landed managerial families. Yet, while there is no systematic relationship between officeholding and belonging to a propertyless managerial family, the pattern is actually reversed for the landless capitalists: the fewer political offices a man has held, the more likely it is for his immediate family to be a landless capitalist family (see Table 5.11). (As we shall see, however,

TABLE 5.9. Percentage of Higher Executives of the Top 37 Nonfinancial Corporations in Chile Who Have Held Political Office, by Ownership of Landed Property or Capital in the Immediate Family, 1964/66

	Offices Held Personally			
	None	One	Two-plus	(*N*)
Landed capitalists	60	20	20	(20)
Landless capitalists	77	15	7	(84)
Landed managers	40	30	30	(10)
Propertyless managers	73	17	10	(115)

NOTE: "Landed capitalists," for instance, includes those executives having both a great-estate owner and a principal capitalist in the immediate family, whereas "propertyless managers" includes those executives having neither a great-estate owner nor a principal capitalist in the immediate family.

TABLE 5.10. Percentage of Higher Executives of the Top 37 Nonfinancial Corporations in Chile Who Have Held a Specific Political Office, by Ownership of Landed Property or Capital in the Immediate Family, 1964/66

	Deputy	Senator	Minister	Party Official	(*N*)
Landed capitalists	20	20	15	20	(20)
Landless capitalists	6	6	6	7	(84)
Landed managers	30	30	30	20	(10)
Propertyless managers	10	4	8	10	(115)

NOTE: See Table 5.9, note.

TABLE 5.11. Percentage of Higher Executives of the Top 37 Nonfinancial Corporations in Chile Whose Immediate Families Own Landed Property or Capital, by the Number of Political Offices Held Personally, 1964/66

	Landed Capitalists	Landless Capitalists	Landed Managers	Propertyless Managers	(*N*)
No offices	7	39	2	51	(165)
One office	10	33	8	49	(39)
Two-plus offices	16	24	12	48	(25)
All executives	9	37	4	50	(229)

NOTE: See Table 5.9, note.

this relationship is not stable, and changes substantially once we consider the ownership of land and capital vis-à-vis political officeholding within the entire close family.)

Looking at their families' ownership of land and capital by the occupancy of specific political offices brings this relationship into even higher relief. For instance, while the landed capitalists constitute only 9 percent of all 229 higher executives, and 7 percent of those who have never held office, they constitute 23 percent of the senators; similarly, the landed managers constitute only 4 percent of the executives and 2 percent of the nonofficeholders, but 18 percent of the senators. While these segments are highly overrepresented in their class's political leadership, however, the others are considerably underrepresented: the landless capitalists constitute 37 percent of all executives and 39 percent of the nonofficeholders, but only 29 percent of the senators; and the propertyless managers are the most underrepresented politically, constituting 50 percent of all executives and 51 percent of the nonofficeholders, but only 29 percent of the senators.

What about other members of the executive's family, then, who have also been active in the political arena? Does their political officeholding vary with the family's ownership of land and capital? The answer, as we can see, is a definite yes: the landed capitalists are the most likely by far to have a father who has held political office, and, again, the propertyless managers are least likely. When the officeholding of any member of the immediate family (i.e. brothers, sons, or father) is taken into account, the landed capitalists and the landed managers again stand out: in both cases, 60 percent belong to an immediate political family (see Table 5.12).

If we examine this relationship conversely, the pattern is more or less the same. Proportionately, of the executives whose fathers have been officeholders compared with those whose fathers have never held office, more than three times as many are landed capitalists. The only other segment that compares is, again, the landed managerial one. Also, as before, the propertyless managers are highly underrepresented: they constitute well over half of the executives whose fathers have never held office, but barely a third of those whose fathers have been officeholders. If the officeholding of anyone in the immediate family is considered, the relationship is similar; but only the landed capitalists stand out as being far more represented (by more than three times) among our executives from political families than among those from nonofficeholding families (see Table 5.13).

The contrast in the representative political activity of our four intraclass types is sharpest and clearest, however, at the level of the entire close family (i.e. including all immediate, secondary, and tertiary relatives). For brevity's sake, and to spare the reader unnecessary tedium (although the relationships along the way are intriguing as well as consistent with what we are about to see), we shall examine the constellation of relationships among family ownership of landed property or capital and political officeholding "symmetrically," i.e. at the

TABLE 5.12. Percentage of Higher Executives of the Top 37 Nonfinancial Corporations in Chile Whose Immediate Families Include Political Officeholders, by Ownership of Landed Property or Capital in the Immediate Family, 1964/66

	Father	Someone in Family[a]	(*N*)
Landed capitalists	40	60	(20)
Landless capitalists	19	29	(84)
Landed managers	30	60	(10)
Propertyless managers	10	23	(115)

NOTE: See Table 5.9, note.

[a] An executive's father, brother(s), or son(s) has/have held political office.

TABLE 5.13. Percentage of Higher Executives of the Top 37 Nonfinancial Corporations in Chile Whose Immediate Families Own Landed Property or Capital, by Political Officeholding in the Immediate Family, 1964/66

	Landed Capitalists	Landless Capitalists	Landed Managers	Propertyless Managers	(*N*)
Father has held office	21	41	8	31	(39)
Father has not held office	6	36	4	54	(190)
Someone in family has held office	18	35	9	38	(68)
No family member has held office	4	37	3	55	(161)

NOTE: See Table 5.9, note.

same kinship distance of within three links (close relatives) for each of these variables.[26]

We find not only that the landed capitalists are by far the most likely of our intraclass types to have several political officeholders in the close family, but also that the vast majority of them—more than three-fourths—do. The landed managers, however, also enjoy rather substantial political representation through their close relatives; half of them have at least two close relatives who have held office. Although the landless capitalists pale politically by contrast to their landed peers, they are scarcely without political representation: more than one-half of them have at least one close relative who has been in political office. Even among the propertyless managers, who are (as expected) the least likely to belong to a close political family, four out of ten do (see Table 5.14).

Finally, if we also examine this relationship conversely, the landed capitalists are again revealed to possess special political weight in their class. The more fully a family is directly involved in the nation's governance (i.e. the more political officeholders it has had), the more likely it is to be a landed capitalist family (although, from this vantage point, the same can be said, albeit not to the same degree, of the landed managers and even the landless capitalists). On the other hand, the propertyless managers are overrepresented only among those executives not having a single close relative who has served in public of-

[26] The full panoply of relationships among the family's landownership, capital ownership, and political officeholding would take us sequentially through the various combinations of these variables at the level of the immediate, secondary, and close family. For instance, the first series of relationships examined would consist of the immediate family's landownership, the immediate family's capital ownership, and the immediate family's political officeholding, followed by the secondary family's political officeholding, the close family's political officeholding, etc.

TABLE 5.14. Percentage of Higher Executives of the Top 37 Nonfinancial Corporations in Chile Whose Close Families Include Political Officeholders, by Ownership of Landed Property or Capital in the Close Family, 1964/66

	Officeholders in Family			
	None	One	Two-plus	(*N*)
Landed capitalists	13	10	77	(62)
Landless capitalists	47	40	13	(62)
Landed managers	20	30	50	(20)
Propertyless managers	60	25	15	(85)

NOTE: See Table 5.9, note.

TABLE 5.15. Percentage of Higher Executives of the Top 37 Nonfinancial Corporations in Chile Whose Close Families Own Landed Property or Capital, by the Number of Political Officeholders in the Close Family, 1964/66

	Landed Capitalists	Landless Capitalists	Landed Managers	Propertyless Managers	(*N*)
No officeholders	9	30	5	55	(92)
One officeholder	10	43	10	36	(58)
Two-plus officeholders	25	46	13	17	(79)
All executives	15	39	9	37	(229)

NOTE: See Table 5.9, note.

fice. Indeed, whereas the probability of a family owning both landed property and capital rises in proportion to the number of political officeholders in it, the probability of a family owning neither form of property falls at the same time: the more political officeholders a family has, the less likely it is to be propertyless (see Table 5.15).

In sum, to belong to a landed capitalist family is to be marked for political prominence, if not preeminence, in Chile's corporate world. At whatever level of complexity and from whatever angle of view the constellation of relations among landownership, capital ownership, and representative political activity is analyzed, we find that the landed capitalists are distinguished by their disproportionate numbers among the most conspicuous political leaders of their class.

The "Coalesced Bourgeoisie"

More than a century ago, Marx analyzed what he called the "coalesced bourgeoisie" of France, and the "two great interests into which [this] bourgeoisie is split—landed property and capital. We speak of the two interests of the bourgeoisie," he wrote, "for large landed property, despite its feudal coquetry and pride of race, has been rendered thoroughly bourgeois by the development of modern society."[27] In the course of capitalist development, Marx noted, "a large part of landed property falls into the hands of capitalists and capitalists thus become simultaneously landowners. . . . Similarly, a section of large landowners become simultaneously industrialists. The final consequence is thus the abolition of the distinction between capitalist and landowner."[28]

It is doubtful that the specific historical form of "large landed property" in Chile—namely, the great landed estate employing tenant labor as well as wage labor—had become "thoroughly bourgeois" by the 1960s. But our analysis here has focused, in any event, on precisely these great landowning families whose members are simultaneously principal owners of capital as well as higher executives of the top corporations. Thus, these landed capitalists surely personify the coalescence of large landed property and corporate capital, and incarnate the "abolition of the distinction between capitalist and landowner." And it is this segment of Chile's dominant class that, above all, has reigned politically within it. The landed capitalists constitute, to borrow Marx's apt phrase, the "aristocratic representatives of the bourgeoisie" in Chile.[29]

The fact that the landed capitalist segment has distinguished itself politically compared with other higher executives is explicable in terms of the historically specific role of large landed estates in Chile's political economy, their basis in the social domination of the peasantry, and the consequent long-standing political power of the great landowning families. To a lesser but significant extent, after all, the landed managers (who are, of course, also "capitalists" in the sense that they are higher *functionaries of capital*) are also distinctively involved politically. For these reasons, it is reasonable to suggest that the landed capitalists are distinguished politically as their class's leaders not because they are landed *capitalists*, but "merely" because they are, in reality, *great landowners* per se, heirs of their own political families' landed political power and propensity to rule. The question, therefore, is whether the intraclass location of this class segment has a specificity of

[27] Marx 1963, p. 48; 1965, p. 43.
[28] Marx 1956, p. 60.
[29] Marx and Engels 1953, p. 353.

its own, rooted in the coalescence of landed property and capital and the consequent "abolition of the distinction between capitalist and landowner." Is this *coalesced segment*, consisting of families who are at once landlord and capitalist, intrinsically different not only from the segment consisting of capitalists who are not landowners, but also from the segment consisting of landowners who are not simultaneously capitalists?

Class segments, it will be remembered, are differentiated not only by their relatively distinct locations in the social process of production as a whole, but also by inherently contradictory interests; in consequence, they are also potential political rivals over state policies that may impinge differently on their specific interests. This formulation applies, in particular, to landowners and industrial capitalists; depending on the specific historical circumstances and phase of capitalist development, their interests often have been in conflict. Chile is surely no exception to this general observation. Such problems as free trade vs. protection, the pattern of public investment in infrastructure, differential taxation on landed property and capital, the alienability of landed property, the mobility of wage labor, the prices of foodstuffs (and, therefore, the relative "wage bill" for industry), the prices of industrial crops grown on the landed estates, ground rent as a deduction from profits, export-import tariffs, controls on agricultural commodities and capital goods, and so forth have figured at different times as sources of political rivalry between landlords and capitalists. Clearly, then, in this sense, the coalesced class segment of landlords and capitalists occupies a self-contradictory intraclass location. What its members' interests as landowners dictate, their interests as capitalists reject, and vice versa.

It is precisely this inherently self-contradictory set of interests, characteristic of the landed capitalists, that gives special impetus, we suggest, to their search for class leadership and direct political representation, so that they can attempt to shape state policy to fit or harmonize with these recalcitrant and double-edged interests. As we saw in the preceding chapter, the great landed and capitalist families are so indissolubly intermingled that neither a "landlord" nor a "capitalist" segment of the dominant class has an autonomous existence. Rather, when contradictions between land and capital have led to clashes over state policy during this century, these arose not between ontologically real rivals, but within the bosom of the same class. Contradictory interests and social cleavages have not coincided. The families who have personified this coalescence of agrarian property and corporate capital, then, are in a very concrete way the bearers of the "general interest" of the dominant class—that is to say, of the common interests of its integrated "central core" of freely intermarrying, great landowning and principal capitalist families. Consequently, they, in particular, have been impelled to assume a distinctive intraclass political role as its leaders and representatives.

If this reasoning concerning the special propensity of landed capitalists to be active in national politics and in the actual formulation and execution of state policy is correct, then they should be politically prominent compared not only with landless *capitalists*, as we have already seen, but also with *landowners* who are not capitalists. Further, to the extent to which the dominant class as a whole holds political power, state policies should tend in particular to coincide with the specific constellation of interests of the coalesced bourgeoisie.

We turn, therefore, to an analysis of the internal differentiation of our 132 top landowners, so as to assess the specific political weight of the coalescence of large landed property and corporate capital. As of the mid-1960s there were 35 top landowners whose immediate family owned capital, and another 8 who sat on the board of one of the Big Five commercial banks or had a Big Five director in the immediate family. So, by these criteria, we define 43 of the 132 top landowners as members of the "coalesced segment" of the dominant class. The question, of course, is how, if at all, the political careers of these landed capitalists may differ from the careers of their noncapitalist peers, i.e. the other 89 (noncapitalist) top landowners.

The answer, as we shall see, is that they differ sharply. Many more, proportionately, of the top landowners whose immediate families are in the landed capitalist (or coalesced) segment have served in public office than their noncapitalist landed peers (see Table 5.16). The gap between them is even wider when those who have personally held several offices are compared, and the differences are also clear and fairly consistent for each of the major offices: all told, 23 percent of the landed capitalists, but only 10 percent of the noncapitalist landed, have served as a senator, deputy, minister, or party official (see Table 5.17).

Conversely, if we take a look at the social composition of the top landowners' political cadre, the coalesced segment is highly overrepresented. Ten of the 19 men (or 53 percent) who personally have served in congress or as a minister or party official, but only 33 of the 113

TABLE 5.16. Percentage of Chilean Top Landowners Holding Political Office, by the Intraclass Situation of the Immediate Family, 1964/66

	Offices Held Personally			
	None	One	Two-plus	(*N*)
Landed capitalists	77	7	16	(43)
Noncapitalist landowners	87	10	3	(89)
All top landowners	83	9	8	(132)

TABLE 5.17. Percentage of Chilean Top Landowners Holding a Specific Political Office, by the Intraclass Situation of the Immediate Family, 1964/66

	Deputy	Senator	Minister	Party Official	DSMP[a]	(*N*)
Landed capitalists	14	9	16	12	23	(43)
Noncapitalist landowners	8	0	1	5	10	(89)
All top landowners	10	3	6	7	14	(132)

[a] Deputy, senator, minister, *or* party official.

men (or 29 percent) who have not held any of these offices, are in the coalesced segment.

The familial political differences are even more acute. Whereas not even one in ten men in a noncapitalist landowning immediate family have a father who has held office, almost three in ten of those men whose immediate family is in the coalesced segment have; if we consider whether there are several political officeholders in the top landowner's immediate family (brothers, sons, or father), the pattern is equally pronounced. It is also worth emphasizing, as a relevant historical fact, that nearly half of the men whose immediate families are in the coalesced segment have at least one political officeholder in the family (see Table 5.18).

Of those top landowners whose fathers have held office, conversely, nearly two-thirds belong to a landed capitalist immediate family, as compared with slightly over a fourth of those whose fathers have not held office. Similarly, as the number of political officeholders in a top landowner's immediate family rises, so (and sharply) do the chances that his family is in the coalesced segment of landed capitalists (see Table 5.19).

TABLE 5.18. Percentage of Chilean Top Landowners Whose Immediate Families Include Political Officeholders, by the Intraclass Situation of the Immediate Family, 1964/66

	Father Has Held Office	Officeholders in Family			(N)
		None	One	Two-plus	
Landed capitalists	28	53	26	21	(43)
Noncapitalist landowners	8	81	15	5	(89)
All top landowners	14	72	18	10	(132)

TABLE 5.19. Percentage of Chilean Top Landowners Whose Immediate Families Are in the Coalesced Segment, by Political Officeholding in the Immediate Family, 1964/66

	Landed Capitalists	(N)
Father has held office	63	(19)
Father had not held office	27	(113)
No immediate family member has held office	24	(95)
Someone in immediate family has held office	46	(24)
Two or more immediate family members have held office	69	(13)
All top landowners	33	(132)

TABLE 5.20. Percentage of Chilean Top Landowners Holding Political Office, by the Intraclass Situation of the Close Family, 1964/66

	Offices Held Personally			(N)
	None	One	Two-plus	
Landed capitalists	73	11	16	(56)
Noncapitalist landowners	91	8	1	(76)
All top landowners	83	9	8	(132)

Extending our analysis to the entire close family reveals an even more pronounced tendency for the landed capitalists to arrogate political leadership to themselves. Proportionately three times as many of the landed capitalists have personally held office as their noncapitalist peers, and the contrast is far sharper for multiple officeholders (see Table 5.20). Most important, the landed capitalists are embedded in a web of close kinship relationships that are simultaneously and inseparably political: about two-thirds of them have at least one close relative who has held office, and well over half have several such relatives, as compared with much less than a tenth among their noncapitalist peers (see Table 5.21).

The converse of these relationships is also remarkable. The more political offices a top landowner has held personally during his lifetime, or the more political officeholders there are in his close family, the more likely by far that his is a landed capitalist family. It is almost literally true to say that if a top landowner has held multiple political offices or has several close officeholding relatives, then he is both a landowner and a capitalist; among the men in that political category, the close family of some 90 percent are in the coalesced segment of their class (see Tables 5.22 and 5.23).

These findings are surely consistent with our theory that the self-contradictory intraclass situation of the landed capitalists drove them into politics; for, insofar as public policy has impinged on the interests of landed property *or* capital, it has always had, given their objective situation, an unavoidable double edge to it, capable of cutting deeply into one or another of their selfsame interests as simultaneous owners of both of these decisive forms of property. The weapon of state policy is thus an especially dangerous one from their standpoint, to be fashioned and wielded with caution. They dare not merely entrust it to the

TABLE 5.21. Percentage of Chilean Top Landowners Whose Close Families Include Political Officeholders, by the Intraclass Situation of the Close Family, 1964/66

	Officeholders in Family			
	None	One	Two-plus	(*N*)
Landed capitalists	36	11	54	(56)
Noncapitalist landowners	78	16	7	(76)
All top landowners	60	14	27	(132)

TABLE 5.22. Percentage of Chilean Top Landowners Whose Close Families Are in the Coalesced Segment, by the Number of Political Offices Held Personally, 1964/66

	Landed Capitalists	(*N*)
No offices held	37	(110)
One office held	50	(12)
Two-plus offices held	90	(10)
All top landowners	42	(132)

TABLE 5.23. Percentage of Chilean Top Landowners Whose Close Families Are in the Coalesced Segment, by the Number of Political Officeholders in the Close Family, 1964/66

	Landed Capitalists	(*N*)
No officeholders	25	(79)
One officeholder	33	(18)
Two-plus officeholders	86	(35)
All top landowners	42	(132)

state's "relative autonomy" or officials whose own immediate interests fail to dictate a special attentiveness to, and consideration for, the interests of landlords and capitalists. It is thus not an accident that the landed capitalist families of Chile have a marked propensity to seek, hold, and wield state power directly, or that they have distinguished themselves as the "hegemonic segment" of their own class.

Analysis of the actual policies pursued by successive Chilean governments in the past several decades will reveal, we believe, that they, indeed, have attempted to reconcile the common, yet contradictory, interests of landlords and capitalists. The worldwide depression of the 1930s and the subsequent world war severed Chile from international trade, and made it possible for the government to spur industrialization based on a policy of import substitution via state subsidies and direct investments in the production of goods formerly imported from abroad. But if it was, therefore, necessary for the government to control the prices of agricultural products, particularly of grain and other food staples, so as to reduce the "wage bill" for industrialists, it was also necessary to put a floor under agricultural prices to prevent them from dropping too low and cutting into the profits of large landowners. To have done one without the other would have meant protecting the interests of one major segment of the same dominant class at the expense of the other; and this problem would have been exacerbated, in particular, for the coalesced segment at the core of that class.

As a result, wholesale and retail price controls on agricultural products, and taxes on their export, were offset by low agricultural land taxes. Not only much private commercial credit, but most public credit, went to the large agricultural producers, who also received large subsidies from the government for improved methods of cultivation, irrigation, and transportation. Perhaps above all, the organization of agrarian labor was effectively prohibited or "efficiently controlled," for instance, by the Peasant Unionization Law of 1947.[30] An increased flow of capital went, nonetheless, from agriculture into industry during the prolonged period from the 1930s on, resulting in the stagnation of agricultural production.[31] But this stagnation coincided with *rising* profits for the large landowners. Between 1940 and 1952 (years for which a careful analysis is available), the "average annual *real earnings* of unincorporated enterprises," which mainly comprised the great landed estates, increased by more than 50 percent while, in contrast, the wages of agricultural workers fell by almost 20 percent.[32]

The historical paradox, however, is that if such state policies tended to coincide with the immediate self-contradictory interests of the "coalesced bourgeoisie," they led at the same time to the long-term erosion of its social-economic base. The decline in the already low subsistence level of agrarian labor, the ruin of small holders, the rapid migration from the countryside into the cities, as well as the other significant changes in rural areas discussed earlier in this chapter tended to create the conditions for the radicalization of the peasantry in the early 1960s, when no issue became more pressing than agrarian reform.

Our systematic quantitative analysis has shown that landed capitalists hold political hegemony in their class: they constitute the core of the dominant class structurally and have been at the center of its leadership historically; and state policies during the first half of this century generally were consistent with their immediate interests. With the advent of open class struggle in the countryside in the 1960s, the political strategy adopted by the dominant class to meet the growing agitation for agrarian reform and to try to stem the increasing militancy and deepening radicalization of agrarian labor, as well as the growing unity, militance, and political initiative of the urban working class, would have portentous implications for the nation. Surely it was the "aristocratic representatives" of Chile's coalesced bourgeoisie who played the decisive role in shaping that strategy and in leading that struggle in order to ensure their continuing class domination.

[30] Echeverría 1969, p. 107; see, also, Castells 1971, pp. 53–55; Aranda and Martínez 1970, pp. 129–134.

[31] Between 1939 and 1964, average agricultural output increased at an annual rate of 2 percent as compared to rate of popultion growth of 2.2 percent (Swift 1971, chap. 2).

[32] Mamalakis 1965, p. 145; italics added.

CHAPTER SIX

The Ties That Bind

IN THE EPOCH of the multinational corporation's ascendancy, the implications of the internationalization of capital have now become both a critical theoretical question and an urgent political issue even for the advanced capitalist countries themselves. In particular, just how foreign capital affects the economy, class relations, and political process of the "host country" is an issue that now faces even the United States, as its global economic preeminence is being challenged by other advanced capitalist countries and as foreign investment is flowing into it at an unprecedented level and accelerating pace. This is an issue, of course, that is endemic to the "less developed" capitalist countries, as well as to the new states of the former colonial world, where foreign penetration (if not domination) of the economy has long been typical, and where their very political sovereignty is often threatened, limited, or subverted by multinational corporations. Thus, in order to grasp the class relations of such countries, "efforts to link class analysis . . . to the facts of international stratification" are not only useful, as Seymour Martin Lipset suggests, but essential. This chapter is such an effort, focusing on the ties of the leading capitalist families and their political cadre to foreign corporations in Chile.[1]

The Question of the "National Bourgeoisie"

This inquiry was provoked by the theory, held by adherents of a "national capitalist model" and of an "antifeudal, antioligarchic, and anti-imperialist revolution" alike, that the historical agency of independent national development in Latin America would be the so-called national and progressive bourgeoisie. This theory originated as a subset of propositions within the Hilferding-Lenin theory of imperialism, out of an effort to understand the tendencies toward the liberation of the

[1] Lipset 1970, p. 201. For a rare thorough study of the nature and extent of foreign capital's ownership and control of the top corporations in a Western capitalist country *and* its interrelations with domestic control groups, see the pioneering work by Wheelwright and Miskelly (1967).

colonial world inherent not only in its foreign subjugation, but, in particular, its penetration by foreign investment. Colonialism led, in this theory, not only to the uneven and combined development of these backward colonial areas, but also to the emergence of a native colonial bourgeoisie split between a "comprador" merchant class, prospering as the local agent of foreign trade, and a "national bourgeoisie" striving to erect local industries in competition with cheap manufactured imports. Thus, the same process that destroys the old handicraft system and self-sufficient agriculture, thereby impoverishing the urban and rural masses, also threatens the national bourgeoisie itself; sharing common interests in opposition to the interests of the compradors, landlords, and foreign capitalists, its members unite in a national movement aspiring to win freedom from foreign domination and to foster independent national development.[2] Whatever the validity of this theory as a guide to understanding the vast anticolonial movement that culminated in the independence of most of the former colonies of Asia and Africa in the aftermath of World War II, it had become, by the late 1930s—and has been since, in one variant or another—the reigning theory of development in Latin America.

While the adherents of "national capitalism" or of "developmental nationalism" advocate a path of independent capitalist development spurred by structural, but nonrevolutionary, reforms, and consequently emphasize the centrality of "the state [as] an agent of the national bourgeoisie,"[3] the adherents of an "anti-imperialist revolution" emphasize that only the national bourgeoisie's participation in a multiclass alliance, in an "ample and concrete labor and popular front," stiffens its "independence in the face of imperialism" and compels it to fulfill its historical mission.[4] Thus, as Helio Jaguaribe has written of the "Brazilian experience," the "national bourgeoisie [is] insufficiently aware of its class interest and of its socio-political role," and has forgotten that "the state should be an agent of the national bourgeoisie," protecting it, "externally, from the overwhelming pressures of the bourgeoisies of the highly developed countries, particularly in the United States." Or, as the theory has been put by a leading Argentine Communist, Ernesto Giudici, the left's political strategy must not be to attack "the bourgeoisie 'in general,' but to deepen the division between

[2] See Sweezy 1956, pp. 305–306; 326–328; Mandel 1968, II, pp. 480–481. Also see Roxborough's penetrating theoretical discussion of class relations and what he refers to as "imperialism and dependency" (1979, pp. 55–69).

[3] Jaguaribe 1969, p. 427.

[4] Giudici 1966, pp. 36–37.

the collaborationist capitalist sector and the sector of the national bourgeoisie"; the latter is "not linked with imperialism and is interested in the independent development of the country, that is, it is oriented, by the necessities of its own development, toward anti-imperialist and democratic positions."[5] This theory, in whatever variant, thus rests on the crucial (and unexamined) assumption (paralleling its other assumption that the landed "oligarchy" and the "progressive bourgeoisie" constitute separate and contending classes) that national and foreign capital are structurally autonomous, that the relationship between them is "external" and their concrete interests contradictory, and that, in consequence, they are driven into conflict over the nation's development.

The theory's critics argue, to the contrary, as Theotonio dos Santos expresses it, that "the tendency of the underdeveloped countries toward integration with international monopoly capital" has made it impossible for "national capitalist classes . . . to lead the struggle for national independence in our countries." This tendency toward integration, André Gunder Frank argues, has been "drawing and driving the entire Latin American bourgeois class—including its comprador, bureaucratic, and national segments—into ever closer economic and political alliance with and dependence on the imperialist metropolis." The result, Paul Baran suggests, is that "native industrial monopolists are in most cases interlocked and interwoven with domestic merchant capital and with foreign enterprise." In short, as Fernando Henrique Cardoso and Enzo Faletto put it, the "internationalization of the domestic market" tends to result in the formation of an "internationalized bourgeoisie"—dominated, in Osvaldo Sunkel's apt phrase, by its "transnational kernel."[6] Thus, in this conception of their

[5] Jaguaribe 1969, p. 427; also see Jaguaribe 1962, 1968; Giudici 1966, pp. 42, 33–34. The original and foremost proponent of the historymaking role of the national bourgeoisie as the leader of a national, multiclass antifeudal revolution developing the forces of production via "state capitalism" and an "anti-imperialist state" in South America was Victor Raúl Haya de la Torre, the Peruvian social theorist and founder of APRA (*Alianza Popular Revolucionaria Americana*); his peculiar blend of liberalism and inverted Leninism ("imperialism is the *first* stage of capitalism in Latin America") dominated much of the Latin American nonsocialist-left's political thought from the early 1950s through the mid-1960s (and, in Peru, may now be ascendant again). See, for instance, Haya de la Torre 1936, 1946. Cf. Alba 1969.

[6] Santos 1968, p. 452; Frank 1969, p. 396 (and see, also, pp. 388–395); Baran 1957, p. 195; Cardoso and Faletto 1973, p. 134; Sunkel 1973. Also see Polit 1968. "Modernization theory" contains an ahistorical psychological variant of the theory of the national bourgeoisie, in its central "image," as Alejandro Portes describes it, "of highly motivated entrepreneurs racing to break the barriers of stagnation." What this

relationship, far from being the "natural enemy of imperialism," the so-called national bourgeoisie has become foreign capital's natural ally; for it is not only unwilling but unable, given their close mutual association and the coincidence of their immediate interests, to act against foreign capital without, at the same time, acting against itself.

In the 1960s, the Communists still considered Chile to be one of the countries of Latin America (along with Brazil, Argentina, Uruguay, and Mexico) where "the progressive groups of the national bourgeoisie, neither connected with the interests of the latifundists nor subordinated to the imperialist monopolies, would join in the pursuit of agrarian reform and resistance to imperialist monopolies."[7] In 1967, Luis Corvalán, the general secretary of Chile's Communist party, declared that "the motor forces of the revolution in Latin America are the working class, the peasantry, . . . the students, the middle strata, and sectors of the national bourgeoisie. Despite some contradictions among these forces," he said, "they have a deepening common interest in the struggle against North American imperialism . . . and their unity in combat is necessary."[8]

Chile's Socialist party, in contrast, wavered in the 1960s between a similar, if less optimistic, conception of the national bourgeoisie as not yet having "exhausted [its] creative possibilities" and one in which it had already become, as Senator Raúl Ampuero argued, a "tributary of foreign investment," whose "organic symbiosis" both with the latter and the "rural oligarchy . . . deprived the industrialists of the political independence to attempt a profound transformation of the structure of the country."[9]

Thus, the empirical question that is of crucial if not decisive relevance for these contending theories of the potential developmental role of a "national bourgeoisie" in contemporary Latin America can now be posed. How, and to what extent, have national and foreign

supposed theory neglects, however, as Portes correctly remarks, is "the fact that individual action is highly conditioned by external social arrangements. . . . Highly motivated modern individuals may be extremely functional for maintenance of existing power structures. They may be hired, for example, as highly paid managers of foreign corporations, as has been increasingly the practice of multinational companies." Thus, to assess "the strategies of development in countries of Latin America, Africa, and Asia," empirical analysis of the relationships between the "emergence of a 'national bourgeoisie' . . . and foreign-based corporate bureaucracies" is indispensable. See Portes 1976, pp. 71–72, 81.

7 Motta Lima 1966, p. 83.

8 Corvalán 1967, p. 199.

9 Ampuero Díaz 1964, p. 6; also see Jobet 1962, p. 9.

capital coalesced within the economy, and in what social forms is this coalescence expressed among the nation's capitalists? Remarkably, despite this question's centrality for the contending theories just described, studies attempting to answer it with any empirical precision are rare.

One of the barriers to carrying out a theoretically relevant empirical inquiry is the slipperiness of the conceptual (let alone real) identity of the "national bourgeoisie" itself. For if the theory of the historymaking potential of this national bourgeoisie is apparently grounded in a conception of the objective contradictions or structural relations that divide national and foreign capital, the actual structure of intraclass relations (i.e. relations within the "bourgeoisie in general") tends to become rather hazy whenever concrete political alliances and conflicts or historical episodes are under analysis by the theory's adherents.

This is true both of the proponents of the national bourgeoisie's role in the development of a "national capitalism" and of the proponents of its role in an "antioligarchical and anti-imperialist revolution." For instance, Celso Furtado, one of the leading authors of the "national capitalism" variant, laments the fact that national industralists tend to "make concessions to the foreign groups as a solution of their immediate problems," an attitude that is "rational" from the standpoint of their own "business interests," but not "from the national point of view." Furtado concludes: "The industrial capitalist class, *closely bound up with the foreign groups* in whom it has always found the key to a solution of its immediate problems, is not in a position to grasp the nature and seriousness of the problem."[10] Thus, the structural relationships that are supposed to separate foreign and national capitalists, and make the latter the driving force of independent capitalist development, are suddenly recognized as the source of their unity instead, thereby leaving even so sophisticated a developmental nationalist as Furtado with an exhortation rather than an analysis. So it is not that the national bourgeoisie actually exists, but that it ought to!

In discussions of this bourgeoisie's supposed anti-imperialist historical role, a concrete "national industrial bourgeoisie" is rarely identified. Rather, a variety of dimly perceived bourgeoisies—"progressive" vs. "reactionary," "combative" vs "conciliatory," a national bourgeoisie that "suffers intensely from imperialist domination," and a big bourgeoisie that serves "the interests of imperialist countries"—make their own abrupt appearance, accompanied by only the vaguest (if

[10] Furtado 1965, p. 120; italics added.

any) reference to their actual social locus or identity. As the penetration of foreign capital in domestic industries has vastly increased in Latin America over the past few decades, and as this neo-Leninist theory has been battered by actual events as well as theoretical critiques, the mantle of the national bourgeoisie seems to have fallen onto the shoulders of the "medium bourgeoisie" or of the "small and medium manufacturers," who are seen as involved simultaneously in a struggle against "spoliation by the monopolies" and by "imperialism."[11]

Such conceptual haziness also tends to afflict the theory of the "national bourgeoisie" in some of the advanced European capitalist countries. For instance, Philippe Herzog writes of France: "We should be careful not to characterize the new step as a struggle of 'national' capital against trans- or multinational capital. . . . At the present time, the major national monopolies have certain common interests with foreign capital, and both 'resistance' and 'competition' have lost their national character. The groups that confront one another have interests that are partially bound up together, and are in the process of becoming cosmopolitan." As Nicos Poulantzas remarks, however, "the problem here is simply shifted; the PCF [French Communist party] still has its own national bourgeoisie, only [now], this is non-monopoly capital or medium capital."[12]

Thus, the empirical *inquiry* in this chapter is not designed as, nor should it be seen as, a "test" of the theory of the national bourgeoisie. Rather, it is an effort to discover and delineate the pattern of concrete

[11] This came out clearly in the senatorial debate of late 1966, over the privileges to be granted the newly established Chilean subsidiary of Ralston Purina, when Volodia Teitelboim remarked on the senate floor: "We Communists don't have our militants among national producers, among Chilean capitalists. But in the contradiction and struggle between them [and imperialism]—that is, the non-monopoly sectors (because there are also Chilean capitalist monopolies, like Edwards and Ross, who are acting in complicity with imperialism)—we cannot remain entirely indifferent" (*El Mercurio*, August 11, 1966). On the "progressive" vs. "reactionary" bourgeoisie and the equation of the "small and medium bourgeoisie" with the "national bourgeoisie" in Latin America, see, for instance, Esteban 1961, pp. 174, 193; Fernández and Ocampo 1974, p. 58; González Casanova 1965, p. 145; Arismendi 1959, pp. 34–35, and throughout the various articles in Arismendi 1966. Also see Puiggros 1967. On Chile, in particular, see Corvalán 1969, pp. 322–325, and Castells 1974, pp. 76–78.

[12] Herzog 1971, p. 148 (as quoted and remarked on in Poulantzas 1975, p. 77). Of the few empirical analyses of the relations between Chilean national capitalists and foreign investors, see Garretón and Cisternas 1970, esp. p. 32–41, and Johnson 1968–1969. On Brazil, see Vinhas de Queiroz, Martins, and Pessoa Queiroz 1965; Vinhas de Queiroz, Evans, Mantega, and Singer 1977; and, in particular, the subtle analysis by Evans (1979, esp. chap. 3) of "the contemporary pattern of differentiation" and the alliances and conflicts between "local and international capital."

structural interrelations between national and foreign capital in an actually existing capitalist class. The present empirical problem, then, can be posed as, To what extent (borrowing Herzog's words) do "the major national monopolies have certain common interests with foreign capital," or do "the [foreign and national] groups that confront one another have interests that are partially bound up together?"

What our analysis reveals to be the internal structural relationship between domestic capitalists and foreign corporations in Chile during the mid-1960s must not, however, be projected onto other countries nor even back into Chile's own past, as if these relationships are a timeless historical reality. Nothing in our analysis is meant to be so interpreted. Luis Vitale has suggested, for example, that "the Latin American bourgeoisie was associated from the beginning with landholders and foreign investors."[13] But even if this were so, what form this association took, how it has varied over time within the same country and among countries, and what its implications have been for a country's (or a region's) development are answers to be found only by historically specific, and theoretically informed, empirical analysis.

For although foreign capital has a long history of participation in Chile's economy, it was Chilean capitalists who developed the nation's resources and controlled its major enterprises, especially from the middle to the end of the nineteenth century, while also playing a significant role in international copper and grain markets. What status foreign investment should enjoy in their country was thus a hotly contested issue among Chileans as early as the 1850s, and it continued to divide the dominant class itself until the pre–World War I era.

Indeed if a genuine national bourgeoisie has existed anywhere in Latin America, it was in nineteenth-century Chile. At mid-century, a coalition of owners of the copper mines and smelters and grain mills articulated and advocated a program of social-political reform and independent capitalist development. Not only did they seek protection against foreign competition and the intrusions of foreign capital, but they demanded state investment to encourage the growth of national industry—and also fought and bled to win their program, in armed struggles against the state. A generation later, the dominant class was again torn apart by fierce political conflict over the issue of foreign capital in Chile, when President José Manuel Balmaceda, a dissident aristocrat and nationalist, attempted to limit the prerogatives of "foreign monopolies" and to use state investment to stimulate rapid mod-

[13] Vitale 1968, p. 42; cf. Frank 1967, pp. 6–7.

ernization and economic development. In that bloody internecine struggle, the civil war of 1891, the Balmacedistas were largely the political incarnation of that same distinctive segment of the capitalist class, the owners of the major copper, silver, and coal mines, who were now beset by economic crisis and were seeking state assistance for their salvation. Only after their defeat, and Balmaceda's suicide, did foreign capital in Chile become more or less secure—and soon, as in copper and nitrates, ascendant.[14] Not until well into the second half of the twentieth century would the status of "foreign monopolies" again become a divisive national issue. But this time a unified dominant class stood at their side, determined to protect their common interests, first against reforms enacted by the Christian Democratic government of Eduardo Frei and then against the Socialist government of Salvador Allende.

The Alliance of National and Foreign Capitalists

Although foreign capital already weighed heavily and cut deeply in Chile's economy long before the 1960s, that decade saw an especially massive inflow of foreign investment, encouraged by new legislation, amounting to about $1.5 billion from 1962 to 1970 alone, compared with less than $200 million during the previous eight years. Manufacturing, in particular, saw a dramatic upsurge in foreign investment, tripling in value between 1960 and 1968, from $22 million to $68 million, when about one in every four (212 out of 833) industrial companies had some foreign stockownership. A couple of U.S. multinationals, Kennecott and Anaconda, controlled the nation's large-scale copper mining; Bethlehem Steel, with minority holdings by Chilean investors, owned the iron mines. In 1968, the value of these 3 U.S. firms' direct investment was estimated to be $586 million. A combination of British and U.S. capital controlled the production of nitrates and iodine. (On the average, copper accounted for some 80 percent, and the other minerals for some 5 percent, of the value of all of Chilean exports in the 1960s.) ITT owned the telephone and telegraph services; a majority of the stock in the consumer electricity utility was also foreign-owned. Perhaps half of all wholesale trade in the country was in the hands of just 3 British and 3 U.S.-owned firms. The value of U.S. direct investment in trade in 1968 came to an estimated $68 million. Among the nation's 16 major commercial banks, there was

[14] See Zeitlin 1984.

little foreign stockownership, but there were 5 foreign-owned banks that held about 10 percent of the aggregate assets of these 21 banks and accounted for 18 percent of Chilean currency loans and 12 percent of foreign currency loans.[15] Only the great estates remained entirely in Chilean hands, though animal husbandry and ranching in the deep south had long experienced substantial foreign involvement.[16]

As of the 1960s, then, Chilean capitalists, although they retained a solid and highly concentrated economic base of their own, appeared to be rapidly becoming at best the coequals of foreign corporations within their own country. This was, paradoxically, welcomed by the business community, which favored unrestricted foreign investment, but was condemned and opposed by the left; the paradox, however, is only apparent.[17] For, as our analysis here will reveal, domestic and foreign capital are intimately involved with each other, and Chile's leading capitalist families have extensive interests in common with the foreign corporations operating in Chile.

Conscious mutual accommodation between Chilean and foreign capital had, by the 1960s, long since replaced the often sharp competition and occasionally acute political differences marking their past relations. Lasting and close business connections between the two appear to have become common; at the same time, Chilean capitalists have sought to buttress and reinforce, often with the assistance of the state, their own independent economic base. If some of the leading families have deliberately entered into an intimate relationship with

[15] Stallings 1978, p. 42–46; Vylder 1974, pp. 14–18. U.S. Department of Commerce estimates of U.S. direct investment (as reported in the *New York Times*, October 4, 1970) also include $270 million in "Other," for a total direct investment of $964 million. For official studies of foreign investment during this period, see CORFO 1970a, 1971; ODEPLAN 1970b. Also see Caputo 1970 and Pacheco 1971, for studies done under the auspices of the centers of economic analysis at Chile's two leading universities.

[16] Perhaps most important are the investments in sheep raising (and meat packing) of the British firms of Duncan, Fox, Ltd. and the Bank of London and South America, in association with the Braun-Menéndez southern landholding family of Punta Arenas; the nation's largest cattle company (and 9th in the top 37), Tierra del Fuego Cattle, is jointly controlled by the family and these firms (see Table 1.6). Ralston Purina of Panama, a subsidiary of the U.S. multinational, is the only recent major foreign incursion in agricultural production, and the provisions of its operations in Chile became a significant political question in late 1966 (on which see notes 11, above, and 24, below).

[17] For thorough discussions of foreign investment and Chilean politics, see Wallis 1970. On the contending "development models" of the left, right, and center in Chile during the 1960s, see Stallings 1978.

foreign capital, others who had previously kept their distance have also found themselves, as the result of mergers and acquisitions, unwittingly involved, through the integration into the new company of the preexisting foreign connections of their erstwhile competitors.

The changing relationships between national and foreign capitalists in Chile since her mid-nineteenth-century economic efflorescence are roughly epitomized by the saga of Chile's quintessential capitalist family: the Edwardses. When, in the fall of 1970, the Socialist Salvador Allende won the presidential election on a platform calling for nationalization of the American copper companies and other foreign and domestic "monopolies," Agustín Edwards Eastman left Chile for New York City to become an international vice-president of the Pepsi-Cola Corporation. As head of the powerful Edwards economic group at the time, and one of the most visible and bitter foes of the newly elected Socialist government, his hasty departure from Chile was one measure of how the propertied now felt about their economic future in Chile. The ability of Mr. Edwards to retreat to a lucrative position as a higher executive in a major U.S. corporation also suggests the close ties that existed between Chile's prominent families and the multinational corporations operating in their country, as well as the confidence the heads of these corporations had in their loyalty.

The Edwards family is particularly interesting because its foreign alliances have shifted with the changing balance of foreign vs. national capital in Latin America. Although the family was founded by an immigrant ship's physician (an Englishman entranced by a young Chilean woman) in the early nineteenth century, the Edwardses made their original fortune as leading participants in Chile's dynamic nineteenth-century economic expansion. The family's ownership of a major bank and large landed estates was supplemented by investments in railroads, telegraph lines, newspapers, copper mines, and nitrate fields, and it was preeminent in the finance and export of copper during an era when Chilean-owned mines dominated in the world copper market.[18]

By the 1880s, however, the Edwardses apparently decided that it would be prudent to temper their continued economic independence by an alliance with increasingly powerful British interests. Agustín Edwards Ross established partnerships between the family's nitrate and railway enterprise and the most powerful English firms. Similarly, the

[18] Ratcliff 1972; 1973, pp. 392–393; O'Brien 1982, pp. 104–143; Figueroa 1925–1931, III, pp. 18–19.

Bank of Edwards (along with other leading private banks in Chile) became extensively involved in the many financial linkages in the nitrate industry among domestic and foreign capitalists. Edwards Ross had long been prominent politically and, as a senator, had successfully influenced state policies that enhanced his family's economic interests.[19]

Agustín Edwards MacClure, his son, and the grandfather of (Pepsi's) Agustín Edwards Eastman, did much to cultivate his family's close economic and social relations with England during his long term as Chile's ambassador in London. Although his own education (following in the tradition of the class that the founder of his family had joined) was in Santiago and Paris, Edwards MacClure sent his son to an elite English secondary school and then to Oxford University. During these years, Edwards MacClure also added to the family fortune by selling its nitrate holdings to British companies and a controlling interest in the Bank of Edwards to the Anglo–South American Bank, which was the forerunner of the Bank of London and South America (BOLSA).[20] The Edwardses were paid a "premium of 90 percent on the purchase of their shares." The prominence of Anglo–South American in Chile was based on the fortune built up over the last two decades of the nineteenth century by the "Nitrate King," Sir John Thomas North, with whom the Edwards interests were long associated. After retiring as ambassador, Edwards MacClure sat on the BOLSA board of directors, surrounded by some of the world's most powerful international bankers. The only other Latin American on the board was Antenor Patiño, the Bolivian tin baron.[21]

But, by the late 1920s, British economic hegemony in Latin America was being challenged by the United States, and the Edwards family began to look in that direction for allies. Agustín Edwards Budge, the son of Edwards MacClure, left England soon after his graduation and settled in Paris, where he worked for several years in a branch of the Morgan Bank. In time, his own sons were to attend Dartmouth and Princeton. By the 1960s, they had made the family into one of the

[19] O'Brien 1982, pp. 104–105.

[20] Joslin 1963, p. 259. This controlling interest (60 percent in 1920) "regularly paid a 16 percent dividend to the parent bank" in the years after 1920 (Joslin 1963, p. 261), but Chileans eventually regained control, probably (we have no documentation) during the Great Depression or World War II, when British economic involvement in Latin America was sharply curtailed. "The years from 1936 to 1950 were an extremely difficult period for the bank," Joslin (1963, p. 288) remarks.

[21] Joslin 1963, pp. 259, 261.

most important allies of U.S. corporations in Chile. In addition to the Pepsi-Cola franchise and a number of other ties to foreign corporations, the family reportedly owned 20 percent of a newly established Ralston Purina subsidiary in Chile,[22] and Agustín Edwards Eastman was the president and a top stockholder of the Chilean subsidiary of the Rockefellers' International Basic Economy Corporation (IBEC).

The ease with which Agustín Edwards Eastman moved between Chile and the centers of international corporate power was, of course, not unique to his family. Other Chilean businessmen in recent years have taken important positions in the headquarters of multinational corporations and financial institutions. For instance, Guillermo Carey Bustamente, a leading banker and industrialist, moved to New York in 1966 to become a vice-president with the Anaconda Corporation, then one of the world's largest multinational companies and one of two U.S. firms that had long dominated Chilean copper mining. Such high-level transfers into the headquarters of major foreign corporations are merely the most conspicuous and prominent of the close ties between Chilean and foreign capitalists.

At home, Chileans can benefit in many ways from aligning themselves and their fortunes with foreign corporations. Those who are most favored benefit from shared ownership, joint ventures, franchises (such as the Edwards Pepsi-Cola plant), and respected and lucrative positions as higher executives of the Chilean subsidiaries and affiliates of foreign corporations. These foreign companies also provide opportunities for top lawyers, consultants, agents, brokers, and—particularly for the young and ambitious, often fresh from colleges and universities in the United States—other managerial, professional, and technical positions. In short, a variety of proprietary, business, and employment connections—not to mention informal intermingling at the "best" clubs and watering places and the most exclusive social gatherings—constitute the bonds between Chile's privileged, propertied, and powerful and the representatives of foreign interests in their country.

These bonds are reciprocal, for the multinationals themselves benefit from this close association with the domestic business and professional community, which becomes a local social bastion of their own interests. At the highest levels, of course, such close local business ties may also have drawbacks for the multinational corporations, for whom it is the net return on their worldwide operations that counts,

[22] *El Mercurio*, August 11, 1966.

regardless of what the consequences might be for the development of any of their "host countries." The multinational corporations' freedom of action is crucial to them, and drawing local capitalists into their operations can limit that freedom, if not compel them to share both local control and profits. At the same time, multinational corporations have long recognized that such associations are important in providing them with "national" roots that can withstand "discriminatory" or even "confiscatory" political winds. In Latin America, from the late 1950s on, local "equity participation" and coinvestment reportedly was increasingly undertaken by the subsidiaries of U.S. corporations.[23]

The question of "imperialism" or foreign domination has, as we know, long been a volatile political issue in Chile, and it has been raised not only from the left but from the right. The concern of Chilean conservatives has been motivated by both a genuine sense of national pride and an aristocratic disdain for the "materialism" and "crudity" of U.S. business (and businessmen), as well as a profound fear of the weakening of their own economic interests and social dominance.[24] Thus, multinational corporations operating in Chile have had

[23] PMPC 1952, p. 65. A *Business Week* special supplement in late 1954, on Latin America's growing market and increasing industrialization, urged more U.S. direct investment in partnership with local industries to counter the reemergent competition of European and Japanese capital (with which the area was now "crawling") and to assuage nationalist sentiment. "There's rising pressure in Latin America," the magazine reported, "to domesticate foreign operations—with local participants, with local capital. Some U.S. companies are already selling shares to local businessmen; others are exploring the possibilities of doing it. Many new investments are taking the partnership form from the start. At the very least, this takes the 'foreign' stigma off the enterprise. . . . A royalty or licensing deal with local investors, perhaps involving stock ownership, is sometimes the best way to begin." The magazine also advised: "Pick local partners carefully. Choosing men solely for their impressive political pull can backfire when another government takes over. Yet you want Latin Americans with ability, reputation, good connections" (*Business Week* 1954, pp. 150–151).

[24] "We Denounce a Grave Menance to National Industry" was the startling headline of a quarter-page advertisement in the Edwardses' *El Mercurio* in 1966. Seven of Chile's major agribusinesses signed the ad, protesting special tax breaks and subsidies to "Ralston Purina of Panama, a subsidiary of . . . the North American enterprise. . . . This foreign enterprise, taking advantage of [a recent decree law], is soliciting a series of concessions . . . that would *constitute illegitimate privileges and mean the ruin of national industry*. . . . There would be no objection to the installation of a foreign enterprise in Chile, in free and legitimate competition with national industry," the signatories wrote, "but it would be a monstrosity to authorize such privileges and advantages as would constitute *disloyal competition* and result in the rapid ruination of Chilean industry—erected through many years of effort and great sacrifice—and the establishment of a veritable *foreign monopoly*" (*El Mercurio*, July 9, 1966; italics added). Ironically, this was a nationalist appeal from the right to the Frei reform govern-

to tap not only the business acumen, knowledge, and contacts of their Chilean associates, but also their capacity to influence state policy or to mollify critics and soothe tensions that have arisen concerning their operations. The efforts of such influential Chileans are often needed to ensure beneficial conditions for foreign investment. Their business and social contacts can be important to the representatives of foreign corporations in gaining access to appropriate politicians and officials. (On occasion, influential Chileans have even acted as intermediaries in bribery or in other clandestine efforts on behalf of foreign capital.)

In turn, of course, a business association with foreign companies has many attractions for local business. While others might long to take the path of "national capitalism," resisting foreign penetration and gaining independence from foreign capital, that route would involve formidable uncertainties and dangers for domestic capital. Even a domestic company's refusal to agree to a foreign offer to acquire a substantial interest in it raises the threat—in the absence of legal or political countermeasures—of unaccustomed foreign competition. Taking these sorts of countermeasures, especially where major left-wing parties and an "anti-imperalist" political climate already exist, could also lead unintentionally not only to a generalized confrontation with foreign capital, but to a sharpening of social tensions and political struggles that also threaten the interests of the domestic business community. Thus, in an international economy dominated by multinational corporations based in the United States and a few other advanced capitalist countries, Chilean capitalists have been likely to see both their

ment, which had utilized precisely such nationalist rhetoric in pushing for its own program of "Chileanization" of the major foreign mining operations in the country—as an alternative to the left's call for "nationalization." When it had become evident that U.S. policymakers strongly supported the Frei government's agrarian reform, spokesmen for Chile's *terratenientes* bluntly warned the United States that their fate and the fate of U.S. business interests in Chile were closely linked. In an open letter to the U.S. ambassador Ralph Dungan, the former Chilean ambassador to Mexico Juan Smitmans López wrote: "Mr. Ambassador, you have put yourself at odds with this country's respectable agrarian sectors whose propertyowners you have attacked unjustly. . . . Our agriculturists are also Chilean citizens and cannot accept being robbed of their properties—properties that they acquired and developed by their efforts and labor—just as the North American mining companies and industrialists, established in Chile under the protection of our laws, would not [want to] be deprived of theirs. One cannot advocate expropriation of the first, Mr. Ambassador, because they are Chilean, without also compromising the privileges . . . of the second, which are foreign" (*El Diario Ilustrado*, June 5, 1966, as reported in *El Siglo*, June 6, 1966).

individual fortunes and their class interests as better served by an alliance than by a confrontation with foreign capital.

The most prominent of them, in any event, given their economic power and influential connections, are prime candidates for recruitment as business associates (and political allies) by foreign corporations. For all these reasons, then, we suggest that the most extensive ties with foreign capital, through investments and participation in the direction of foreign-owned firms, have probably been forged by the families located at the very core of Chile's "coalesced bourgeoisie."

The relationships between national and foreign capital take the simultaneous form of relationships between national and foreign *firms* and relationships between national and foreign *capitalists*. Not only interlocking directorates and interpenetrating ownership between these firms, but also social intermingling, close personal relationships, and even intermarriage may bind together the families at the higher spheres of the national and foreign corporate world, thereby cementing "international," inter*class* loyalties that are far deeper than any constituted by the cash nexus alone. Thus, for instance, John D. Rockefeller, Sr.'s granddaughter Margaret Strong married Jorge ("George") de Cuevas, "in an international romance that John D. found somewhat shocking."[25] And Agustín Edwards Eastman probably could have counted, in a pinch, on the "old boy network" of his alma mater Princeton University and on personal friendships with business leaders in the United States to facilitate his search for a fittingly lucrative position there after the election of Salvador Allende. Just how extensive such personal ties are is one question we have not attempted to answer. We do examine, however, not only the coalescence of national and foreign capital within the top firms, but the extent to which the members of those families at the core of Chile's capitalist class are part and parcel of the corporate apparatus of foreign appropriation in their own country.

Foreign Stockownership in the Top 37 Nonfinancial Corporations

The top 37 nonfinancial corporations are relatively free of foreign stockownership. Government data for 1966 show only 4 with foreign shareholdings of 20 percent or more. In another 3, foreign shareholders have less than 20 percent but at least 10 percent of the stock; there

[25] Collier and Horowitz 1976, p. 72.

are 6 more with at least 5 percent but less than 10 percent foreign-held stock; and the rest have less than 5 percent (including 20 firms with no major foreign shareholdings). Of course, the extent of foreign penetration of a corporation can be hidden by stock held through nominees acting as the local agents of foreign interests. A number of minor holdings can also be significant when these are combined in the same hands. Our own analysis of the stockownership of the top 37 reveals that government figures, limited to the 10 major stockholders-of-record, tend slightly to understate foreign stockownership, especially when it is distributed among a number of smaller holdings. (Although the official figures show no foreign stockownership in 20 of the top 37 corporations, we found that 10 of them actually have between 1 and 5 percent of their stock held by foreign shareholders.)

While local nominees can, and often do, obscure foreign ownership, we also found that holding companies registered *abroad* can mask the actual locus of control at *home*. Of the 4 companies in the top 37 in which "foreign investors" hold at least 20 percent of the shares, according to government figures, 2 are, in fact, almost certainly controlled by a Chilean resident and his associates: Mantos Blancos Mining Enterprise and Oruro Mining Co. (see Table 1.5). A complex façade of foreign holding companies masks their actual control by Mauricio Hochschild, in and of himself a veritable multinational corporation, based mainly in Chile. When the tin mines bearing his name were expropriated in Bolivia in 1952, *Business Week* reported that "Hochschild is largely held in Chile." His biographical entry in the *Diccionario biográfico de Chile*, Chile's equivalent of *Who's Who*, notes that Hochschild has "firms established in Chile, Peru, Bolivia, Brazil, and Argentina, as well as agencies in the United States and Great Britain."

The U.S. Department of Commerce reported in 1960 that the copper mines at Mantos Blancos had been "under development since 1956 by the Mauricio Hochschild interests." But Hochschild did not appear among the principal stockholders-of-record in Mantos Blancos, although the following did: Marvis Corporation, S.A., Panama, with 46 percent of the stock; Empresas Sudamericanas Consolidadas, S.A., Panama, with 23.2 percent; and Mantos Blancos itself, with 9.7 percent. Our inquiry at the time to the international banking division of one of the world's largest commercial banks, based in San Francisco, brought the following confidential reply concerning these firms: "Marvis Corporation, Panama is the holding company of subject [Mantos Blancos], and they [sic] in turn are wholly owned by the Empresas Sudamericanas Consolidadas, S.A., Panama. . . . [The latter] was formed in 1950 as a holding company in order to centralize control over the large group of mining, industrial and commercial interests of Dr. Mauricio Hochschild and associates. These enterprises comprise a network of companies in South America, as well as the U.S., Canada, U.K., Germany, France, and Belgium."

In Oruro Mining Co., Empresas Sudamericanas Consolidadas is the second-ranking shareholder, with 17.6 percent, and the top stockholder is Cía. Mercantil Corona, S.A., with 34.7 percent (about which the British Registry yields no useful information); the other principal shareholders in Oruro are also holding companies. Given Dr. Hochschild's proclivities for control through holding companies registered in foreign (low-tax or no-tax) jurisdictions, Oruro is probably also under his control (perhaps in association with the Anglo–South American Bank, through its nominee Bolsa de Nominees [sic] Ltd., which, according to the British Registry, holds 13.5 percent of Oruro's stock). Thus, despite appearances, Mantos Blancos and Oruro are not foreign-controlled, but are, in fact, under the control of a centralized multinational holding-company complex based in Chile.[26]

Two other top-37 corporations illustrate the complexity of the form that can be taken by the coalescence of national and foreign capital: Yarur Chilean Cotton Products and Glassware of Chile. Yarur Cotton, the 12th largest company owned by Chileans in 1966, is probably under the joint control of the Yarur family and W. R. Grace interests. One of Chile's major industrial and banking families, the Yarurs dominate the company's board and have the largest combined Chilean holding; but the single-largest holding, 24.5 percent, is in the name of the Chase Manhattan Trust Department. This may, of course, be held for the Yarurs, if not for the Chase Manhattan Bank itself, but it seems likely, instead, that it is held for W. R. Grace and Co.: Yarur and Grace have close interests in at least two other top manufacturing firms, Caupolicán Textiles and Bella Vista–Tomé Cloth Factory, which rank 22nd and 34th, respectively, among the top 37 corporations. The board of directors of Caupolicán Textiles is dominated by Grace representatives; indeed, we could not identify one Yarur representative among its officers and directors. Yet Caupolicán's dominant holdings

[26] *Business Week* 1952, p. 149; *Diccionario biográfico de Chile, 1947–1948* (1950, p. 577); Bohan and Pomeranz 1960, p. 88; confidential March 29, 1968, letter to authors from San Francisco–based bank; British Registry, from the April 1967 Annual Return.

are apparently in the hands of the Yarurs: Yarur Enterprises (a holding company owned entirely by three Yarur brothers in 1964) holds 21 percent of Caupolicán's shares, and another 49 percent is held by Yarur Cotton. If our educated guess is correct, i.e. that Yarur and Grace share control of Yarur Cotton, then this would explain the absence of any Yarur representatives on Caupolicán's board as well as its domination by Grace agents. Indeed, we found a similar situation in Bella Vista–Tomé, where a complicated pyramidal holding-company arrangement is at work.

Glassware of Chile is the country's biggest manufacturer of glass (80 percent of the container tonnage and 40 percent of the household glassware tonnage) and ranks 24th in the top 37. Although most of its shares are held by Chileans, the two largest holdings as of 1964 belong, respectively, to Corning Glass Works, with 19.5 percent, and Pittsburgh Plate Glass International, with 8.8 percent. (Another principal U.S. interest, fourth largest at 6.5 percent, is the First National City Bank of New York.) It might be supposed that the first two holdings represent the competing interests of two U.S. multinationals: in 1964, PPG ranked 73rd and Corning 201st by sales among U.S. industrial corporations. Thus, although they were aware that these two corporations have minority holdings in Glassware of Chile, U.S. Department of Commerce specialists could nonetheless write that it is "controlled by Chilean interests."[27] The fact is, however, that PPG and Corning have a long-standing business association. In 1937, they organized the Pittsburgh Corning Corporation, of which they are co-owners (fifty-fifty); the latter, in turn, owns the Pittsburgh Corning Export Corporation. Therefore, the "separate" shareholdings of PPG and Corning in Glassware of Chile likely form a coordinated controlling block of 28.3 percent. In fact, it is listed in Moody's *Industrial Manual* as an "associated company" (as distinguished from a subsidiary or affiliate) of Corning Glass—though no such connection is noted for PPG[28] (This indicates, incidentally, one way in which putatively rival multinational corporations extend their "co-respective behavior" to foreign countries in order to secure their joint control of ostensibly independent and nationally owned firms. In this case, the Chilean firm had already established a monopoly of the national industry before coming under the control of foreign corporations.)

Production of glass is one of Chile's oldest industries, pioneered by

[27] Bohan and Pomeranz 1960, p. 157.

[28] Moody's 1970b, p. 2165.

Matías Cousiño, who established glass factories and refractories as early as the 1850s. Cousiño was the founder of the Lota Coal and Industrial Company (merged in 1964 as Lota-Schwager to become the 10th largest of the top 37 nonfinancial corporations in Chile in 1966). The heirs of Cousiño, through personal and indirect holdings, and through their strategic representation in management, hold significant interests in Glassware of Chile. The president is married to the first cousin of Arturo Cousiño Lyon, the grandson of Matías Cousiño, and is an officer or director of at least 3 other Cousiño-controlled firms (including Lota-Schwager). Three other directors have been close associates of the Cousiños for many years. Cousiño and associated interests in Glassware of Chile, aside from their strategic representation in management, amount to 9.2 percent as of 1964. (One of Glassware's directors is also a director of Lota-Green Refractories, and the president of Glassware is also its president, while another Glassware director is its vice-president. Lota-Green was founded [under another name] by Matías Cousiño in 1854. The president and three directors of Glassware also rank among Lota-Green's 10 largest stockholders, as do the firms of Glassware of Chile and Lota-Schwager themselves. Lota-Green, in turn, is also exemplary of the ascendance of foreign over domestic capital within a major national firm. The A. P. Green Firebrick Company went from being merely a technical-advisory firm in 1953 to the holder of 76.8 percent of Lota-Green [along with Metropolitan Refractories, Inc.] in 1966.)[29]

The other principal domestic interest that is prominent in Glassware of Chile is the Edwards family and its associates. Like the Cousiños, the Edwardses, it will be remembered, have been a major power in Chile's economy since the mid-nineteenth century, and in the decade of the 1960s they were still one of the few most important capitalist families in Chile. The Edwards family and associates hold 9 percent of the stock of Glassware of Chile, although they apparently have no representation in its management. The Edwards interests in Glassware probably date from the early 1900s, when the Gubler and Cousiño Brewery merged with the Edwards-controlled United Breweries.[30] Decades later, these powerful capitalist families now find themselves acting as "junior partners" of foreign capital in a firm that they built. Given their long history of business leadership in Chile and their dominant position in several large corporations as of the mid-1960s, these

[29] Bohan and Pomeranz 1960, p. 158.

[30] Figueroa 1925–1931, I, p. 473.

families probably act with relative independence in Glassware of Chile, and not as mere subordinates. Given the technological integration of the firm with U.S. industry, however, coupled with the presence of the dominant PPG and Corning interests, the Edwardses and the Cousiños, even in association with other large Chilean investors in Glassware, almost certainly have to share control with these U.S. multinationals.

The Coalescence of National and Foreign Capital

The actual pattern of interrelations between foreign and domestic capital, as these cases among the top 37 suggest, can be obscured if one simply counts the percentage of foreign vs. domestic stockownership in the large corporation. A variety of other business arrangements, not necessarily involving stockownership, can serve to bind together domestic and foreign investment: financial agreements; licensing, technical, and marketing contracts; subcontractor or customer-supplier deals; and interlocking directorates. Thus, the implications of, for instance, even a minor foreign shareholding in a Chilean company (or vice versa) will differ to some unknown extent depending on such business arrangements and, in addition, on that company's relative national and international competitive standing. Bearing this in mind, the coalescence of ownership of the large corporation remains a decisive way of integrating the concrete interests of national and foreign capital.

How extensive, then, is this coalescence in our top 200 corporations in Chile as of 1966? It is, to lay down the answer immediately, not especially extensive in the top *Chilean-owned* corporations but, in contrast, is quite extensive in the top *foreign* corporations, where the ownership of stock by Chileans is, in fact, marked. Among these top 200 corporations, it will be remembered, 11 are state enterprises, 6 are financial companies (5 Chilean-owned and 1 foreign), and 1 is not identified. Of the 182 top nonfinancial corporations, 43 are "foreign-owned" and 139 are "Chilean-owned—that is to say, 50 percent or more of the stock is held, respectively, by foreign and domestic shareowners.[31] What, then, is the relative distribution of foreign vs. domestic stockownership in these top 43 foreign and top 139 nonfinancial corporations?

Merely 5.3 percent of the worth of all outstanding shares of the top 139 Chilean corporations is in foreign hands; 112 of them (80.6 per-

[31] For a detailed description of these top 200, see note 14, Chapter 1.

cent) have no identifiable foreign shareholders, but a block of at least 5 percent of the stock is foreign-held in 21 corporations (15 percent), and a block of at least 10 percent is so held in 16 corporations (11.5 percent). Foreign-held blocks of at least 10 percent of the stock are far more frequent in the largest of the top 139 corporations: there are 8 among the top 50 and 7 among the next 50, but only 1 among the bottom 39. The pattern is similar if we consider what can be defined as a "joint venture" involving a foreign holding of at least 20 percent of the stock. A holding of this size not only indicates that the interests of foreign investors in the activities of that firm are substantial, but also suggests that they share in its actual control. Such joint ventures in the top 139 are few: among the top 50, there are 4; among the next 50, 7; and in the bottom 39, only 1 (see Table 6.1).

If the top 139 Chilean-owned nonfinancial corporations appear to be relatively free of foreign ownership, the top 43 "foreign" corporations are, paradoxically, the site of a marked coalescence of Chilean and foreign capital. Of the market worth of the outstanding shares in the top 43 foreign firms, 10.9 percent are held by Chileans. They hold more than 40 percent (but less than 50 percent) of the stock in 11 (25.6 percent) of the top 43, and hold 20 percent or more (but less than 40 percent) of the stock in another 10; that is to say, Chileans own a substantial joint holding in just about half of the top 43 ostensibly foreign corporations. While the foreign holdings in Chilean corporations tend to be in the largest firms, the pattern is reversed here. Most of the principal Chilean shareholdings are in the smaller foreign companies: among the bottom 23, Chileans hold a block of 40 percent

TABLE 6.1. Distribution of Foreign Ownership of the Top 139 Chilean-Owned Nonfinancial Corporations, in Manufacturing and Other Industries, 1966

	Manufacturing Firms		Other Firms		All Chilean Firms	
% Foreign Ownership	*N*	%	*N*	%	*N*	%
0	66	77.0	46	88.5	112	80.6
under 1	2	2.3	1	1.9	3	2.2
1–4.9	2	2.3	1	1.9	3	2.2
5–9.9	2	2.3	3	5.8	5	3.6
10–19.9	3	3.4	1	1.9	4	2.9
20–29.9	6	6.9	0	0	6	4.3
30–39.9	2	2.3	0	0	2	1.4
40–49.9	4	4.6	0	0	4	2.9
TOTAL	87	100.0	52	100.0	139	100.0

(but less than 50 percent) of the stock in 9 companies, compared with holdings of that size in only 2 of the top 20. The sizable shareholdings by Chileans also tend to be in manufacturing rather than in other industries: of the 21 foreign companies in which Chileans hold at least 20 percent of the stock, two-thirds are in manufacturing. Conversely, Chileans hold at least 20 percent of the stock in the vast majority of the top 20 foreign manufacturing firms (70 percent), but in just less than one-third (30.4 percent) of the top 23 nonmanufacturing firms (see Table 6.2).

The origins of this marked coalescence of domestic and foreign ownership within the top foreign corporations can only be surmised here. On the one hand, multinational corporations often use host-country capital to establish overseas subsidiaries, since this minimizes their own investment (and risk). It can be to a multinational's advantage, as one *Fortune* writer notes, to start foreign operations "with a limited amount of equity and a generous supply of debt," because "foreign lenders will often provide . . . far more money, as a percentage of equity, than will U.S. lenders."[32] Substantial shareownership by "nationals" is also a hedge against nationalist "interference" in or "discrimination" against the operations of foreign companies; not only does it provide protective coloration, but it also establishes a concrete community of interest with influential domestic capitalists. This must have been—in what was an epoch of sharpening class conflict and growing nationalism in the Chile of the 1960s—an important consid-

TABLE 6.2. Distribution of Chilean Ownership of the Top 43 Foreign-Owned Nonfinancial Corporations, in Manufacturing and Other Industries, 1966

	Manufacturing Firms		Other Firms		All Foreign Firms	
% Chilean Ownership	*N*	%	*N*	%	*N*	%
0	3	15.0	13	56.5	16	37.2
under 1	1	5.0	2	8.7	3	7.0
1–4.9	0	0	0	0	0	0
5–9.9	1	5.0	1	4.3	2	4.7
10–19.9	1	5.0	0	0	1	2.3
20–29.9	2	10.0	3	13.0	5	11.6
30–39.9	5	25.0	0	0	5	11.6
40–49.9	7	35.0	4	17.4	11	25.6
TOTAL	20	100.0	23	100.0	43	100.0

[32] Rose 1968, p. 104.

eration for the multinationals in opening themselves up to substantial Chilean stockownership. On the other hand, the 1960s were also characterized, as we noted earlier, by a considerable surge of foreign investment in Chilean manufacturing; and these sizable Chilean shareholdings in the top 43 foreign corporations may well represent the still significant remnants of what once was predominant Chilean ownership.

This was the trend in Latin America generally, where nearly half of the manufacturing firms established by the top 187 U.S. multinationals during the 1960s were "established" by buy-outs of existing local firms. The figure would have been even higher, *Business Latin America* observed, except for the "scarcity of local firms remaining in particular industries." Chile's capitalists resisted the establishment of foreign firms that would compete with their own already existing companies, and their resistance was usually supported by state policy. But many of the leading families had also long since acquired a habit of investment in association with foreign capital; so it is likely that many of the top 43 foreign-owned corporations with substantial minority shareownership by Chileans resulted from such Chilean-foreign joint ventures or partnerships. Whichever of these tendencies the pattern reflects, the pattern itself is clear: a substantial coalescence of national and foreign capital among the top 43 foreign corporations.[33]

Foreign Corporations and Intraclass Relations

While revealing, these findings do not sufficiently gauge the depth of foreign penetration into the inner structure of Chile's dominant class. The question is how and to what extent its decisive segments are involved with the largest foreign corporations. To answer it, we gathered information on the stockownership and higher executive offices held in several dozen large foreign corporations by the 229 officers and directors of the top 37 nonfinancial corporations. Aside from the top 43 foreign corporations (in our top 200), we also included the 11 foreign firms that appear among the top 50 firms originally selected for this study, as well as 15 firms on a "trade list," compiled by the U.S. Department of Commerce, of U.S. subsidiaries having a "substantial

[33] Rose 1968, p. 105. Also see Moran 1974; Barnet and Müller 1974, p. 139, citing *Business Latin America*, January 15, 1970. On Chile, see Burbach 1975, p. 126. See, also, Vaupel and Curhan 1969, on multinational corporations' local acquisitions in Latin America.

direct capital investment" in Chile.[34] Among the latter are subsidiaries of RCA, Singer, Mobil Oil, and American Screw.

We find that a mere 7 percent of the 229 higher executives of the top 37 nonfinancial corporations personally have a principal shareholding in a large foreign corporation (2 percent hold substantial stock in 2 foreign firms); but three times that many sit on a foreign board (11 percent sit on one, 4 percent sit on two, and 7 percent on three).[35] Whether this latter figure is said to amount to "fully" 22 percent or "only" 22 percent, the fact is that, by this measure, the overwhelming majority of the higher executives of our top Chilean corporations have no concrete stake in the interests of the largest foreign corporations. But, as we have emphasized throughout this analysis of the inner structure of the dominant class, an exclusive focus on the individual tends to obscure the real dimensions and contours of social economic relations within the dominant class. Further, the *location* of individuals and families within this ensemble of social relations is crucial in determining other attributes of their intraclass situation.

As the reader now knows all too well, the detailed presentation of these complex inner-structural relations in multivariate tabular form involves some unavoidable tedium. To reduce that tedium to a minimum while maximizing the clarity of the relationships, especially as this book draws to a close, stockownership and occupancy of a seat on a foreign corporate board have been combined into a single measure we call "the ties that bind" or, more prosaically, "ties to foreign corporations." A "foreign tie" is constituted by ownership of a principal

[34] On the original "top 50," see note 14, Chapter 1. The trade list (Bureau of International Commerce 1970) provides the names of the firm's "principal officials" in Chile, its number of employees, and the name of its controlling U.S. company; 67 wholly- or majority-owned nonfinancial firms are on the list; of these, 43 appear among the "top 200" firms of 1966, from which we drew a random sample of the 15 U.S. firms included in the present study.

[35] The data in Table 6.3 understate the linkages of the top 37 executives to foreign-controlled corporations in Chile because we have here defined only corporations over 50 percent foreign-*owned* as "foreign-controlled." But foreign *control* can certainly be exerted on the basis of ownership of a substantial minority block of shares. If we assume that working control can be exerted when foreign ownership amounts to at least 20 percent, the percentage of higher executives with seats in foreign-controlled firms would be as follows: 68 percent in none; 19 percent in one; 4 percent in two; 9 percent in three or more. Note that only 204 executives are considered here. Excluded are 25 top-37 executives who have seats only in foreign-controlled firms according to this 20 percent criterion. If these 25 men are included here, then 40 percent of the 229 higher executives would be defined as having seats on the boards of foreign-controlled corporations in Chile.

stockholding *or* by occupancy of a position in a foreign corporation, whether by an individual or by a close relative.

THE "INNER GROUP"

The "inner group" of those men who interlock several of our top 37 corporations are thereby charged, we have argued, with a disproportionate responsibility for managing the common affairs of the entire business community; they have, in other words, a distinctive role in fashioning an intercorporate strategy that serves not only the narrow interests of particular firms or families, but the broader interests of their class. For this reason, they are especially well situated to act as intermediaries or representatives of their class in its relations with foreign capital.

We find, in fact, that it is precisely the men in this inner group who are by far most closely tied to large foreign corporations, both personally and through their families. The pattern is the same at each kinship level: the men who sit in the management of only one top-37 corporation are much less likely to have a personal or familial tie to a foreign corporation than are the men in the inner group, i.e. those who hold two or even three or more top-37 seats. For example, among the men in the "inner group within the inner group," i.e. the 16 men who sit on three or more top-37 boards, fully half have personal foreign ties, in contrast to slightly over a sixth of those having a single top-37 seat; similarly, 75 percent of the men "within the inner group" have foreign ties within the close family, compared to 39 percent of those having one top-37 seat.

It is also obvious that taking the ties of the close family into account profoundly alters our view of the depth of the community of interest shared by Chilean capitalists and foreign corporations. Thus, the overall percentage having foreign ties nearly doubles, from 23 percent having personal ties to 43 percent having close family ties. And for each category, the tendency is the same: as the foreign ties of family members are taken into account, the extent of foreign ties is revealed to be far greater than when only the individual's foreign ties are considered (see Table 6.3).

FINANCE CAPITAL

The interlocking directorates tying together the major banks and the top nonfinancial corporations have an especially crucial political-economic role. They must try to integrate the simultaneous and poten-

TABLE 6.3. Percentage of Higher Executives of the Top 37 Nonfinancial Corporations in Chile Who Have Personal or Family Ties to Foreign Corporations, by the Number of Top-37 Management Seats Held, 1964/66

	Personal Foreign Ties	Immediate Family Foreign Ties	Secondary Family Foreign Ties	Close Family Foreign Ties	(*N*)
One seat	17	25	31	39	(166)
Two seats	36	38	40	49	(47)
Three-plus seats	50	56	62	75	(16)
All executives	23	30	35	43	(229)

tially contradictory financial, industrial, and commercial interests of the principal capitalist families whose various investments span these apparently independent institutional realms. We found, indeed, that the "finance capitalists," who interlock the boards of the banks and corporations, simultaneously disposing of loan and productive capital, are a distinctive intraclass type and occupy a special place in their class. For this reason, we suggest, they are especially well suited to deal with foreign capital, to assess its impact not merely on the immediate, narrow interests of the firms or industry, but on the broad economic and political interests of their class, and to try to act to protect and advance both. Further, as men of finance, able to facilitate commercial bank loans or credits, or even equity investments, for foreign firms, the latter would consider it desirable to establish close business ties with them.

The contrast in the extent of the foreign ties of finance capitalists and other executives is, in any case, striking. Ordinary corporate executives are less likely to have personal or close family ties to the large foreign corporations than either the "secondary" or the "primary" finance capitalists. Furthermore, not only are the primary finance capitalists far more likely than either of the former to have foreign ties, but most of them have personal as well as familial foreign ties. The differences in the extent of the foreign ties of ordinary executives, primary finance capitalists, and secondary finance capitalists are consistent at each kinship distance (though it should be noted that these differences shrink as the foreign ties of close relatives at increasing kinship distance are successively taken into account). (See Table 6.4.)

PRINCIPAL OWNERS OF CAPITAL

The men who are both higher functionaries and principal owners of capital have a special stake in ensuring that foreign investment and the operations of foreign corporations in Chile reinforce, rather than

TABLE 6.4. Percentage of Finance Capitalists and Other Higher Executives of the Top 37 Nonfinancial Corporations in Chile Who Have Personal or Family Ties to Foreign Corporations, 1964/66

	Personal Foreign Ties	Immediate Family Foreign Ties	Secondary Family Foreign Ties	Close Family Foreign Ties	(*N*)
Primary finance capitalists	57	60	63	73	(30)
Secondary finance capitalists	22	37	41	48	(27)
Ordinary executives	17	23	29	37	(172)

NOTE: See pp. 125–126, above, for definition of "primary" vs. "secondary" finance capitalists.

TABLE 6.5. Percentage of Higher Executives of the Top 37 Nonfinancial Corporations in Chile Who Have Personal or Family Ties to Foreign Corporations, by the Number of Principal Capitalists in the Secondary Family, 1964/66

	Personal Foreign Ties	Immediate Family Foreign Ties	Secondary Family Foreign Ties	Close Family Foreign Ties	(*N*)
No capitalists	21	22	23	27	(114)
One or two capitalists	28	37	47	58	(74)
Three-plus capitalists	20	39	46	61	(41)

undermine, the existing patterns of corporate ownership, concentration of capital, monopolistic competition, and overall balance of class and intraclass power. In consequence, we suggest, they would be especially likely to seek (and to be sought out for) an active role in the boardrooms of the large foreign corporations. Known to be members of wealthy families, their social credentials also qualify them as impeccable representatives of foreign capital within the domestic corporate world. If this reasoning is correct, then the top-37 executives who are members of a principal capitalist family would tend, in comparison to noncapitalists, to be tied to foreign corporations.

When it comes to having their own foreign ties, however, we find that the differences are minor: 21 percent of the noncapitalists, and 25 percent of the principal capitalists, have personal foreign ties. When, however, we consider the foreign ties of *family* members, the differences between the foreign ties of propertied and nonpropertied executives are consistent, and sharp, at each kinship distance. Further, even a family's specific number of principal capitalists affects the chances that it will have ties to foreign capital. Among those men whose families have three or more principal capitalist members, the proportion whose families also have foreign ties is consistently higher than it is among those having only one or two principal capitalists in the family (see Tables 6.5 and 6.6). At the level of the close family for both capital ownership and foreign ties, for instance, we find that one-quarter of the nonpropertied have familial foreign ties; but of those who have one or two principal capitalists in the family, slightly over half, and of those who have three or more, nearly two-thirds, have close family ties to foreign corporations (see Table 6.6).

TABLE 6.6. Percentage of Higher Executives of the Top 37 Nonfinancial Corporations in Chile Who Have Personal or Family Ties to Foreign Corporations, by the Number of Principal Capitalists in the Close Family, 1964/66

	Personal Foreign Ties	Immediate Family Foreign Ties	Secondary Family Foreign Ties	Close Family Foreign Ties	(*N*)
No capitalists	21	22	22	25	(105)
One or two capitalists	29	34	42	52	(59)
Three-plus capitalists	22	39	49	65	(65)

THE "INNER GROUP," FINANCE CAPITALISTS, AND CAPITAL OWNERSHIP

Both their location as functionaries of capital, in the intercorporate and banking–corporate managerial apparatus, and their families' ownership of capital affect the top-37 executives' propensity to form foreign ties. The question, then, is how these variables, when we consider them together, affect the formation of foreign ties—especially, as we also know from earlier chapters, since the men of the inner group and the finance capitalists tend disproportionately to be members of principal capitalist families. Remarkably, remember, nearly all of the finance capitalists in the inner group belong to a capitalist family.

Both the family's capital ownership and the number of top-37 seats held by the higher executive affect the chances that he or his family will have foreign ties. The differences between the personal and familial foreign ties of the men inside and outside the inner group are especially sharp among the principal capitalists. Among these latter, only 14 percent of the men holding a single seat have personal foreign ties; but 45 percent of those holding two seats, and 50 percent of those holding three or more seats, have foreign ties. Similarly, the pattern of foreign ties within the immediate, secondary, and close capitalist family, is also clear: men of property inside the inner group are consistently more likely than those outside it to have close relatives with ties to foreign corporations. At the same time, the family's ownership of capital also weighs heavily in the establishment of foreign ties: holding the number of top-37 seats constant, we find that those men from capitalist families are consistently more likely than nonpropertied executives to have personal foreign ties or to have immediate, secondary, or close family members with such ties. Thus, for instance, among those men holding a single top-37 seat, 54 percent of the principal capitalists, but only 23 percent of the noncapitalists, have foreign ties within the close family. And, though the numbers in the relevant cells are very small, the pattern is the same for men holding multiple seats: 62 percent and 83 percent, respectively, of the principal capitalists, compared with 28 percent and 50 percent of the noncapitalists holding two seats vs. three or more seats, have foreign ties within the close family (see Table 6.7).

The pattern is similar with respect to differences between finance capitalists and ordinary executives. Both being a finance capitalist and belonging to a principal capitalist family affect the chances that a man or his family will have foreign ties. The finance capitalists—especially the primary finance capitalists—stand out preponderantly, among capitalist and noncapitalist higher executives alike, as the decisive intermediaries between their own and foreign corporations. Those finance capitalists and ordinary executives who belong to principal capitalist families are also more likely than their noncapitalist counterparts to have close relatives with foreign corporate ties. Note also that spreading the kinship net more widely among the noncapitalists does not yield additional close relatives with foreign ties; but it does among the

TABLE 6.7. Percentage of Higher Executives of the Top 37 Nonfinancial Corporations in Chile Who Have Personal or Family Ties to Foreign Corporations, by the Number of Top-37 Management Seats Held and Ownership of Capital in the Close Family, 1964/66

	Personal Foreign Ties	Immediate Family Foreign Ties	Secondary Family Foreign Ties	Close Family Foreign Ties	(*N*)
Principal capitalists					
one seat	14	29	41	54	(83)
two seats	45	48	52	62	(29)
three-plus seats	50	58	67	83	(12)
All executives in capitalist families	25	36	46	59	(124)
Noncapitalists					
one seat	19	20	20	23	(83)
two seats	22	22	22	28	(18)
	} 27	} 27	} 27	} 32	
three-plus seats	50	50	50	50	(4)
All executives in noncapitalist families	21	22	22	25	(105)

principal capitalists, where, as the kinship distance probed increases, the percentage of close relatives having foreign ties also increases. What is certain is that the primary finance capitalists, the consummate "business leaders" of their class, drawn from the core of intermarrying capitalist families and managing their common interests at the interlocking helms of the big banks and top corporations, are also the segment most thoroughly tied to the foreign corporations operating in Chile (see Tables 6.8 and 6.9).

Political Hegemony and Foreign Capital

But what of the explicit *political* leaders of the dominant class? What are their relations with the major foreign corporations? Although the issue of the rights and responsibilities of foreign capital had gravely divided the dominant class in the second half of the nineteenth century, it was not uncommon as early as the 1880s to find members of congress in the employ of foreign companies, as their advisers, attorneys, or agents—and, of course, as advocates of their interests within the government itself. If an air of impropriety once attached to such activities, however, they became—as accommodation with foreign capital proceeded in Chile's business community and as foreign corporations became dominant in some areas of the nation's economic life during the twentieth century—both accepted and respectable. Much as passage through the portals of Pentagon procurement offices or armed services general staffs and defense contractor boardrooms has

TABLE 6.8. Percentage of Finance Capitalists and Other Higher Executives of the Top 37 Nonfinancial Corporations in Chile Who Have Personal or Family Ties to Foreign Corporations, by Ownership of Capital in the Secondary Family, 1964/66

	Personal Foreign Ties		Immediate Family Foreign Ties		Secondary Family Foreign Ties		Close Family Foreign Ties		(*N*)
Principal capitalists									
primary finance capitalists	54	43	59	54	64	59	77	70	(22)
secondary finance capitalists	27		47		53		60		(15)
ordinary executives	17		30		44		54		(78)
all capitalist executives	25		37		47		59		(115)
Noncapitalists									
primary finance capitalists	63	35	63	40	63	40	63	45	(8)
secondary finance capitalists	17		25		25		33		(12)
ordinary executives	18		18		19		23		(94)
all noncapitalist executives	21		22		23		27		(114)

TABLE 6.9. Percentage of Finance Capitalists and Other Higher Executives of the Top 37 Nonfinancial Corporations in Chile Who Have Personal or Family Ties to Foreign Corporations, by Ownership of Capital in the Close Family, 1964/66

	Personal Foreign Ties	Immediate Family Foreign Ties	Secondary Family Foreign Ties	Close Family Foreign Ties	(*N*)
Principal capitalists					
primary finance capitalists	54 } 40	59 } 50	64 } 55	77 } 67	(22)
secondary finance capitalists	22	39	44	56	(18)
ordinary executives	18	30	42	55	(84)
all capitalist executives	25	36	46	59	(124)
Noncapitalists					
primary finance capitalists	62 } 41	62 } 47	62 } 47	62 } 47	(8)
secondary finance capitalists	22	33	33	33	(9)
ordinary executives	17	17	17	20	(88)
all noncapitalist executives	21	22	22	25	(105)

become a common career line in the United States, circulation between the executive suites of top Chilean corporations, public office, and foreign boardrooms had likewise become common in Chile long before the 1960s. Surely few could be chosen who would more "naturally" and effectively represent the community of interest of the top domestic and foreign corporations than those higher corporate executives who had also served as leaders of their parties, or in congress, government ministries, the judiciary, or other public office—where the laws governing the operations of these corporations were made and enforced. Inside experience with the workings of government and "old boy" ties with former colleagues ensured even out-of-office politicians a measure of access and influence denied to others. For these reasons, we should find that, proportionately, far more political officeholders than nonofficeholders among our top-37 higher executives have served on the boards of foreign corporations.

Although this is, in fact, what we find, the differences in the extent of their personal foreign ties are small. Extending our probe to the foreign ties of their immediate families does not change the picture; and, although including the foreign ties of other close relatives does widen the gap, the differences remain modest: 53 percent of the officeholding, and 39 percent of the nonofficeholding, top-37 executives have foreign ties (see Table 6.10).

What these figures obscure, however, is the importance of the *polit-*

TABLE 6.10. Percentage of Higher Executives of the Top 37 Nonfinancial Corporations in Chile Who Have Personal or Family Ties to Foreign Corporations, by Political Offices Held Personally, 1964/66

	Personal Foreign Ties	Immediate Family Foreign Ties	Secondary Family Foreign Ties	Close Family Foreign Ties	(*N*)
Executive has held office	31	36	45	53	(64)
Executive has not held office	20	27	31	39	(165)

ical family in the placement process. If a prominent congressman or cabinet minister may not find it convenient or possible to attend simultaneously to the affairs of state and the affairs of business, others in the family can attend to the latter in his stead; no doubt, an illustrious family name enhances one's prospects of being appointed to the board of a major foreign corporation or of being invited to invest in it. Many of the men who appear (as in Table 6.10) to be "apolitical," then, are actually from political families; the full impact of these families on the establishment of foreign connections has been obscured by an exclusive focus on personal officeholding. Once we separate out the men having no close relatives in politics from the men who belong to political families, however, systematic and sharp differences in the extent of their foreign ties become evident.

TABLE 6.11. Percentage of Higher Executives of the Top 37 Nonfinancial Corporations in Chile Who Have Personal or Family Ties to Foreign Corporations, by the Number of Political Officeholders in the Secondary Family, 1964/66

	Personal Foreign Ties	Immediate Family Foreign Ties	Secondary Family Foreign Ties	Close Family Foreign Ties	(*N*)
No officeholders	16	20	21	25	(103)
One officeholder	25	30	37	48	(60)
Two-plus officeholders	32	44	54	67	(66)

What is revealed, indeed, is that the more close political relatives a higher executive has, the more likely he is to be tied to a foreign corporation, either personally or through his family (see Tables 6.11 and 6.12). Of those who have no political officeholders within the close family, for instance, a mere 14 percent have personal foreign ties; but 22 percent of those with one officeholding close family member, and 34 percent of those with two or more officeholding close relatives, have *personal* foreign ties. As the foreign ties of our executives' close family members are taken into account, moreover, far sharper differences emerge. At each kinship distance, from primary through ter-

TABLE 6.12. Percentage of Higher Executives of the Top 37 Nonfinancial Corporations in Chile Who Have Personal or Family Ties to Foreign Corporations, by the Number of Political Officeholders in the Close Family, 1964/66

	Personal Foreign Ties	Immediate Family Foreign Ties	Secondary Family Foreign Ties	Close Family Foreign Ties	(*N*)
No officeholders	14	16	17	20	(92)
One officeholder	22	31	36	43	(58)
Two-plus officeholders	34	44	54	71	(79)

TABLE 6.13. Percentage of Higher Executives of the Top 37 Nonfinancial Corporations in Chile Who Have Personal or Family Ties to Foreign Corporations, by the Number of Political Officeholders and Ownership of Capital in the Secondary Family, 1964/66

	Personal Foreign Ties	Immediate Family Foreign Ties	Secondary Family Foreign Ties	Close Family Foreign Ties	(*N*)
Principal capitalists					
no officeholders	21	30	33	35	(43)
one officeholder	28	38	52	69	(29)
two-plus officeholders	28	44	58	77	(43)
all executives in capitalist families	25	37	47	59	(115)
Noncapitalists					
no officeholders	13	13	13	18	(60)
one officeholder	23	23	23	29	(31)
two-plus officeholders	39	44	48	49	(23)
all executives in noncapitalist families	21	22	23	27	(114)

tiary relatives, the number of political officeholders in a man's family is directly and highly associated with the likelihood that his family also has foreign ties. So, for instance, among those men having no political officeholders in their close families, only 20 percent have foreign ties within the close family. But 43 percent of those having one officeholder in the close family—and 71 percent of those having two or more officeholders in the close family—have foreign ties within the close family (see Table 6.12).

What is especially important, theoretically and historically, is that it is precisely among those higher executives who belong to *politically active principal capitalist families* that personal and family ties to foreign corporations are most extensive (see Tables 6.13 and 6.14). Belonging to a political family and belonging to a capitalist family both contribute independently to an executive's chances of having personal or family foreign ties. Among men of property as well as among the nonpropertied, the more political officeholders one has in his close family, the more likely he is to have personal or family ties to foreign corporations. But in each political category, men of property are more likely than the nonpropertied to have personal or family ties to foreign companies. For instance, among those men whose close families have no political officeholders, 24 percent of the principal capitalists, but only 16 percent of the noncapitalists, have foreign ties within the close family. The comparable figures for those having one political officeholder in the close family are 61 percent of the principal capitalists, but only 22 percent of the noncapitalists; and for those so related to two or more officeholders, the figures, respectively, are 80 percent and 48 percent (see Table 6.14). Thus, the politically active capitalist family, of which several members have held political office, is also the quintessential family in the corporate world whose interests are bound up with foreign capital.

For historical reasons having to do with their estates' territorial predominance—which has endowed them with social power over tenants as well as small holders and other residents in the estates' surrounding rural areas—the great landed families of Chile are, as we know, also political families. In particular, the families who are simultaneously owners of the vast landed estates and principal owners of the top corpo-

TABLE 6.14. Percentage of Higher Executives of the Top 37 Nonfinancial Corporations in Chile Who Have Personal or Family Ties to Foreign Corporations, by the Number of Political Officeholders and Ownership of Capital in the Close Family, 1964/66

	Personal Foreign Ties	Immediate Family Foreign Ties	Secondary Family Foreign Ties	Close Family Foreign Ties	(*N*)
Principal capitalists					
no officeholders	14	19	22	24	(37)
one officeholder	26	42	52	61	(31)
two-plus officeholders	32	45	59	80	(56)
all executives in capitalist families	25	36	46	59	(124)
Noncapitalists					
no officeholders	14	14	14	16	(55)
one officeholder	18	18	18	22	(27)
two-plus officeholders	39	44	44	48	(23)
all executives in noncapitalist families	21	22	22	25	(105)

rations are distinguished as the active political cadre of their class. These "landed capitalists" are impelled by their self-contradictory class location to strive for political hegemony within their class and power within the state, so that they might push through policies that enhance the peculiar interests of their own coalesced segment. Only foreign capital constitutes a parallel (and potentially threatening) bastion of economic and political power; accommodation with it is thus an economic imperative and a political necessity, if their mutual interests are to be served both through business strategy and state policy. We would expect to find, therefore, that the landed capitalists—above all the politically active landed capitalists—stand out in their class as the segment most extensively tied to foreign capital.

We find, first, that—whether landed or not—the "capitalists" among the higher executives are considerably more likely than the "managers" to have foreign ties within the immediate, secondary, and close family. Second, the landed managers and propertyless managers scarcely differ in the extent of their foreign ties, and the managerial families' foreign ties scarcely increase as the kinship distance increases. Third, and most important, the landed capitalists are by far the most likely of these four intraclass types to belong to close families that have foreign ties: the close families of only one-quarter of the landed managers and one-quarter of the propertyless managers, but roughly half of the landless capitalists and over two-thirds of the landed capitalists, have foreign ties (see Table 6.15).

The question now is how a family's involvement in Chile's governance, together with its ownership of landed property and capital, has

TABLE 6.15. Percentage of Higher Executives of the Top 37 Nonfinancial Corporations in Chile Who Have Personal or Family Ties to Foreign Corporations, by Ownership of Landed Property or Capital in the Close Family, 1964/66

	Personal Foreign Ties	Immediate Family Foreign Ties	Secondary Family Foreign Ties	Close Family Foreign Ties	(*N*)
Landed capitalists	27	39	53	69	(62)
Landless capitalists	23	34	39	48	(62)
Landed managers	20	20	20	25	(20)
Propertyless managers	21	22	22	25	(85)

NOTE: "Landed capitalists," for instance, includes those executives having both a great-estate owner and a principal capitalist in the close family, whereas "propertyless managers" includes those executives having neither a great-estate owner nor a principal capitalist in the close family.

affected the likelihood that it also collaborates closely with foreign capital. (Alas, the absolute numbers in two crucial categories from among our higher executives whose close families have no political officeholders are too small to compute reliable percentages: only 8 landed managers and 4 landed capitalists. What is to be made of the fact that their close families have no foreign ties is thus unclear.) Certainly what is clear, and remarkably so, is that, first, those men who belong to a political family are far more likely, in each intraclass type, also to have foreign ties within the family (especially at the level of the close family). Second, among those who belong to a political family, the "capitalists" are again much more likely than the "managers" to have foreign ties in their families. Third, and of special theoretical and historical significance, not only are those landed capitalist families who have participated actively in governing the Chilean nation the most likely by far of our intraclass types to be associated with foreign capital, but, indeed, the overwhelming majority of them—80 percent—are so associated (see Table 6.16). The epitome of the dominant class both socially and politically, the landed capitalist families who are most deeply involved in the affairs of state are also the ones that most fully

TABLE 6.16. Percentage of Higher Executives of the Top 37 Nonfinancial Corporations in Chile Who Have Personal or Family Ties to Foreign Corporations, by Political Officeholding and Ownership of Landed Property or Capital in the Close Family, 1964/66

	Personal Foreign Ties	Immediate Family Foreign Ties	Secondary Family Foreign Ties	Close Family Foreign Ties	(*N*)
Someone in family has held office					
landed capitalists	32	44	61	80	(54)
landless capitalists	27	42	48	64	(33)
landed managers	25	25	25	31	(16)
propertyless managers	29	32	32	35	(34)
all executives in political-officeholding families	29	39	47	59	(137)
No family member has held office					
landed capitalists	0	0	0	0	(8)
landless capitalists	17	24	28	31	(29)
landed managers	0	0	0	0	(4)
propertyless managers	16	16	16	18	(51)
all executives not in political-officeholding families	14	16	17	20	(92)

collaborate with the foreign corporations, sharing sovereignty with them over the nation.

On the eve of an unprecedented historical challenge to their common dominion, i.e. by the *Unidad Popular* government, the lives and fortunes of these self-conscious, politically active landlord-and-capitalist families were all but indissolubly bound up with foreign corporations. What is remarkable, indeed, is that the decisive axes of the inner structure of the dominant class, successively revealed in our foregoing chapters, are here disclosed as being the axes of that class's integration with foreign capital. The network of interlocking directorates among the top nonfinancial corporations, and between them and the biggest banks; the ownership of capital and of landed property, especially the simultaneous ownership of both; and the actual exercise of intraclass political hegemony—each of these has significantly enhanced, in its own way, the formation of close relations between the dominant class and the multinational corporations operating in the country. The men in the inner group, the finance capitalists, the principal owners of capital, and, above all, the landed capitalist families and their leading political cadre are especially—and closely—integrated into the corporate apparatus of appropriation those multinationals have established in Chile.

EPILOGUE

The Color of the Rose

THIS study of Chile's landlords and capitalists focuses on them, as we now know, at a time when their class dominion was, albeit for an ephemeral moment, about to be called into historical question. In 1958, Dr. Salvador Allende, the presidential candidate of a coalition led by the Socialist and Communist parties, had narrowly failed—by a margin of 35,000 votes—to win election. In 1964, Eduardo Frei won the presidency on a Christian Democratic program explicitly designed as an alternative to socialism; his campaign spoke in a populist idiom and called for a "revolution in liberty." With its rhetoric of mass participation in reconstructing Chilean society, its emphasis on the dignity of the poor and the need for vast reforms, its demand for the "Chileanization of [U.S.] copper" and even for a "noncapitalist path of development," Christian Democracy's sudden rise and assumption of government, side by side with the growth of the socialist left, was a palpable measure of the accelerating erosion of the political legitimacy of Chile's landlords and capitalists. Confronted by the moderate social reforms pushed by the Christian Democrats early in Frei's presidency, the leaders of the dominant class were already speaking about their immediate future—as did the National Manufacturers Association president Eugenio Heirmans Despouy (a top-37 higher executive)—publicly and in apocalyptic language: "At this moment we are playing our last card, to decide whether the progress of Chile will be made through private enterprise or by means of the socialism of the State."[1]

With Allende's election to the presidency on September 4, 1970, on a program calling for the "peaceful construction of socialism," the social resilience and political skill of the dominant class was to be tested as never before, for its very existence as a class now appeared to be in jeopardy. In this epochal class struggle, the political leadership of this "coalesced bourgeoisie" must surely have been in the hands of the great landlord-and-capitalist families at its core, who were threatened

[1] *El Mercurio*, July 23, 1966.

in the cities and the countryside alike by workers and peasants united behind Allende's socialist government.

If, as Marx once said, our analysis "paint[s] the capitalist and the landlord in no sense *couleur de rose*" and deals with particular individuals "only insofar as they are the personifications of economic categories, embodiments of particular class relations and class interests,"[2] then something must now be said about the specific political role played in the struggle against socialism by particular individuals who are, indeed, the "personifications" of their class. It would take detailed historical research to disclose how the individuals represented in this study—particularly those from landed capitalist families having close ties to foreign capital—have participated in shaping the political strategy of the dominant class in the struggle to retain its social ascendancy. But fragments of what is already known about the clandestine as well as the open political activities of leading members of two of Chile's most prominent landed capitalist families, the Mattes and the Edwardses, suggest what thorough historical research, guided by the results of the analysis in this work, would reveal.

The Mattes controlled 2 of the top 37 nonfinancial corporations and, together with the closely related Claros and Vials, were at the very center of the "central core" of their class. The Edwardses, aside from their ownership of the Bank of Edwards and of *El Mercurio* (Chile's most influential daily newspaper) and of an entire chain of daily and weekly publications, also controlled 3 other top-37 corporations and shared control of a 4th, as well as owning large landed estates and enjoying close business associations (as we noted earlier) with such major U.S. corporations as the Rockefellers' International Basic Economy Corporation (IBEC, Chile), Pepsi-Cola, and Ralston Purina.

Both families were deeply involved not only in open leadership of the right, but also in covert action aimed at bringing about a military coup to prevent Allende from taking office. When Allende won the presidential election on September 4, 1970, despite a massive CIA propaganda campaign and covert political organizing in assistance of his opposition, the "reaction on the right in Chile, among the multinationals, and in the White House," as Thomas Powers puts it, "was all but identical: alarm verging on panic. . . . Something had to be done to stop Allende. This sentiment was fully shared by the multinationals."[3] At least one such alarmed multinational, namely ITT, was directly im-

[2] Marx 1973d, p. 86.

[3] Powers 1979, p. 291.

plicated in a conspiracy to prevent Allende's inauguration. ITT's fellow conspirators in Chile featured Arturo Matte Larraín, the octogenarian head of the Matte family interests (whose brother-in-law, Jorge Alessandri, a former president of Chile, was a defeated presidential candidate on September 4), and Agustín Edwards Eastman, titular head of his own family. ITT was in constant communication with the U.S. Central Intelligence Agency (through William V. Broe, chief of the CIA's Clandestine Services in the Western Hemisphere), urging CIA intervention even before the agency embarked on its own "tracks" to military intervention. The "thesis" (Broe's term) of their secret discussions was "a plan to create economic chaos" that would provide the justification for military intervention.[4]

An ITT operative in Latin America by the name of Hal Hendrix (a former Scripps-Howard correspondent) reported to ITT Senior Vice-President E. J. Gerrity that one of the key points agreed on at "a meeting with Arturo Matte at his residence Sunday September 13 [1970]" was the need for a "constitutional way out" to stop Allende "that doesn't preclude violence—spontaneous or provoked. A constitutional solution [*sic*!], for instance, could result from massive internal disorders, strikes, urban and rural warfare. This would morally justify an armed forces intervention for an indefinite period." But, Hendrix also reported, "The Marxists will not be provoked. 'You can spit in their face in the street,' Matte said, 'and they'll say thank you.' "[5]

Discussed in plentiful detail at this and subsequent meetings were seditious scenarios—for creating "economic chaos" by having U.S. public financial agencies and private banks withhold loans and credits from the Allende government, for penetrating the armed forces, for providing a "moral justification" for a military coup through the creation of mass confrontations, employer lockouts, hoarding, and sabotage of production and distribution. These set the pattern for events soon to follow, culminating with the deadly military coup of September 11, 1973.

Arturo Matte's nephew, Benjamín Matte Guzmán, head of the National Agricultural Society, which vociferously opposed even Frei's modest reforms, was also a clandestine leader of the fascist terrorist organization *Patria y Libertad*, or the Fatherland and Freedom Nation-

[4] U.S. Congress 1973, p. 10; also Szulc 1973. On the CIA's role in Chile at the time, see U.S. Congress 1973, 1975a, 1975b, 1975c, 1976a, 1976b. On the murderous repression during and after the coup, see U.S. Congress 1973–1976.

[5] ITT memorandum of September 17, 1970, as reprinted in NACLA 1972, pp. 8–9; also see U.S. Congress 1973.

alist Front. Their swastika-like spider and scrawled threats of "Djakarta" (a reminder of the slaughter of some 300,000 "leftists" in Java, Indonesia, in 1965) were appearing on Santiago walls, in counterpoint to coup plots, gunrunning, bombings, assassination attempts, and sabotage, from the early months of 1973. Matte Guzmán was one of the *Patria y Libertad* leaders involved in organizing the June 29, 1973, attempted coup by General Roberto Souper and other officers of the Second Armored Regiment, the so-called *tancazo* (or tank coup). After it was quelled by General Carlos Prats, Allende's loyal head of the armed forces, Mr. Matte took asylum in the Ecuadorian embassy, acknowledging that he had tried, "together with a heroic unit of our army," to overthrow the government.[6]

Immediately after Allende's election, the CIA station chief in Santiago, Henry Heckscher, had been visited by Agustín Edwards Eastman, "a longtime ally of the CIA," who asked him to arrange a meeting with U.S. Ambassador Edward Korry. At the embassy, Mr. Edwards bluntly asked Korry, "Will the U.S. do anything militarily—directly or indirectly?"[7] In fact, while the CIA did not inform Ambassador Korry of their effort to mount a military coup in order to prevent Allende from taking office, Mr. Edwards was to play a pivotal role in getting that CIA effort launched. Two days after meeting ITT and CIA officials at Arturo Matte's home in Santiago, Mr. Edwards was in Washington, D.C., having breakfast with Pepsi-Cola's Donald Kendall and President Nixon's national security adviser Henry Kissinger, to ask that the U.S. government do something to block Allende. CIA Director Richard Helms was then asked (by either Nixon or Kissinger) to meet with Edwards and Kendall in a Washington hotel. "The two men made quite an impassioned appeal for CIA help in blocking Allende, and Helms concluded," Powers reports, "that they must have made the same appeal to Nixon, with some success."[8]

[6] Davis 1985, pp. 152–153, 172; NACLA 1973, p. 5.

[7] Powers 1979, p. 228 (citing former Ambassador Edward Korry's article, "The sell-out of Chile and the American tax-payer," *Penthouse* [!], March 1978). On the Edwards-CIA long-time alliance, see U.S. Congress 1975b, pp. 13, 22–23, 29.

[8] Powers 1979, p. 234. See, also, the testimony of former CIA Director Richard Helms on his meeting with Edwards and Pepsi-Cola's Donald Kendall (U.S. Congress 1975a, p. 228n). Another conspirator reportedly involved in the coup planning during that infamous September 13, 1970, meeting in Matte's residence was the Kennecott Copper Company attorney Guillermo Carey Tagle (Varas 1972, p. 132), who is the son of Guillermo Carey Bustamente (mentioned in Chapter 6), a Chilean promoted in 1968 to the post of senior vice-president for Latin America in Anaconda's New York office. Perhaps incidentally, but worth noting, Mr. Carey Tagle was also at the

After CIA efforts to mount a coup failed, and as political polarization over Allende's policies sharpened, the Edwards family's newspapers and magazines grew increasingly strident in their opposition. Soon they began more and more openly to advocate sedition and antigovernment military action, which they continued to call for until the September 11 coup itself. The Edwards newspaper group was paid a "subsidy" of at least $1.6 million by the CIA to keep it publishing during Allende's presidency.[9] "CIA-inspired editorials [ran] almost daily in *El Mercurio*"; and one CIA "project renewal memorandum" concluded, as a U.S. congressional investigation disclosed, that "*El Mercurio* and other media outlets [many also Edwards-owned] supported by the Agency had played an important role in setting the stage for the September 11, 1973 military coup which overthrew Allende."[10] The only newsman permitted by the military *junta* to view Allende's body after he was shot and killed resisting the coup was an *El Mercurio* reporter (even Allende's wife was not permitted to see the body). *El Mercurio* was the only major daily allowed to continue publication, almost without interruption, even as the massive violent repression of Chile's citizenry was under way; and the newspaper's general manager, Fernando Leniz, became the only civilian minister in the new military regime.

Two months after the coup, the prominent Conservative senator Francisco Bulnes Sanfuentes, Mr. Matte's second cousin and a member of a "central core" landed capitalist family, summed up what must have been the view of his social peers concerning the new military regime: "Sometimes there rises to the top a providential man, as was the case of Franco in Spain, but this is not what happens for each nation. . . . We must detoxify Chile of the venom that was spread by Marxism and cure her damaged economy. All this takes years and could not have occurred in a democratic regime."[11]

Nearly a century earlier, in 1891, another visionary nationalist pres-

---

time a director of Andina Bottling Company in Chile (of which his father had also been a director), a majority-controlled affiliate of the Coca-Cola Company.

[9] U.S. Congress 1975b, p. 29.

[10] U.S. Congress 1976a, p. 12, and 1975b, p. 8. The CIA also ". . . exerted substantial control over the content of that paper's [*El Mercurio*'s] international news section" (1976a, p. 12).

[11] *La Segunda* (Santiago), November 2, 1973, as translated in IDOC 1973, p. 43. Senator Bulnes's father, Francisco Bulnes Correa, was a "top landowner," a director of 2 U.S.-owned subsidiaries, and an officer of 3 top-37 corporations; Manuel Bulnes Sanfuentes, the senator's brother, was a director of 3 and an officer of another 2 top-37 corporations.

ident, José Manuel Balmaceda, not a man of the left but a dissident aristocrat who had sought to stem the ascendance of British capital in Chile's nitrates industry and to use massive public investment to propel the country's modernization and independent capitalist development, was overthrown in a terrible civil war. Among the most important leaders of the conspiracy against Balmaceda's government—who were also the insurgents' most active agents abroad—were Augusto Matte Pérez, uncle of Arturo Matte Larraín, and Agustín Edwards Ross, great-grandfather of Agustín Edwards Eastman. These men and their families thus uncannily personify the structural continuity and political hegemony of the coalesced segment of their class—as another of Mr. Matte's uncles, the banker Eduardo Matte Pérez, summed up faithfully several months after the defeat and suicide of Balmaceda, in words again appropriate today: "We, the owners of land and capital, own Chile. The rest, the masses, do not matter."[12]

[12] *El Pueblo* (Santiago), March 19, 1892. On the role of Messrs. Matte and Edwards in the successful rebellion against Balmaceda, see Yrarrázaval Larráin 1940, II, pp. 211, 226, 229; also see Zeitlin 1984, pp. 118, 169.

REFERENCES

Adams, Bert

1968 *Kinship in an Urban Setting.* Chicago: Markham.

Alba, Victor

1969 *The Latin Americans.* New York: Praeger.

Allen, Michael P.

1974 "The structure of interorganizational elite cooptation: Interlocking corporate directorates." *American Sociological Review* 39 (June): 393–406.

1976 "Management control in the large corporation: Comment on Zeitlin." *American Journal of Sociology* 81 (January): 885–893.

Allende Gossens, Salvador

1964 "Principios de orden político del Partido Socialista de Chile." In *El proceso chileno: Pensamiento teórico y político del P. Socialista de Chile,* ed. Alejandro Chelén Rojas, pp. 123–143. Buenos Aires: Quatro Editores, 1974 (as reprinted from "Respuesta de Salvador Allende a Sergio Guilisasti Tagle para su libro *Partidos políticos chilenos, 1964*").

Althusser, Louis, and R. Etienne Balibar

1970 *Reading Capital.* London: New Left Books.

Álvarez Andrews, Oscar

1936 *Historia del desarrollo industrial de Chile.* Santiago: Imprenta y Litografía la Ilustración.

Amin, Samir

1974 *Accumulation on a World Scale.* 2 vols. New York: Monthly Review Press.

1976 *Unequal Development.* New York: Monthly Review Press.

Ampuero Díaz, Raúl

1964 "1964, año de prueba para la revolución chilena." *Arauco* no. 49 (February): 3–23.

Angell, Alan

1972 *Politics and the Labor Movement in Chile.* London: Oxford University Press.

Anuario ejecutivos (no editor given)

1964 *Anuario ejecutivos de sociedades anónimas, bancos, cías. de seguros y corredores de la Bolsa de Santiago, 1963.* Santiago: Editorial del Pacífico.

Aranda, Sergio, and Alberto Martínez

1970 "Estructura económica [de Chile]: Algunas características fundamentales." In *Chile, hoy,* ed. Aníbal Pinto Santa Cruz et al., pp. 55–172. Santiago: Editorial Universitaria.

Arismendi, Rodney
1959 "On the role of the national bourgeoisie in the anti-imperialist struggle." *World Marxist Review* 2 (June): 31–39.
1966 *América Latina: Problemas y perspectivas de la revolución.* Prague: Editorial Paz y Socialismo.

Auburn, H. W., ed.
1960 *Comparative Banking.* London: Waterlow and Sons.

Bain, Joe S.
1966 *International Differences in Industrial Structure: Eight Nations in the 1950's.* New Haven, Conn.: Yale University Press.

Baltra, Miereya
1973 "La gauche dresse son bilan." *Les Tempes Modernes* (June): 2066–2098.

Baltzell, E. Digby
1958 *Philadelphia Gentlemen: The Making of a National Upper Class.* New York: Macmillan.
1966 " 'Who's Who in America' and 'The Social Register': Elite and upper class indexes in metropolitan America." In *Class, Status, and Power,* ed. Reinhard Bendix and S. M. Lipset, pp. 266–275. 2nd ed. New York: Collier-Macmillan.

Baran, Paul A.
1957 *The Political Economy of Growth.* New York: Monthly Review Press.
1961 "A non-communist manifesto." *Kyklos* XIV, as reprinted in his posthumous collection *The Longer View: Essays toward a Critique of Political Economy,* ed. J. O'Neil, pp. 52–67. New York and London: Monthly Review Press, 1969.

Baran, Paul A., and Paul M. Sweezy
1966 *Monopoly Capital.* New York: Monthly Review Press.

Barnet, Richard J., and Ronald Müller
1974 *Global Reach: The Power of Multinational Corporations.* New York: Simon and Schuster.

Barraclough, Solon
1973 *Diagnóstico de la reforma agraria chilena (noviembre 1970 – junio 1972).* Santiago: Instituto de Capacitación e Investigación en la Reforma Agraria (ICIRA).

Barraclough, Solon, et al.
1966 *Chile: Tenencia de la tierra y desarrollo socioeconómico del sector agrícola.* Santiago: Comité Interamericano de Desarrollo Agrícola.

Barros Borgoño, Luis
1912 *La Caja de Crédito Hipotecario.* 2 vols. Santiago: Imprenta Cervantes.

Bauer, Arnold J.
1975 *Chilean Rural Society from the Spanish Conquest to 1930.* Cambridge: Cambridge University Press.

Bearden, James, et al.
1975 "The nature and extent of bank centrality in corporate networks." Paper presented at the annual meeting of the American Sociological Association, August.

Bell, Daniel
1958 "The 'Power Elite'—reconsidered." *American Journal of Sociology* 64 (November): 238–250.
1961 "The breakup of family capitalism." In his *The End of Ideology*, pp. 37–42. New York: Collier.

Bendix, Reinhard
1952 "Bureaucracy and the problem of power." In *Reader in Bureaucracy*, ed. R. K. Merton, Alisa P. Gray, Barbara Hockey, and Hanan C. Selvin, pp. 114–134. Glencoe, Ill.: The Free Press.
1964 *Nation-Building and Citizenship*. New York: John Wiley and Sons.
1970 *Embattled Reason: Essays on Social Knowledge*. New York: Oxford University Press.

Berle, Adolf, Jr., and Gardiner C. Means
1967 *The Modern Corporation and Private Property*. New York: Harcourt, Brace, and World (originally published in 1932 by Macmillan).

Bernstein, Eduard
1961 *Evolutionary Socialism*. New York: Schocken (originally published in Germany in 1899).

Blakemore, Harold
1974 *British Nitrates and Chilean Politics, 1886–1896: Balmaceda and North*. London: University of London (Institute of Latin American Studies), Athlone Press.

Bohan, Merwin, and Morton Pomeranz
1960 *Investment in Chile: Basic Information for United States Businessmen*. Department of Commerce. Washington, D.C.: U.S. Government Printing Office.

Bonbright, James C., and Gardiner C. Means
1932 *The Holding Company*. New York: McGraw-Hill.

Bonfield, Patricia
1980 *U.S. Business Leaders: A Study of Opinions and Characteristics*. New York: The Conference Board.

Brady, Robert Alexander
1943 *Business as a System of Power*. New York: Columbia University Press.

Brandeis, Louis D.
1913 "The endless chain: Interlocking directorates." *Harper's Weekly* 58 (December 6): 13–15.

Bunting, David, and Tsung-hua Liu
1977 "Economic and social aspects of interlocking." Paper presented at the annual meeting of the American Sociological Association, August.

Burbach, Roger J.
1975 "The Chilean Industrial Bourgeoisie and Foreign Capital, 1920–1970." Ph.D. dissertation, University of Indiana.

Burch, Phillip H., Jr.
1972 *The Managerial Revolution Reassessed.* Lexington, Mass.: D. C. Heath.

Bureau of International Commerce
1970 *American Firms, Subsidiaries and Affiliates—Chile.* Washington D.C.: United States Department of Commerce (mimeographed).

Business Week
1952 "Boliva takes over tin." November 15: 148–150.
1954 "Latin America: The market grows, but so does the competition." November 20: 142–151.
1971 "The board: It's obsolete unless overhauled." May 22: 50–58.

Cademartori, José
1963 "El imperio de las sociedades anónimas." *Principios* no. 95 (May–June): 28–44 (written under pseudonym of "Jerónimo Ugarte").
1968 *La economía chilena.* Santiago: Editorial Universitaria.

Caputo, Orlando, and Roberto Pizarro
1970 *Dependencia e inversión extranjera en Chile.* Santiago: Centro de Estudios Socio-Económicos; Facultad de Ciencias Económicas, Universidad de Chile.

Cardoso, Fernando Henrique, and Enzo Faletto
1973 *Dependência e desenvolvimento na America Latina: Ensaio de interpretacão sociologia.* Rio de Janeiro: Editora Zahar.
1966 "The entrepreneurial elites of Latin America." *Studies in Comparative International Development* 2, no. 10: 147–159.

Castells, Manuel
1974 *La lucha de clases en Chile.* Buenos Aires: Siglo XXI Argentina Editores.

Cavan, Ruth
1963 *The American Family.* New York: Thomas Y. Crowell.

Chinchilla, Norma S.
1973 "Strata and Class Consciousness in the Chilean Peasantry." Ph.D. dissertation, University of Wisconsin.

Chinchilla, Norma S., and Marvin Sternberg
1974 "Reform and class struggle in the [Chilean] countryside." *Latin American Perspectives* 1 (Summer): 106–128.

CIDA (Comité Interamericano de Desarrollo Agrícola)
1966 *Chile: Tenencia de la tierra y desarrollo socioeconómico del sector agrícola.* Santiago: CIDA.

Clement, Wallace
1975 *The Canadian Corporate Elite.* McLelland and Stewart.

Clubok, Alfred, F. Berghorn, and N. Wilensky
1969 "Family relationships, congressional recruitment, and political modernization." *Journal of Politics* 31: 1035–1062.

Collier, Peter, and David Horowitz

1976 *The Rockefellers: An American Dynasty*. New York: Holt, Rinehart, and Winston.

Connell, R. W.

1979 "A critique of the Althusserian approach to class." *Theory and Society* 8: 321–345.

CORFO (Corporación de Fomento)

1966 *Geografía económica de Chile*. Primer apéndice. Santiago: Talleres de Editorial Universitaria.

1970a *Inversiones extranjeras en Chile*. Santiago: Talleres de Editorial Universitaria.

1970b *Participación del capital extranjero en las sociedades anónimas industriales*. Santiago: Gerencia de Industrias; División de Planificación Industrial.

1971 *Las inversiones extranjeras en la industria chilena (1960–69)*. Santiago: Gerencia de industrias; Division de Planificación Industrial.

Correa Vergara, Luis

1938 *Agricultura chilena*. 2 vols. Santiago: Imprenta Nascimento.

Corvalán, Luis

1967 "Unión de las fuerzas antiimperialistas." *Nuestra Época* (June). In Corvalán 1971, pp. 192–213.

1969 "Unidad Popular para conquistar el poder." In Corvalán 1971, pp. 293–336.

Corvalán, Luis, ed.

1971 *Camino de victoria*. Santiago: Sociedad Impresora Horizonte.

Cuadra Gormaz, Guillermo de la

1950 *Familias chilenas: Origen de doscientos familias coloniales de Santiago; y Familias coloniales de Santiago* (published as a one-volume edition), revised and enlarged. Santiago: Editorial Zamorano y Caperan.

Dahl, Robert A.

1970 *After the Revolution?* New Haven, Conn.: Yale University Press.

Dahrendorf, Ralf

1959 *Class and Class Conflict in Industrial Society*. Stanford, Calif.: Stanford University Press.

Dahse, Fernando

1979 *Mapa de la extrema riqueza: Los grupos económicos y el proceso de concentración de capitales*. Santiago: Editorial Aconcagua.

Davis, Nathaniel

1985 *The Last Two Years of Salvador Allende*. Ithaca and London: Cornell University Press.

Debray, Régis

1971 *The Chilean Revolution: Conversations with Allende*. New York: Pantheon.

Diccionario biográfico de Chile (no editor given)

1936–1961 Ediciones 1–12. Santiago: Empresa Periodística Chile.

DiTomaso, Nancy

1980 "Class politics and public bureaucracy: The U.S. Department of Labor." In *Classes, Class Conflict, and the State*, ed. Maurice Zeitlin, pp. 135–152. Boston: Little, Brown.

Domhoff, G. William

1967 *Who Rules America?* Englewood Cliffs, N.J.: Prentice-Hall.

1970 *The Higher Circles: The Governing Class in America*. New York: Random House.

1978 *The Powers That Be*. New York: Random House.

1980 *Power Structure Research*. Beverly Hills, Calif.: Sage.

1983 *Who Rules America Now? A View for the '80s*. Englewood Cliffs, N.J.: Prentice-Hall.

Domínguez Barros, Arturo

1968 *Domínguez, 1818–1968: Descendencia de Don Francisco Domínguez Heras*. Santiago: privately printed.

Dooley, Peter C.

1969 "The interlocking directorate." *American Economic Review* 59 (June): 314–323.

Dpto. de Impuestos Internos

1963 "Predios agrícolas con avalúos de mas de E°40,000, 1961." Santiago: República de Chile (a copy of the unpublished original list of 1,848 *predios* [compiled in 1963 by Department of Internal Revenue employee José González] was retained in the files of the Land Tenure Center, Santiago; a list of the top 100 *predios* of 1961 and their tax-assessed valuations, by internal revenue code number and taken from the full list, is in the possession of Zeitlin and Ratcliff).

Dunn, Marvin G.

1980 "The family office." In *Power Structure Research*, ed. G. William Domhoff, pp. 17–45. Beverly Hills, Calif.: Sage.

Duque, Joaquín, and Ernesto Pastrana

1972 "La movilización reivindicativa urbana de los sectores populares en Chile 1964–1972." *Revista Latinoamericana de Ciencias Sociales* (December): 259–293.

Dye, Thomas R.

1976 *Who's Running America?* Englewood Cliffs, N.J.: Prentice-Hall.

Eaton, John

1949 *Political Economy*. New York: International Publishers.

Echeverría, Roberto

1969 "The Effect of Agricultural Price Policies on Intersectoral Income Transfers." Ph.D. dissertation, Cornell University.

ECLA (U.N. Economic Commission for Latin America)

1971 "Public enterprises: Their present significance and their potential in development." *Economic Bulletin for Latin America* 16, no. 1: 1–70.

Ehrman, Libert

1966 *Opportunities for Investment in Chile: A Program for Encouragement of Private Industry*. New York: Praeger.

Escobar Cerda, Luis

1959 *El Mercado de Valores*. Santiago: Editorial del Pacífico.

Esteban, Juan Carlos

1961 *Imperialismo y desarrollo económico*. Buenos Aires: Editorial Palestra.

Evans, Peter

1979 *Dependent Development: The Alliance of Multinational, State, and Local Capital in Brazil*. Princeton, N.J.: Princeton University Press.

Feder, Ernest

1960 "Feudalism and agricultural development: The role of controlled credit in Chile's agriculture." *Land Economics* 36 (February): 92–108.

Fellmeth, Robert

1973 *Politics of Land*. New York: Grossman Publishers.

Fernández, Raúl, and José F. Ocampo

1974 "The Latin American revolution: A theory of imperialism, not dependence." *Latin American Perspectives* 1: 30–61.

Figueroa, Pedro Pablo

1888 *Diccionario biográfico general de Chile (1550–1887)*. 2nd ed. Santiago: Imprenta "Victoria" de H. Izquierdo y Cía.

1887–1901 *Diccionario biográfico de Chile*. 3 vols. Santiago: Imprenta y encuadernación Barcelona.

1900 *Diccionario biográfico de extranjeros en Chile*. Santiago: privately printed.

Figueroa (Talquino), Virgilio

1925–1931 *Diccionario histórico, biográfico y bibliográfico de Chile*. 5 vols. in 4. Santiago: Balcells.

Firth, Raymond

1964 "Family and kinship in industrial society." *The Sociological Review*. Monograph no. 8: 65–87.

Fischer, Gerald C.

1968 *American Banking Structure*. New York: Columbia University Press.

Fitch, Robert, and Mary Oppenheimer

1970 "Who rules the corporations?" *Socialist Revolution* 1, no. 1: 73–107; also 1, no. 5: 61–114, and 1, no. 6: 33–94.

Florence, P. Sargant

1961 *Ownership, Control, and Success of Large Companies: An Analysis of English Industrial Structure and Policy, 1936–1951*. London: Sweet and Maxwell.

Frank, André Gunder

1967 *Capitalism and Underdevelopment in Latin America: Historical Studies of Chile and Brazil*. New York: Monthly Review Press.

1969 *Latin America: Underdevelopment or Revolution*. New York: Monthly Review Press.

1972 *Lumpenbourgeoisie: Lumpenproletariat; Dependence, Class, and Politics in Latin America*. New York: Monthly Review Press.

FTC (Federal Trade Commission)
1951 *Report of the Federal Trade Commission on Interlocking Directorates*. Washington, D.C.: U.S. Government Printing Office.

Fuentes, Jordi, and Lía Cortés
1963 *Diccionario histórico de Chile*. Santiago: Editorial del Pacífico.
1967 *Diccionario político de Chile (1810–1966)*. Santiago: Editorial Orbe.

Furtado, Celso
1965 *Diagnosis of the Brazilian Crisis*. Trans. Suzette Macedo. Berkeley and Los Angeles: University of California Press.

Galbraith, John K.
1967 *The New Industrial State*. New York: New American Library.
1971 "Introduction." In *The New Industrial State*, 2nd ed. New York: Houghton Mifflin.

Galdames, Luis
1964 *A History of Chile*, Trans. I. M. Cox. New York: Russell and Russell.

Garretón, Oscar Guillermo
1971 "Concentración monopólica en Chile." *Cuadernos de la Realidad Chilena* no. 7 (March): 143–164.

Garretón, Oscar Guillermo, and Jaime Cisternas
1970 *Algunas características del proceso de toma de decisiones de la gran empresa. La dinámica de concentracíon*. Santiago: Oficina de Planificación Nacional (mimeograph).

Giddens, Anthony
1971 *Capitalism and Modern Social Theory*. Cambridge: Cambridge University Press.
1973 *The Class Structure of the Advanced Societies*. New York: Harper and Row.

Gil, Federico G.
1962 *Los partidos politícos chilenos: Genesis y evolución*. Buenos Aires: Ediciones de Palma.
1966 *The Political System of Chile*. Boston: Houghton Mifflin.

Gillin, John
1958 "Some signposts for policy." In *Social Change in Latin America Today*, ed. Philip Mosely, pp. 14–62. New York: Vintage (Council on Foreign Relations).

Giudici, Ernesto
1966 "El proceso revolucionario en América Latina." In *América Latina: Problemas y perspectivas de la revolución*, ed. Rodney Arismendi, pp. 28–43. Prague: Editorial Paz y Socialismo.

Glade, William
1969 *The Latin American Economies*. New York: Van Nostrand–Reinhold.

Glasberg, Davita S., and Michael Schwartz
1983 "Ownership and control of corporations." *Annual Review of Sociology* 9: 311–332.

Goldsmith, Raymond W.

1969 *Financial Structure and Development.* New Haven: Yale University Press.

Goldsmith, Raymond W., and Rexford C. Parmelee.

1940 *The Distribution of Ownership in the 200 Largest Nonfinancial Corporations.* Monograph no. 29 of the Temporary National Economic Committee's Investigations of Concentration of Economic Power. Washington, D.C: U.S. Government Printing Office.

Góngora, Mario

1960 *Origen de los 'inquilinos' de Chile central.* Santiago: Editorial Universitaria.

Góngora, Mario, and Jean Borde

1956 *Evolución de la propiedad rural en el valle del Puangue.* 2 vols. Santiago: Editorial Universitaria.

González Casanova, Pablo

1965 *La democracia en México.* Mexico: Siglo XXI.

Goode, William J.

1963 *The Family.* Englewood Cliffs, N.J.: Prentice-Hall.

Goode, William J., Elizabeth Hopkins, and Helen McClure

1971 *Social Systems and Family Patterns: A Propositional Inventory.* Indianapolis: Bobbs-Merrill.

Gordon, Robert A.

1966 *Business Leadership in the Large Corporation.* Berkeley: University of California Press (originally published in 1945 under the auspices of the Brookings Institution).

Guttsman, Wilhelm L.

1965 *The British Political Elite.* London: MacGibbon and Kee.

Hacker, Andrew

1961 "The elected and the anointed: Two American elites." *American Political Science Review* 55: 539–549.

1975 "What rules America?" *New York Review of Books.* May 1: 2–13.

Hagen, Everett E.

1962 *On the Theory of Social Change.* Homewood, Ill.: Dempsey.

Haya de la Torre, Victor Raúl

1936 ¿Adonde va Indoamérica? Santiago: Biblioteca América.

1946 ¿Y después de la guerra, que? Lima: Editorial Talleres PTCM.

Herman, Edward S.

1973 "Do bankers control corporations?" *Monthly Review* 25: 12–29.

1981 *Corporate Control, Corporate Power.* Cambridge, Eng.: Cambridge University Press.

Hernández, Silva

1966 "Transformaciones tecnológicas en la agricultura de Chile central. Siglo XIX." *Cuadernos del Centro de Estudios Socioeconómicos* (Santiago) 3: 1–31.

Herzog, Philippe

1971 *Politique économique et planification en régime capitaliste*. Paris: Éditions Sociales.

Hilferding, Rudolf

1910 *Das Finanzkapital: Eine Studie über die jüngste Entwicklung des Kapitalismus*. Berlin: Verlag JHW Dietz (1947 reprint of the original edition). An English translation of this monumental work finally was published in 1981: *Finance Capital: A Study of the Latest Phase of Capitalist Development*, ed. with an introduction by Tom Bottomore; trans. Morris Watnick and Sam Gordon. London: Routledge and Kegan Paul.

Hoselitz, Bert F.

1960 "Social structure and economic growth." In his *Sociological Factors in Economic Development*. Glencoe, Ill.: The Free Press.

Hurtado, Carlos

1966 Concentración de población y desarrollo económico: El caso chileno. Santiago: Universidad de Chile (Instituto de Economía).

ICIRA (Instituto de Capacitación e Investigación en la Reforma Agraria)

1966 "Predios, propietarios, superficie total en e./ir entre las provincias de Aconcagua a Ñuble, 1964." Santiago: ICIRA (unpublished original list in authors' possession).

ICSPS (Institute for the Comparative Study of Political Systems)

1963 *Chile: Election Factbook, September 4, 1964*. Washington, D.C.: Operations and Policy Research, Inc.

IDOC (International Documentation on the Contemporary Church)

1973 *Chile: The Allende Years; The Coup; Under the Junta*. New York: IDOC–North America.

Imaz, José Luis de

1970 *Los que mandan*. Albany: SUNY Press.

Institute for the Comparative Study of Political Systems

1963 *Chile: Election Factbook, September 4, 1964*. Washington, D.C.: Operations and Policy Research, Inc.

Jaguaribe, Helio

1962 *Desenvolvimento econômico e desenvolvimento político*. Rio de Janeiro: Editora Fundo de Cultura.

1968 *Economic and Political Development: A Theoretical Approach and a Brazilian Case Study*. Cambridge: Harvard University Press.

1969 "Political strategies of national development in Brazil." In *Latin American Radicalism*, ed. I. L. Horowitz, Josue de Castro, and John Gerassi, pp. 390–439. New York: Vintage.

James, David, and Michael Soref

1981 "Profit constraints on managerial autonomy: Managerial theory and the unmaking of the corporate president." *American Sociological Review* 46 (February): 1–18.

Janowitz, Morris
1968 "Political sociology." *International Encyclopedia of the Social Sciences* 12: 298–397. New York: Macmillan.

Jobet, Julio César
1962 "Esquema de las contradicciones económicas y sociales de América Latina." *Arauco* no. 34 (November): 5–10.

Johnson, Dale
1967–1968 "Industrialization, social mobility, and class formation in Chile." *Studies in Comparative International Development* 3, no. 7: 127–151.
1968–1969 "The national and progressive bourgeoisie in Chile." In *Dependence and Underdevelopment*, ed. J. D. Cockroft, A. G. Frank, and D. Johnson, pp. 165–217. New York: Anchor.

Johnson, John
1958 *Political Change in Latin America: The Emergence of the Middle Sectors.* Stanford, Calif.: Stanford University Press.

Johnson, R. W.
1973 "The British political elite, 1955–1972." *Archives Europeenes de Sociologie* 14: 35–77.

Joslin, David
1963 *A Century of Banking in Latin America.* London: Oxford University Press.

Kaufman, Robert R.
1972 *The Politics of Land Reform in Chile, 1950–1970.* Cambridge: Harvard University Press.

Kay, Cristobal
1974 "La participación campesina bajo el gobierno de la U.P. (Unidad Popular, Chile)." *Revista Mexicana de Sociología* (April–June): 279–295.

Kennedy, R.
1944 "Single or triple melting-pot? Intermarriage trends in New Haven, 1790–1940." *American Journal of Sociology* 49, no. 4: 331–339.

Kolko, Gabriel
1962 *Wealth and Power in America.* New York: Praeger.

Kotz, David M.
1978 *Bank Control of Large Corporations in the United States.* Berkeley: University of California Press.

Kuh, Edward
1963 *Capital Stock Growth: A Micro-econometric Approach.* Amsterdam: North Holland Press.

L.A.C. (pseudonym)
1950 *Dos cartas y artículos sobre política y economía.* Santiago: Casa Nacional del Niño.

Lagos Escobar, Ricardo
1961 *La concentración del poder económico.* Santiago: Editorial del Pacífico.

Lambert, Jacques

1967 *Latin America: Social Structure and Political Institutions*. Berkeley and Los Angeles: University of California Press.

Larner, Robert J.

1970 *Management Control and the Large Corporation*. Cambridge, Mass. University Press, Dunellen.

Lenin, Vladimir I.

1967 "Imperialism, the highest stage of capitalism: A popular outline." In *Selected Works in Three Volumes*, vol. 1, pp. 675–777. New York: International Publishers.

Levine, Joel H.

1972 "The sphere of influence." *American Sociological Review* 37 (February): 14–27.

Lipset, Seymour Martin

1960 *Political Man*. Garden City, N.Y.: Doubleday.

1970 *Revolution and Counter-revolution*. Garden City, N.Y.: Doubleday/ Anchor.

Loveman, Brian

1973 "Property, Politics, and Rural Labor: Agrarian Reform in Chile, 1919–1972." Ph.D. dissertation, Indiana University.

1976 "The transformation of the Chilean countryside." In *Chile: Politics and Society*, ed. A. Valenzuela and J. S. Valenzuela, pp. 201–237. New Brunswick, N.J.: Transaction Books.

Lundberg, Ferdinand

1946 *America's Sixty Families*. New York: Citadel (originally published in 1937 by Vanguard).

1968 *The Rich and the Super Rich*. New York: Bantam.

Luxemberg, Rosa

1970 *Reform or Revolution*. New York: Pathfinder (originally published in Berlin in 1899).

Mace, Myles L.

1971 *Directors: Myth and Reality*. Cambridge: Harvard University Press.

Mamalakis, Markos

1965 "Public policy and sectoral development: A case study of Chile, 1940–1958." In *Essays on the Chilean Economy*, ed. Markos Mamalakis and Clark Reynolds, pp. 1–200. Homewood, Ill.: Richard D. Irwin.

Mandel, Ernest

1968 *Marxist Economic Theory*. Vol. 2. New York: Monthly Review Press.

Manteola, José, ed.

1966 *Guía de la administración pública de Chile, y de los principios organismos del sector privado*. Santiago: Editorial Salesiana.

Marcus, George E.

1980 "Law in the development of dynastic families among American business elites: The domestication of capital and the capitalization of family." *Law and Society Review* 14 (Summer): 859–903.

Mariolis, Peter

1975 "Interlocking directorates and the control of corporations. *Social Science Quarterly* 56: 425–439.

1978 "Bank and Financial Control among Large U.S. Corporations." Ph.D. dissertation, SUNY at Stony Brook.

Marx, Karl

1948 *The Class Struggles in France: 1848 to 1850*. Moscow: Foreign Languages Publishing House.

1952 *The Civil War in France*. Moscow: Foreign Languages Publishing House.

1956 *Economic and Philosophic Manuscripts of 1844*. Moscow: Foreign Languages Publishing House.

1963 *The Eighteenth Brumaire of Louis Bonaparte*. New York: International Publishers.

1965 *Der 18. Brumaire des Louis Bonaparte*. Berlin: Sammlung Insel 9, Insel-Verlag.

1967 *Capital*. Vols. 1–3. New York: International Publishers.

1973a "The class struggles in France: 1848–1850." In *Karl Marx and Frederick Engels: Selected Works in Three Volumes*, vol. 1, pp. 205–299. Moscow: Progress Publishers.

1973b "Die Burgerkrieg in Frankreich." In *Karl Marx. Friedrich Engels Werke*, vol. 17, pp. 313–365. Berlin: Dietz Verlag.

1973c "Die Klassenkampfe in Frankreich." In *Karl Marx. Friedrich Engels Werke*, vol. 7, pp. 9–108. Berlin: Dietz Verlag.

1973d "Preface to the first German edition of the first volume of *Capital*." In *Karl Marx and Frederick Engels: Selected Works in Three Volumes*, vol. 2, pp. 86–90. Moscow: Progress Publishers.

1976 "The poverty of philosophy." In *Karl Marx and Frederick Engels: Collected Works*, vol. 6, pp. 105–212. New York: International Publishers.

Marx, Karl, and Frederick Engels

1942 *Selected Correspondence: 1846–1895*. New York: International Publishers.

1953 *Marx and Engels on Britain*. Moscow: State Publishing House.

1958 *Marx-Engels Selected Works*. 2 vols. Moscow: Foreign Languages Publishing House.

McConnell, Grant

1966 *Private Power and American Democracy*. New York: Vintage.

McKinley, Donald G.

1964 *Social Class and Family Life*. Glencoe, Ill.: The Free Press.

McLelland, David

1961 *The Achieving Society*. Glencoe, Ill.: The Free Press.

Merton, Robert K.

1959 "Notes on problem-finding in sociology." In *Sociology Today*, ed. R. K. Merton, Leonard Broom, and Leonard S. Cottrell, Jr., pp. ix–xxxiv. New York: Basic Books.

Metcalf, (Senator) Lee, and Vic Reinemer

1971 "Unmasking corporate ownership." *The Nation* 213 (July 19): 38–40.

Miliband, Ralph

1969 *The State in Capitalist Society*. New York: Basic Books.

1973 "Poulantzas and the capitalist state." *New Left Review* 82: 83–92.

Mills, C. Wright

1956 *The Power Elite*. New York: Oxford University Press.

1962 *The Marxists*. New York: Dell.

1963 "Review of the social life of a modern community." *American Sociological Review* 7 (April 1942): 264–271. In *Power, Politics, and People: The Collected Essays of C. Wright Mills*, ed. I. L. Horowitz, pp. 39–52. New York: Oxford University Press.

Mintz, Beth, and Michael Schwartz

1985 *The Power Structure of American Business*. Chicago: University of Chicago Press.

Mokken, R. J., and F. N. Stockman

1974 "Interlocking directorates between large corporations, banks, other financial companies and institutions in the Netherlands in 1969." Amsterdam: Institute for Political Science, Department of Research Methodology, University of Amsterdam.

Moody's

1970a *Bank and Finance Manual*. New York: Moody's.

1970b *Industrial Manual*. New York: Moody's.

Moore, Barrington, Jr.

1966 *Social Origins of Dictatorship and Democracy*. Boston: Beacon.

Mora Valverde, E.

1966 "La situación económica de América Latina y el desarrollo de la revolución." In *América Latina: Problemas e perspectivas de la revolución*, ed. Rodney Arismendi, pp. 44–60. Prague: Editorial Paz y Socialismo.

Moran, Theodore H.

1974 *Multinational Corporations and the Politics of Dependence: Copper in Chile*. Princeton, N.J.: Princeton University Press.

Motta Lima, Pedro

1966 "Problemas de la democracia en el proceso revolucionario de América Latina." In *América Latina: Problemas y perspectivas de la revolución*, ed. Rodney Arismendi, pp. 79–97. Prague: Editorial Paz y Socialismo.

Moyano, Eduardo

1972 "Notas sobre el pago de licencias industriales en Chile." In *Proceso a la industrialización chilena*, ed. Oscar Muñoz. Santiago: no publisher given.

Muñoz, Oscar

1968 *Crecimiento industrial de Chile, 1914–1965*. Santiago: Universidad de Chile (Instituto de Economía y Planificación).

Murdock, George P.

1949 *Social Structure*. New York: Macmillan.

NACLA (North American Congress on Latin America)

1972 "Secret memos from ITT." *Latin America and Empire Report* 6 (April): entire issue.

1973 "Chile: The story behind the coup." *Latin America and Empire Report* 7 (October): entire issue.

Nadler, Paul S.

1968 *Commercial Banking in the Economy*. New York: Random House.

Nash, Manning

1963 "Introduction: Approaches to the study of economic growth." *Journal of Social Issues* 19 (January): 1–5.

National Resources Committee

1939 *The Structure of the American Economy*. Pt. 1, app. 13. Washington, D.C: U.S. Government Printing Office (app. 13, written by Paul M. Sweezy, is reprinted in Sweezy 1953).

Nef, Jorge

1974 "The politics of repression: The social pathology of the Chilean military." *Latin American Perspectives* 1 (Summer): 58–77.

Nehemkis, Peter

1964 *Latin America: Myth and Reality*. Rev. ed. New York: Mentor.

Neumann, Franz

1944 *Behemoth*. New York: Oxford University Press.

1957 *The Democratic and the Authoritarian State*. Glencoe, Ill.: The Free Press.

Newcomer, Mabel

1955 *The Big Business Executive—The Factors That Made Him: 1900–1950*. New York: Columbia University Press.

Nichols, W.A.T.

1969 *Ownership, Control, and Ideology*. London: Allen and Unwin.

Norich, Sam

1980 "Interlocking directorates, the control of large corporations, and patterns of accumulation in the capitalist class." In *Classes, Class Conflict, and the State*, ed. Maurice Zeitlin, pp. 83–106. Boston: Little, Brown.

Norman, E. Herbert

1940 *Japan's Emergence as a Modern State*. New York: Institute of Pacific Relations.

O'Brien, Thomas F.

1982 *The Nitrate Industry and Chile's Crucial Transition: 1870–1891*. New York and London: New York University Press.

O'Connor, James

1968 "Finance capital or corporate capital?" *Monthly Review* 20 (October): 3–35.

ODEPLAN (Oficina de Planificación Nacional)

1970a *El crédito externo como fuente de financiamiento del sector privado.* Santiago: República de Chile.

1970b *El capital privado extranjero en Chile en el período 1964–1968 a nivel global y sectorial.* Santiago: República de Chile.

Ostrander, Susan A.

1980 "Upper-class women: Class consciousness as conduct and meaning." In *Power Structure Research,* ed. G. William Domhoff, pp. 73–96. Beverly Hills, Calif.: Sage.

Pacheco C., Luis

1971 *La inversión extranjera y las corporaciones internacionales en el desarollo industrial de América Latina: El caso Chileno.* Santiago: Centro de Estudios de Planificación (CEPLAN), Universidad Catolica de Chile.

Palmer, Donald

1983 "Broken ties: Interlocking directorates and inter-corporate coordination." *Administrative Science Quarterly* 28: 40–55.

Palmer, John

1973 "The profit performance effects of the separation of ownership and control in large industrial corporations." *Bell Journal of Economics and Management Science* 4: 293–303.

Parkin, Frank

1979 *Marxism and Class Theory: A Bourgeois Critique.* New York: Columbia University Press.

Parsons, Talcott

1953 "A revised analytical approach to the theory of social stratification." In *Class, Status, and Power,* ed. Reinhard Bendix and S. M. Lipset, pp. 92–128. Glencoe, Ill.: The Free Press.

1954 "Social classes and class conflict in the light of recent sociological theory." In his *Essays in Sociological Theory,* rev ed., pp. 323–355. Glencoe, Ill.: The Free Press.

1970 "Equality and inequality in modern society; or, Social stratification revisited." *Sociological Inquiry* 40, no. 2: 13–72.

Parsons, Talcott, and Neil Smelser

1957 *Economy and Society.* London: Routledge and Kegan Paul.

Pennings, Johannes

1978 "Interlocking relationships: The case of interlocking directorates." Paper presented at the annual meeting of the American Sociological Association, August.

1980 *Interlocking Directorates: Origins and Consequences of Connections among Organizations and Boards of Directors.* San Francisco: Jossey-Bass.

Petras, James

1969 *Politics and Social Forces in Chilean Development.* Berkeley: University of California Press.

Petras, James, and Maurice Zeitlin

1967 "Miners and agrarian radicalism." *American Sociological Review* 32 (August): 578–586.

1968 "Agrarian radicalism in Chile." *British Journal of Sociology* 19: 254–270.

1969 "Mineros y la política de la clase obrera." *Revista Latinoamericana de Sociología* (March): 121–126.

Petras, James, and Maurice Zeitlin, eds.

1968 *Latin America: Reform or Revolution?* Greenwich, Conn.: Fawcett.

Pfeffer, Jeffrey

1972 "Size and composition of corporate boards of directors: The organization and its environment." *Administrative Science Quarterly* 17 (June): 218–228.

Pike, Fredrick B.

1963 *Chile and the United States, 1880–1962.* Notre Dame, Ind.: University of Notre Dame Press.

Pinto Santa Cruz, Aníbal

1959 *Chile: Un caso de desarrollo frustrado.* Santiago: Editorial Universitaria.

Playford, John

1972 "Who rules Australia?" In *Australian Capitalism*, ed. John Playford and Douglas Kirsner, pp. 108–155. Harmondsworth, Eng.: Penguin.

Plotke, David

1973 "Coup in Chile." *Socialist Revolution* 3, no. 4: 99–124.

PMPC (President's Materials Policy Commission)

1952 *Resources for Freedom.* Vol. 1. Washington, D.C.: U.S. Government Printing Office.

Polit, Gustavo

1968 "The Argentinian industrialists." In *Latin America: Reform or Revolution?* ed. James Petras and Maurice Zeitlin, pp. 399–430. Greenwich, Conn.: Fawcett.

Portes, Alejandro

1976 "On the sociology of national development: Theories and issues." *American Journal of Sociology* 82 (July): 55–85.

Poulantzas, Nicos

1973a "On social classes." *New Left Review* 78: 27–54.

1973b *Political Power and Social Classes.* London: NLB with Sheed and Ward.

1973c "The problem of the capitalist state." In *Ideology in Social Science*, ed. Robin Blackburn, pp. 238–262. New York: Vintage.

1975 *Classes in Contemporary Capitalism.* London: NLB.

Powers, Thomas

1979 *The Man Who Kept the Secrets: Richard Helms and the CIA.* New York: Alfred A. Knopf.

Projector, Dorothy, and Gertrude Weiss

1966 "The distribution of wealth in 1962." In *Survey of Financial Characteristics of Consumers* (August), pp. 33–36, 98–99. Washington, D.C.: Federal Reserve System (reprinted in Zeitlin 1977).

Przeworski, Adam

1977 "Proletariat into class: The process of class formation from Karl Kautsky's *The Class Struggle* to recent controversies." *Politics & Society* 7, no. 4: 343–401.

Puga Vega, Mariano

1964 *El petróleo chileno.* Santiago: Editorial Andrés Bello.

Puiggros, Rodolfo

1967 *La izquierda y el problema nacional.* Buenos Aires: Jorge Álvarez.

Ramírez Necochea, Hernán

1956 *Historia del movimiento obrero. Siglo XIX.* Santiago: Empresa Editora Austral.

1960 *Historia del imperialismo en Chile.* Santiago: Empresa Editora Austral.

Ratcliff, Richard Earl

1972 "The ties that bind: Chilean industrialists and foreign corporations." In *New Chile*, ed. NACLA, pp. 79–81. Berkeley, Calif.: NACLA (North American Congress on Latin America).

1973 "Kinship, Wealth, and Power: Capitalists and Landowners in the Chilean Upper Class." Ph.D. dissertation, University of Wisconsin, Madison.

1974 "Capitalists in crisis: The Chilean upper class and the September 11 coup." *Latin American Perspectives* 1 (Summer): 78–91.

1979/80 "Capitalist class structure and the decline of older industrial cities." *Insurgent Sociologist* 2, no. 3: 60–64 (reprinted in *Power Structure Research*, ed. G. William Domhoff. Beverly Hills, Calif.: Sage, 1980).

1980a "Banks and the command of capital flows: An analysis of capitalist class structure and mortgage disinvestment in a metropolitan area." In *Classes, Class Conflict, and the State*, ed. Maurice Zeitlin, pp. 107–132. Boston: Little, Brown.

1980b "Banks and corporate lending: An analysis of the impact of the internal structure of the capitalist class on the lending behavior of banks." *American Sociological Review* 45 (August): 553–570.

Ratcliff, R. E., M. E. Gallagher, and K. S. Ratcliff

1979 "The civic involvement of bankers: An analysis of the influence of economic power and social prominence in the command of civil policy positions." *Social Problems* 26: 298–313.

Reynolds, Clark

1965 "Development problems of an export economy: The case of Chile and copper." In *Essays on the Chilean Economy*, ed. Markos Mamalakis and Clark Reynolds, pp. 207–361. Homewood, Ill.: Richard D. Irwin.

Rheinstein, Max
1967 "Intestate succession." *Encyclopædia Britannica* 12. Chicago: Encyclopædia Britannica.
Robertson, Ian
1983 *Sociology*. New York: Worth Publishers.
Rodríguez Arena, Aniceto
1966 El socialismo y la unidad (cartas del Partido Socialista al Partido Comunista). Santiago: Prensa Latinoamericana.
Rodríguez Brieba, Tomás Eduardo
1955 "El desarrollo de las sociedades anónimas." In *Medio siglo de Zig-Zag: 1905–1955*. Santiago: Zig-Zag.
Rose, Sanford
1968 "The rewarding strategies of multinationalism." *Fortune* (September 15): 101–105, 180, 182.
Rostow, W. W.
1971 *The Stages of Economic Growth: A Non-communist Manifesto*. Cambridge University Press.
Roxborough, Ian
1979 *Theories of Underdevelopment*. London: Macmillan.
1984 "Unity and diversity in Latin American history." *Journal of Latin American Studies* 16: 1–26.
Roxborough, Ian, Philip O'Brien, and Jackie Roddick, assisted by Michael González
1977 *Chile: The State and Revolution*. London: Macmillan.
Roy, William G.
1981 "From electoral to bureaucratic politics: Class conflict and the financial-industrial class segment in the United States, 1880–1905." *Political Power and Social Theory* 2: 173–202.
Santos, Theotonio dos
1968 "Foreign investment and the large enterprise in Latim America: The Brazilian case." In *Latin America: Reform or Revolution?* ed. James Petras and Maurice Zeitlin, pp. 431-453. Greenwich, Conn.: Fawcett.
1970 "The structure of dependence." *American Economic Review* 60, no. 5: 235–246.
Sayers, R. S., ed.
1962 *Banking in Western Europe*. London: Oxford University Press.
Schuby, T. D.
1974 "The Divine Right of Property: An Analysis of the Transmission of Positional Power by the Established Upper Socio-economic Class of Detroit, 1860–1970." M.A. thesis, Wayne State University.
1975 "Class power, kinship, and social cohesion: A case study of a local elite." *Sociological Focus* 8 (August): 243–255.
Schumpeter, Joseph
1955 "Social classes in an ethnically homogeneous environment." In *Imperialism and Social Classes*. New York: Meridian Books (originally published in German in 1923).

1962 *Capitalism, Socialism, and Democracy*. New York: Harper and Row.

Scott, John

1979 *Corporations, Classes, and Capitalism*. London: Hutchinson.

1985 *Corporations, Classes, and Capitalism*. 2nd ed. London: Hutchinson.

Scott, John, and Catherine Griff

1984 *Directors of Industry: The British Corporate Network, 1904–1976*. Cambridge, Eng.: Polity.

Secretariado del Partido Comunista, Comisión de estudios históricos, Anexa a su comité central

1952 *Ricardo Fonseca: Combatiente ejemplar*. Santiago: Ediciones 21 de julio, Talleres Gráficos Lautaro.

Segall, Marcelo

1953 *Desarrollo del capitalismo en Chile*. Santiago: privately printed.

Sepúlveda, Sergio

1956 *El trigo chileno en el mercado mundial*. Santiago: Editorial Universitaria.

Sepúlveda Acuna, Adonis

1966 "El Partido Socialista en la revolución chilena." In *El proceso chileno: Pensamiento teórico y político del P. Socialista de Chile*, ed. Alejandro Chelén Rojas, pp. 19–50. Buenos Aires: Quatro Editores.

Shonfield, Andrew

1965 *Modern Capitalism: The Changing Balance of Public and Private Power*. London: Oxford University Press.

Smith, Ephraim, and Louis R. Desfosses

1972 "Interlocking directorates: A study of influence." *Mississippi Valley Journal of Business and Economics* 7: 57–69.

Smith, Thomas

1961 "Japan's aristocratic revolution." *Yale Review* (Spring): 370–383.

Soref, Michael

1976 "Social class and a division of labor within the corporate elite: A note on class, interlocking, and executive committee membership of directors of U.S. industrial firms." *Sociological Quarterly* 17 (Summer): 360–368.

1979 "The Internal Differentiation of the American Capitalist Class." Ph.D. dissertation, University of Wisconsin, Madison.

1980 "The finance capitalists." In *Classes, Class Conflict, and the State*, ed. Maurice Zeitlin, pp. 62–82. Boston: Little, Brown.

Soref, Michael, and Maurice Zeitlin

1988 "Finance capital and the internal structure of the capitalist class in the United States." In *Structural Analysis of Business*, ed. Mark S. Mizruchi and Michael Schwartz. New York and Cambridge: Cambridge University Press.

Sorokin, Pitirim

1953 "What is a social class?" In *Class, Status, and Power*, ed. Reinhard Bendix and S. M. Lipset, pp. 87–92. Glencoe, Ill. The Free Press.

Stallings, Barbara

1978 *Class Conflict and Economic Development in Chile, 1958–1973*. Stanford, Calif.: Stanford University Press.

Stanworth, Philip, and Anthony Giddens

1975 "The modern corporate economy: Interlocking directorships in Britain, 1906–1970." *Sociological Review* 23: 5–28.

Stavenhagen, Rodolfo

1968 "Seven fallacies about Latin America." In *Latin America: Reform or Revolution?* ed. James Petras and Maurice Zeitlin, pp. 13–31. Greenwich, Conn.: Fawcett.

Sternberg, Marvin J.

1962 "Chilean Land Tenure and Land Reform." Ph.D. dissertation, University of California, Berkeley.

Strachey, John

1956 *Contemporary Capitalism*. New York: Random House.

Strang, Roger A., and Roger A. Harberge, Jr.

1980 *Privately Held Firms: Neglected Force in the Free Enterprise System*. Los Angeles: University of Southern California (Center for the Study of Private Enterprise).

Stunzi, Jacques R.

1968 "Banking and financing considerations: Financing in Chile." In *Doing Business in Latin America*, ed. Thomas A. Gannon, pp. 67–68. New York: American Management Association.

Subercaseaux, Guillermo

1920 *El sistema monetario i la organización bancaria de Chile*. Santiago: Sociedad imprenta Literaria Universo.

Sunkel, Osvaldo

1973 "Transnational capitalism and national disintegration in Latin America." *Social and Economic Studies* 22: 132–176.

Superintendencia de Bancos

1964 *Chile: Estadística bancario* no. 182 (December 31). Santiago: República de Chile.

Sweezy, Paul M.

1953 *The Present as History*. New York. Monthly Review Press.

1956 *The Theory of Capitalist Development*. New York: Monthly Review Press.

Swift, Jeanine

1971 *Agrarian Reform in Chile*. Lexington, Mass.: D. C. Heath.

Szulc, Tad

1973 "U.S. and ITT in Chile." *New Republic* (June 30): 21–23.

Tarasov, K.

1966 "Finanzovaja oligarchija Cil" ("The Chilean financial oligarchy"). Unpublished translation by Albert Zeitlin. *Mirovaia Ekonomika* 1, no. 9 (September): 66–76.

Thompson, James D.

1967 *Organizations in Action*. New York: McGraw-Hill.

Time

1960 "Trouble in green gold." May 16: 34.

U.S. Congress, Senate Subcommittee on Anti-trust and Monopoly

1964 *Overall and Conglomerate Aspects [of Economic Concentration]*. Pt. 1. 8th Cong., 2nd sess. Washington D.C.: U.S. Government Printing Office.

1965 *Interlocks in Corporate Management. Staff Report to the Anti-trust Subcommittee of the Committee on the Judiciary, House of Representatives.* 89th Cong., 1st sess. Washington D.C.: U.S. Government Printing Office.

U.S. Congress, House Committee on Banking and Currency

1967 *Control of Commercial Banks and Interlocks among Financial Institutions. Staff Report for the Subcommittee on Domestic Finance.* 90th Cong., 1st sess. Washington, D.C.: U.S. Government Printing Office.

1968 *Commercial Banks and Their Trust Activities: Emerging Influence on the American Economy. Staff Report for the Subcommittee on Domestic Finance.* 2 vols. 90th Cong., 2nd sess. Washington, D.C.: U.S. Government Printing Office.

U.S. Congress, Senate Committee on Foreign Relations

1973 *The International Telephone and Telegraph Company and Chile, 1970–1971. Staff Report for the Subcommittee on Multinational Corporations.* 93rd Cong., 1st sess. Washington, D.C.: U.S. Government Printing Office.

U.S. Congress, Senate Select Committee to Study Governmental Operations with Respect to Intelligence Activities

1975a *Alleged Assassination Plots Involving Foreign Leaders: An Interim Report.* 94th Cong., 1st sess. Washington, D.C.: U.S. Government Printing Office.

1975b *Covert Action in Chile: 1963–73. Staff Report.* 94th Cong., 1st sess. Washington, D.C.: U.S. Government Printing Office.

U.S. Congress, House Committee on Foreign Affairs

1975c *United States and Chile during the Allende Years, 1970–1973. Hearings before the Subcommittee on Inter-American Affairs.* 94th Cong., 1st sess. Washington, D.C.: U.S. Government Printing Office.

U.S. Congress, Senate Committee on the Judiciary

1973–1976 *Hearing before the Subcommittee to Investigate Problems Connected with Refugees and Escapees. Refugee and Humanitarian Problems in Chile.* Pts. 1–3. 93rd Cong., 1st sess.–94th Cong., 1st sess. Washington, D.C.: U.S. Government Printing Office.

1976a *Supplementary Detailed Staff Reports on Foreign and Military Intelligence. Final Report.* 94th Cong., 2nd sess. Washington, D.C.: U.S. Government Printing Office.

1976b *Hearing [on] Covert Action.* 94th Cong., 1st sess. Washington, D.C.: U.S. Government Printing Office.

U.S. Congress, Senate Committee on Governmental Affairs

1978 *Interlocking Directorates among the Major U.S. Corporations*. Washington, D.C.: U.S. Government Printing Office.

Useem, Michael

1978 "The inner group of the American capitalist class." *Social Problems* 24 (February): 225–240.

1979 "The social organization of the American business elite and participation of corporation directors in the governance of American institutions." *American Sociological Review* 44 (August): 553–572.

1980 "Which business leaders help govern?" In *Power Structure Research*, ed. G. W. Domhoff, pp. 199–225. Beverly Hills, Calif.: Sage.

1984 *The Inner Circle: Large Corporations and the Rise of Business Political Activity in the U.S. and U.K.* New York: Oxford University Press.

Valdés Solar, Manuel

1966 "En la hora de las definiciones." *Punto Final*, anexo no. 16, 2[a] (November 15).

Valencia Avaria, Luis

1951 *Anales de la República*. Vols. 1 and 2. Santiago: Imprenta universitaria.

Valenzuela, Arturo, and Julio Samuel Valenzuela, eds.

1976 *Chile: Politics and Society*. New Brunswick, N.J.: Transaction Books.

Valenzuela, Julio Samuel

1976 "The Chilean labor movement: The institutionalization of conflict." In *Chile: Politics and Society*, ed. Arturo Valenzuela and J.S. Valenzuela, pp. 135–171. New Brunswick, N.J.: Transaction Books.

Vance, Stanley C.

1964 *Boards of Directors: Structure and Performance*. Eugene: University of Oregon, School of Business Administration.

Varas, Florencia

1972 *Conversaciones con Viaux*. Santiago: Varas.

Vaupel, J. S., and J. P. Curhan

1969 *The Making of Multinational Enterprise*. Boston: Harvard Business School.

Vilar, Pierre

1973 "Marxist history, a history in the making: Towards a dialogue with Althusser." *New Left Review* 80 (July–August): 65–106.

Vinhas de Queiroz, Mauricio, Peter Evans, Guido Mantega, and Paul Singer

1977 *Multinacionais: Internacionalização e crise*. Cuaderno CEBRAP no. 28. São Paulo: Editora Brasiliense/CEBRAP.

Vinhas de Queiroz, Mauricio, Luciano Martins, and Jose Pessoa Queiroz

1965 "Os grupos econômicos no Brasil." *Revista do Instituto de Ciências Sociais* 2, no. 1.

Vitale, Luis

1968 "Latin America: Feudal or capitalist?" In *Latin America: Reform or Revolution?* ed. James Petras and Maurice Zeitlin, pp. 32–43. Greenwich, Conn.: Fawcett.

Vylder, Stefan de

1974 *Chile 1970–73: The Political Economy of the Rise and Fall of the* Unidad Popular. Stockholm: Unga Filosofers Forlag.

Wallis, Victor

1970 "Foreign Investment and Chilean Politics." Ph.D. dissertation, Columbia University.

Warner, W. Lloyd, and Darab Unwalla

1967 "The system of interlocking directorates." In *The Emergent American Society: Large-scale organizations*, vol. 1, ed. W. L. Warner, D. Unwalla, and John H. Trimm, pp. 121–157. New Haven, Conn.: Yale University Press.

Weber, Max

1946 *From Max Weber: Essays in Sociology*, ed. C. Wright Mills and Hans Gerth. New York: Oxford University Press.

1961 *General Economic History*. Trans. F. H. Knight. New York: Collier.

1968 *Economy and Society*. Ed. G. Roth and C. Wittich. New York: Bedminster.

Wheelwright, E. L.

1957 *Ownership and Control of Australian Companies*. Sydney: The Law Book Company.

Wheelwright, E. L., and Judith Miskelly

1967 *Anatomy of Australian Manufacturing Industry: The Ownership and Control of 300 of the Largest Manufacturing Companies in Australia*. Sydney: The Law Book Company.

Whitaker, Arthur P.

1964 *Argentina*. Englewood Cliffs, N.J.: Prentice-Hall.

White, Shelby

1978 "Cradle to grave: Family offices manage money for the very rich." *Barron's* (March 20): 9, 18, 20–21.

Whitley, Richard

1974 "The city and industry: The directors of large companies, their characteristics and connections." In *Elites and Power in the British Class Structure*, ed. Philip Stanworth and Anthony Giddens, pp. 65–80. London: Cambridge University Press.

Wolf, Eric R.

1955 "Types of Latin American peasantry." *American Anthropologist* 57: 452–471.

Wright, Erik Olin

1978 *Class, Crisis, and the State*. London: NLB.

Yago, Glenn

1980 "Corporate power and urban transportation: A comparison of public transit's decline in the United States and Germany." In *Classes, Class Conflict, and the State*, ed. Maurice Zeitlin, pp. 296–323. Boston: Little, Brown.

Yrarrázaval Larraín, José Miguel

1940 *El presidente Balmaceda*. 2 vols. Santiago: Editorial Nascimento.

Zald, Mayer, N.

1969 "The power and functions of boards of directors: A theoretical synthesis." *American Journal of Sociology* 75 (July): 97–111.

Zeitlin, Maurice

1967 *Revolutionary Politics and the Cuban Working Class*. Princeton, N.J.: Princeton University Press.

1968 "The social determinants of political democracy in Chile." In *Latin America: Reform or Revolution?* ed. James Petras and Maurice Zeitlin, pp. 22–34. Greenwich, Conn.: Fawcett.

1969 "Cuba—Revolution without a blueprint." *Transaction* 6, no. 6 (April): 38–42, 61.

1971 "Chilean revolution: The bullet or the ballot." *Ramparts* (April 1): 20–28.

1972 "Camilo's Colombia: The political, economic, and religious background to revolution." In *Father Camilo Torres: Revolutionary Writings*, ed. Maurice Zeitlin, pp. 1–46. New York: Harper and Row.

1974a "Corporate ownership and control: The large corporation and the capitalist class." *American Journal of Sociology* 79 (March): 1073–1119 (reprinted in Zeitlin 1977).

1974b "Economic concentration, industrial structure, and national and foreign capital in Chile in 1966." *Industrial Organization Review* 2: 195–205.

1976 "On class theory of the large corporation." *American Journal of Sociology* 81 (January): 894–903.

1977 *American Society, Inc.: Studies of the Social Structure and Political Economy of the United States*. 2nd ed. Chicago: Rand McNally.

1981 "Class, state, and capitalist development: The civil wars in Chile (1851 and 1859)." In *Continuities in Structural Inquiry*, ed. Peter Blau and Robert K. Merton, pp. 121–164. London and Beverly Hills, Calif.: Sage.

1984 *The Civil Wars in Chile (or the bourgeois revolutions that never were)*. Princeton, N.J.: Princeton University Press.

Zeitlin, Maurice, ed.

1980 *Classes, Class Conflict, and the State*. Boston: Little, Brown.

Zeitlin, Maurice, Lynda Ann Ewen, and Richard E. Ratcliff

1974a " 'New princes' for old? The large corporation and the capitalist class in Chile." *American Journal of Sociology* 80 (July): 87–123.

1974b "The 'inner group': Interlocking directorates and the internal differentiation of the capitalist class in Chile." Paper presented at the annual meeting of the American Sociological Association, August.

1975 "Propiedad y control de las grandes empresas en Chile." *Papers: Revista de Sociología* (Universidad Autónoma de Barcelona) 4: 111–161.

Zeitlin, Maurice, W. Lawrence Neuman, and Richard E. Ratcliff

1976 "Class segments: Agrarian property and political leadership in the capitalist class of Chile." *American Sociological Review* 41 (December): 1006–1029.

Zeitlin, Maurice, W. Lawrence Neuman, Richard E. Ratcliff, and Lynda Ann Ewen

1974 "Politics and the capitalist class in Chile: The 'inner group' and the state." Paper presented at the annual meeting of the American Sociological Association, August.

Zeitlin, Maurice, and Samuel Norich

1979 "Management control, exploitation, and profit maximization in the large corporation: An empirical confrontation of managerialism and class theory." *Research in Political Economy* 2: 33–62.

Zeitlin, Maurice, and James Petras

1970 "The working-class vote in Chile: Christian Democracy versus Marxism." *British Journal of Sociology* 21 (March): 16–28.

Zeitlin, Maurice, and Richard E. Ratcliff

1975 "Research methods for the analysis of the internal structure of dominant classes: The case of landlords and capitalists in Chile." *Latin American Research Review* 10: 5–61.

1976 "The concentration of national and foreign capital in Chile." In *Chile: Politics and Society*, ed. Arturo Valenzuela and J. S. Valenzuela, pp. 297–337. New Brunswick, N.J.: Transaction Books.

INDEX

LIBRARY OF CONGRESS CATALOGING-IN-PUBLICATION DATA

ZEITLIN, MAURICE

LANDLORDS AND CAPITALISTS: THE DOMINANT CLASS OF CHILE / MAURICE ZEITLIN AND RICHARD EARL RATCLIFF.

P. CM.

BIBLIOGRAPHY: P.

INCLUDES INDEX.

ISBN 0–691–07757–6 (ALK. PAPER) ISBN 0–691–02276–3 (PBK.)

1. CAPITALISTS AND FINANCIERS—CHILE. 2. LANDLORDS—CHILE. 3. ELITE (SOCIAL SCIENCES)—CHILE. 4. CAPITALISM—CHILE. 5. CHILE—ECONOMIC CONDITIONS—1918– 6. CORPORATIONS—CHILE. 7. WEALTH—CHILE. I. RATCLIFF, RICHARD EARL, 1943– . II. TITLE.

HG185.C5Z45 1988

305.5′232′0983—DC19 87–33010

CIP